A LIFE IN
THE SQUARE MILE

A LIFE IN
THE SQUARE MILE

KEVIN PARKER

BROWN
DOG
BOOKS

Published under licence by Brown Dog Books and
The Self-Publishing Partnership Ltd, 10b Greenway Farm, Bath Rd, Wick,
nr. Bath BS30 5RL

www.selfpublishingpartnership.co.uk

ISBN printed book: 978-1-83952-457-8
ISBN e-book: 978-1-83952-458-5

Cover design by Kevin Rylands
Internal design by Andrew Easton

Printed and bound in the UK

This book is printed on FSC certified paper

CONTENTS

THE BEGINNING

The bulk of these memoirs are concentrated on my working life in financial markets in the City of London, otherwise known as the Square Mile.

My journey requires context, and I decided early on to start with my college life at Totton College in Southampton and my first experience of employment at Waitrose supermarket in Hythe. The reason for this is simply that there are people and events from those college days that impacted heavily on my early life in London.

It was important to explain the complicated path that resulted in me working in an industry that I knew nothing about beforehand. My life could have been vastly different to the one detailed in this book.

To start this tale, though, I should explain a little about my parents and my early formative years.

My mother was born Rosemarie Nebel on 6 May 1938 in Hamburg, Germany. You do not need to be a great historian to realise that being born in Hamburg in 1938 it is remarkable I have a mother at all. It would be an understatement to say that Rosemarie did not have a normal childhood.

The youngest of four children, she had three elder brothers. Her father was conscripted into the German military, and her mother was working as best she could to keep food on the table. When the war finished, the Nebel family was remarkably intact. But with her father in internment and Germany an occupied ruin of its former self, survival became the overriding priority.

Rosemarie's mother, my grandmother Martha, divorced her husband in 1946, met and fell in love with an English soldier of occupation named David Pallett, and subsequently became pregnant. With his tour of duty in Germany over, David Pallett took Martha and their son Walter back to England, leaving Rosemarie and her three brothers behind in war-torn Hamburg.

This did not mean Rosemarie was forgotten, and once Martha had fully settled in Edgware, northwest London, she sent for Rosemarie to join them.

In early 1954 and aged fifteen, Rosemarie received a ticket to come to England on a one-year work visa. It should not be underestimated how daunting this must have been for Rosemarie, a native German, unable to speak anything other than her native language, leaving for England immediately after WW2 and moving to London of all places.

This placement was with a rich, London-based family, as an au pair, and the idea was for Rosemarie to learn English and to temporarily take her out of Hamburg. Once the visa expired, Rosemarie returned to Hamburg and life with her brothers. However, the boys had moved on with their lives and were struggling to feed themselves and so Rosemarie was left to fend for herself.

In 1956, now aged eighteen, Rosemarie was sent another work visa by her mother Martha, this time to work at Stanmore Hospital as an auxiliary nurse. Rosemarie quickly taught herself English but did not stop at that. Determined to fit into her new home and distance herself from all the negativity that came with being a German national at that time, she managed to lose all traces of her German accent.

In my childhood years, nobody would have suspected my mother was anything other than English. Her place of birth was something Rosemarie kept to herself. The only people who knew, other than my English grandparents, were people mother was happy to tell. Over the years, German tourists who said something disparaging about the English in Rosemarie's earshot, would be totally surprised when she reprimanded them in perfect German.

Rosemarie settled into her new home in Edgware, and one night, while out for an evening's entertainment in Harrow, had a life changing encounter with David Parker, my father.

The Parker family historically was affluent gentry. My grandfather Kenneth was the youngest of six siblings and was born in Thetford, Norfolk.

The family owned a successful grocer and draper's business and a large home called Commerce House, complete with servants. So successful were the Parkers that Kenneth and his elder brother were despatched to Harrow School for their private education. However, Kenneth did not get to complete his education at Harrow because unfortunately for him the family fortune evaporated due to his father's gambling and drinking.

David, my father, was born in December 1936 to Kenneth and Betty Bushell. David was a great athlete, playing cricket at county level and football. He did his national service and just avoided being involved in the Suez Crisis, reaching the rank of sergeant. He did consider joining the Army full-time but was subsequently demobbed when his national service finished.

David started a career as a window dresser for men's tailors Horne Brothers in London's West End. Horne Brothers was a leading menswear retailer with branches all over London and with plans to expand and open branches on most high streets. Horne Brothers main competitors on the highstreets were Moss

Brothers and Burton's. In the 1960s, most employers insisted their employees wore suits, collared shirts, and ties, so men's tailoring shops were phenomenally successful and profitable.

David and Rosemarie married in June 1958, just six months after meeting. In the early years of their life together, they lived in a rented house in South Norwood.

I was born in the Mayday Hospital in April 1962. My dad happily tells anyone who wants to hear that I was the result of him celebrating one hundred runs in a cricket match.

My brother Robin was born in the same hospital in 1964, after which our parents bought their first house in Hilltop Road, Frindsbury, Strood, Kent.

The semi-detached 1950s-style house in Hilltop Road will always be home to me – the first house you remember as a child is always special. Robin and I started our lives in a road where we had lots of children our age around us, living in neighbouring houses. Our first school was just a short walk down Hilltop Road.

Ken and Betty Parker,
Dad, Mum, Martha and
David Pallett

Our house 80
Hilltop Road,
Strood

Hilltop Junior School was also an infant's school, so I started attending aged five and enjoyed my first taste of education, but I use the word loosely.

Education in the 1960s was in flux; the education system was distancing itself from the old grammar system and had embraced the American comprehensive system. But the headmaster at Hilltop had ideas that went beyond just mixed-ability classes.

Mr James, the headmaster at Hilltop Junior School, was a pioneer of new 'trendy' 1960s-style education. The theory went something like this: if you split a classroom in two and put toys at one end and books and educational equipment at the other and give children the choice, they will eventually gravitate towards the educational end of the room. The idea was that a child who chooses to learn, rather than play, will be able to achieve much more than a child who is compelled to learn. The idea sounds good in theory but ignores one important thing: a child's psychology. We played with the toys and kept on playing.

My father was unhappy, and when I reached seven years of age and still could not read properly, he decided he had to do something about it. My parents bought the complete set of Ladybird reading books, which were available in class, if I had been inclined to use them.

Each and every night after he got home, my dad sat down with me, and I was forced to read. I was not incredibly happy about it, but little by little I started to learn.

At the very next parent-teacher evening, my dad let the teacher trap herself when she enthused about how well they were doing with me and how my reading was vastly improved. That's when he let the teacher have both barrels. My dad was so verbally damning on their efforts to educate me that he was never invited back to another parent-teacher evening.

Needless to say, the quality of the education at Hilltop Junior School did not improve and having tried to have both Robin and myself moved to another local school without success, our parents decided they had no choice but to remove us from the Kent educational system altogether.

We relocated from Hilltop Road to a flat in Rodwell Close, Eastcote, west London in 1970. This meant changes; the flat was two-bedroomed, so Robin and I now shared a bedroom in bunk beds. We had no garden, although the flats had green spaces all around them and garages in a big block that now became our football pitch.

Our new school was Newnham Junior School, a short walk from Rodwell

Close. Ordinarily, a change of school would involve the new one communicating with the old one to do an educational handover. Our parents had a meeting with the principal at Newnham and explained that the reason for the move of home was based on the poor education we had been receiving in Kent.

The school reserved judgement and did their own assessment of me in particular and concluded I was 18 months behind my peers. An accelerated learning program was devised, meaning I had frequent one-to-one lessons with teachers aimed at helping me catch up. The result of this intensive teaching was that I was quickly able to catch up and bridge the educational gap with my classmates. I made new friends, and Robin and I settled down at Rodwell Close and Newnham Junior School. But this was not to last.

Just 18 months later, we were on the move again; this time it was dad's job that was the driver behind the move. From his window-dressing role, dad had progressed via a sales role on the shop floor, to deputy manager at one of Horne Brothers' flagship branches in London's West End. Now dad had been offered his first manager's position at a new shop in Guildford. The shop was just off the prestigious Guildford High Street in a new shopping mall called Tunsgate Square. The chance to manage his own shop was something dad could not turn down.

For Robin and myself this meant another change of home and school, and it was not something either of us was happy about. Home was to be a new-build semi-detached house on the Grange Park estate in Worplesdon, in a road called Burden Way. Robin and I were to attend Stoughton Junior School, in Grange Road, a twenty-minute walk from our new home.

I was unhappy, wondering what the point of making new friends was. At the start of life at my new school, I was very much the outsider, with my classmates having established friendships forged over time. With one class of 30-odd pupils per year group, my teacher was Mr Graham for all subjects. Mr Graham was on the verge of retirement and as such was classified as 'old school' in his approach. But after my experience at Hilltop, I was more than happy with these traditional-style lessons.

I ended up making friends with another 'outcast,' a lad by the name of Gary Luck who was a little socially inept and not good at football, both of which left him on the fringes of the social mix in class. All the other lads used to call him 'Lucky Jim,' which he just accepted. Lunchtime in the playground was always a game of football, the two captains picking a side from the year group. Gary Luck was always the last to be selected and told to 'stay out the way' during the games.

Stoughton Junior School did an annual trip for the fifth-year children at the end of their last year at the school. This trip was a week away to Dymchurch in Kent, and I was signed up for it.

This was my first real trip away from my parents for any length of time, but it proved to be enjoyable, with a visit to the Romney, Hythe and Dymchurch steam railway and frequent trips to the nearby beaches.

The move from junior school to senior school was a little less daunting at Worplesdon, as the first year was at the 'Larch Avenue Annex,' which was opposite the Stoughton school entrance. This meant you were able to mix with only first-year students and get to grips with secondary school education before the move to the nearby, and much larger, Larch Avenue Secondary School. The mix of Stoughton students with four other junior schools in the Larch Avenue catchment meant I was now no longer an outsider, and I was accepted into the Stoughton fold.

For the following year of my secondary education, I was off to Larch Avenue Secondary School. This was a larger school and a modern facility. It was by far the biggest school I had ever been to, with each year group having around a hundred pupils. For the first time, I was in mixed-year tutor groups for registration, and it was a vastly different educational experience from anything I had encountered before.

In 1974, we had our first experience of the troubles in Northern Ireland on our doorstep. The IRA bombed the Horse and Groom and Seven Stars public houses in Guildford.

Guildford was very much an Army town. Our house in Burden Way was opposite the Women's Royal Army Corp barracks, and frequent armed patrols could be seen around the perimeter fences after the bombings. Luckily, Dad never went drinking after work, and none of his staff were caught up in the blasts which killed six, including two Women's Royal Army Corp soldiers from the barracks opposite our house.

My time at Larch Avenue Secondary School was to come to another premature end. Just as we settled into life at our new school and area, another move of home was upon us. This time, dad was offered the chance to manage one of Horne Brothers' other regional branches, Southampton.

Horne Brothers' Southampton branch was one of their premier regional branches that benefitted from one of the best shopping centres outside of London. Southampton High Street enjoyed having the nearby affluence that resided in the New Forest and all the commercial liner traffic that came to Southampton Port. The Southampton branch was consistently one of Horne Brothers' top-earning branches, usually eclipsed only by their central London and City of London flagship branches.

Such was the speed of this move that our parents did not have time to find a house they wanted to buy. When our house in Burden Way sold quickly, we relocated into a rented house. This rented house was a huge, detached 1970s four-bedroomed property called 'The Pines'.

This house was set back from a quiet, wooded road called Roman Road and overlooked the New Forest. 'The Pines' got its name from the four huge pine trees that were situated in the large back garden and the group of smaller versions bordering the Roman Road which screened the house.

Roman Road itself was in a village called Dibden Purlieu, positioned on what is known as the Forest Front, with Beaulieu a short drive down the road. Dibden Purlieu is on the opposite side of the Solent to Southampton and was either a 35-minute drive down the Marchwood bypass or a more attractive ferry ride away from the nearby town of Hythe. The Ferry conveniently docked at the end of Southampton High Street.

We moved to Dibden Purlieu in time for me to complete the last two weeks of my second year of secondary education at Applemore Secondary School. Dibden Purlieu had two local secondary schools; one, called Noadswood, which was closer to the village, and Applemore which was a little further out and on the fringes of the village. The parents' choice was Applemore, at the suggestion of the local estate agent they were house hunting with.

Applemore accepted children from the Butts Ash estate in the village, as well as the local village of Marchwood, which was primarily an Army base. My first experience of life at Applemore was being escorted to meet my house tutor, Ms Martin, an art teacher, by the head of Nightingale House, Mr Ainsworth. As we walked into the classroom, I could see a boy being held upside down, two stocky lads holding a leg each, one of whom had a pretty developed moustache and looked far too old to be in school uniform. The head of the boy held upside down was being 'dunked' in and out of a dustbin, and Ms Martin was telling the victim to stop making so much noise! My misery at attending yet another strange school instantly multiplied, and I concluded my new school was an actually a lunatic asylum.

The parents' decision to send me to Applemore for these final two weeks of the second year was, in hindsight, a huge blessing. These two weeks gave me the opportunity to form a friendship with a boy called Ian Tuckwell. I spent the majority of the summer holidays exploring the New Forest on my bicycle with Ian, usually accompanied by his younger sister Elaine. My friendship with Ian and Elaine also led to my parents making friends with Ian's parents, Maureen, and Dennis Tuckwell.

Upon my return to Applemore school after the summer holiday, to start the third year of secondary education, I was replaced as the new boy in Ms Martin's tutor group. The newcomer was an Army boy from Marchwood, Steve Dickinson.

Steve's dad had been posted to Marchwood from an Army base in West Germany. For this reason alone, Steve was christened 'Kraut' by the other kids, and this nickname stuck. As two new members of the school, Steve and I quickly formed a bond of friendship.

Robin also joined us at Applemore after the summer holiday for his first year of secondary education, and we finally moved into our new home. We made the short move from The Pines in Roman Road to a three-bedroomed detached Swiss-style house at 3 Froghall Close on the Butts Ash estate.

I spent the first couple of years in Dibden Purlieu expecting to be told we were on the move again. However, the parents quickly fell in love with New Forest life. The feeling that we had finally settled was further cemented when mother was able to arrange a 'swap' of council accommodation for our grandparents. Betty and Kenneth were able to move from their council flat in Honey Pott Lane, Stanmore, west London to a bungalow in a new exclusive development of five purpose-built retirement bungalows tucked at the end of an established road in Dibden Purlieu village.

In 1975, now aged thirteen, I started to come out of my shell a little and travelled on Saturdays, with my friend Ian Tuckwell, to watch Southampton FC play football. We would catch the ferry from Hythe, drop into my parents working at Horne Brothers in the high street and then head off for the short walk to The Dell, home of Southampton FC.

Ian and I would go to the Milton Road end to stand and watch the games. This started me off with my great love of watching live football. Attending music and sports events is a much more rewarding experience than watching on the television. You go along as much for the atmosphere and the camaraderie as the match.

Ian and I attended most of the Southampton FC home matches over the next couple of years, and we always made for the same place at The Dell each time, this being in the corner under the scoreboard next to the away supporters.

Ian and I were befriended by the much older regulars around us, who also headed for the same place. Positioned just behind the corner flag, we had a magnificent view, as The Dell was a very compact football ground. Ian and I joined in all the songs and good-natured banter that usually went on during matches. We got to see a number of footballing legends during our time there, including Georgie Best and Rodney Marsh.

As well as discovering live football at 13, another development that year was that I started to discover GIRLS!

Steve Dickinson and I had many of the same classes and so spent a great deal of time together. We were classified as 'nice' boys and started receiving invitations to girls birthday parties. One girl in particular, Julie Ross always invited Steve and I to join her at all her family's regular house parties.

Julie was the same age as us, a quiet, slim, studious girl who always seemed happier in the company of boys. That is not to say she was a tomboy – she was always very feminine in dress and behaviour. Julie lived just a ten-minute walk away from Froghall Close, and her parents were always very welcoming. Another big plus of afternoons and evenings at the Ross family home in Partridge Road was that they owned a snooker table which sat in their conservatory.

Steve Dickinson's home in Marchwood was not exactly convenient for trips to the Butts Ash estate, requiring either a parent driving him or a bus to Hythe and another on to Butts Ash. This was usually not possible for Steve and so I would occasionally set off by myself and knock on Julie Ross's door, we would play cards, snooker, or just watch TV.

In 1976, Ian and I had attended all of Southampton FC's home games, including a cup run that took the team to the FA Cup Final against Manchester United. As a team in the then Second Division, and Manchester United being a major force in football and in the league above us, the odds were firmly stacked against our team.

Ian and I were too young to be allowed to head off on the long journey to Wembley. Instead, I joined Ian and his family for the weekend of the cup final and we headed off to Ian's Aunt's pub just outside Basingstoke.

FA Cup Finals in the 1970s were one of the biggest events of any year, drawing huge television audiences. Television coverage usually started at midday and were star-studded events leading up to the three o'clock kick-off.

At kick-off, Ian and I were wearing our Southampton scarfs in the public bar, surrounded by Manchester fans and a lot of neutrals. We watched Lawrie McMenemy and his team upset the odds and win. By the time the final whistle sounded, Ian and I were hoarse with all the shouting and singing we had done.

On the drive back toward Southampton, we decked the Tuckwell car in red and white with ribbons and scarfs, and all the way home horns sounded, lights flashed, and people waved.

Dad told me that when the referee blew the whistle for full-time, all the ships in Southampton harbour sounded their horns and sirens, and this was followed by the buses and cars, with people coming out of the pubs and dancing in the street. Despite working at Horne Brothers on the day, he was left in no doubt that Southampton had won the cup.

In my final year at secondary school, my friend Ian Tuckwell and his family moved out of the village to Godalming in Surrey. I was upset to say the least at losing not only yet another friend but also my football companion.

I eventually made friends with two other lads from Dibden Purlieu, who went on to become particularly important to me. Nick Cringle and Stephen Breen were different characters, but the three of us had formed a close bond by the end of secondary school. I am still in contact with both of them and we meet up occasionally in Dibden Purlieu.

I sat my exams at the end of my time at Applemore Secondary School feeling more secure than ever, happier, and finally at home. But I had to say farewell to another friend when Steve Dickinson was accepted into the Metropolitan Police Cadets at 16 and moved to Hendon Police College soon after the summer holiday.

$$\wr\wr\wr$$

In the summer of 1978, having sat my O-level exams and finished secondary school, like any other 16-year-old I was contemplating my future and it was daunting. What to do next?

Employment opportunities at 16 existed if you were determined to leave education and start work. Many fellow school leavers did just that. Jobs were available in retail as Southampton had a huge shopping centre, and another major employer in the city was the docks. Fawley Refinery was another big local employer, just 20 minutes down the road from Dibden Purlieu, perched on the banks of the Solent. It offered apprenticeships to school leavers, although the majority of these went to friends and family of existing workers.

At 16 years of age, I wasn't mentally prepared for any of those options. I wanted to go to college, and when my O-level exam results came in, the desire became a necessity because they were a very disappointing mixed bag. I had managed passes in English, History, Drama and Geography, but crucially failed

Maths with a D. After a painful conversation with my parents, we agreed that I needed to go to Totton College, but my dad was not going to let me spend two years just retaking my O-levels. I applied to Totton College for an A-level Geography course, English, and Maths O-level courses (my pass in English was a narrow one!) and an offered trial A/O-level course in Current Affairs.

Another condition on attending college for two years was to find part-time work for evenings and/or weekends.

In our area, there were only three major employers taking on students. One of these was the infamous 'chicken factory,' which was just that: a food factory processing chickens. Not my favoured option. Then there was Dreamland, a bed manufacturer down the road in the Hythe Industrial Park, which was also not exactly inspiring. My third and much-preferred option was a position at the local Waitrose supermarket, also based in Hythe.

At the first opportunity, a sunny Saturday morning, I set off on my bike to cycle down to Hythe. It was a pleasant ride, heading out of the house in Froghall, out of the estate and across to Frost Lane, a long winding country lane that plunged downhill to the Solent marshes and then along the waterfront into Hythe town.

Hythe is a very quaint town with the then-famous Hythe Ferry, which ran twice hourly across the Solent into Southampton. The Hythe Ferry service consisted of three old navy-blue and white ferry boats, all called Hotspur. These boats had sailed across the English channel to pick up soldiers at Dunkirk during WW2.

Lots of people who worked in Southampton but lived on our side of the Solent, including my parents, used the ferry to commute to work. The alternative to the ferry was an often-painful car journey down the Marchwood bypass, which was a single-lane road all the way to Southampton, and often nose-to-tail during the rush hour.

I cycled past the American naval base, Dreamland and the famous Hovercraft development area that had seen Dr Christopher Cockerell's designs developed in the 1950s. I cycled on, into Hythe town and the car park located at the rear of Waitrose supermarket. I peddled over to the railings to chain my bike just as the lovely vision of Sue Eason cycled into the car park. When she saw me, she headed over to join me..

Sue Eason was a girl I had often had my eye on in our secondary school. She was very pretty, with freckles and mousey brown hair that was straight but curled inwards at shoulder level, as was the fashion of the time. She had been a quite polite, studious girl who had not attracted attention from my fellow male pupils. That was until Sue hit her mid-teens when she had simply blossomed. Suddenly, she became very noticeable, but any male attention just made her blush and retreat into her shell.

Sue and I had never really mixed in the same circles at secondary school, so I had never had the opportunity to get to know her beyond nodding terms. Even if the opportunity presented itself, I was too shy to have acted upon it. But here was an excellent chance to engage with her socially, and I wasn't about to turn it down.

'Hi Sue,' I said as she daintily dismounted her bike.

Sue smiled as she chained her bike next to mine. 'What are you doing in Hythe so early?' she asked.

'I'm just off to see if I can get a weekend job at Waitrose,' I replied.

Sue smiled. 'Me too … are you going to college then?'

'Yes, Totton … but on the condition I get a job for the weekends and holidays,' I replied.

With her bike secured next to mine, Sue stood there, her smile broadening. 'I'm off to Totton as well,' she explained. 'So, we'll be on the same coach picking up and dropping off from the Butts Ash bus stop.'

We both started to walk towards the arch that led from the rear car park to Hythe's high street. I nodded. 'Well, if we both get jobs here and we're both going to Totton, we'll be seeing a lot of each other.' The prospect was growing on me by the minute.

Once through the arch and into the high street, we turned left into the main doors of Waitrose, which was already busy with Saturday morning shoppers. We entered the supermarket and looked around for anyone in authority. Without a suit in sight, we walked slowly down the aisles and towards the back of the supermarket. Still not seeing anybody of obvious authority, we headed for the tills, and then finally I spotted a suited gentleman. He was short, with short jet-black hair, thick, black-rimmed glasses, a navy pinstriped suit and a crisp white shirt, finished off with a plain navy-blue tie. He was armed with a clipboard and seemed to be taking an inventory of the baked beans.

Sue and I walked up to him, and I got his attention. 'Excuse me,' I said.

The gentlemen turned enough for me to see a badge pinned to his breast pocket, which stated, 'Mr Gowe, Deputy Manager.'

'Mr Gowe, Sue and I were interested in Saturday jobs if you have any available.'

Mr Gowe looked us both up and down for a moment and then inclined his head. 'We have nothing available immediately, but over the summer our older existing weekenders will be heading off into full-time jobs and university, then we'll be taking on new weekenders. We have a couple of names on the list already, but I expect we can add you to it. Are you both off to college?'

'Yes,' Sue replied, 'we're both going to Totton College for two years.'

Mr Gowe nodded. 'Well then, if you would like to come with me, I'll take a few details and get you on the list.'

We followed Mr Gowe down the rows of aisles to a door next to the fruit-and-veg aisle. He keyed in a four-digit code and opened the door, standing aside to let us pass into the bottom of a staircase. We headed up to the first floor, and at the top of the stairs we went through a fire door and into a long corridor. Three doors to the left went into offices, while the corridor continued onwards before turning right.

Mr Gowe walked down to the furthest of the doors and entered. He asked us to sit and then walked round to take his seat on the other side of the table. He pulled a clipboard with forms out of a tray on his desk, turned a few pages to a blank form, and looked at Sue.

'Ladies first,' he said before asking Sue for her address, home phone number and confirmation of the school she had recently left and the college she was going to.

Then he asked me for the same information. Having taken down my details, he smiled for the first time.

'Good, well I don't think you'll have to wait too long. I know a number of our existing weekenders have to leave soon to find digs at their universities, and we have a couple who have already indicated they are leaving for full-time employment. We also have two who are joining us here at Waitrose – one is off to management training in Bracknell, and the other is joining us full-time. We'll give you both a phone call when a vacancy comes along.'

With that, he stood, and we followed him back down the stairs onto the shop floor.

Having said goodbye to Mr Gowe, Sue and I walked back around to the Waitrose car park to collect our bikes. We cycled back to the village together, and during the cycle ride Sue told me she was keen to get into nursing. I explained I didn't have a clue what I wanted to do and that was another reason college had been a saviour. I really wasn't ready to make any life-determining decisions at this stage. I was still a kid at heart and not ready to join the adult world just yet.

It was three weeks later when, returning home after a day out with my mates, my mother told me we had received a call from Waitrose. Mum told me that I was expected back at Waitrose in Hythe on Saturday morning at nine o'clock precisely, and to ask for Mr Gowe.

I decided against cycling and leaving my bike outside the shop all day. I left home at eight-thirty for the healthy walk down to Hythe, arriving with five minutes to spare and having to wait for the shop doors to open.

At nine o'clock, a lady in the trademark light-brown till overall unlocked and opened the main doors, and I walked inside along with a couple of shoppers. I made straight for the lady still holding the shop door keys and explained that I had an appointment with Mr Gowe. She told me to head towards the office door and that she would call up to the office and let Mr Gowe know I was here.

As I walked towards the same door that Sue Eason and I had taken last time, I spotted Sue at the end of the shop, working on the deli counter. Dressed in a crisp white overall and with a hat over a hairnet, Sue gave me a shy wave and was immediately questioned by an extremely attractive brunette working alongside her.

I waved back and hovered by the door until Mr Gowe appeared, he shook my hand, and led me back up the stairs to his office. There, waiting seated at Mr Gowe's desk, was a broad, middle-aged lady with a mass of black curly hair flecked with grey, again dressed in the light-brown overall.

'This,' Mr Gowe gestured to me, 'is Kevin Parker.' The lady stood and offered a hand. 'And this is Valerie Cottrell, the head of our non-food department.'

I took the offered seat next to Valerie.

'Now, Mr Parker, you'll be working on Thursday evenings from five-thirty until eight and on Saturdays eight-thirty to six, and as holiday cover when needed. I have assigned you to work with Valerie and Joanne Basham on non-food.'

I nodded as Mr Gowe continued.

'Non-food is unique. It only has one weekender assigned to it, which means you need to be able to run the department on your own sometimes. I have also put you on non-food as you will be in sight of your girlfriend, who, as I'm sure you know, is working on the deli counter.'

I realised Mr Gowe had made a bit of an assumption about my relationship with Sue Eason, but I wasn't about to correct him – it sounded like it had been a factor in me getting my job!

'Oh,' said Valerie, 'which one is Kevin's girlfriend?'

I was now in a difficult position, but Mr Gowe didn't miss a beat. 'Susan Eason. They came together to enquire about positions, and the deli job came up soon after.'

Valerie gave me a surprised look and a little grin. 'Good, Susan will be able to keep an eye on you from the deli. She seems to be a lovely girl. I haven't been able to talk to her much in the brief time she's been here, but Debbie seems incredibly happy with her.'

I now had a name for the brunette!

With that, Mr Gowe ceremonially turned to the table behind him, lifting a dark-brown overall and presenting it to me. 'If you go with Valerie, she'll start to show you the ropes. Valerie, if you can take him round to Lucy at some point today to complete the formalities.'

'Of course, Mr Gowe,' Valerie said as she stood and gestured for me to follow her out of the office.

Instead of turning right for the shop floor, Valerie turned left, then right at the end of the corridor, and immediately on the left was a set of double doors that led into a large canteen. She told me this was where I could get complimentary cups of tea and coffee at breaktime and purchase a subsidised lunch. Further along and to the right was a ladies' changing room, followed by a door into the men's changing room, and then a large door at the end took us into the stockroom.

The stockroom was a cavernous area with floor-to-ceiling shelves stretching down the entire length of the building. Halfway down these long rows of stocked shelves, like the trunk of a huge tree, was a large, tilted set of rollers, forming a conveyor belt. Boxes taken from the shelves and dropped onto the rollers travelled down and out of sight. Valerie told me this was the grocery area and that the boxes ended up on a marking bench where they were expertly sliced open with Stanley knives. I could hear the clicking of the pricing guns going at an alarming speed. The boxes, once open, exposing the tins or packets inside, were all individually priced and then stacked onto trollies. Once a trolley was full, a waiting staff member would head to the lifts and travel down to the shop floor to replenish the shelves.

Non-food had a much smaller but similar setup. Valerie explained that our section dealt with all non-edible products, such as soap powder, toilet roll, shoe polish, tampons, and deodorant. Our job was to keep the shop floor stocked by going down, writing up a list of the products that needed topping up, heading back up to the stockroom, finding the required products, pricing them, loading a trolley, and then heading back down to the shop floor to fill the shelves.

Additionally, we had to make sure the stockroom itself was kept stocked by filling in a 'stock control' sheet to order replacement stock from head office when required.

Complications came in the shape of special offers. Valerie pointed to a noticeboard. On set dates, special offers came into play, often with a price displayed on the product itself. When this happened, the shop floor shelves had to be cleared of standard packed items and replaced with the special-offer product, and all these had to sell before reverting back to the standard packaging and pricing.

It all sounded simple enough, but it was not. The use of the Stanley knife, for example, was an art – push too hard and you could damage the product inside. Soap powder was especially prone to this, and if the product's packaging was damaged in any way, it had to be discounted, and you had to fill in a form to explain the damage. If you didn't press hard enough with the knife you couldn't open the box. Once you became an expert in the art you could slice through box after box without ever damaging the product inside.

The pricing gun was another art. You had to set the price by turning the numbers on the flywheel, and then armed with a huge roll of blank pricing tickets, you priced each item in the box. Within weeks, you didn't need to consult the pricing sheets stapled to the noticeboard – you knew the prices of the standard goods off by heart.

Everyone started pricing with the guns at a slow, methodical, one-click-at-a-time pace carefully pricing each and every item. But you quickly became adept at a high-rhythm pricing that was totally intimidating and daunting on your first day.

I watched in awe as Valerie strode around our four shelving units in the stockroom, pulling the stock off the metal shelves, cutting the boxes open, setting the pricing gun to the required price, and then blitzing the tickets before stacking the boxes onto the trolley.

A full warehouse box of soap powder was heavy, but Valerie just carted them around with ease. The bulky items such as soap powder, toilet rolls and kitchen roll were all at floor level, while washing-up liquid, bleach, etc. tended to be on the second- and third-level shelves. Lighter items like shoe polish, shoe laces, toothpaste, etc. were all on the higher shelves. Pulling down boxes from these top shelves, balanced on a stepladder, could be tricky at times.

Valerie set up my first trolley for me and led me to the nearby small lift, which went down to the shop floor. It was a tight fit with a full trolley and two people, but we managed to climb in and hit the button. As the lift doors opened, we emerged between the two meat chiller cabinets. We went through them, past the meat aisle and into non-food. Non-food was one continuous aisle with the tills at one end and the deli counter at the other. We also had four corner units on the main customer walkway which dissected our aisle halfway down the shop.

I got a wave from Sue Eason as Valerie and I pushed the trolley down the aisle, heading for the soap powder. The soap powder was the nearest product to the deli counter. Valerie explained that new stock always went to the rear of the shelves, so you had to do a bit of clearing up first, moving the old stock forward to get access, but it was a quick job once you got the hang of it.

Once the trolley was clear, Valerie pulled out a notepad, and we slowly walked down the long aisle, itemising the products that needed topping up. These would be on our next shop-floor-bound trolley.

This was the shape of my day, interspersed with two 15-minute tea breaks and an hour for lunch.

Then at 4.30 precisely, all the staff hit the shop floor for a ritual called 'facing forward.' This involved moving the stock on the shelves in such a way as to give the appearance that they were fully stocked. Customers always seemed intent on destroying your efforts, but when the till manager made the announcement over the public address system that the store was closing, and could all customers make their way to the tills, you were able to plug any gaps before the inevitable quick inspection from Mr Gowe or the shop manager, Mr Dailey.

I started the routine of working at Waitrose on a Thursday night, straight from college, and all-day Saturday. Valerie Cotterill was a particularly good and patient boss, and Saturdays were fun.

Not only did Sue Eason look nice in her white deli coat and hat, she had not one, but two lovely colleagues on the deli counter. Both of them were from Hardley village, which was a 15-minute drive further down the Marchwood bypass from Dibden Purlieu.

Debbie Frazer was a year older than Sue and me, and she already had one year's experience at Waitrose behind her. Debbie managed the deli counter on a Saturday, and she was in a relationship with one of the full-timers, Ian Shrive, who was a genuinely nice guy and worked in the grocery department.

The other member of the deli team was Jane Whatney. Jane was the same age as me but went to a college in Southampton. Jane took an instant liking to me and was not shy in making that clear from the moment I started at Waitrose. Jane was always smiling, waving, and taking every opportunity to chat with me. But she was so forward, especially in front of Sue and Debbie, that I initially got flustered by her flirtatious advances. Far from putting her off, this just encouraged Jane even more, much to Sue and Debbie's amusement. Eventually, I started returning the banter.

After each trolley of items was delivered to the non-food aisle of shelves and duly emptied (except for the empty boxes, which were destined for the 'bailing room' to the rear of the shop), I would spend time chatting to the deli girls.

After a couple of weeks, I had things pretty well under control, to the point where Valerie told me I had my first solo Saturday on the horizon. Mr Gowe would be keeping an eye on me.

Sadly, he was not the only one; the 'meat room boys' also had their eyes on me. You see, like many workplaces there were certain 'traditions' that they were keen to make sure were observed. They had been waiting patiently for Valerie to be out of the way, as she was a little protective of me. The guys in the meat department were rough diamonds. They took immense pleasure in their notoriety, and, as the only all-male department, they were renowned as 'animals.'

Sure enough, with my guardian Valerie Cotterill out of the way, I was pounced on and 'initiated.' This involved being held down while a broom was inserted via the left arm of my brown Waitrose overall and through to the right arm, rendering my arms useless. Now standing up and resembling a scarecrow, a meat hook was inserted behind my neck, pointing outwards under the broom handle, I was physically lifted, and the meat hook connected to tracks fixed to the ceiling.

The tracks the meat hooks ran on went from the ground floor loading bay to the rear of the shop, up via a choice of two lifts into the stockroom and on into the meat department. Another track then continued out and into a lift that went down to the shop floor. Hanging helpless on the hook I was given the tour, and round I went until they got bored. At this stage, I was taken along the track to the shop-floor lift and left hanging in there to go up and down. Staff came and went, snickering or rolling their eyes as I swung from the hook.

Eventually, Ms Fallon got into the lift. She was the till manager and the senior member of the shop-floor staff. In her late fifties, she was very much of the Penelope Keith variety – prim, proper and no-nonsense. She needed to be to keep all of her 'girls' in line – most of the full-time till staff were ladies in their twenties and thirties.

As Ms Fallon got into the lift on the first floor, having been up to the canteen for coffee, she took one look at me hanging there and shook her head in a disappointed way. As the lift doors closed, she looked up at me and said, 'You must be Kevin from non-food.' I nodded. 'Good, I'm glad to have bumped into you. I have you down for till training. You're going to be one of my queue busters on Saturdays.' When the lift arrived at shop-floor level, she took one more look, shook her head and left, the doors closing behind her.

As it turned out, Ms Fallon let Mr Gowe know the 'new boy' was in the cargo lift hanging from a meat hook. Mr Gowe played the game and went to the meat room to suggest I was now initiated and needed to get on with my non-food duties. Two of the smirking meat room boys promptly walked into the lift, and I was unhooked and released to get back to my work.

There were two huge advantages associated with working at Waitrose back in the day. Firstly, the staff parties, held quarterly, these consumed food that was going out of date, alcohol minus labels and dented or end-of-promotion lines, and doubled as team-building exercise. Neither Mr Dailey, the manager, nor Mr Gowe, his deputy, ever attended. Instead, these evenings were organised by John Totts, the grocery department head. John was in his late twenties, a big strapping guy. Totts was a well-known family name in the area, as John's mum ran the Dibden Purlieu florists.

The other advantage of my time at Waitrose was pure statistics. The branch had a daytime staff of around fifty, of which two thirds were ladies, plus twenty-odd Saturday staff, the majority of whom were also female. Male attendance at these functions was more or less compulsory, and we did not put up much of a fight.

The only problem was the obvious tugs of war that developed after a few drinks. You see, being sixteen- to seventeen-year-old boys, we were too naive to understand the attractions of more mature ladies. The full-time ladies always seemed very keen to get to know the male weekenders. These friendships tended to manifest themselves when the inevitable slow dances started at the staff parties.

As teenage lads, we only really had eyes for our fellow female weekenders who were our own age. But they were not usually interested in us, as they considered us to still be a little immature. Apart from Jane Whatney, who, as I mentioned, seemed to have taken an instant shine to me, but who scared me. Don't get me wrong, Jane was attractive, but I was not mentally geared at this stage to cope with someone who not only liked me, but also seemed to be actively and very publicly pursuing me. I had a great deal of growing up to do.

The full time Waitrose ladies were mostly married and of varying ages from mid-twenties to late forties. I enjoyed the playful banter and flirtation, and I was safe in the knowledge that they really were only playing, but you could never be certain.

There is something very intimidating to a naive teenage boy about a group of mature ladies fired up on alcohol in an enclosed space – especially with music and the added encouragement of their friends. Luckily, on disco nights, I had a guardian angel – a lady called Josie Smart.

The Waitrose staff parties followed the same pattern. Everyone would gather in groups, chatting as the alcohol flowed. Then the disco music would start, and eventually, after more drinks, the disco music would make way for the more edgy music of the day. The boys would then 'Grebo' to the likes of Status Quo's 'Paper Plane' or Rainbow's 'Since You've Been Gone.'

Once the male showboating was over it would give way to a free-for-all of dancing to the current dance music. The meat room boys circled the teenage female weekenders like sharks, and we all waited for the inevitable slow dances at the end of the evening.

When the slow music came on, the fun commenced. Be it 'I'm Not in Love' by 10CC or 'Nights in White Satin' by The Moody Blues, we froze on the dance floor as the slightly tipsy middle-aged women pounced. The lovely Josie did not always manage to save me, and I had dances with the Waitrose canteen staff or the slightly wilder till ladies. In particular, Dorothy 'Dot' Murray, who, with her rotund figure, would delight in a bear-like grip on her 'dance' partner.

Josie Smart was a quiet, petite, five-foot lady in her mid-thirties. She had a noticeably short 'elven' hairstyle, and I always suspected that she was not happily married. I was occasional lunch cover for Josie on the tills, and we had started chatting on the handovers.

One Thursday evening Josie had passed me in her car as I was walking home, she pulled over and offered me a lift. From that point on, I enjoyed a regular lift with her, as her journey to the Netley View estate, where she lived, took her past the Butts Ash bus stop, a short walk from my home.

After a couple of months of traveling home in her car, Josie often parked up at the bus stop as we chatted. We made a point of sitting together if our lunchtime or teatime breaks coincided. Towards the end of my time at Waitrose we reached a point where we always parted with a kiss on the cheek, be it from the Waitrose canteen or when I was getting out of her car. At that stage we did become the subject of some shop-floor gossip.

Till training was the only thing that occurred away from the branch. Ms Fallon waited until there was a couple of us and then hired a cab to take us to Southampton train station, and off we went. At the training centre we met people from all the other local branches of Waitrose, including our deadly rivals at the Lymington branch.

The Waitrose social club had lots of competitive inter-branch sports competitions – football, netball, and pool and then the local branches enjoyed a combined Christmas party in Southampton. Inevitable local rivalries flourished, and this extended even to the till training. In the pep talk from the branch manager Mr Dailey, we instructed to make sure we got better results than Lymington branch.

I set off with Trudy Tawnie, another girl from Applemore secondary school, Nick Goodman from fruit and veg, and Christine Cittern, who was a new full-time addition to the drinks department.

At that time, an era of an extremely basic pre-computerised tills, you had to key the price of each item manually. Once you had keyed all the items and hit the total button, the till displayed the final cost of the shop. Then you had to take the cash, cheque, or credit card. In those days, the vast majority of the payments were cash, so you then had to calculate mentally what change to give from the till.

The till workers worst nightmare was the pensioner with a fistful of coupons that they had cut diligently from the newspapers and product packages and saved for the next big shop. When you saw them in your till line, your inner voice screamed 'Noooo,' you rang your bell and Ms Fallon would walk over with a big smirk and close the till behind the pensioner concerned. This was simply because you were going to be ages making sure the coupons were in date and that the shop actually stocked the items concerned. Each coupon discount had to be manually keyed into the till – it took forever.

Each person had their own 'float' which they had to collect from the accounts department. As you sat down at a till, you had to take a 'till' reading before you started your shift and then another reading when you left with your float. The accounts department would then calculate how much money should be in your float. When they cashed up, if you were over or under, you got a 'yellow' warning. Three yellows meant you got a red and were banned from the tills.

The till training at Waitrose HQ was just a simulated version of a real shop. One third of the trainees would sit on the tills, while the other two thirds would take baskets and trollies of pre-loaded fake shopping to tills and pay with monopoly money.

At the end, you your float was checked. You had to learn how to process credit cards and what to look for, such as expiry dates. It was the same for cheques, which had to be accompanied by a guarantee card for purchases over £25. Then you had staff discounts and of course the dreaded 'money off' promotional coupons.

I am pleased to report all the Hythe branch staff members passed with flying colours. Upon our return, Ms Fallon was delighted with four new recruits.

Once you had taken your till training, you were officially part of Ms Fallon's team, and then we all had to listen out for the shop-floor announcement of, 'All queue busters to the tills please.' When you heard this, you had to make your way to the front of the shop and take your place at the empty tills.

Luckily, my solo role on non-food meant I was normally excluded from 'queue buster 'duties. I did perform lunchtime cover for the permanent till staff, but that required an individual announcement for a select person to head for the tills.

Two months after the till training, Ms Fallon realised my initials were KP, so her usual announcement immediately changed to, 'Can all queue busters, excluding Nutty, please come to the tills.' She never faltered thereafter, finding it just as amusing eighteen months later. If the queues were really long, my non-food exclusion went, then 'Can Nutty come to the tills please' was broadcast to the shop floor.

I was not a great fan of being on the tills, but it did make the time go quickly. The relentless queue of customers and occasional face you recognised from the village – a parent of a friend or the occasional teacher – would appear before you.

I got a couple of yellow cards for slight till discrepancies in my time at Waitrose, but I never got the red card. Some of my colleagues did, others went out of their way to get the three yellow cards so they could deliberately avoid till duty.

As time passed, you went from a junior weekender to being treated like full-time staff. Indeed, I was working full-time during part of my school holidays as this enabled Waitrose mums to have time off while their children were off school. The added income put more beer money in my pockets.

My flirtation with the deli girls went on unabated, and it was just as well, as it saved me when my good friend Nick Cringle became engaged to Carol Picketts.

Nick and Carol were in my year at school, and both now attended Totton College. We all considered them to be mad to get engaged at such a youthful age, but what did we know? I can report they are still happily married, proving us all wrong.

With Nick and Carol's engagement party approaching, the pressure was on, all my college friends were bringing dates. I was determined not to be the only singleton at the party. To fail to bring a date would be an abject humiliation and had to be avoided at all costs. Added to this pressure was the fact that it was a 'village' event, meaning that all the parents were going to be there, including mine.

After a great deal of thought and a sleepless night, I decided that humiliation could only be avoided if Jane Whatney was really interested in me, and not just having a great deal of fun at my expense! I decided I had to call her bluff; she was my only realistic option.

The Saturday after receiving the party invitation, I went down to the Waitrose shop floor with my loaded trolley. The soap powder was the nearest product to the deli, and so I lingered, stacking the shelves with the various brands of soap powder, gazing over from the aisle at Debbie, Sue, and Jane.

I waited nervously for an opportunity and, when the coast was clear and there were no customers in earshot, I resolutely strode over from the safety of my aisle to the deli. Leaning on the counter, I called Jane over to me. I could feel my heart thumping in my chest – this was alien territory for me, and I was incredibly nervous. Both Sue and Debbie stopped what they were doing as Jane approached the counter, they watched intently.

I was basing my invitation on the winks and smiles and flirting that Jane, and to a lesser extent I, had been engaging in since I started working at Waitrose. I had never asked a girl on a date before and certainly never imagined doing so in such a public place, and with an interested audience watching avidly.

I could sense both Debbie and Sue rooting for me – this just made me more nervous. Red-cheeked with embarrassment I looked over at a grinning Jane. I blurted out, 'I have a party to go to in two weeks' time. It's a Saturday night, and I wondered if you would like to go with me.' I waited anxiously for her answer.

Jane leaned further forward, and asked, 'Is this a date, Parky?' Parky being her nickname for me.

'Well, yes,' I stammered, flustered as this was not going the way it was supposed to go. I was looking for a binary answer, preferably yes, but Jane seemed to be enjoying me being so far out of my comfort zone.

'What sort of party?' she innocently asked with a mischievous twinkle in her eye.

'It's an engagement party at Hardley Community Hall. All my mates are going to be there. There's a DJ and bar.' I figured it best not to mention the parents at this stage.

Jane hesitated; she was not going to let me off lightly. She leaned a little closer over the counter and whispered, 'I will only go if you give me a kiss.' With both her colleagues watching, I leaned over and planted a kiss on her waiting lips.

I could hear Sue and Debbie laughing, and as I pulled away, Jane was grinning triumphantly as she said loudly, 'Then you have a date, Parky.'

Relieved that I had received a positive answer, I replied, 'Great.'

I quickly retreated to the safety of the soap powder, attempting to look casual, and trying even harder not to look back at the deli counter. I could hear the three girls giggling and chatting in a huddle. You would have thought I had just asked Jane to marry me!

I felt happy that I had plucked up the courage from somewhere and immensely relieved that I now had an actual date – especially a date who was going to surprise a few people.

As the day went on and I continued to think about the pending party, my happiness was replaced with growing anxiety. All my mates and my parents were going to be at the party, and I had this very unpredictable girl on a first date. If the date went badly I was going to have to face Jane at Waitrose afterwards.

On the Saturday of Nick Cringle and Carol Pickett's engagement party, I was nervous about what lay ahead. I went down to the shop floor with a trolley of washing-up liquid and toilet rolls, and I remember glancing at the deli counter at the end of the aisle and panicking when I saw just Sue and Debbie – no Jane???

I waited briefly for the lone customer to clear the deli counter, I quickly walked over to a beaming smile from Sue, but it was Debbie who crossed the counter to talk. 'Looking forward to your date tonight?' she asked.

'Yes, where is Jane?' I replied nervously.

Debbie laughed, as it was obvious I was concerned Jane was not in view and might not have been at work. Debbie quickly reassured me that Jane was in the chiller up in the stockroom and would be on the shop floor shortly. I was relieved. Then Sue came over, telling me I was 'in for a treat' as Jane had described to them both the dress she had lined up for the party.

I beat a hasty retreat back to the safety of the non-food aisle. Before I left the shop floor with my empty trolley, I spotted the three girls chatting, so I went back over. Jane walked to the counter as I approached, "I hope you're picking me up, Parky. I can't walk through Hardley village in my dress and high heels.'

At this stage, I had not passed my driving test. I had, like all the boys in the village, flirted with a 50CC Yamaha FS1E as this was the standard mode of transport when a New Forest boy hit sixteen. But two very swift wipe-outs had convinced me that this was not for me, I had two options for picking Jane up: my parents or Gary Highton. Gary was my only school friend with his own car at that stage, albeit a Morris Minor!

'Sure Jane,' I replied. 'Give me your address and I'll come over. Shall we say seven-thirty?'

With a very worryingly cheeky grin, she nodded and passed me a piece of paper. On it was her address and phone number with two exceptionally large X's on the bottom.

That night as Waitrose closed and I left the shop I did not see Jane. I hopped into the car with Josie and was delivered, as usual, to the Butts Ash bus stop before rushing home to get ready.

My parents made a fuss about my mysterious girlfriend, and I told them to behave. I dressed smart casual, which I had already double-checked with Nick and Carol was the preferred dress code, whereas my parents were suited and booted, as all the parents had opted to go formal.

Gary Highton lived on the Butts Ash estate, just a five minute walk away from Froghall.

Gary is one of life's quiet, unassuming guys who, straight from secondary school, had started work as an apprentice at Fawley Refinery.

Fawley Refinery had been important in the development of local villages. Hardley is the closest village to the refinery, it sits just outside the New Forest borders, which enabled housebuilders to develop a Wimpey estate to house workers in the 1970s. The majority of the population in Hardley were either directly or indirectly connected to the refinery.

The drama group I belonged to was based in the 'Esso Cinema' in Hardley. This doubled as the local theatre, and, as the name implies it was built by oil giant Esso for the local community.

So why is this important? Well, Gary set off with me in his Morris Minor, and our first stop was to pick up his 'girlfriend' for the night.

Like me, Gary had been compelled to improvise on this front, asking out our schoolfriend Keith Lomas's younger sister, Megan. Megan was just fifteen at the time, but as her elder brother Keith was going to the party, and Gary being classified as 'safe' by Megan's parents, they were happy with her attending.

As we headed out of Dibden Purlieu towards Hardley, Gary asked for the address we were driving to. When I told him, he almost choked, and he immediately asked for Jane's surname. I said, 'Whatney.'

It turned out Jane's father was one of the senior managers at the refinery.

Ten minutes later we had turned into what was obviously a very affluent, gravelled road. Each house that we passed seemed to get bigger the further we went down the small country lane. Eventually, we pulled up outside a large wooden bar gate, behind which, a gravel drive led up to a very stately house, set in, and partially obscured by, large established broadleaf trees and bushes.

Gary pulled up alongside the gate, gate and I clambered out. Gary drove away to find a spot in the lane where he could turn the car around. I opened the gate and crunched down the gravel drive towards the house.

I did not even get a chance to knock as the impressive wooden door swung open before I got to it. In the doorway stood a willowy well-manicured middle-aged lady with wavy brown hair and big-rimmed glasses. Seeing the likeness, I immediately knew it was Jane's mum.

A hand was promptly offered. 'Call me Wendy,' she said. 'And you must be the famous Parky we have been hearing about.' I was ushered into a huge hallway dominated by a winding staircase. 'Jane is almost ready. Would you like a drink or anything?' I shook my head, and just as I was about to be guided into the lounge, Jane appeared on the upstairs landing.

As previously stated, Jane was attractive, but very much the girl-next-door type. That said Jane was blessed with a fantastic figure. She was tall – an inch taller than me – and as she started to come down the stairs, I glimpsed for the first time a feature about her that I had never seen before: perfect model-grade legs that just went on forever.

I would not say I was, or have ever been, a 'leg' man, but you could not help but be impressed at the way the dress highlighted her legs. The dress was bright red in colour with spaghetti straps and two thin red ties at bust level, knotted in a large bow. From the back you could see bare skin from her shoulders to just above her hips, meaning no bra.

As Jane continued walking down the stairs, I realised that not only did she have amazing legs but that they were clad in stockings, and she was wearing a suspender belt.

Janes mum laughed at my open jaw. 'Jane darling, my little girl looks fabulous tonight,.' I nearly jumped out of my skin as a very deep male voice added, 'Jane, you look amazing.' Jane's dad had appeared from the lounge and moved beside me while I had been totally distracted by his daughter gliding down the stairs.

He was a huge, imposing man, easily over six feet tall, with broad shoulders. I could not take my eyes off Jane in her dress, and all I could think about was getting her to this party as soon as possible so I could show her off!

As Jane reached the hallway, she looked me straight in the eye and huskily whispered, 'Well?' Before I could say anything, she did a little twirl, giving me another chance to enjoy a glimpse of her amazingly long, nylon-clad legs.

'Wow,' was all I could muster. I have to say she looked beautiful, with bright red lipstick, a little eye shadow and a cheeky grin. It was an embarrassment taking her out of this mansion, dressed as she was, and expecting her to clamber into a Morris Minor.

Jane's dad was not going to let his daughter walk down the gravel drive in heels, so I was despatched to open the gate. With her father's added encouragement, a very sheepish Gary drove his car up the drive to the doorstep of the house.

Jane prepared to get into the back seat with as much dignity as the dress would allow. I quickly volunteered to clamber into the back with Megan and allow Jane the more dignified front passenger seat.

Once Jane was seated in Gary's none-too-impressive car – I say that, but to Gary it was the most impressive thing on four wheels, I made brief introductions and explained to Jane that Gary was an apprentice at the refinery.

Gary gingerly pulled around the driveway and back into the narrow country lane.

Luckily, the trip from Jane's house to the venue was short, and just ten minutes after leaving her house we had parked. As we climbed back out of Gary's car and walked the short distance to the hall, I could hear the music. I spotted my parents' car, so I knew Mother was going to have her eyes glued to the door.

As we walked in with Jane on my arm, dozens of eyes homed in on us. I could see my group of mates over in the corner farthest from the door and conveniently close to the bar. Jane's attendance that evening was to have a significant impact. You see, I was one of those poor lads girls would like to have as a 'friend' or considered to be 'like a brother' which to your average teenage boy is the ultimate insult.

Jane Whatney, looking as she did that evening, moved the goalposts for me and opened the door to my first serious girlfriend.

All my close friends were in attendance: Lisa Davis, Charlotte Luke, Steve Breen, Keith Lomas (Megan's brother), Pete Helms, Suzie Jones, and of course

Gary, Nick, and Carol. This was the first time my Dibden village college friends had ever seen me with a girl on my arm with romantic inclinations.

I introduced Jane to my friends and their partners, and I found her a chair at the table. With trepidation, I left her as I went to the bar to get the 'white wine spritzer' she had requested.

I had considered walking Jane over to the parents knowing they would expect an early introduction. But I decided to let the poor girl settle and have a sip of her drink first.

I rushed back to Jane as fast as I could, to monitor the conversation and ensure no embarrassing stories were being bandied about. The moment I sat down, and Jane had her drink, she grabbed my hand and held it.

I remember little about the initial flow of conversation, but after Nick had made a quick speech to the gathered guests, the music started in earnest and Jane immediately dragged me up onto the dance floor.

With more abandon than I had ever witnessed at a Waitrose disco, she let her hair down. The fact that she did not know anybody at the party encouraged her to be a little more 'expressive' than normal as she danced. I was as mesmerised as everyone else as she wiggled, spun, and glided around the dance floor, the dress flying, the legs flashing. Not that I was complaining at all – the more people watched us, the bigger my esteem grew.

For the next three hours or so, we alternated between sitting at the table, drinking, eating, and hitting the dance floor.

As we returned once again to our table, my mum could contain herself no longer. She had given up on me bringing Jane over by that time, and so she came over to introduce herself. I had still not warned Jane that my parents were at the party, but she took it in her stride.

As my mother started to chat with Jane, I was sent for drinks with dad. When we arrived at the bar, dad just slapped me on the back, and like Butch from the *Tom and Jerry* cartoons, it more or less said, 'That's my boy.'

I quickly returned to ensure that, yet again, events were not moving out of my control as Jane and Mum exchanged pleasantries. Luckily, before too long, the slow dances were on, and I held out my hand and escorted my date back onto the dance floor.

Desperate to ensure none of my 'mates' cut in, I held onto Jane for all I was worth. We danced through Eric Clapton's ' Wonderful tonight' and the Bee Gees 'How deep is your love,' but it was Leo Sayer's 'When I Need You' that I remember most.

Jane was, by this stage, a little tipsy, and she snuggled remarkably close. She had dispensed with her high heels early on, and I was desperately trying not to step on her toes. Jane felt great in my arms. I could feel the heat of her body, her hair slightly damp from perspiration, and her face slowly tilting up. Naturally, our lips moved ever closer, and we engaged in our first real kiss.

Everything else in the room vanished from thought. In that moment, I could have been anywhere – this kiss was all that mattered. When we finally stopped kissing, we just looked at each other for a moment, and without a word we left the dance floor and walked back to the table holding hands.

Not long after that, people started packing up. Gary had already departed, being under orders to return his young date at a respectable time. To my parents' delight this left them as my only option for getting Jane home.

I could tell the parents were impressed as we pulled up at the barred gate outside Jane's house. Jane did not hesitate in getting out of the car and encouraging me to walk her down the gravel drive to her front door, all concern for her high heels gone.

Once I had escorted Jane to the front door, I thanked her for her company and made to turn back. My dad had opted to turn the car around at that stage, but Jane was not going to let me go that easily. With her trademark grin and emboldened by the white wine spritzers she had downed; Jane pulled my lips to hers and another very enthusiastic kiss ensued.

I was like a rabbit in headlights; not just because my parents could have returned to the end of the drive by now but the prospect of her dad choosing this moment to open the door – he was a man mountain! With our final kiss of the evening over, we once again said our goodbyes and I walked back towards my parents' car. I heard the front door open, and Jane's voice call out 'See you at work on Thursday, Parky!'

The funny thing is that 'Parky' stuck after that night – both Charlotte and Lisa started calling me by that name. Although I do not see Lisa anymore, I am in contact with Charlotte and when she writes or calls me Parky, I remember Jane Whatney and her red dress.

Jane was an only child, and as you may have gathered, her parents were affluent. She was most definitely the apple of their eyes. I would not say Jane was spoilt, but what she wanted she usually got, one way or another. Jane had all the confidence in the world.

Seventeen-year-old New Forest boys usually dated younger girls. The height of passion was a kiss on the lips, and if you were ultra-lucky a quick fumble.

Seventeen-year-old New Forest girls dated older boys and were, shall we say, much more experienced than us boys. That said, very few had surrendered their innocence totally.

These factors weighed on my mind. A relationship with Jane could quickly move beyond my comfort zone. I also assumed that Sue and Debbie would always get a full update on the current state of our relationship. This made me very wary and reluctant to jump into another date with Jane.

In hindsight, what a twit I was! But at that time in my life, it seemed like the safest choice was to take a step back.

On the trip to college the following Monday, the back seats of Coach 3 was full of talk about the party, and, in particular, both Lisa and Charlotte seemed intent on finding out more about Jane and our 'relationship'. The main pressure, however, was on the home front. My mother was keen for me to bring Jane round for a 'meal.'

Let me explain a little about Charlotte Luke.

I had known Charlotte since my family first moved into the village and I started at Applemore Secondary School. Charlotte was the middle of five sisters. Her father was a famous, if eccentric, New Forest artist.

The Luke family owned a large, detached house called Heatherdene, on the main road into Dibden Purlieu village. Charlotte's parents had a very colourful and fiery relationship. Often, their fights would be so spectacular that Charlotte would walk out, and I would get a phone call to meet her, or she would just move in with Lisa Davis for a night or two.

This happened so often that after an unfortunate house fire, her father bought a static caravan and parked it in the back garden, and Charlotte quickly moved in.

To Charlotte, I developed into a confidant and a shoulder to lean on. We would often just meet up after college and walk and talk. Throughout our college years, Charlotte had an on-off relationship with Lisa Davis's much older brother David.

This relationship with David Davis meant Charlotte was close to Lisa. Charlotte did not seem to confide in her siblings, and with a house full of females, her father aside, she always seemed happier to find male company.

We knew that anything we said to each other would go no further, and so that Monday lunchtime, after Nick and Carol's engagement party, I explained to Charlotte all my concerns about a relationship with Jane Whatney.

I went on two more, very tame, dates with Jane – one to see *Alien* at the Odeon in Southampton, which with hindsight was not the most romantic movie to take a young lady to. Having said that, *Alien* did give us an excuse for plenty of hugging and hand holding. At the time it came out, this film was publicised as 'the scariest movie ever made' and there had been anecdotal news reports of people being sick in cinemas and walking out.

On the other occasion, I took Jane out to a Chinese restaurant in Hythe.

I think the long gaps between dates and my lack of frequent phone contact finally communicated to Jane. I was partially relieved when she told me she had moved her attentions to a guy from Hardley village and away from Waitrose.

In the meantime, the last singleton on the Waitrose deli counter, Sue Eason, had become romantically entangled with a member of the Waitrose fruit-and-veg team – a 'gentleman' called Nigel Carlton, who was a horrible individual. It was a toxic relationship that would come back to bite both Sue and me in the years ahead when we both lived and worked in London.

For a while, I went back to my bachelor student life, and my relationships at college changed slightly post Nick and Carol's engagement.

Out of all the male friends I had at college, Nick Cringle was the closest. I had been present when Nick asked Carol out on their first date. I watched as Nick and Carol just got closer and their relationship developed, and other friendships were slowly side-lined. Carol was close to both Charlotte and Lisa, and I believe seeing Carol and Nick's relationship bloom had been a revelation for Lisa.

Prior to Nick and Carol's engagement, Lisa Davis had been firmly in the 'older boys only' camp with Charlotte. But seeing two of our close friends having such a happy relationship changed her perception of boys our age.

To explain a little about the young lady concerned, Lisa was a 'mistake,' and was much younger than siblings. Lisa's sister, Angie, was Seven years older, and her brother, David, was five years older. Lisa's parents were genuinely nice, but because of their advanced years were detached from their youngest daughter, letting her do whatever she wanted.

To make matters worse, Lisa was an exceedingly early developer. At the age of thirteen, she had a figure that meant she easily passed as a much older teenager. Indeed, I always thought, prior to Totton College, that Lisa was significantly older than us. I had no classes with her at Applemore, and we never mixed in the same circles at school, so it was a surprise to see her getting onboard our coach on our first day at Totton College.

Lisa's relationship with Charlotte and Carol meant she became an immediate part of our Totton College group, and we mixed increasingly at college and socially. I quickly developed a bit of a crush on her. Lisa was always very pleasant to me, and I guess in hindsight because she 'forbidden fruit' and a rebel, she was very appealing to a boring conformist boy like me.

During many conversations with Lisa, I learned that she lost her virginity at an incredibly early age while dating a boy in his late teens. Lisa's experience with her much older boyfriends meant she experienced more at an early age than she should have.

Lisa had very expressive eyes and I quickly spotted that underneath the facade of confidence was an insecure girl who had grown up way too quickly. She always smoked, and not just cigarettes – throughout the time I knew her, she was smoking dope and taking the odd 'pill.' All of this merely made me want to take her under my wing, convinced that I could be a positive influence.

One evening, Lisa just turned up on my parents' doorstep. My mother shouted that 'someone' was at the door for me as I sat in my downstairs bedroom. (The house was a strange Swiss style with two upstairs bedrooms, and mine was downstairs.)

I am sure that if it had been Charlotte at the door then Mum would have warmly invited her in and made her feel at home. Lisa, however, was left standing at the front door. I was never sure if my mother had heard the rumours about Lisa or if it was her not-very-tactful way of showing displeasure at this older-looking girl turning up unannounced.

I was as shocked as my mother to see Lisa on the doorstep. I remember distinctly she had on a powder-blue V-neck jumper and her usual blue jeans. For a moment, we just looked at each other, Lisa's eyes sparkled, and she gave me a lovely smile.

When my senses returned I quickly ushered her into the house, down the corridor and into my bedroom. I put on an LP record, and we sat and chatted. My conversations with Lisa always flowed easily – we never experienced any uncomfortable silences.

I remember that Lisa looked slightly nervous, but the warm smile never left her lips, and I was mesmerised by her. On my mother's third interruption, we decided to leave the safety of 3 Froghall Close and go for a walk.

Over the years that followed, this evening took on an almost surreal, mystical aura.

It had rained while we had been chatting in my bedroom, so when we left the house all the trees and lamp posts seemed to glisten. As we walked, the spiders' webs on the lamp posts seemed to sparkle, and there was this mist everywhere swirling around us. Even the most mundane sights became somehow magical.

We walked through the estate and turned towards the village; Lisa took my hand. It just felt very natural and made me amazingly happy. We entered the village itself, and I remember desperately wanting to be seen by someone, anyone, but everyone seemed to have vanished. No people, no cars, just Lisa and me walking hand in hand.

We continued through to the forest front, chatting endlessly, and ambled down Roman Road towards Applemore School. Roman Road was a mostly unlit wooded road that ran between Dibden Purlieu village and the New Forest.

Eventually, we came to a secluded wooded section, and Lisa practically pulled me in. We went a little deeper into the wood, just out of view of any passing cars, where Lisa backed herself against a large oak tree. Despite the dampness and the occasional raindrop falling from the leaves at that stage, I did not care – it could have been pelting down and I would not have cared.

We chatted on for a long while until Lisa laughed aloud, looked me straight in the eye, threw her arms around my shoulders and said, 'Parky, for goodness' sake, shut up and kiss me!'

It was not that I had not wanted to; it had occurred to me, but I was desperate not to overstep the boundaries or make a mistake. This voice kept telling me I was reading too much into the situation, I was in complete disbelief that I was there, alone, with Lisa Davis.

Our very first real, full-on, enthusiastic kiss was quickly followed by more, and those magical moments always stayed vividly in the memory. Once we started and I realised I had 'permission,' I could not stop kissing her. I did not want to stop kissing her. But eventually, she asked me to walk her home, and that evening was the start of a defining relationship.

Just an hour beforehand, I had been bored in my bedroom, contemplating an uneventful evening, and here I was, walking home this incredibly sexy girl. It all seemed too good to be true – these things just did not happen to me.

Thereafter, much to my delight, Lisa and I started spending increasing amounts of time together. We sat together on the coach to and from college and spent breaktimes and lunchtimes together. We spent evenings together, either in the company of the others or alone. If alone we spent a lot of time in her bedroom listening to music, as Lisa was determined to broaden my musical taste beyond ABBA.

When in company more often than not Lisa would come to my house with Nick and Carol, Charlotte, or Steve Breen. I am not sure how apparent it was to my parents that Lisa and I were in a relationship. My parents really liked my circle of friends at college. In particular, my mother liked Charlotte, and I am sure she secretly hoped Charlotte and I would get together.

As a group of seventeen year-olds gathering socially in numbers, we quickly wore out our welcome at our various homes, and so we needed to find ourselves a venue for our social get-togethers.

Dibden Purlieu had four local public houses within walking distance. The Jester was the decent-quality village pub group and was the venue of choice for our parents, so we avoided it.

The Travellers Rest was a small real-ale venue and home to the socially inept and the rougher crowd of bikers and punk rockers.

The Croft was more of a restaurant than a pub and was always terribly busy.

That left the Heath Hotel, which was known as the grandads' choice.

The Heath Hotel sat at the very edge of the village, next to a roundabout on the Marchwood bypass and the main road to Beaulieu and the plentiful New Forest pubs.

The Heath Hotel was a little run-down and noticeably quiet. Its two bars were always empty and therefore perfect for us and so became our social venue.

The proprietor knew we were borderline underage but was not about to turn away a dozen regular customers. He was rewarded with our custom at least three times a week, on Wednesday, Friday, and Saturday nights.

The thing I remember most about our nights at the Heath Hotel was the jukebox, with its selection of Johnny Cash, Ms Mills, Dolly Parton, Kenny Rogers, and the like. We all groaned when one of the old guys headed for the jukebox armed with a handful of coins!

It was at these drinking evenings at the Heath Hotel that my relationship with Lisa blossomed. She impacted on all aspects of my teenage life. I started listening to music I would never have previously considered getting into – the Undertones, the Sex Pistols, the Clash, the Jam, XTC and the Buzzcocks.

My newfound love of punk music impacted on my clothes. My dad's old donkey jacket became a favourite, along with ripped jeans and even black eyeshadow.

However, on that fateful day I came home with a Mohican hairdo – manufactured by Lisa with sugar water to evaluate the look – my dad finally drew the line. He looked up briefly as I walked into the lounge, turned back to the TV he was watching, and in a very level, calm voice said, 'Nice haircut, son, but by this time tomorrow either the haircut goes, or you do.'

Needless to say, punk or not, the Mohican quickly went. My new rebellious streak was not about to challenge my father's sincerity on being potentially homeless.

My first live music concert was with Lisa. We set off one Saturday for the Southampton Gaumont Theatre to see the Stranglers play live. This was the first of many concerts I attended over the next decade.

Inevitably, my frequent nights out drinking was followed by my first dabble with cannabis. On the night in question, after a long drinking session at the Heath Hotel, Lisa and I staggered homeward, and Lisa offered to share her 'spliff.' This time, and the few times that were to follow, I can state clearly that I was completely unaffected.

It did not do anything for me, but as we walked, my arm around Lisa, I can only conclude that it had an effect on her. We stopped walking and kissed, and Lisa whispered in my ear that she wanted me to take her to bed.

Up until this fateful moment, we had been going further and further when alone, but this was the moment – no going back.

I was stunned. This was a very experienced Lisa, and I was a complete novice. Being a virgin was something I would never have admitted, but it must have been blatantly obvious to Lisa. Plus, I had just downed five or six lager and limes. But there was no ducking out of this. Once we got back to her house and her bedroom, she started undressing and all concerns vanished.

Lisa was amazing. Without going into any detail, I enjoyed many firsts that night, and Lisa was absolutely the right person at the right time. I know there are clichés about the first time, but I will always be a little in love with Lisa for making that moment the absolute best introduction to sex anyone could have had.

But as with all things, after the peak came the crash.

That evening was Lisa's parting gift to me. I went home thinking this was it, she was the one, we were on a path to a life together. But everything I had done to put distance between Jane Whatney and myself, was now coming my way from Lisa.

Lisa had decided to move on, and a gentleman called Graham Smythe started joining us all at the Heath a couple of weeks later, as her new boyfriend.

Hindsight being the wonderful thing that it is, I can see what happened. Lisa had enjoyed our four-and-a-bit months together, but she was a restless soul. The fact we were at college together five days a week, as well as all our social time together, had made her feel claustrophobic.

Prior to her relationship with me, her love life and social circle were kept far apart. Lisa had never invited her previous boyfriends to any social gatherings. Her boyfriends had just been names. We never met them, and I suspect, because they were much older, they had no interest in meeting or socialising with us.

Graham Smythe was three years older, working full time and actually a really nice guy, so he was the perfect compromise between Lisa's previous older boyfriends and me.

Lisa and I did not break up as such; we never had that discussion. I have to conclude that this was because she was concerned our mutual friends would be caught in the middle of any acrimony. It just went cold and ended when Graham appeared.

Lisa did not do confrontation, and when she just stopped coming round and being available to me, I was distraught. To me, this was 'the' girl. I was totally besotted, and I remember thinking the world had ended. The pain was physical and mental, but I tried to put a brave face on and hoped she would come back.

When it was obvious Lisa was not coming back, my answer was to avoid all social contact with her. That meant not going to the Heath Hotel to meet my friends, sitting elsewhere on the coach to college and avoiding all contact, all of which was a very public show of my feelings.

Charlotte was immediately there for me, talking sense and telling me frankly that I was only punishing myself by cutting all contact and isolating myself. To all intents and purposes, Charlotte told me straight that by acting so immaturely, I was telling Lisa she had done exactly the right thing. The best thing I could do was 'man up,' take it on the chin and move on. Charlotte did not just give me a strong talking to – she followed it up with action and demanded that we go to the Heath together that evening.

Looking back, I suspect an element of collusion may have gone on between Lisa and Charlotte.

That night, Charlotte and I walked together through the village to the Heath Hotel. The moment I walked in, Graham Smythe came over and insisted on buying me a pint and officially introducing himself. This just made me feel even worse about my behaviour.

It turned out Lisa had told him about me and that she felt guilty and was worried about the potential fallout. Graham put himself in the firing line, for which I admired him. As I say, he was genuinely a good guy.

As much as I wanted to dislike him, he was actually incredibly good for Lisa. Graham bridged the gap for her – he was happy to socialise with us, but at the same time he was not a consistent element of our social circle, so Lisa could pick and choose.

Years later, on one of my visits back to the New Forest, I invited Lisa out for a meal, and we chatted about the past and our short time together. She explained that despite the relationship being short, we had given each other what we needed at that time. I couldn't argue with her summary.

Years after this meal, by which time I had bought a one-bedroom flat in Kingsbury, northwest London, unexpectedly Lisa Davis asked if she could visit for a 'few weeks.' Not knowing what was going on, I let her have my bed, and I slept on the sofa bed in the lounge.

I could only get one week of the two weeks Lisa stayed with me off work, so for first week Lisa contented herself with exploring London alone. For the second week we did all the usual tourist sights together. Then Lisa left, and I did not see or hear from her ever again.

I discovered that soon after her visit to me in Kingsbury, Lisa had left Dibden Purlieu and vanished.

I believe now that she had been evaluating, to see if I was still interested and would invite her to move in. I did not know at the time that her parents had sold their house on the Butts Ash estate, and that Lisa was looking for a new home and direction.

That was Lisa, and sadly that was me – as always, I missed the signals, and Lisa was expecting me to read between the lines.

For a long time after my short but eventful relationship with Lisa, I played safe in relationships, not wanting to get hurt like that ever again. It was a long time before my next 'serious' relationship.

College was getting evermore serious, and as much as I wanted to avoid thinking about work and my future, I couldn't. Taking only one A-level meant the end of the road was approaching in terms of education.

Steve Dickinson's decision to join the Metropolitan Police Cadets at 16 had given me a firm interest in looking at a career in the police force. Steve made frequent visits back to his parents in Marchwood village during my time at Totton College.

He owned a green Hillman estate car and so, being a short drive from Dibden Purlieu, we socialised whenever he was in the area. Steve always got along well with my parents, and they were always pleased to see him.

That said, my dad had serious reservations about me taking a career in the Met Police, preferring me to apply to county forces. I hedged my bets and applied to Avon and Somerset, Devon and Cornwall, and the Met Police. The first to reply was Devon and Cornwall, inviting me to a four-day induction course in Exeter during the summer.

I also investigated a career in the Royal Navy. Being in a port town like Southampton, and with Portsmouth just down the road, some of my schoolmates had joined the Navy. The Navy careers office was just below the Bargate in Southampton High Street.

One Saturday I took myself off onto the Hythe Ferry, over the Solent, and after a short walk up the high street, I went in. The sailor behind the desk, dressed in full Naval attire, gave me a brief look up and down and invited me to sit. He started handing over brochures about Navy life. He asked what courses I was taking at college, then he sat back, crossed his arms, and said very plainly that joining as a normal able seaman was not going to work. He said I was too 'posh,' that able seamen were rough-and-ready types, and he could not see me fitting in.

His second thought was I could join as an artificer, but as I had dropped all sciences this was not going to be an option either.

Then he produced the only other alternative, based on my A-level being in Geography – I could join the Navy and serve on their survey ships. Pleased with his solution, he then gave me a mixed sales pitch. Serving on survey ships meant no uniforms, a much more relaxed service, and people I would be able to mix with.

The unwelcome news was that 'normal' Navy vessels would sail into big foreign ports like Sydney where the sailors could disembark and enjoy quality R&R, but a survey vessel would often pull into a remote port where the only inhabitants were penguins.

As I walked out of the office with brochures and my 'Life in the Navy' carrier bag, I considered this to be an option but very much a plan B. My mind was now, more than ever, focused on the police as a career. As luck would have it, had I taken this Navy path, there was a good chance I would have been on HMS Endurance, which involved in the start of the Falklands War in 1982.

I had a trip to the Devon and Cornwall Police in Exeter pencilled into my diary and returned to college life with my weekend and evening job at Waitrose. Those happy, relaxed college days whistled past.

I rekindled my relationship with Julie Ross. We had been good friends during my early days at secondary school. With Steve Dickinson out of the way, I did not have to put up with him teasing me relentlessly about Julie having a crush on me.

Despite this teasing, I had sneaked around to Julie's house from time to time during my time at secondary school. Julies parents had taken a liking to me and were always more than happy for me to come in and spend time with her.

When I attended Totton College my social circle changed, and I did not socialise with Julie, who was also there, at all.

The goalposts had moved – aged thirteen you could just be friends with a girl, but at sixteen any fraternisation with a girl meant you were 'going out.' Julie had boyfriends and mixed with, what was considered to be, the more 'swotty' highbrow elements of Totton College.

With my friend/tormentor safely out of the way at police cadets in Hendon and my relationship with Lisa over, I started straying back to Partridge Road and socialising with Julie once more.

I felt safe with Julie, and she was an extremely sweet and tactile young lady. Neither of us wanted rumours to start, and from my viewpoint it gave me the best of both worlds.

Taking a leaf firmly out of Lisa Davis's book, I kept my love life and social life apart. Not very gentlemanly in retrospect, but things with Julie did get serious in later years.

I was approaching the end of my college days in the summer of 1980, and eventually the time came to make the trip to Exeter for the daunting prospect of four days with the Devon and Cornwall constabulary.

I remember dad driving me to Southampton Central train station – the journey was long and required a change at Reading.

I arrived extremely late that afternoon. The police headquarters was huge, and I was immediately shown to the training wing and my bedroom. We were encouraged to settle quickly and make our way to a meeting room to have a light meal and mix with the other attendees.

There were thirty of us, a comprehensive mix of males and females and a range of ages and backgrounds. I was one of the youngest, still being at college, but there were ex-forces, second jobbers, including a schoolteacher looking for a career change, and a couple of university types. But this was 1980 and height restrictions for applicants to the Police were still in force – males had to be a minimum of 6ft 1in – there was a distinct lack of racial minority interest.

The people on the course were a good bunch, and we bonded immediately. Post meal, we went to the 'social club,' which was a subsidised police bar where we could mix with off-duty police officers This was something we needed little encouragement to do.

That night at the bar, I heard a couple of anecdotes that set the tone for the four days. The first was that up until a year or so before my trip, the attendees on the induction course had been supplied with police uniforms. However, a couple of enterprising criminals had attended the course, run off with the uniforms and conducted a heist in them. To this day, I do not know if it was true.

The other more graphic story came from a very stocky police officer who said that they had regular problems with off-duty sailors getting into fights with locals in the bars and clubs. This meant sailors ending up in Police cells overnight and subsequently being loaded into police vans, driven to the dockside, and 'delivered' to the Navy Shore Patrol. It was a regular part of their routine, and this tickled the ex-forces guys in particular.

The next day, we did a street run and had a series of school-style lectures on the police as a career, the law, and the judicial system. These lectures were consistently attended by three senior officers who were evaluating us.

There were question-and-answer sessions, and one that has stayed firmly in the mind was an exercise that involved spending half an hour writing a speech on something we felt strongly about. We had to give this speech to the panel of officers and the other attendees, and then answer questions.

Again, hindsight being a wonderful thing, I fell into the trap of picking a topical subject and something that had been a regular cause of heated discussions in the Totton College common room: the pros and cons of unilateral nuclear disarmament.

My mistake became very apparent when the clever teacher stood up and gave a speech based on the pros and cons of owning a formal dinner jacket over hiring one! As you can imagine, the Q&A on his speech was brief.

When the time came to give my speech, I went up and delivered an enthusiastic case for maintaining our nuclear deterrent, and then the barrage began. Everyone had a viewpoint, and even the hitherto quiet panel of three senior police officers weighed in, challenging my position, and asking lots of questions.

One senior officer on the panel asked me firmly if I had heard the phrase 'Better red than dead'! Nobody else spent the time up front, defending their position, or answering questions as I did. By the time I sat down, I was convinced I had blown it; a police officer is supposed to be politically neutral, and I felt an idiot for having picked one of the political hot potatoes of the age.

As we filtered out, the teacher slapped me on the back and told me I was brave for picking such a topic and he felt I had managed it well. Sadly, I did not think his opinion was going to count for much.

The medical must go down as one of the most embarrassing events of my life, as it all took place in front of a panel of three doctors. Standing in just my Y-fronts and being incredibly skinny at that time, one of them looked over and said, 'You do know, Mr Parker, that you will have to face some exceptionally large, often hostile individuals in the line of normal police work.'

I remember losing my temper at that stage due to the frustration of the earlier Q&A still playing on my mind and now having to stand in just my Y-fronts and answer more questions. I fired back at him, 'If you're saying all confrontations inevitably end up in violence, then I think I will have failed completely as a police officer.' The doctor did not reply, but as panic struck, I noted one of his colleagues chuckling, so I figured I might have got away with it.

At the end of the induction, we were told our attendance would be evaluated and that we would be contacted by post.

I bid my fellow attendees goodbye and headed for the train station and my long journey home. I was not sure if I had done enough gain acceptance, but at that stage I did not know that I had already shot myself in the foot in my first couple of hours at Exeter.

On arrival, we had all filled in a quick 'getting to know you' questionnaire, and one of the questions was to list any other constabularies to which we had applied. I had dutifully listed Avon and Somerset and the Met Police.

A week later when proudly telling Steve Dickinson about my trip to Exeter, he told me to expect a rejection from the two county forces. It turned out that there was an unofficial understanding that if any candidate had applied to the Met Police, the country forces would defer.

Steve was right, a letter arrived from the Devon and Cornwall declining to offer me a position. Soon after, a letter arrived confirming that I had been provisionally accepted into the Met Police.

After sitting my exams at Totton College, I was contemplating the summer holidays and waiting for the exam results. This had been the longest period of time my parents had stayed in one location.

In the summer of 1980, dad was offered the manager's position at one of his company's premier London branches. This branch was located on the corner of Tottenham Court Road and Oxford Street, directly opposite the Dominion Theatre.

The new job required my parents to move to London immediately and this meant them temporarily moving into a company-owned flat in Islington. Our house in Froghall was put up for sale.

My younger brother, Robin, was already in the Army at this stage, doing a two-year apprenticeship as a vehicle engineer at the Army Apprentice College Arborfield in Berkshire. There, he was learning blacksmithing, welding, vehicle electrics, hydraulics, and light vehicle mechanics.

That just left me and our dog, Chipper, living in the house in Froghall. (Chipper had been named after the dog in the TV programme *Land of the Giants*.)

I was very reluctant to immediately leave Dibden Purlieu and all my friends and so I reached an accommodation with my parents. I would stay at Froghall, keep the house clean for the estate agents and if needed show people around the house. I would take a temporary full-time position at Waitrose, and I would move to join my parents in London once the sale of house had been completed.

In the meantime, my police career was on hold, as I had received a letter from the Met saying there was no room on the next police intake, meaning I had at least a 12-month wait for the next intake.

I was transferred from my weekender position in the non-food department at Waitrose to the grocery department for my full-time position. This meant occasionally working on the tills full-time, giving Ms Fallon plenty of opportunities to use her 'Can Nutty come to the tills please' trademark PA announcement.

It was on one of these days, sitting in the Waitrose canteen soon after my parents had left for London, when Sue Eason sat next to me. Sue told me that she was leaving Waitrose and Dibden Purlieu to head off to London to start a position as a trainee nurse.

Suddenly, the move to London was not as unattractive as it had been. I eagerly told Sue that my parents had already left for London, and I would be there soon as well, and that my plan was to join Steve Dickinson in the Met Police.

Sue gave me her new London address, Hopkinson House in Vauxhall Bridge Road, Victoria, and we agreed to meet up as soon as I was in London. Sue was as pleased and relieved as I was at the prospect of having someone from the village to meet up with in London.

With my parents out of sight and their ongoing concerns about me having house parties, or worse still, for the house to be in a mess, my grandparents were mobilised. Their small bungalow was just 15 minutes down the road, tucked onto the end of one of the most exclusive roads in Dibden Purlieu village. They would turn up at the Froghall unannounced; usually gran would come bearing food on the basis a teenage boy would not be able to cook for himself. Grandad would often turn up just to kidnap Chipper on the pretence of taking him for a walk and then head off to the Royal Oak Pub just outside Beaulieu for a couple of sneaky pints.

One of my dreads was gran's notorious fish soup.

Gran had been a great cook in her day; in my early impressionable years, her Sunday roasts were amazing.

However, she was past her best, and her wartime habit of making the most of anything meant that any carcass or bone was boiled and turned into soup. Even her salads managed to give me wind. I have no idea how she managed it!

Chipper was a typical dog, and he would eat anything in double-quick time, unless it was gran's soup. Even cunningly mixed into his dog food and soaked into his dog biscuits, he was not having any of it. One sniff and off he went in a huff.

I was reduced to waving gran off, immediately emptying the contents of the bowls down the toilet, washing the bowls up and advising her how good it had been upon her next visit.

One quick tale about gran's cooking was when my parents made a rare return trip to Froghall during this period. Gran arrived early, determined to cook a full Sunday roast and dessert as, on my parents' instructions, the freezer was being emptied prior to the move.

We all sat down and ate a hearty dinner, and then gran announced that, to follow, she had made an apple and blackberry crumble from the contents of the freezer. Just as the custard was being poured into the bowls, Mum asked where the apples had come from, she could not remember any being in the freezer.

Just in time, Mum realised that we were all about to tuck into gran's blackberry and chip crumble!

The day eventually came, and the estate agent hammered the SOLD board outside the house in Froghall. My life in the New Forest was ending.

By now my close friends were all starting their adult lives and heading in various directions. Our regular gatherings ended as everyone moved into full-time employment.

My parents had not managed to buy a house in London by the time the sale of Froghall went through, and so everything went into storage. I loaded up my clothes and personal bits and set off to start my new life in central London, joining my parents in their company flat in Islington.

Fate now played a big hand in the next chapter of my life. Dad was not about to let me do nothing while I waited for my place in Met Police. One evening, he came home and slapped a copy of the *Evening Standard* in front of me, with jobs ringed in pen.

For the majority of the job vacancies dad had highlighted, a phone call was all that was required for me to get a rejection.

My college results meant I ended up with a mixed bunch of exam passes. One A-level, one A/O-level and five O-levels meant I was overqualified for some jobs and underqualified for others.

The dozen potential jobs dad had picked out for me quickly became two. One was a clothes importing business that had a showroom in Dean Street in the heart of London's West End. The other was a back-office position with a commodity brokerage company in the City that required me to go to a recruitment company in Holborn. I booked appointments with both, scheduled for the same day.

Dad told me to come round to his new branch of Horne Brothers where he would 'lend' me a suit for the two upcoming interviews.

As I stood in the changing room of his shop in Tottenham Court Road, being measured, dad gave me a pep talk.

Firstly, he suggested including in the conversation with the clothes importers that he was in the 'business.'

As far as the commodities company went, dad casually told me that my godfather, Dave Ritchings, had worked at a company that had something to do with commodities. He said Dave worked at a place called the 'Clearing House' as a messenger and that it might be worth throwing that into the conversation.

I was kitted out with a fashionable three-piece pinstriped suit, brilliant white shirt, and blue tie; dad told me that should I get either job, I could pay him back for it over the first couple of months of my employment.

With the addresses in hand, I set off for Dean Street.

The shop front, when I found it, was full of colourful ladies' clothes, and as I went in, ladies were browsing the packed aisles and racks of dresses, skirts, and blouses.

I walked over towards the checkout and told the extremely attractive sales assistant I was there for an interview with the owner. I was rewarded with a big smile as she called over a young blonde-haired lady.

I guessed her to be only a year or two older than me, she was heavily made up with thick black eyeliner, blue eyeshadow, and rich red lipstick. The blond-haired lady asked me to follow her.

We walked to the back of the shop and through a door that was cleverly disguised to blend into the fittings in such a way that you would not know it was there.

I followed the young lady out into a stairwell, which was pretty grotty, damp, and cold compared with the flash shop we had just left.

As she started to climb the stairs ahead of me, I realised that her skirt was incredibly short, and it was almost impossible to miss the stocking tops and glimpse of inner thigh as I followed her up the stairs. After a moment of embarrassed shock, I lowered my gaze, concentrated on the stairs, and tried to avoid another glance upwards.

On the second floor was another door out into a stockroom filled with clothes and boxes. I followed my guide as we weaved in and out and towards a glass office where a middle-aged man with noticeably slicked back black hair sat at a desk, speaking on the phone.

Glancing up as the young girl led me in, the man gestured for me to take a seat on the other side of the desk. At a nod from the man, the young lady turned and left us, heading back the way she had come.

As he was finishing his phone call, I could not help but notice the flamboyant nature of his attire. He wore a bright yellow shirt and a tie with a dazzling swirl pattern in yellows and greens, topped off with red braces. He had a large sovereign ring on his finger, a chunky watch, and an overpowering aftershave.

He placed the phone down and offered his hand over the desk. With a firm handshake, he introduced himself and started to explain about the business in an unexpectedly plummy voice.

He was in partnership with a German national, and they were importing innovative ladies' fashion from Europe, primarily Germany and Italy. As well as having their own shop downstairs, they supplied boutiques and shops all around London. They were looking to expand as they were struggling to meet the current demand. Ultimately they had a desire to move beyond London and out into the county towns and cities.

I passed over my CV, he scanned it and quickly handed it back. He explained he was more about personality and first impressions than exam results. Then he asked if I could speak any languages. Sadly, despite having a German mother, languages had never been of interest to me, I had dropped them at the first opportunity at school. I could feel the enthusiasm of the man quickly wane as he explained that, with the main supplier being based in Germany, he ideally wanted someone fluent in German, but he would keep me in mind.

I felt suitably deflated as I left and made my way back down the grotty staircase.

I glanced at my watch; I had an hour to kill before I was due at the recruitment company in Holborn. I jumped on the Tube, and once at Holborn found the office and then went for a cup of tea at a nearby coffee shop to kill time.

This period to myself did me no favours; after what I considered my first rejection earlier, my nerves were building, so I headed back to the recruitment office early.

I pressed the reception button on the street-level entry system, the door buzzed, and I walked up the two flights of stairs and into the office. I explained I was here for an interview for the commodities position, the receptionist asked me to take a seat.

After a thankfully short wait, a very dapper man in his fifties came out, looked me up and down and offered a hand. 'The interview isn't here,' he explained. 'We made you come here first because we wanted to make sure you were presentable. This lot are very conservative. They only stopped wearing bowler hats a few years ago.'

He went on to explain that the trip to Holborn was purely to make sure I did not have multicoloured hair and a safety pin through my nose!

Turned out as I was, in my new suit, I had passed inspection, and so he went on to explain that the job interview was with a company called C. Czarnikow Ltd and they were based at Mark Lane in the City. He said I had half an hour to get there, which should be plenty of time. 'When you get there, ask for John Gollop. He's the head of recruitment.'

Armed with a name and address, I went out the door into Holborn, quickly flagged down a black cab, and set off on the short drive to 66 Mark Lane. The building I arrived at was a very 1960s six-storey office block on the corner of Mark Lane and Hart Street. It was a light-green marble-clad building, and the name 'Czarnikow' and '66' was etched in gold to the right of the entrance doors.

As I entered through the doors into the ground-floor reception, to my immediate right, a large man stood behind the reception desk and asked if he could help me.

A group of another four or five men milled around behind him, indulging in jokey conversation inside what was obviously a post room. I explained that I was here to meet with a John Gollop.

I waited at the desk as he picked up the phone and pressed four digits on the phone keypad. 'John, it's reception. I have a young man here who says he's here for an interview … Oh, OK, I'll give him a call.'

With a slight frown, he redialled. 'Paul, John Gollop asked me to tell you that a young man is here in reception for the interview.' He listened for a second and then put the phone down. Looking back to me he explained 'You're actually having an interview with Paul Thompson. He runs terminal accounts. He'll be down shortly.'

I waited, wondering what 'terminal accounts' was?

Two lift doors lay beyond the reception desk. People were coming and going, and it had the feel of a busy office. Moments later, a friendly looking man in his thirties with a mop of light-coloured hair came out of one of the lifts, smoking a cigarette. His smile was broad and genuine, and he immediately offered his hand.

'You must be Kevin,' he said. 'I'm Paul Thompson. If you would like to follow me, we're pinching one of the directors' offices.' I followed him back into the lift and he hit five. 'We work on the fourth floor, which is the sugar floor,' he said. 'That's our core business, but we also trade cocoa, coffee, soya, palm oil, potatoes and rubber.' The doors opened onto a corridor, and we turned left, beyond a fire door into another corridor with doors left and right, and then we went left into a small office. 'Take a seat,' Paul said. 'You're fresh out of college I understand.'

I explained about my college results and my recent move from the New Forest.

Paul then explained about the position I was applying for. Czarnikow was a commodities clearing and broking company acting on behalf of large companies. Their biggest client was CSR Sugar (Colonial Sugar Refining Company), but they also had major clients in Japan and Europe for whom they cleared and executed orders on the London Commodity Exchange (LCE).

As a result of being members of the LCE, Czarnikow had built brokerage and clearing operations on all the contracts that the LCE traded.

Paul went on to explain that Czarnikow had recently joined the International Petroleum Exchange (IPE), and as a result of that, one of his staff members had transferred onto the IPE trading floor to join the team there.

He then asked the question I had been patiently waiting for: did I know anything about the commodities markets?

I said no, not really, but my godfather had been employed by a company involved in the business.

Paul stubbed out his cigarette and said, 'Oh that's interesting. This is a small community – maybe I know him. What's his name?'

'Dave Ritchings,' I replied. 'I was told that he worked at a place called the Clearing House.'

Paul immediately replied, 'I know Dave really well. It must be the same person – the name is not a common one.'

That was not what I was expecting, and I was on the back foot for a moment, but I decided to elaborate. 'Dave is married to Shelia, and they have two sons, Stewart and Andrew.'

Paul nodded as he lit another cigarette, politely offering me one which I refused. 'Well, I know Shelia as well. She also works at the ICCH. I can't say I know much about the children though. That seals it then – we're talking about the same man.'

He leaned back in his chair for a second in silence and seemed to be studying me before continuing. 'Dave Ritchings is a director at the International Commodities Clearing House (ICCH). He's an important man.'

Without taking a breath, Paul started to talk about the working hours – nine till six with an hour for lunch – and then he paused. 'Salary is not great for your first year, but the bonuses are usually around ten per cent, and you get thirty-five pence a day in luncheon vouchers and a turkey at Christmas.'

I listened intently; did this mean I had the job?

'Starting salary,' Paul went on, 'is three thousand, two hundred pounds for the first year, but the boys supplement their money with overtime, which is paid in cash monthly.' He looked at me. He was offering me the job!

'Great,' I said, 'when do you want me to start?'

'Monday,' Paul replied. 'That will give me the chance to get a contract ready for you to sign and to get payroll sorted. Do you have a bank account?'

I replied I did not, so Paul suggested taking a walk to the nearby branch of William & Glyn's Bank across the road on the corner of Mincing Lane and Fenchurch Street.

He escorted me back down to reception where he called over to the gentleman I had met earlier.

Paul explained that I was joining his department on Monday, and I would need a staff pass. With that, he shook my hand once again and said he would see me on Monday and to get a 'messenger' to show me up to the department when I got there.

Sid, the guy on reception, turned out to be a messenger. Messengers walked all around the City of London, delivering, and picking up mail and important documents. They were an essential communication system in the City at this point in time.

I made my way over to William and Glyn's in Mincing Lane and signed up for a bank account, explaining I needed it for my new job at Czarnikow. After 15 minutes of filling out a form, I walked out. I had a bank account. A cheque book and paying-in book was on its way to my home address, as well as a nifty binder to keep all the statements in.

I felt that life had just changed, and I was officially an 'adult.'

1981

I went home buzzing with the fact I had a job, and my parents were delighted. My euphoria about being in full-time employment partially burst when dad said.

'Well done, son. That's great news. Now how much are you going to pay your mum in housekeeping a month?'

I was horrified. It had not occurred to me that there would be a parent tax on my new income. In a panic, I said £60, and Dad immediately agreed. I cursed to myself. I needed to work on my negotiating skills.

But I had a nagging question: why hadn't I seen my now-famous godfather?

It transpired that my parents had first met Dave and Shelia Ritchings soon after their wedding when they set up home at Norwood near Crystal Palace. Being neighbours and similar ages, the Ritchings and Parkers quickly became firm friends. At that stage, Dave Ritchings had indeed been a messenger at the ICCH and had met Shelia there.

Both couples started families at around the same time, and it was this combination of factors that resulted in Dave Ritchings being selected to be my godfather.

However, as Dave's career progressed quickly, and his income increased, the Ritchings had moved to a new build in Sittingbourne. My parents moved soon after themselves to the 1950s semi in Strood, Kent.

The gap in disposable income between the couples grew, and my parents had increasingly felt like poor relations. When we moved from Hilltop Road in Strood to our flat in Rodwell Close, Eastcote, the parents made the decision not to pass the new address on to the Ritchings and so had deliberately lost contact.

I felt sure my godfather had been the reason I had just walked into a job in the City, and I was not about to let this slide. I was determined to make an early visit to the ICCH to meet him.

It was soon after my employment that my parents found a house in their preferred location of Eastcote, an area we knew well. This time, they purchased a period semi-detached house in Cardinal Road.

The parents were cash buyers so there were not expected to be any problems, and the move was just months away. This move meant an immediate dent to my disposable income, as the negligible cost of my Tube travel from Islington to Tower Hill was going to increase when I started to commute from Eastcote.

In 1981, there were no mobile phones, no personal computers and not even fax machines.

At that time, Czarnikow was an innovative company with a main frame computer that filled half the basement floor.

As well as a computer processing team working in shifts, it had half a dozen full-time software developers.

The state-of-the-art communication at that time was telex. All messages to clients and exchanges were manually typed out on a keyboard by telex operators.

The telex network was a customer-to-customer switched network of teleprinters, using telegraph-grade connecting circuits for two-way text-based messages. The typed message would be converted into a long paper strip with punched holes that, once completed, would be fed into a transmission machine, and at the other end the receiver's keyboard would type the message.

Czarnikow had the second biggest telex department in the country – only the Bank of England's was larger. I was told anecdotally that the Harold Wilson government had Czarnikow on its list of companies to be nationalised, based purely on its huge financial turnover and the size of its telex department.

My first day of work was one of the most daunting of my life. I felt like I was jumping out of a plane with no parachute. I had no idea what to expect or how I was going to take to life in a City office.

I arrived early on my first day, stopping at the reception desk as a stream of people filed in behind me and queued for a lift to their various floors.

One of the messengers slapped a blue pass in my hand and told me to go to Tower Hill Tube station at lunchtime to get a passport photograph taken, as there was a photo kiosk on the concourse. My task was to bring back the picture so they could laminate it onto my LCE floor pass.

I was led to the lift; I could feel the eyes of the other people who entered the lift behind us.

As we stepped out of the lift on the fourth floor, immediately in front of us were the toilets, to the left was a set of double doors, to the right was a small open-door-sized space with a drinks machine and a single door alongside.

To the right of the drinks station was a short corridor that led to the stairs. If we had taken the double doors to the left and the Mark Lane-facing windows, we would have entered a large open-plan trading floor that housed the sugar desk and traders; to the right, the direction we went, was the trading support area and my new home: terminal accounts.

We passed a small office in which two ladies sat at typewriters. They were Sandra Fallows, and her friend Sue Hockley.

We continued past them, through another door and in front of us was my department.

Immediately to the left were two desks facing each other. One seated figure I recognised as my new boss, Paul Thompson. In front of him was a slim, dark-haired gentleman with a large moustache in his mid-twenties. This gentleman was introduced as Paul's deputy, Ken Boyles.

To their right was a block of four desks, and sitting here was a young, smiling, short lad with curly black hair, this was Gavin Brodie. Opposite Gavin was a young, bespectacled, fair-haired youth who held out his hand. He was Keith Baker.

Keith explained that I had replaced his best friend John Morris, the gentleman Paul had mentioned in my interview, who had recently transferred down to the International Petroleum Exchange (IPE) floor as a trader.

It had already been agreed that Keith would follow John down to the IPE floor. This meant that I would not be the new boy for long, as another person would be employed to replace Keith.

Keith was obviously very keen to make the move to the IPE floor as soon as possible, but Paul Thompson had told him that I needed to be fully trained before he could go.

The internal training at Czarnikow was excellent and intensive. The first thing I learned was the most obvious: what are the derivatives markets?

Derivatives are financial products that derive from an underlying commodity or financial instrument. Two examples are 'futures' and 'options.'

I was given an example of how futures worked on the cocoa market.

The cocoa future was a derivative of the physical cocoa market. Cocoa historically originated in South America, but now 75 per cent was produced in West Africa, specifically Côte d'Ivoire, Ghana, Cameroon, and Nigeria. Cocoa is a labour-intensive crop, meaning the grower needs a set price in order to harvest the crop and achieve a profit.

Any agricultural crop is at the mercy of weather conditions and nature, and as such the quality and quantity of the crop varies with each and every harvest. As with any agricultural market, there are supply-and-demand factors that determine the price, and so a 'bumper' crop is not necessarily a good thing for the cocoa grower.

An oversupply of cocoa inevitably reduces the price and may move the price below the level at which the producers can recover their costs. This is where the futures markets come into play. The growers can sell their crops before they harvest them and can in fact sell two or three crops in advance.

Let's assume the grower needs £10.00 per tonne to cover the price of harvesting and sells the crop at £12.50 a tonne on the futures markets. When they get their cocoa harvest to the market, let's assume the price is £9.00 due to an oversupply.

The futures price at delivery will be the same as the physical market price. When the grower sells their crop at £9.00 on the physical market, they would also buy back their futures position at £9.00. This negates their obligation to deliver to the futures market.

Using this example, the producer realises £9.00 per tonne on the physical market and £3.50 on the futures market. (Their original sell price of £12.50 less the £9.00 they paid on the futures market to close out their position and cancel their delivery obligation.)

Likewise, if there was a poor crop when the grower gets to market and the price has gone up to £15.00, they will sell at that price on the physical market.

However, they still have a futures obligation at £12.50 against which they either need to deliver the cocoa or close their position. Having sold their crop on the physical market, they would have to buy on the futures market at the £15.00 market price.

They have made £15.00 per tonne on the physical market but lost £2.50 per tonne on the futures market, meaning once again they realise £12.50 per tonne.

On the other side of the equation, you have the chocolate manufacturer, who also has costs associated with making a profit; these include the factory, the staff costs, and the ingredients, the key one being cocoa.

They have a delicate balancing act to perform – they need a steady supply of cocoa at a consistent price. They cannot afford to be changing the price of their chocolate bars in the shops every few months, and they know that there is a price at which customers would stop buying.

To avoid constant price fluctuations and to guarantee a steady supply of cocoa, the chocolate manufacturer would buy their cocoa on the futures market for the next year or longer. Let's assume they buy their cocoa on the futures market at £12.50 per tonne for the next 12 months.

When the first delivery month is reached, assume once again that the cocoa producers have had a bumper crop and the price has fallen to £9.00 per tonne. The chocolate manufacturer buys the cocoa at £ 9.00 on the physical market and to close out their futures position sells at £ 9.00.

They have paid £12.50 per tonne for their cocoa; £9.00 on the physical market and £3.50 to close out their futures position.

If we assume there has been a bad crop and the price of physical cocoa had gone up to £15.00 per tonne, the chocolate manufacture would still end up paying £12.50 because, despite paying £15.00 on the physical market, they will make a profit of £2.50 a tonne by selling out their futures position at £ 15.00 for which they had paid £12.50.

This is called 'hedging' and removes the danger of short-term price fluctuations.

This same mechanic is applied to all the agricultural and energy markets, and enables airlines, for example, to hedge the cost of their oil requirements over a 12-month period. As and when their planes land and refuel, regardless of the price of the refuelling at the airport, the airline has already covered the price by hedging on the futures markets.

Options are another form of derivative, and these give companies a different form of price insurance.

If you are a cocoa grower and you do not see the price of cocoa changing much over the next 12 months, you may decide to save the cost of hedging your crop on the futures markets. But at the same time, you do not want to leave yourself totally exposed to the price falling below your break-even point of £10.00.

The cocoa grower could buy a 'put' option. A 'put' is the option to sell at a future date at a fixed price.

For example, if your crop was due to be harvested in September, you would buy a September £10.00 'put' option, giving you the ability to 'exercise' your option. If the market price is below £10.00 in September, you exercise the option and sell your crop at the pre-agreed £10.00.

The company that grants you this option would charge a cash option premium, which is a commission amount agreed at the point of trade. This commission is theirs regardless of whether you exercise the option or let it lapse. This option writer would be taking the view that the price will stay above £10.00, and you will not exercise your option, and in September you will let it expire.

Likewise, the chocolate company may take the view that the price of cocoa will remain below the £12.50 per tonne they require and that they do not need to hedge on the futures market. They may decide to take an option contract instead just in case the price of cocoa spikes.

The chocolate manufacturer would want an option to buy, which is known as a 'call' option. If we assume they are worried the September delivery price may spike, they will negate this risk by buying a September £12.50 call option.

Once again, they would pay the writer of the option a premium commission for this. If the price remains below £12.50 in September, the option will expire and be worthless. However, if the price was £15.00 then the chocolate manufacturer would exercise their option and buy the cocoa at the pre-agreed £12.50 per tonne.

The options markets are less liquid because of their complexity and the fact you have to negotiate the premium with the writer of the option.

When I finally got to sit down with Keith Baker to learn more about my immediate role, he explained that the main function of the office juniors job involved running around the City to the various trading floors and the ICCH.

Twice a day, the junior would go around all the markets, collecting the floor traders 'cards.' These were cardboard records of the trades they had executed.

The 'run,' as it was known, involved heading the end of Mark Lane to an imposing building called the Grain Exchange and picking up the tickets from the soya and potato floors.

Then over to Mincing Lane and the impressive Plantation House, a vast building with a network of corridors and shops on the ground floor. Located at basement level we had to go to coffee and cocoa markets, then the all-important sugar floor.

Lastly we headed off to Dunster House, opposite our office in Mark Lane, and the IPE floor before heading across the road to the Czarnikow office.

These trading cards were then handed over to each of the respective office-based trading desks. Here the trades recorded on the Cards were matched against the orders taken over the phones in the office. These agreed trades were then written onto three-ply input sheets. Each input sheet had twelve trades and were colour coded.

Often the floor traders did not know who they were actually executing for when accepting orders from the trading desks at Mark lane. This provided key institutional clients the anonymity they may require when trading.

For example, if the sugar desk in Mark Lane took an order from Japanese client Mitsui to buy twenty lots at the market price (each lot is 112,000 pounds of raw sugar), then this order would be relayed down to the sugar trading floor: 'Buy twenty lots.'

The trader on the sugar floor would buy from sellers but could end up trading with multiple counterparties. The floor trader would then phone back to the office with a price: 'Filled at £12.50.' Later in the day the terminal accounts would complete its 'run' to the trading floors to bring back the sugar trading cards which would include the trades executed to complete this order.

If we assume the floor trader traded with two counterparties and bought ten lots from Woodhouse, Drake & Carey (WDC) at £12.25 and bought another ten lots at £12.75 from EDF Man Group (EDF). Sandra Larwood on the sugar desk would then write up an 'input' sheet for terminal accounts to process. This would have three lines: the buys from WDC and EDF and the sale to Mitsui at the consolidated price of £ 12.50 plus whatever commission had been agreed with Mitsui for the trade.

Trades executed on the raw sugar contact were on light-blue sheets, the white sugar trades were deep blue, cocoa was yellow, coffee was orange, IPE trades were red, and any others were green. These completed input sheets were placed by the respective departments into trays, which the office junior, yours truly, then gathered up and walked back to terminal accounts for processing.

Processing involved entering these trades via one of four computer stations equipped with vast chunky VDU green-screen computer monitors, into our state-of-the-art clearing system.

Each trade was keyed, one at a time, into the computer system and entered. Each accepted trade produced an 'input number' which was diligently written alongside the trade on the coloured input sheet. When all the trades on the input sheet had been entered it was filed into the appropriate folder.

The other duty of the junior was to head off to the ICCH to collect the 'Business Done Sheet' (BDS) report. This report recorded all the trades executed on the various trading floors by Czarnikow and was utilized to cross-check that the trades executed in the market matched those we had entered into the Czarnikow clearing system.

Equally important, the BDS reports were used to record 'give-up' trades. These were trades executed by our floor traders that were destined for another member company and had to be transferred from Czarnikow's account at the ICCH and placed onto the other member's account. This was achieved by 'writing' the other member's three alpha mnemonic code, which identified them, next to the trade concerned. For example, WDC was the code for Woodhouse, Drake & Carey.

When we had agreed all the trades and allocated what we needed to, the BDS had to be 'signed off' by Paul Thompson or Ken Boyles and then walked back to the ICCH for processing.

Keith Baker was obviously very keen to get rid of all this running about between the trading floors and the ICCH. This was fair as he had been doing it for over a year.

However, Paul asked him to let me settle in a bit first and to concentrate on the internal collection of the input sheets for the first week. This enabled me to get to know all the characters on the various trade desks at Mark Lane.

Wasting no time at all, Keith took me on the internal tour, the first stop being the all-important sugar desk.

The sugar desk was managed by Geoff Mirams and Arthur Blundel, who everyone just called 'Arb.' Arb had been on the sugar trading floor for years before moving to the sugar desk in the office.

Also working at the sugar desk were Tony Curtis, whose nickname was Parrot because he really did like the sound of his own voice, Paul Harper, who ran the white sugar book, John Payne, who looked after the US book, and the all-important Sandra Larwood, who was the office trading-floor liaison.

Arb was good enough to take the time to explain how the desk worked.

In front of all the traders were vast 'key and lamp' dealer boards. Each key was a direct line to a different client. There was also a 'broadcast' key which enabled the trader to talk to all the clients at once. During busy times, this enabled a verbal call of the market prices from the trading floor, as sometimes the prices on the screens could lag behind the actual prices. At the centre of the trading desk were screens showing not only the price of sugar on the London trading floor but also in Paris and in the US, where the equivalent contracts were traded.

The traders phoned their respective client base throughout the day to talk about the day's trading and to elicit orders; often the orders would come unsolicited. When an order was received, the desk trader would hit a direct line to the trading floor where one of the three Czarnikow traders would take the order, execute it, and confirm back the price of the completed trade.

In busy market conditions, one floor trader would keep the phone line to the office open and would signal any orders to the other two traders on the trading floor, using a trading form of sign language. This unique sign language had been developed on the trading floors because often the volume of noise would quickly drown out shouted orders. It was a similar system to that used by bookies at racecourses.

The office-based desk traders would communicate their orders to Sandra, who diligently recorded them on a huge 'blotter.' Sandra would then cross-check filled and working orders with the floor periodically.

When the market was busy and the desk traders were occupied taking orders over the phones, Sandra was an essential linchpin who enabled the desk traders to concentrate on taking orders and the floor traders on trading them.

When the terminal accounts junior returned to the office with the traders cards from the sugar trading floor, Sandra would cross-check each recorded trade against the blotter. If she found a discrepancy, she would phone the trading floor, and they could check with the other floor traders and amend the trade if required.

All the trade desks in the office used the same tried-and-tested system, and Keith walked me around the building down to the ground floor where the cocoa and coffee trading desks were, then on to the palm oil desk which also covered the soya markets, of which there was one in London and three in Chicago (soya bean, soya meal and soya oil).

The last desk we visited was the oil desk. This was on the second floor and run by Chris Bell, an ex-Guards officer. Also on the oil desk was Peter Hadsley, Guy Morrison, and Katherine Demarco, who had the same duties on the oil desk as Sandra Larwood had on sugar.

During my second week in the office, the pressure was on as Keith was keen to lose his trading-floor duties and speed his departure to the IPE floor. Paul Thompson agreed, and so that Monday I set off to experience the trading floors for the first time.

Having watched the screens and seen little activity on the soya and potato markets that day, Keith headed straight for the imposing Plantation House.

We walked across from Mark Lane, down past Dunster Court, into Mincing Lane, across the road and through the fancy doors into Plantation House. Having walked into the heart of the building and then down the staircase, we turned right towards the coffee market.

As we approached the double doors that opened out onto the coffee trading floor, we stopped so I could take a look through the glass panels.

I was amazed by the scale of the trading floor. The brightly coloured, cavernous room was ringed on the outside by 'booths.' These were telephone boxes large enough to accommodate two traders with phones and bi-folding doors required when the noise of the floor was such that you needed to mute it by closing them.

About five feet further into the room was a ring of desks in a horseshoe pattern around the actual trading floor.

At the head of the horseshoe was a bank of four desks. These desks faced out into the trading floor and were occupied by 'rostrum' staff who kept the market screens up to date by continuously keying in prices as trades were executed.

Eight gigantic screens hung down from the roof and were at the dead centre of the trading floor. They were in a square shape, facing out to all four corners of the market and relaying real-time prices from the London and New York coffee trading floors.

Behind the four rostrum desks, and elevated, was a single empty desk which was used by the 'call chairman' who orated prices and trades on the 'opening' of each trading session and at the 'close' of the market at the end of the day. This 'call' was broadcast to all the market participants and desks around the world that traded coffee.

Keith pointed out a guy in his late-twenties. 'That's Rowland Dunn, our coffee trader. I'll get the coffee tickets and then we'll move on to cocoa, sugar, and IPE. I'll point out our traders, and you get the tickets, OK?' I nodded, and so Keith pushed his way through the double doors and made for Rowland on the other side of the trading floor.

Had we been a little more observant, we may have noted that it was not just the soya and potato markets that were having a quiet day. The two dozen or so bored coffee traders were milling about, and there were very few shouts for prices, let alone deals being done.

Knowing that Keith was soon off to join the trading community on the IPE floor, these bored coffee traders had decided to give him a send-off he would not forget.

Just as Keith was halfway on his journey across the trading floor to a smiling Rowland, a shout went up: 'Debag him!' The coffee traders from all sides pounced on my unsuspecting colleague and wrestled him to the floor.

As I watched on in horror, they pulled his trousers off, held him at bay and then threw them up into the air in an attempt to get them hooked onto the screens hanging twelve feet in the air. On the third attempt, they managed to do so.

The traders holding Keith down then let him up and started rolling around with laughter. I watched in horror from the safety of the other side of the double doors as poor Keith stood in the middle of the coffee market in his suit jacket, underpants, socks, and shoes, looking up at his trousers, wondering how he was going to get them back down.

At this stage, I decided it was best to head back to Mark Lane, convinced now that the stories I had heard about the traders all being animals were true. I was wondering if there was a better way of earning a living.

I walked back through the entrance to Czarnikow's office, past the bemused messengers who had watched me set off with Keith, and back into the terminal accounts department alone.

Paul Thompson gave me a quizzical look, and I explained what I had just witnessed. The entire back office fell about laughing and the story quickly went around the other areas like wildfire.

Paul Thompson then phoned down to the coffee floor and suggested to Rowland that if Keith was still there, minus his trousers, that the joke was over, and he should assist him and send him on his way.

Being a true professional and demonstrating why Keith would make such a good floor trader, having recovered his trousers, he completed his run. When Keith finally made it back to the office with all the trading cards for processing, he was given a rapturous round of applause from all the trading desks as he delivered them.

For the next couple of days, Keith continued to campaign for me to make a return to the trading floors, which I refused. Eventually, Paul took me to one side and pointed out that Keith had been picked on because he had been doing the run for over a year. The traders knew him, and they also knew he was off to a rival trading floor. Paul assured me that this was a one off.

For better or worse, I reluctantly agreed to try again. Keith and I set off, and as we arrived at the doors of the coffee floor, I insisted Keith walk out onto the trading floor. If anything was going to happen, I figured it would be here.

Keith pushed the doors and entered the floor collecting the trading cards from Rowland. Feints by various traders in his direction kept him nervous, but Keith returned victorious with trousers intact.

On we went, this time to the doors of the cocoa floor. The layout was much the same as coffee. Keith pointed out a tall, imposing man in his thirties – Dave Moore, our head cocoa trader. (Dave Moore's floor name was "FA Cup" because his ears protruded).

With a little trepidation, I headed onto the trading floor.

Word of Keith's escapade on the coffee trading floor had spread beyond Czarnikow. Seeing a new face walking in the direction of Dave Moore was the signal, and before I knew what had happened, I had been barrelled over.

Despite my best attempts, my pinstriped trousers were off, and as a cheer went up, the traders headed for the screens hanging from the centre of the trading floor.

All I could think about was how lucky it was I that I had selected boxers to wear that day and not my Y-fronts!

As the traders were about to throw my trousers up onto the screens, Dave Moore shouted in a commanding voice, 'Enough guys. The poor lad has only just started. Let's not traumatise him.'

Dave strode over, took my trousers off the offenders, and despite grumbles about being a spoilsport, he handed me my trousers in one hand and his trading cards in the other.

I made a hasty exit with trousers in hand. Despite trying not to laugh, Keith took the trading cards and let me pull my trousers back on before we set off for the sugar market.

Luckily, the sugar and IPE floors were always much busier and far too populated for anything similar to happen, and so I made it back to the office without being debagged a second time.

Nothing like that ever happened again, and the rest of my short stint making the floor runs was mostly uneventful. However, there were two colourful events I witnessed during this short spell that have stayed in my mind.

There was the day that a soya trader had taken three casks of his very potent 'home brew' down to the floor where it was discreetly tucked away in an unused trading booth.

By the time I walked onto trading-floor for the afternoon run, the entire soya floor community, including rostrum staff and our trader Tom Falkner, were all totally inebriated. They were having 'hopping races' across the trading floor by holding onto the bottom of their stools and bouncing towards a finish line. Soya was never the busiest of markets in London.

The second event I witnessed was the retirement of Harry Banks, a popular call chairman on the coffee floor.

A fitting tribute was decided upon, and at lunchtime the City shops were cleared of M&M's and Smarties, the chocolate sweets.

As stated previously, the closing call of any market was audio broadcast internationally to anyone with an interest in that underlying product. As the unwitting Harry Banks started his final closing call on the coffee floor, the traders started throwing handfuls of the sweets at him in a doomed attempt to make him falter in his impeccable broadcast.

As a true professional, he never wavered. I watched in utter amazement from the side-lines as the bombardment of handfuls of M&M's and Smarties continued for the full fifteen or so minutes. By the end of the broadcast, he was nearly knee deep in sweets and was rewarded with a roar of approval and round of applause.

Tremendous changes were to unfold on the trading floors in the years ahead, but those early experiences sealed my determination that a career on the trading floors was not for me. I would decline two offers to join the trading community in the years to come.

My job as office junior was threefold. First thing in the morning was filing; the computer department would deliver a mass of green printouts about a foot deep. These printouts had to be separated into different 'reports.'

One was a list of all the trades, another was a list of all the positions Czarnikow held on the international markets, then there was a list of all the client positions we held, followed by 'master reports,' which listed all the amalgamated positions the company held at the various clearing houses. The biggest of these was the ICCH, but we also held positions on markets we cleared via other companies.

Czarnikow were members of the Coffee, Sugar and Cocoa Exchange (CSCE) based in New York and had an active New York office. Czarnikow cleared soya oil, meal and beans traded on the Chicago Mercantile Exchange (CME) and palm oil on the Kuala Lumpur Exchange via EF Hutton. We also had currency positions cleared via Drexel Burnham Lambert.

We had individual reports on all the positions held at these clearing venues.

Once these individual reports were separated, they were filed in various binders.

The next job I had was to split 'contract' notes.

Again, these were delivered by the computer department in boxes.

They were A4-sized and had printer 'holes' down each side that could be removed via a perforation.

After carefully tearing away the superfluous printer holes, you were left with the A4 contract note. These had to be separated by client. Once you had a contract note per client, they had to be carefully folded and tucked into windowed envelopes and placed into a tray for delivery down to the ground-floor post room.

Once you completed the contract notes you started the first run to the markets to collect the trading cards and deliver them back to the office, after which it was lunch time.

Lunchtimes gave you two alternatives. Firstly, armed with your company allocation of thirty five pence a day worth of luncheon vouchers, you could head to Benji's for one of their sandwich/roll combos and then head down to the basement staffroom. Or you could do what most of us did and head off to the local pubs for a hot meal and a couple of pints.

The afternoon started with the arrival of the first 'input' sheets from all the various trade desks. These input sheets had been prepared from the first batch of trade tickets delivered earlier from the trading floors.

Later you had the second run around the trading floors followed by more inputting.

As the markets closed the traders would return to Mark Lane with the last of their trading cards which was the same time at which the office junior was heading down to the ICCH to collect the BDS reports before returning to the ICCH with the signed off BDS reports, and any allocations required.

Interspersed with the above was numerous drink runs which inevitably fell to the 'junior.'

The coffee machine was out in the reception hallway next to the lifts. This 'refreshment station' dispensed powdered coffee with or without sugar, chocolate, powdered tea, and lemon tea.

As you would expect, the powdered tea was disgusting, so everyone stuck to the coffee.

The small plastic cups, however, were pretty useless as they were so thin that picking up a hot coffee in them would result in third-degree burns, and so everyone double skinned, taking two cups so that you could actually pick it up.

Within weeks, I had made friends with two partners in crime: Andrew Mersh, who was the same age as me and was in the coffee documents department, and Rowland Dunn, our coffee trader. Inevitably at lunch time we would head to the City Yeoman pub which was located immediately behind our office in Mark Lane. Here, after eating, and armed with a pint, the remainder of the lunch hour was spent on the Space Invaders machine.

Evenings out in the City at this point in time were short-lived, the pubs closed at nine o'clock as the City cleared out. That meant if you had set your heart on a night out, you had to move east to Shoreditch, or to Brick Lane for a curry, or to the west end.

The problem was that wherever we went, east or west, you had to keep a keen eye on the time.

This was because the Tube trains started shutting down at 10:30 pm on weekdays, and it was often a desperate sprint to Baker Street to catch my last train on the Uxbridge-bound Metropolitan Line train, back to my parents' house in Eastcote.

Just weeks after my start at Czarnikow, I was asked to take cocoa warrants to the ICCH and wait while the 'rent' was updated and then return them back to the office. This provided the perfect opportunity to meet with my godfather, Dave Ritchings, and so I set off with the warrants concealed in a large envelope.

The guys in the office had been busy winding me up prior to this journey to Crutched Friars.

The warrants I would be carrying were bearer warrants, meaning the holder was the actual owner.

These warrants had a large cash value, so the surprise was that muggers were not descending on the City in droves and knocking messengers on the head for them. Thankfully, the walk from our office in Mark Lane to Crutched Friars, the home of the ICCH, was short.

As I arrived at the reception of the ICCH, I asked for Vic Neary, who was the operations contact tasked with updating the warrants. Updating warrants involved Vic cross-checking the ICCH database to confirm that we had paid the rent and then signing and stamping each warrant accordingly.

As Vic vanished with my warrants, I asked the receptionist if Dave Ritchings was in the office. I got a shake of the head; he was away on business. At this time, the ICCH was setting up a Paris office called the Banque Centrale de Compensation, under their rising star Gilbert Durieux, a good friend of my godfather's.

The receptionist asked if anyone else could help me, and I explained my relationship, at which point I was told that Dave's wife, Shelia, was just round the corner, and he would let her know I was here.

Shelia was both surprised and delighted to see me. She asked what I was doing, where I was working, and how my parents were. Shelia then said that she would make sure Dave gave me a call the following week. Vic returned with my updated warrants, and I set off back to the Czarnikow office.

A week later, Dave Ritchings phoned me and invited me for a 'business lunch.' I asked Paul Thompson if I could accept. He leaned back in his chair, gave me a broad smile and said, 'Do you know how long I had to wait for my first business lunch, Mr Parker? Two years.' I could see the rest of the team avidly listening to the conversation. 'And you,' he continued, 'get invited out by a director of the ICCH after just a month!' Then with a chuckle he said, 'Of course, Dave called me first to make sure it was OK to invite you!'

So off I went. The restaurant Dave picked was actually at the end of Mark Lane. It was a fish restaurant called Wheelers. I entered the restaurant and told the waiter that I was joining Dave Ritchings from the ICCH and was guided to a table where Dave was already sitting sipping on a Gin and Tonic.

Dave was a large man – not fat, but stocky and tall, he gripped my hand in a firm hearty handshake.

During the lunch, he told me I was working at a good company and that staff at both Czarnikow and the ICCH tended to be poached by other futures companies. He explained that as traditional family-style companies, both Czarnikow and the ICCH were at the lower end of the pay scales. But that both companies were renowned for training their staff really well, and I should expect calls offering me jobs once I was established.

He also advised me to get into the commodities social scene, explaining that Czarnikow and the ICCH had teams competing in pool and darts leagues and that there was an established inter-company football league, with both companies entering teams in the GAFTA (Grain and Feed Trade Association) Football Cup.

Dave then went on to tell me I had joined at just the right time as both he and his good friend Gilbert Durieux were working with a UK team to establish a new market in London that would deal in financial futures and options. He said that these financial contracts were already established and successful in America and that they were expected to be an enormous success in London.

However, at that point in time, launching financial contracts in London required a change of law in the UK. Currently, these markets would fall foul of the existing UK gambling laws.

Dave explained that all the current derivatives markets were deliverable. A coffee/cocoa/sugar/oil contract held to 'expiry' would result in the seller having to deliver to the buyer the underlying contracted commodity. For example, one lot of a coffee futures contract held to expiry meant the delivery of five tonnes of coffee.

In reality, the coffee was stored in bonded warehouses in the UK and Europe, and what actually passed hands were bearer warrants of ownership. These were the very same documents I had taken to Vic Neary for updating.

The oil contracts traded on the IPE floor worked the same way, but the oil was stored in huge tanks in Rotterdam. Once again, ownership of the oil was a paper bearer warrant.

Financial contracts had no such underlying product and were 'cash settled,' meaning that when these futures contracts expired, a final closing price was used to calculate the cash value that settled all outstanding positions. As such this activity would be deemed to be gambling under the UK law at that time.

At the end of a very satisfying lunch, my head was spinning, and not just because of the lager I had consumed during the meal nor the large glasses of port that followed, but mainly because of the volume of information I had been given. Dave obviously loved what he was doing and was positively excited at the pending, as yet unnamed, new financial market.

After this initial lunch Dave Ritchings and I started to meet up every three or four months.

Dave was extremely disappointed that neither of his sons had been inclined to follow their parents into financial services. Stewart, Dave's eldest son, was still trying to make money in the music industry as a musician and lead singer in a band. Stewart's band never achieved any commercial success, and eventually Dave set him up in a landscape gardening business.

Andrew, Dave's youngest, was in the print industry in Wapping. Dave was therefore delighted to have his godson in the industry, and in these early days he just adopted me, and I was incredibly pleased to have his support.

Things changed a little in April 1981 when Keith left the department for the IPE floor, and we saw the arrival of Steve Robertson.

Steve was a slim, fresh-out-of-school 17-year-old chap with small round spectacles, which unfortunately for him meant he was immediately nicknamed 'Scooter' by the sugar desk, after the bespectacled character from *The Muppets*.

Scooter's arrival meant I was no longer the office junior, so I could leave the market and ICCH runs behind me and move on.

Ken Boyles, the department's deputy manager, started to introduce me to reconciliations and margin calls which meant ensuring our in-house position printouts agreed with those of other clearing accounts we held. If they did not agree you had to investigate why and correct any discrepancies. The biggest of these reconciliations was the ICCH, but we also held accounts with EF Hutton,

Drexel Burnham and the New York-based Coffee, Sugar, and Cocoa Exchange. This job was much more interesting than filing and the daily trips to the trading floors.

'Margin calls' involved going through all of our clearing accounts with both clients and brokers and checking to see if the overnight change of valuation prices and/or positions had resulted in a surplus or deficit of cash on the accounts.

For example, if our Japanese client had made money on their sugar position, and wanted me to pay them the funds, we would agree the balance on the account and the amount of money they required. Once agreed, I would set up a payment for Ken or Paul to approve.

However, this payment to the client would mean that by default I had an equal surplus, either at the clearing house or Czarnikow New York, or both, and so I would need to call sufficient funds back from them to cover the client payment.

I would go through our entire 'margins' report, calling all the clients or brokers where we had deficits to make sure we received payments. I would also wait for expected calls from clients or brokers sitting on surplus funds to call them off.

Each client or broker would have a minimum balance agreed which meant small movements would be ignored. We also often had to execute foreign exchange trades, usually US dollars into sterling or the reverse.

Sometimes a 'margin call' would not be agreed, usually because a trade was missing, had been entered wrongly or booked onto the wrong account. This would require an investigation, and the required correction would be instructed into the clearing system.

All of this became a part of my daily routine.

At the end of April 1981, I came home to find a letter from the Metropolitan Police inviting me to join them in September. Two things convinced me to turn them down. The most important of these was that between the 10th and 12th April 1981, London had witnessed the Brixton Riots.

The main riot on 11th April, dubbed 'Bloody Saturday', resulted in 279 injuries to police and forty-five injuries to members of the public. More than a hundred vehicles were burned out, including fifty-six police vehicles. 150 buildings had been damaged and thirty of these had been set on fire. There were eighty-two arrests and subsequent reports suggested that up to five thousand people were involved.

This proved to be just the start, with other riots following in Chapletown in Leeds, Toxteth in Liverpool, Moss Side in Manchester, and Handsworth in Birmingham. The sight of bricks and petrol bombs being thrown at police officers dressed in normal police uniforms was a huge factor in my decision.

The other reason was simply that I had a job, and I was enjoying life at Czarnikow, so it really wasn't a hard decision for me to say no to the Metropolitan Police.

Once again, fate had played its part. Chances are that had I joined in 1980 as planned, I would have been involved in the horrific scenes that unfolded in Brixton.

As I got more settled at Czarnikow, my social circle developed to include Lesley Neenan from the cable room. Lesley was, is, and always will be, a force of nature. This very tall, striking blonde was your very typical no nonsense Londoner.

Lesley lived in a Spacious 1930's council flat in Peckham, and with the City pubs and bars closing as early as they did at that time; we quickly developed a regular habit of heading off to Peckham on the bus.

Once there, we would inevitably end up buying a Chinese or Indian takeaway and taking it back to Lesley's flat where we ended up crashing the night on her sofa and spare bed.

Even if Lesley was not out with us for the evening, if we missed our last tube or train home, we would just turn up, uninvited, at Lesley's door in the early hours of the morning. She never turned us away, although we did usually receive good-natured abuse before she headed off back to bed and left us to get on with it.

On the romance front, with my new job and a steady income, I quickly set about renewing my acquaintance with Susan Eason. Sue was already four months into her nursing training at her new base in Hopkinson House, Vauxhall Bridge Road.

I phoned Sue from the parents one evening after getting home from work. After speaking to a grumpy-sounding lady, I was put through to Sue's room. She was delighted to hear from me, and we quickly arranged a get-together.

I wanted to impress Sue with my newfound wealth and job status, and so I suggested I take her for a meal. We agreed that I would head over to Victoria to meet her at her nursing residence on the following Thursday evening. I planned

Lesley with my surprise Birthday Cake. Andrew Mersh (L) and Tony Ford (R)

Sue Eason at Hopkinson House

to take her to TGI Friday's in Covent Garden. On the day, I finished work, jumped on the Tube at Tower Hill, and made my way to Victoria.

After the healthy walk from Victoria train station and down Vauxhall Bridge Road, I started looking for Hopkinson House. Finally, I arrived at 86-88 Vauxhall Bridge Road, a very impressive Victorian building, midway between Victoria and Vauxhall Bridge itself.

Opposite Hopkinson House was a very 1960s-style block, and a pub called the Lord Nelson, which I noted for future visits.

I walked up the concrete stairs, and as I went through the double doors, I saw another set of internal doors in front of me, and to the right was a desk with a very fierce-looking lady who just silently stared at me.

'I'm here to meet a friend,' I said, as a couple of young ladies came through the internal door behind me and headed out into the street.

'Name,' she barked.

'Kevin Parker,' I replied.

She looked at me as if I was a total idiot. 'The name of the person you're visiting, not your name.' She continued to stare at me as I blushed.

'Sue … Susan Eason.'

I watched as she pulled out a printed sheet and ran a finger down the list. 'Third floor, room 337.'

I nodded and started to turn towards the internal doors.

'You have to sign in,' she demanded, pointing to the large red book on the desk in front of her.

The pen was on a chain, and the book listed dates and times of entry, the names of the visitors, the nurses being visited, and the nurses room number.

I quickly added my name, noting that three names preceded mine with today's date – two guys and one lady visitor. I finished and then hesitated just in case any new orders followed.

Sure enough, having scanned my addition in the book, she stared straight at me. 'All visitors must be signed out and off the premises by 10.30. Is that understood?'

I nodded. 'Yes, no problem.'

With that, she reached down, out of eyesight, and pushed a button. A dull buzz came from the internal double doors, which were now released, I rushed through before she changed her mind.

As I went through into the dimly lit lobby area, I saw another set of large internal doors to the left and right, and in front a large staircase that swept up and turned to the right. I started up the stairs and continued up to the third floor.

Once I arrived at the third floor I was presented with doors to the left and right. I scanned for room numbers. Sue's room was to the left, three doors down. I went through the double doors and arrived outside her door.

I knocked, noting the door opposite Sue's was open, and a young couple were just leaving – obviously one of the two guys who had signed in before me. The young, short, pretty girl smiled at me as Sue opened her door.

A quick round of introductions followed, as Sue introduced Alison and her slightly balding boyfriend, Paul. They were on their way across the road to the Lord Nelson to meet some of the other resident nurses.

Sue's room was the size of a normal double bedroom and looked out onto Vauxhall Bridge Road, whereas Alison's backed onto Douglas Street, a quiet backstreet. Sue had a bed, an Amstrad music centre, a large wardrobe, shelving units and a small portable TV. She looked lovely as always in a light-grey skirt and silky plum blouse.

Sue quickly applied lipstick, picked up a navy puffer jacket and asked with a smile, 'Where are we going?' I said that I was thinking of Covent Garden. Sue quickly explained that a group of her fellow nurses had recently been to a burger place called Maxwell's in Covent Garden and it was particularly good, so I switched plans. I needed this night to go well.

We headed off down the stairs and through the double doors at the ground-floor reception. As we went to leave, I heard a distinct clearing of the throat coming from behind the desk.

'Oh,' Sue said, 'I forgot, you have to book yourself out.'

I walked over to the desk and the red book, noting Paul had also signed out, I checked my watch writing down the time alongside my previous entry and signed. I got another glare.

As we left, Sue explained that at 10.30 precisely, the front doors were closed and any visitors who had not left were promptly rounded up and escorted off the premises A night porter ensured that only residents entered after hours.

I found out much later that there were ways around the tight security, used primarily by police officers from the nearby Rochester Row police station, and involving the fire escapes and metal staircases to the rear of the property.

As Sue and I walked out onto the busy Vauxhall Bridge Road, we did not have to wait long to find a black cab, and off we went.

The evening was an immense success. We chatted away about our time at Waitrose, Totton College and the mutual friends and acquaintances from school and the village.

The evening was made even more enjoyable by the unexpected entertainment that came from the kitchen staff at Maxwell's. The restaurant was terribly busy, and we had been seated in the basement-level dining area, where the kitchen was visible, enabling customers to see the kitchen staff at work.

Piped disco music was playing around the establishment, and when certain music tracks from the repetitive soundtrack started, the kitchen staff launched into superbly choreographed dance routines.

It was obviously a tongue-in-cheek copy of the cocktail bar staff's routines at rivals TGI Friday's. The chefs danced, burgers were flicked, and sauce bottles were spun and thrown between staff, with entire plates of food being crafted in perfect time to the music. Each time they did so, appreciation was shown with a round of applause from all the diners in view.

Sue confessed to me during our meal that since she had arrived in London, she had not ventured out beyond the Lord Nelson, across the road for her accommodation. I quickly took the opportunity to promise regular visits, which she seemed happy about.

We caught a black cab back to Hopkinson House, and arriving back just after 10 o'clock, I stayed in the cab, stealing a quick kiss on the cheek. I watched Sue enter the large door of Hopkinson House as my cab headed off for Baker Street and my Tube ride back to Eastcote.

My old school friend Steve Dickinson started turning up at my parents' house at Cardinal Road, Eastcote, soon after we had moved in.

He was now a probationer on his two years as a uniformed police constable. He still had his green Triumph Herald and was now based at West Drayton. Steve was living in a house with a landlady provided by the police for new PCs. His new warrant card gave him free travel on London public transport and, as I was to find out later, other benefits.

Although Steve was still disappointed that I had not stuck to the plan of joining the Met myself, having me living just down the road meant frequent visits and trips to local pubs.

Once Steve learned Sue Eason was in town, and better still was in nursing accommodation, he was keen to visit and asked me to have a word with Sue and encourage her to invite a few of her 'friends' out as well.

I delayed as long as I could – I liked Steve, but he could be a little unpredictable, especially as a probationer PC, and I really did not want him muddying the waters while I was building my relationship with Sue.

One little anecdotal example of Steve's unpredictability was when we were driving back towards my parents' having been down to the local chip shop to get a takeaway. As we passed down Eastcote High Street, a gang of three large youths kicked over a large bin, spewing rubbish all over the pavement.

Steve immediately speeded up to pull slightly ahead of them, braked, threw on the hazard warning lights, and shouted for me to 'back him up.'

As quickly as he could, Steve leapt out of the car to confront these three large individuals who were obviously drunk.

All I could think was that he had been watching far too many episodes of the American TV show *Starsky and Hutch*.

Pulling out the ever-present warrant card, he announced, 'Met Police, pick up all that rubbish and the bin now.' As always, these three surprised individuals assumed that, due to my short haircut, I was also a police officer.

Astonishingly, considering their size and inebriation, and the fact that they had us outnumbered, they just set about doing what Steve had told them.

Watching the three of them chasing crisp packets and newspapers down the road under Steve's watchful gaze, while our fish and chips went cold in Steve's car, is an enduring memory.

At work, another revelation was about to take place.

The ICCH, with the increased volume created by the International Petroleum Exchange, launched 'INTERCOM.' This was an automated matching system that allowed the office to see matched trades. It replaced the printouts that previously we had collected daily from the ICCH and enabled localised printing of reports.

The 'give-up' trades still required us to write the clients name in pen on the BDS report and deliver this back to Crutched Friars. INTERCOM was an indicator of the way the markets were going, and with the new financial futures market looming, further automation was certain.

This required the Czarnikow IT department to up its game, and under the leadership of the department head, Ken Maloney, a development team was employed to begin the complete overhaul of the internal computer clearing system.

All of Czarnikow's market competitors were using an American clearing system called GMI. But Czarnikow was determined to develop its own system, the costs of this development would cause them problems in the years ahead.

For now, this updating of our clearing processes meant additional work for those of us working in the back office. For regular spells during the testing phases the back office were required to double key the days trades into both the live and development systems and then cross-check the resulting computer printouts.

Czarnikow established a new 'general trading desk.' This facilitated trading on the growing number of derivatives contracts being launched in London and the US. Established office desk traders were transferred onto this new desk.

They included Norman Kerrigan, who had traded rubber, David Nesbit, who had been trading potatoes, and Dave Peart, who had started in the cable room before becoming a floating floor trader, covering holidays and sickness.

Dave Peart had worked on coffee, cocoa and even the rubber trading floors over the years. During his time on the trading floors, and in keeping with the tradition of all traders having a nickname, Dave had been christened 'Rubik'.

Dave's nickname was based on his ability to master the Rubik's Cube, which was the puzzle craze at that time. Floor traders who had been frustrated or defeated by the puzzle simply tossed them over to Dave, who promptly returned them completed.

The remainder of 1981 drifted past with regular excursions to the West End, frequent evenings at Lesley's in Peckham and weekly visits to Sue Eason in Vauxhall.

To supplement my income, and to pay for all these evenings out drinking, I started doing the 'overtime' Paul Thompson had mentioned during my interview.

This involved covering the sugar department's trading on the New York Coffee, Sugar and Cocoa Exchange, working out manually what the CSR Sugar accounts position were on the close, including the profit and loss on each position. Once we had finished we sent the calculations to the cable department who telexed them to CSR in Australia.

Sending messages to be telexed involved placing the message in a sealed "tube" which was placed into a transparent system of pipes that had a constant air suction system circulating. Placing the tube into the pipe sent the message pinging its was down to the basement cable department.

Once we had completed all the New York processing, we 'gave the system back' to the basement computer department so they could start the overnight processing.

At the end of the month, Tony Curtis from the sugar department walked around with a little notebook and a wad of cash, with five pounds for each member of staff who had worked an evening shift. Over a calendar month this was a significant top-up to the finances.

I was overjoyed when Paul Thompson told me that I was to receive a ten per cent bonus for Christmas and pay rise to four thousand one hundred pounds per annum to start on 1 January 1982.

But that was not all, Paul Thompson had mentioned a free turkey at my interview, and it turned out that Czarnikow owned a turkey farm for reasons unknown to me at the time.

Later, I learned from David Peart that the company founder, the wonderfully named Julius Caesar Czarnikow, loved Charles Dickens' tale *A Christmas Carol* so much so that he was determined that nobody who worked for his company would ever go without a fresh turkey at Christmas, and so he bought a turkey farm to ensure this never happened.

The messengers would come around to each member of staff in mid-November, asking each in turn how big a turkey they would like. Once they arrived in terminal accounts, they started with Paul Thompson and Ken Boyles, then worked down the staff in order of importance. At this stage, I had no idea about joints of meat or sizes, and it was, as I discovered later, one of the perverse pleasures for the messengers when new members of staff were asked this very question.

Eventually, Sid came up to me and asked how big a turkey I would like. Not noticing the knowing smiles around me, I fell straight into the trap. 'How big can I have?' I asked innocently. Sid made a great play of flicking a couple of pages in his notebook. 'Well, Kevin, you're in luck. We have a 28lb turkey available.'

I did not hesitate and put my name down for it.

That evening, I proudly told my parents they didn't need to worry about buying a turkey this year as the company would give me a fresh one that I would collect on the day we closed for Christmas.

That year, the last working day was Wednesday, 23 December, and we expected to finish work at lunchtime. I neglected to tell my parents how big the turkey was, and they did not ask.

Christmas at Czarnikow had its traditions, including a champagne breakfast at The Ship public house in Hart Street.

This event was organised annually by Jon McFarland, who worked in the sugar documents department. It involved a full English breakfast accompanied by bottles of champagne and was very much a taster for the day ahead.

The messengers delivered festive presents from the ICCH, the various derivatives exchanges, EF Hutton, Drexel, and clients. More often than not, these presents involved bottles of alcohol.

In addition, the internal trade desks all delivered presents to the back office to thank us for the work for that year.

Paul Thompson gathered all the bottles together and then split them amongst his staff. A couple of the bottles were opened and immediately consumed.

I had two bottles of wine on my first year and put them to one side, not being a wine drinker myself and intending to take them home along with my turkey.

At 11 o'clock, a group of messengers turned up with wicker-style bags loaded with turkeys. We all patiently waited for ours, and when my name was called, I nearly fainted on the spot.

This could not be a turkey, I thought, it was a bloody emu, a dinosaur, it was absolutely huge!

I could barely pick it up, and there was no way I was going to get it all the way to Aldgate Tube, let alone all the way from Eastcote station down Field End Road and back to Cardinal Road.

On top of this monster, I had two bottles of wine!

My fellow staff members in terminal accounts were all laughing at the size of my turkey.

I found out later that Keith Baker had made the very same mistake on his first year. He had given up trying to get his turkey home and, in a state of inebriation, had promptly deposited his into the Thames.

I knew my parents had not bought a turkey on the back of my announcement, I had to get this beast home somehow.

I put my two bottles of wine into my desk, and when 12.00 arrived, I declined the chance of a Christmas tipple down the City Yeoman with Andrew Mersh and Rowland Dunn and set off for home.

Even with two hands, I could only get a dozen paces before having to put the bag containing the turkey down, wait for the circulation to return to my fingers, and then set off again.

It took forever to stagger to Aldgate Tube station, but I felt huge relief when I finally got onto the Uxbridge-bound Tube.

However, with my turkey taking a full seat next to me, as it was too big and too heavy to heave into the overhead luggage space, I watched in horror as the train started to fill up, station by station.

By the time the train pulled into Baker Street, I was forced to drag the monster onto my lap. I could feel pins and needles in my legs and was relieved when the person next to me got off at Wembley Park and I could push the monster over into the empty seat.

At Eastcote Tube station, I had to start my 12-paces stagger once again, up the concrete staircase to the street-level ticket hall and out past the bemused ticket inspector, who, seeing my distress at the prospect of having to stop and find my season ticket, waved me through.

Out I went into Field End Road and turned left on the tortuous journey that would ordinarily take me 15 minutes. By the time I got to my parents' door and put the monster down for the umpteenth time to fish for my door key, I was exhausted.

When I dragged the monster into the kitchen, the look on my mother's face was priceless.

I doubt any of us had ever seen such a huge bird.

When Dad returned from work later that night, it had become apparent that the turkey would not fit in the oven, and even if it did, we would have been eating it for months!

My dad promptly went out into the garage, came back with a large wood saw and cut the turkey in half. One half went into a carrier bag and was deposited into the chest freezer for Easter.

Needless to say, it was a painful lesson learned, and I never made that mistake again. However, like the others, I would keep a knowing silence in the years ahead when the department took on new staff members.

1982

1982 was a good year for me, but it started modestly enough with me getting my very first car.

My parents had bought me driving lessons for my 18th birthday, but I never saw the need for a car in London, as I could get everywhere I needed on the Tube and save on the cost of insurance and maintenance.

However, Steve Dickinson's frequent visits in his car, and the added cost of my train tickets for my regular visits back to the New Forest to see my old friends, had planted the seed, and then once again fate played its part.

My brother, Robin, was finishing an equipment course at the School Of Electrical Mechanical Engineering in Borden, Hampshire, learning how to repair armoured fighting vehicles and getting his HGV driving licence.

This meant he had parked his pride and joy, a plum-coloured Opel Manta, in our parents' garage.

Once his training had finished, Robin was posted to 16 Tank Transporter Workshop in Fallingbostel, West Germany, which was part of the 7th Armoured Brigade of the British Army on the Rhine. The Army used ageing Antar tank transporters to move all the Chieftain and later the Challenger 1 tanks around Germany, back and forth from firing ranges, battle exercise training areas and the Allied sector of Berlin.

Robin no longer needed his car, and he offered me the chance to buy his Opel Manta for £500. This was a bargain, as Robin had spent the summer installing a reconditioned two-litre Vauxhall engine, and the car ran beautifully. There were few Opel Mantas about, and its style and design meant it was a head turner. The bodywork was in excellent condition, and I jumped at the chance to buy it, which also pleased my dad.

My dad had always wanted a sports car, but as a father had always had to opt for practical cars. Robin's car was as close as he had ever got to realising his dream, and so, under the pretext of keeping the car ticking over, he had frequently used the Opel at weekends on trips to get his newspaper and for any other excuses he could think of, such as getting DIY tools.

Equipped with my new car, I set about calling my grandparents and asking if I could stay with them the following weekend. I then called all my college mates to tell them I would be coming down to the village.

That weekend, I set off on my first ever journey on a motorway for what would become regular weekend trips back to the New Forest. The journey was straightforward – from Eastcote High Street, a short trip to the Western Avenue, then onto the M25 for the short hop onto the M3, then motorway more or less all the way down to Eastleigh and the M27 into Southampton.

Things did not start very well; I stalled the engine at a major junction. I was aware of the significant power under the bonnet, and my unfamiliarity with the car and subsequent flapping meant I missed the lights.

The cars behind quickly leaned on their horns. I got away the next time, but then I could see the blue flashing lights as a police car tucked in behind me. I pulled over at the first opportunity and climbed out.

The police officer approached and asked if the car was mine. I sheepishly nodded and handed over my documents. I explained it was my first real journey in it. When I told him I was heading for the New Forest, he looked a little alarmed. He said a car like mine would be a target for thieves and my obvious unfamiliarity with it meant they had been obligated to check it out.

He handed back my documents, saying that I should be all right when I got onto the motorway, but to take it easy.

The M3 at that stage was not actually a motorway all the way to Southampton, it went back to a single-lane road in a section of motorway that had not been upgraded due to a long, controversial battle with environmentalists.

That stretch of the M3 was known as the 'Winchester bypass' section. Having made the journey a couple of times as a passenger with the parents, I knew that this section could quickly choke up and come to a standstill.

Once on the motorway, my main problem was not breaking the speed limit. The car just wanted to 'go,' and it was so easy to slip up to 85 miles per hour as the drive was smooth and quiet. There seemed to be no difference to the cars noise, handling, or driveability at 60 mph or 85 mph, which meant constant vigilance to speed was required. I didn't want to be stopped twice by the Police on my first trip out in the car.

As I hit the Winchester bypass, the motorway went down from three lanes to a dual carriageway, then the infamous single-lane section, and then the hill.

On this stretch, the road plunged down a steep hill, bottomed out and then went back up again on an equally steep climb on the other side.

On this single-lane section, the traffic bunched because anything of any size, such as a lorry, would struggle on the subsequent climb. Cars with any acceleration would watch carefully for a gap in the oncoming traffic and quickly pull out, overtake the queue behind the lorry, truck, or coach, and get back in front of them in the inevitable gap.

Armed as I was with a car that had plenty of horsepower, I could see ten cars in front and then a lorry as we plunged down the hill. There was temporarily no oncoming traffic and so I pulled out, hoping that none of the ten cars in front of mine would be tempted to do the same.

The moment the lorry in front of the queue of traffic hit the incline up the hill, its speed dropped off, so I floored the pedal, and my car took off, passing everything with ease. Then, to my absolute pleasure, the car continued pulling away just as fast as I hit the climb. In a regular event for this section thereafter, I was able to leave the trail of traffic behind me effortlessly.

I had a great weekend, driving round to see Charlotte Luke, picking her up in my car and meeting my college crowd at their new preferred venue of the Royal Oak, just outside Beaulieu – my grandad's pub.

Meeting my old Dibden Purlieu friends at the weekends became a regular monthly event during 1982, and I loved my new car.

Another social outlet commenced in early 1982 when one of my co-workers from Waitrose appeared in London.

On my first weekend visit back to the New Forest, I bumped into another ex-Waitrose colleague, Andy Hind, and I had told him I worked in the City of London. Andy told me Simon Cullen, who had worked on the grocery department, had started a course at the London School of Economics, which was based in Holborn.

As Andy was a close friend of Simon's, I gave him my work phone number to pass on, and sure enough I got the call from Simon.

Simon and I met up in Holborn after work for a drink, and he introduced me to a group of his fellow students. Not long after that, I joined them as they headed off to the Hammersmith Odeon to see The Jam play live, the first of what became a string of concerts over the next couple of years.

All of our trips to see the current big bands playing live were subject to a tight timetable. We would meet up at the Coal Hole in The Strand for a few beers then walk the short distance to Embankment Tube station where we would jump on the Hammersmith and City line to Hammersmith station and then walk, with the considerable number of 'mods' heading to the gig.

The Jam were always brilliant live; they never shied from playing their numerous hit tracks. The dancing, singing, and shouting went on for the full duration of the gig, and we always left exhilarated, tired, and sweating for the sprint back to Hammersmith Tube.

Usually packed with other concert goers, it was always very fraught to get to Baker Street in time for the last Uxbridge train home to Eastcote.

1982 started uneventfully at work. Gavin Brodie began teaching me how to manage the frequent coffee and cocoa warrant deliveries.

This involved a lot of form filling as we had a number of clients who ran their positions to delivery, and this was made more complicated by what was called 'sifting.'

Sifting meant that if a client wanted a particular grade and origin of cocoa, they would hold a long position, and as this position became 'prompt' for the short period until expiry. During this delivery window they could be 'delivered' at any time.

Delivery was made by a seller sending warrants to the ICCH to settle their outstanding selling obligations. These warrants would then be prorated to the companies holding outstanding buying contracts or 'long' positions. This meant you could get a mix of quality and country-of-origin cocoa from the Ivory Coast, Ghana, Cameroon, Nigeria, Ecuador, and Togo.

Buyers who got a mixture but only wanted Ivory Coast, for example, would keep the Ivory Coast warrants, sell back on the market in the prompt month sufficient lots to deliver back the unwanted warrants to the ICCH and then go long again and wait for the next batch of warrants to be delivered.

Buyers could keep doing this in the hope they would end up with what they wanted. If they did not manage to get what they wanted by the time the delivery window closed, they would just put any unwanted warrants into a safe and start the process again on the next delivery month.

There were five delivery months per calendar year, so there was always plenty of work to do. As well as the form filling for the actual deliveries, the seller also had to make sure the 'rent' (the cost of storing the cocoa) was all paid up on the warrants prior to delivery to the ICCH.

The other duty was to make sure the cocoa or coffee warrant was in date because the commodity could spend a great deal of time in a warehouse before ending up with a manufacturer, and as such could degrade.

The futures contracts traded on the LCE required that the goods be of a stated deliverable quality, this meant that if the cocoa or coffee sat for any length of time in a warehouse it would have to be 'regraded' by specialists at the ICCH.

If the warrant you held told you the grading was out of date, you had to contact the warehouse and give them the warrant number and the warehouse would send you a new sample. This new sample would duly be delivered to the ICCH for grading along with the associated warrant. The quality would then be checked, and if the goods remained of deliverable quality, the warrant would duly be updated.

Importantly, the sample would be returned to you by the ICCH once it had been graded.

The coffee department was very particular about this return of samples, as just down the road an entire business had been established on the back of samples.

An enterprising individual had set up a coffee grinding business, and when sufficient samples were collected, they would be delivered to him. He returned 60 per cent of the resulting ground coffee to the company, and the rest he sold in his shop. He quickly had the market sewn up with all the local commodity companies who had no other use for the samples.

Our cocoa samples, however, were taken down to the basement at 66 Mark Lane and locked away – nobody had any use for them.

In April 1982, war broke out. The Argentinians invaded the Falklands, and we all watched on in a mixture of puzzlement and growing patriotic fervour on 5 April 1982 when we saw TV images of the Naval Task Force setting off to confront the invaders. My family's main concern was whether my brother would be caught up in the conflict.

Robin remained, for the time being, in West Germany, watching across the border at the East German and Soviet forces.

Preparations for the new London financial futures market were moving along at a pace, and Czarnikow had confirmed its intention to be a founder member of this new trading exchange.

Plans for the new contracts were starting to crystallise. There would be a FTSE 100 future based on the stock index that would give companies the opportunity to hedge against stock market swings. This was aimed at the pensions markets.

There were going to be European versions of successful US contracts, such as the Eurodollar and Treasury bond contracts, which would enable traders around the world to continue trading these products 24 hours a day, with Singapore also listing these contracts for trading.

There would be a new UK gilt futures contract and foreign exchange contracts, and there were plans for options on these products as well. I found all of this out at my regular quarterly lunches with Dave Ritchings.

Dave explained to me that there was one new contract that had been the source of a few interesting discussions – a proposed 'interest rate' futures contract.

He explained that if you wanted to invest your money with someone, you wanted an interest return that was as high as possible, and so the same would be true of any futures contract based on interest rates.

But that meant this contract would be the exact reverse of every other futures contract on the new trading floor, where you always wanted to buy low and sell high. With interest rates, you wanted to buy high and sell low, and this was a real concern.

To avoid this, it had been decided to use the same model of existing interest rate contracts trading in the US. There, they had hit upon a simple solution: the interest rate would be deducted from one hundred, so a 7.5 per cent interest yield would be priced on the market at 92.5, and 6.25 per cent would be 93.75, meaning the contract would now work like all the others – buy low and sell high.

The new trading floor was going to be based in the historic Royal Exchange opposite the Bank of England. It was considered prestigious and a fitting venue, but more importantly it already had the required open floorspace.

For the first time, all the UK banks were applying for membership, and established US trading companies were flocking to London to create a trading presence on the new exchange.

Rumours soon started that the new exchange was considering bringing another American concept to London: the 'local' trader. Local traders were individuals who traded for themselves.

In America, on the floors of the Chicago Board of Trade (CBOT) and the Chicago Mercantile Exchange (CME), these local traders made up a large chunk of the floor trading community. These traders were deemed to be essential for adding liquidity, and they could trade their own books and also function as brokers, executing trades for clients.

However, they could not do both simultaneously, as even back in the days before regulation, it was an obvious conflict of interest. It was therefore determined that locals would be single capacity and would have to report to the exchange which role they were performing before entering the trading floor.

The problem with the concept of local traders was that the new market, like the already established commodity exchanges, would be using the ICCH as a central counterparty.

This simply meant that on all futures markets, when two members traded with each other and the trade matched, the ICCH became the counterparty to both legs of the trade. The buyer bought from the ICCH; the seller sold to the ICCH. In this way, counterparty risk was removed, and the ICCH functioned as a guarantor to all the executed trades.

But how could that apply to lots of individual local traders?

The answer was that these local traders would have to find a clearing member to sponsor them and take the risk on all their trading activities.

Conservative companies like Czarnikow immediately set themselves against any such activity; they did not want local traders.

But even Czarnikow realised that if these local traders proved to be successful, then there was a real danger they could quickly start to lose their own traders or brokers as they would inevitably move to local status themselves. This conundrum was passed internally to rising star David Peart to resolve.

David had started reinventing himself as a 'risk and market data' department. With the use of one of the company's first personal computers and new state-of-the-art software called 'LOTUS,' he set about keying in market data as well as looking at charts for trading patterns. He was assisted by a relative newcomer called Harry Deane.

Harry was the latest example of the 'blue bloods' who filled the company at that time. We were told that this dapper young man with a trademark dicky bow had been the 'chicken correspondent' for *Pig Farmer Weekly*. I have no idea if this was true or another Czarnikow yarn.

The public schoolboys seemed to all be related one way or another to senior management as part of a 'friends and family' recruitment policy that had been in existence since the company had first been established.

Usually, these young gentlemen moved from department to department until they 'stuck' or found a vocation that suited them. The sugar and oil department had a few examples of this.

Harry, however, had yet to 'stick,' and he was subsequently working with David to help establish this new department.

David was providing daily charting and market commentary for large clearing clients, including MM Rothschild, using a system called COMTREND. Now he was starting to show Harry how market data could be used to find trading opportunities and how trading patterns often repeated.

David's pride and joy was a huge graph he had built up on the Treasury bond contract traded on the floor of the CBOT and soon to be listed on the new financial market. This carefully penned 'candlestick' chart was drawn onto large A2 sheets of paper, and with each day's high price, low price and settlement price going back years, it showed plenty of 'head and shoulders' trading patterns, for example.

Harry quickly decided his best route to advancement was to apply this new skill set and logic to the company's primary contract, sugar.

Weeks after he had started working with David, Harry formed an opinion on the sugar price and marched up to the fourth floor and the sugar trading desk and proudly described what he considered the price would do in that day's trading session, supported by his charts and price analysis.

Harry's visits thereafter became a daily event. However, after a couple of weeks, he came back down to his desk, fuming and saying that the sugar desk had not taken him seriously.

He explained that he had advised the sugar desk that, based on his chart analysis, he thought the sugar contract price was too high and would finish lower on the day's trading. He then went on to say that Paul Harper, on hearing this, had picked up the phone to one of his clients and said clearly that he felt the price would be going up!

Too much chuckling all round from the other members of the general trading desk, Harry marched off to one of the company directors.

Together, an irate Harry Deane and the accompanying director went up to challenge the sugar trading desk. The director confronted Arb Blundell, the head of the sugar trading desk, saying that Harry's work was not being taken seriously. Arb vehemently denied this. 'Oh no,' Arb quipped, 'we don't want Harry to change anything, and we want him to keep up the good work.' A puzzled expression crossed the directors face as Arb went on. 'It's a genuine gift to be one hundred per cent wrong all the time, and we value it highly.'

As word of this exchange went around the office like wildfire, Harry became a bit of a legend, and other departments started to ask for him to chart their contracts as well.

On 14 June 1982, the Argentinians surrendered. We had watched the Falklands War unfold on the TV news bulletins, and with the final victory, the country felt a wave of relief and pride.

On 30 September 1982, the City of London changed forever as the new financial futures market opened for trading. Christened the London International Financial Futures Exchange (LIFFE), the market broke the mould for the London derivatives markets.

Firstly, copying from its American cousins, all the trading was facilitated on one vast open floor with trading 'pits' rather than the isolated markets London had become accustomed to. Each tradeable contract had its own pit, meaning that all the trading in a particular contract had to be executed in its associated pit.

Pits included a short Sterling interest rate pit, a UK Gilt pit, a US Eurodollar pit, a US T-bond, key foreign exchange futures including Dollar/Sterling, Dollar/Yen, Sterling/Yen, Sterling/German Deutsche Mark, Sterling/French Franc, and a FTSE Index pit.

The pits were side by side flanked by desks on either side of the pits that took the role of the booths on the other floors. Banks of phones on the desks would take the orders from the office or clients directly. This order was then communicated into the pit by the trader's unique sign language. This was even more necessary on LIFFE because the sheer volume of noise on the trading floor meant this sign language was the only effective form of communication.

All the traders had to pass a pit exam before being allowed to trade. This showed they were proficient at the hand signal method of communication and trading in general.

All of this had been ongoing in dummy trading sessions in the weeks and months prior to the market going live. Even experienced traders who had been trading on commodity markets for years for Czarnikow had to pass a LIFFE trading exam before they were given a treasured and unique three alpha trading mnemonic and the official LIFFE trading badge.

For many of Czarnikow's young traders, such as Cliff Donovan, who had been trading on the cocoa exchange with Dave Moore, the opening of this new market presented a huge opportunity.

Another huge innovation on the LIFFE market was the vast number of young ladies on the trading floor. Prior to LIFFE, the trading floors had been male dominated. LIFFE had not only a handful of female traders, but a high percentage of the vast army of new 'yellow jackets,' denoting admin staff, were young ladies.

The new local traders, all wore 'red jackets,' contrasting with the mass of multicoloured corporate trading jackets, each LIFFE member having its own unique and patented designed jacket. Czarnikow had a conservative jacket with blue and white vertical stripes.

The old established futures trading companies sent down some of their most senior and experienced traders to the opening of the LIFFE market. It proved to be a masterstroke.

The big UK and European banks and trading companies, for whom this was a first experience of running a futures trading operation, had sent down an army of Oxbridge-educated graduates and inexperienced traders. Most of these had breezed through the pit training and dummy trading, but nothing could prepare them for the commencement of serious trading.

The experienced traders from the established markets turned the initial days of LIFFE into a bloodbath. They cleaned up and quickly forced the banks and financial institutions into retreat and a major rethink.

Some of these major institutions just decided to put their LIFFE business through the established companies, such as Czarnikow, who picked up a number of institutional clients in these early days.

Others decided to recruit experienced local traders and pay them in guaranteed brokerage commission, rather than have salaried traders on the floor and in the pits.

Others just set about poaching experienced traders from the old derivatives companies, offering larger salaries and associated bonus incentives.

In the aggressive and noisy live market conditions, there was no substitute for the confidence and arrogance of the experienced futures traders. For that reason, the new LIFFE floor belonged to the Essex Boys, South Londoners, and East Enders, as well as the small group of experienced traders who had come over from America. It remained that way right up to the end.

Soon after LIFFE opened, Paul Thompson announced that he wanted to have a team meeting after hours. This was the first time he had ever suggested such a meeting.

After the day's work, we all sat bemused in the office waiting for him to tell us what was going on. Paul sat on the edge of a desk and told us that due to the increased trading and sheer volume of inputting now required, he had asked our line director, Nick Grason, for approval to hire a dedicated input clerk. This new member of the team's job would be making corrections and amendments and managing the bulk of the daily trade input.

We were all relieved to hear this, we had been working flat out since LIFFE started, especially as our trader Cliff Donovan was trading all three legs of a Eurodollar contract. This meant he was trading the contract on LIFFE, on the CME and on the Singapore Exchange, making full use of the new 'follow the sun' trading hours. It was a wonder he had any life outside trading, but he was making significant sums of money. We also had new clearing clients doing much the same.

To a lesser extent, we also had trading in the Chicago Board of Trade's (CBOT) T-bond contract, again because clients trading the London contract sometimes wanted the ability to trade out of positions or indeed put on new positions during the US trading window.

For this reason, our new financial futures desk was open until the close of the US markets at nine o'clock in the evening. This new US trading volume had meant opening a new clearing arrangement with a company called Transmarket in Chicago and this in turn meant a new daily reconciliation for this clearing account.

The increased evening workload meant the numbers on the overtime roster had gone up.

That however was not really what Paul had called the meeting to discuss. I could tell by the look on Ken Boyles face that he knew what was coming.

'So,' Paul said, 'as most of this new work is inputting, I would like to suggest we employ a young lady.' There was an awkward silence as Paul ploughed on. 'Look at LIFFE. Most of the yellow jackets and floor admin staff are young ladies because, well, they're just much better with keyboards.'

Scooter was the most put out, as he realised that he would still be left with the trading floor and ICCH runs. It was unlikely a young lady would be allowed to go down to the commodity trading floors.

But as Paul waited for us all to start nodding and making positive noises, he went on. 'There will have to be a few changes.' We all looked a little puzzled. 'Linda will have to go,' he said, pointing at the Linda Lusardi calendar on the wall. 'And the magazine collection.' He pointed at our historic pile of men's magazines.

Faces dropped a little. 'And' he added, 'we'll need to clean up some of the conversational office banter.' We all shifted a little uncomfortably, but I could see in the shrugs and acceptance from my fellow team members that indicated that we were willing to make the sacrifices required.

'Now,' Paul said, concentrating our attention, 'I have to confess a self-interest.' He lit a cigarette before continuing. 'I have a young lady in mind, and I think you will all like her, but she's my niece.'

The following Monday, with the office tidied up of any potentially offensive material, a young 17-year-old Paula started in the office. Paula was an attractive, shy addition to the team and was the first of many young ladies who would join the back office in the years to come.

A Falklands victory parade took place on 12 October 1982, four months after the Argentine surrender. It was the first time the City of London had celebrated a military event since it had entertained the crew of HMS Amethyst in 1949.

As many as 300,000 people lined the City streets to cheer the parading veterans of the Falklands War as Britain celebrated its successful military campaign in the South Atlantic. It was too good to miss, passing so close to the office, and so with special dispensation from Czarnikow, a batch of us headed to Cheapside to get a view of the soldiers, sailors, trucks, and armoured cars as they passed by.

The parade began at Armoury House, off City Road, near Finsbury Square and progressed via Finsbury Pavement, Moorgate, Lothbury, Bartholomew Lane and Threadneedle Street, past Mansion House, then along Poultry, Cheapside, and King Street to Guildhall. As we stood behind the crowds, we could only see the tops of heads as they passed by, but people leaned out of all of the windows, and Union Jacks waved everywhere. It was difficult not to get caught up in the atmosphere.

The new LIFFE market was continuing to have a major impact on my working day, with the increased volume of trades on these new financial contracts added to increased volume on the IPE.

Our department was rebranded 'central operations,' and we had a new division of labour, as the daily reconciliations and margin calls were split into three: coffee, sugar, cocoa, soya, and potatoes were designated 'soft commodities' and was one section, oil was another, and financials another.

The new LIFFE market had also seen a huge merry-go-round in terms of staff in the City. The banks and financial companies started poaching back-office staff heavily from the existing futures companies, and our deputy manager, Ken Boyles, left to join our huge rivals ED&F Man.

Ken's departure meant Gavin Brodie was promoted to deputy manager.

Rather than just employing new staff, Czarnikow made the decision to inject some 'experience' into our department internally. Joining our team was Ron Wallis from the accounts department and John Brown from palm oil documents.

Ron Wallis was in his late fifties, a delightful soft-spoken gentleman and one of the only openly gay staff members at the company. John Brown was in his early forties and was determined to grasp this opportunity to join an increasingly important team within the company.

Both were welcome additions. John Brown was taken under Gavin's wing to be trained on margins and reconciliations. John started on the new financial market reconciliations and margin calls.

I was given the 'soft' commodities, which was all Czarnikow's historical accounts, and Gavin Brodie took on the oil reconciliation.

Because the LIFFE market was structured in such a different way, it was quickly concluded that getting Scooter to make periodic trips onto the LIFFE floor and run around all the pits collecting trading cards was not going to work.

Instead, the LIFFE floor admin team would gather up the cards from the various pits, write up the input sheets and then despatch one of their number to run them back to the office. This delivery of input sheets would take place when there was deemed to be a sufficient number of sheets to process, although they frequently needed reminding in the early days.

These input sheets then went to Dave Peart's new department which was a 'middle office,' where the standard trading blotter was kept by a new member of staff, Wayne Holloway. Operating in the same way as Sandra did on Sugar and Katherine on Oil, Wayne checked the trades and completed the input sheets which were delivered to us in central operations for processing.

It was a huge relief to all of us in the back office when Ken Maloney and his team finally unveiled a new trading input screen.

Instead of a line-by-line input, we could now input an entire sheet of twelve trades, and once submitted, we would get one input reference for the entire page. We could also amend trades, and this meant no more cancelling and reinputting, instead we could now recall an entire page of input and make a change to the data where required.

My day was now split into two. The morning was spent with my reports, reconciling positions and phoning clients and broking companies, and the ICCH calling and paying funds (margin calls), as well as processing warrants and samples for deliveries.

From lunchtime onwards, I was just inputting trades with Paula, Scooter, Gavin, and John Brown, and then cross-checking trades on Intercom and sending allocations via the BDS to the ICCH.

Another innovation occurred at Czarnikow, once the LIFFE market was up and running. As previously stated It quickly became obvious that with the big banks desperate to secure experienced traders to work for them on the LIFFE floor, Czarnikow was in danger of losing some of their best traders.

Dave Peart's answer to this challenge was a trader incentive scheme which involved them being able to trade their own accounts and take a share in any resulting profits.

This was a hard sell as many directors stated clearly that they could not see why a salaried trader should be paid again for doing their job. Nick Grason was able to convince his fellow directors that they had to agree or lose all their top traders from the various trading floors.

In addition to LIFFE, the traders on the coffee, cocoa, sugar, and IPE floor were also provided with trading accounts, and all quickly made use of them and enjoyed a profit share from the results.

With the back office's growing importance and workload, another good bonus and pay rise followed at Christmas. This time, I ordered a modest turkey, which enabled me to join the festive cheer in the City Yeoman, before staggering off home to Eastcote.

1983

Early in 1983, I had the usual company of Andrew Mersh, Rowland Dunn, and Lesley Neenan, as well as some of our extended settlements family at lunchtime. This included Tony Ford from Bache Securities.

During one lunchtime drink, I asked Tony casually what Bache did with their cocoa samples, as ours were on the verge of filling an entire stockroom. Tony looked more than a little surprised as he said that he sold the cocoa samples to a guy who collected them and took them off to a chocolate manufacturer. Taken aback by this revelation, I asked if he could give me the phone number, which he promptly agreed to do.

I was a little anxious about just selling the samples, especially as we had a room full, so I decided to check first.

I had a quiet chat with Paul Thompson, asking what the plan was to reduce the vast number of cocoa samples in the basement. Paul shrugged and said, 'historically we dump them. The powers that be just want them periodically cleared from the basement, but we have to leave the last six months of samples just to be safe.'

He thought for a second before adding, 'If you have a home for them, I don't want to know the details. If asked, I'll just tell people that I asked you to tidy the room up.'

I made a phone call to the number Tony Ford had provided and told them Tony had given me the number. I explained we had a load of cocoa samples that we were happy for him to collect, and I gave him our address in Mark Lane.

The next day, I recruited Scooter to assist me, and after we had finished our morning jobs, we headed down to the basement.

I unlocked the door to the heaving stack of cocoa samples and carefully moved the last six months samples out of harm's way. With that done, we then started lugging the hundreds of other bags of cocoa samples out of the room, down the corridor and out into the basement car park.

From Hart Street, you had to take a very tight left-hand turn which took you down a ramp under our building and into the basement-level car park. The car park had a turntable that enabled two cars to park, with space for another to remain on the turntable.

As Scooter and I lugged another batch of samples onto our growing pile, I was horrified to see a Ford Capri turn up and stop on the turntable. A scruffy individual climbed out, looking shocked at the stack of cocoa samples we had already piled up.

There was no way a Ford Capri had anywhere like enough space to be able to take away all the samples we were hoping to get rid of. Evidently they did not usually pick up this many samples in one go. I pointed out that the pile represented only half of what we had. Undeterred, we started loading up his car. We started with the boot, which was soon full, and then we moved onto the rear seats, the front passenger seat and the footwells.

The guy held up his hands and said, 'I'll come back tomorrow with a bigger car for the rest.' And with that, he slapped an envelope in my hands. We switched on the turntable, and the Capri was turned to face up the ramp. As the guy started the car up, a plume of smoke shot from the exhaust. This was followed by a screeching as the car's exhaust dragged across the ramp before he vanished up into Hart Street.

I opened the sealed envelope and to our joy saw £100 in notes inside the envelope. I gave Scooter £40 and pocketed the rest.

The next day, I had a phone call to say the guy would be returning at 11 am to collect the rest of the samples. Scooter and I set off back down the basement, carting the last of the old samples from the storeroom and piling them up in the basement garage. This time, the man returned with an assistant and a Volvo estate car, which was a tight fit on the turntable. But we loaded the last of the samples into the large boot, with a few on the back seat.

Another envelope was handed to me with the promise of more when we had another batch of samples to deliver. We turned the ramp slowly, cleared the front bumper with an inch to spare, and finally watched as the Volvo vanished into Hart Street. Scooter and I could not believe it as we opened up the envelope to see yet another £100, which was divided between us.

I bought Tony Ford lunch the next day as a thank you and felt immensely proud of my achievement.

That was until a few days later when Paul Thompson said that Nick Grason, our director, wanted a word. Panic set in as, accompanied by Paul, I made my way down to the second floor, onto the financial futures trading floor and down to the corner where Nick Grason had his office.

Nick was a stocky man in his late forties. He was always immaculately turned out with sharp pinstriped suits and braces. He had a very dominating persona and a no-nonsense attitude to everything, but he also possessed a very dry wit, which I was about to encounter for the very first time.

Paul and I took our seats opposite Nick, who was sat at his large desk in a big black padded chair. 'Mr Parker,' he began, 'I'm here to congratulate you. I went downstairs to the basement yesterday and it's all very tidy.' A wry little smile crossed his lips. 'Very good of you to tidy away all those cocoa samples. I understand that the moths were becoming a bit of an issue. But it's very unusual for staff to take that level of initiative, so thank you!'

I could feel the cold sweat of panic as I smiled back. 'No problem, Mr Grason. I understand they've been piling up for a long time and we were close to running out of space.'

'Quite so,' Nick said. 'But tell me, where did all those samples go?'

I could feel Paul Thompson shifting uncomfortably next to me.

'Well, Nick, via my settlements contacts, I found out that there is actually a market for them. We had a gentleman willing to pick them up.'

Nick sat back and took a few moments before continuing. 'I see.' He leaned in towards me. 'And did he do this for free?'

Here it was – the trap was laid out before me, and I was not about to walk into it. 'Actually, Mr Grason, he paid me for the samples, but I …'

Before I could say any more, Nick held up his hand to stop me. 'I don't need to know the details, Mr Parker.'

He then paused for a few seconds, but it felt like it stretched forever.

Finally, he looked me in the eye and said, 'You do understand that technically those samples were company property.' Paul attempted to come to my rescue at that point, but Nick held up his hand again and silence fell. I feared what would follow next, but Nick surprised me.

'I applaud your initiative and entrepreneurial nous, Mr Parker. In future, however, the company will make use of your contact to dispose of the cocoa samples. That is of course when they have built up again, which is likely to be a while given how few now remain.' He smiled. 'That's all gentlemen.'

With that, Paul and I left. I'm not sure which one of us was the most relieved.

During 1983, I was making frequent visits back to the New Forest in my Opel Manta, staying with my grandparents and visiting Charlotte, Nick and Carol, and Julie Ross.

Julie Ross was engaged to an older divorcee called Keith Moore. Keith was an intense character and seemed very controlling. He tolerated me because I was friendly with Julie's parents.

On the personal front, things came to a bit of a head with Sue Eason early in 1983.

I had been a regular visitor to Hopkinson House and had finally relented in involving Steve Dickinson on many of my visits. I would head for Victoria from the office, and Steve would drive his new Ford Cortina from west London, down the A40, and park up in the square behind the nursing home. I would get a lift home to my parents with Steve, which meant I could now stay until the 10.30 ejection of visitors at Hopkinson House.

Towards the end of 1982, Steve had started to bring a police colleague called Mark along, and Mark had quickly formed a close relationship with Bev, one of Sue's best friends. Another of Sue's friends, Elizabeth, was very attracted to Steve, although this attraction was very one sided. But that all suited me as it left me to focus on Sue.

I had still failed to pluck up the courage to actually ask Sue out officially as a girlfriend, and apart for the exceedingly rare occasion when we were alone in her room and had indulged in an occasional kiss and cuddle, it was a platonic friendship.

It was not that I did not find Sue attractive, because heaven knows I did. In fact, this attraction dated way before we worked together at Waitrose, and back to when we shared Mr Hollies' history class at Applemore Secondary School. But the fear of being turned down and the prospect of losing a friendship and key social avenue meant I was too cowardly to push the point.

This came back to bite me in January 1983 when Sue informed me that on her Christmas trip back to Dibden Purlieu to visit her parents, she had 'bumped' into her old flame Nigel Carlton, and they were once again an item.

I was horrified because back at Waitrose, I and all the male workers had listened as Nigel had boasted of cheating on Sue on numerous occasions. If he could do that when she was at home and just down the road, what on earth would he be doing when Sue was in London, and he was back in the New Forest.

In late March 1983, Sue Eason booked a large table at a pizza venue in Covent Garden for her 21st birthday. Steve Dickinson and I were invited, and Mark was there with Bev. Sadly, Nigel Carlton was also in attendance, having made his way up on the train from the New Forest and staying with family in Acton.

A few of Sue's close friends from Dibden Purlieu had made the journey as well, so there were people I recognised amongst a lot of nurses I didn't. To my horror, Sue showed everyone an engagement ring. Nigel had gone down on one knee and presented it for her 21st birthday.

Mark and Bev, well aware of my concerns, told me I was wrong and if Nigel had been a rat back in the day, he had changed. I remained unconvinced, and as Michael Jackson's 'Thriller' blasted out around the venue, I could not help but think that this was all going to end in tears.

Nigel and Sue wasted little time setting a rough date for the wedding, which was scheduled for summer the following year. This coincided with Sue finishing her nursing training in London. It fundamentally changed her career plans. Now instead of her original objective of working at a major London hospital, she planned to return home and work at Southampton General Hospital.

I told Steve Dickinson that I was going to start to ease up on my visits to Hopkinson House. Luckily, a new social avenue was not far away, the opening of BB's.

On 14th May 1983, I was back in the village to attend the wedding of Julie Ross and Keith Moore in Hythe, followed by the reception at Dibden Hall.

It marked a sea change in my contact with Julie. Once married, the couple moved into a maisonette midway between Dibden Purlieu and Hythe. Keith then set about isolating Julie and started to object to my phone calls, to a point where my contact with her was reduced to an occasional phone call and a covert exchange of letters.

In June 1983, a general election saw the return of Margaret Thatcher for another term in government and the start of the privatisation of lots of state owned companies. As a cash-strapped office junior, I was unable to get involved in this conveyor belt of flotations that started to be offered to the general public.

My colleague Gavin Brodie was not shy in asking anyone in the central operations department, who was not applying for the shares themselves, to do so on his behalf. Gavin offered lunch and a drink as incentives to apply for the shares for him, which we all duly did.

Gavin did not miss any of them – he was a keen buyer of all the denationalised companies. Although Gavin was very astute and a typical City worker of the age, he was also quiet and unlike Harry Enfield's 'Loadsamoney' representation of the Thatcher-style entrepreneur of the time. Gavin did not flash his cash about, but I am sure he made a very tidy sum from the flotations.

My good friend Andrew Mersh was living in a rented room at the top of an imposing Victorian house in Herne Hill at this time.

He was a member of a darts team at The Commercial public house, directly opposite Herne Hill station and based at the end of the Railton Road, which had become notorious during the recent Brixton Riots.

Andrew had a reputation for giving some great excuses for being late to work. On one occasion when arriving late, he told his boss that it was because 'Tower Bridge' had been raised. After a few moments, his boss pointed out that Andrew came into London Bridge station, to which Andrew replied yes he did walk across London Bridge, but he had never seen Tower Bridge raised so he stopped and watched.

Andrew phoned me one morning to tell me he was going to be late, and could I let his boss know. This time he had a top-rated excuse.

I had enjoyed a few evenings drinking with Andrew in The Commercial after work, but I never met the most colourful regular at the pub. He was a gentleman who dressed as a cowboy, complete with spurs, Stetson and six guns. "Buffalo Bill" as he was known, used to walk in dressed in his cowboy outfit and sit quietly at the bar.

One day the gentleman concerned walked into the bar without his cowboy outfit, and Andrew asked him why, to which he replied simply that he was no longer a cowboy. Andrew then enquired if he still wanted his six gun, to which the gentleman replied he didn't and was Andrew interested in buying it? They settled on a price, and it was agreed that on the next darts night they would complete the deal.

On the night of the darts match, the ex-cowboy walked in with the revolver in a carrier bag. Andrew paid for it and put the bag on the bar, next to his pint, as he completed his darts match.

Later in the evening as Andrew was watching the end of the darts match, half a dozen uniformed police appeared, and Andrew was arrested. One of the bar staff had been cleaning the bar, and in moving the carrier bag had looked inside. Convinced someone was waiting for closing time to steal the takings, the landlord had called Brixton police.

Andrew called me at work to say he had been held in Brixton police station overnight on an armed weapons offence. This made for an interesting discussion with his boss in the coffee documents department!

Luckily, a ballistics test by the police proved the gun was a replica and couldn't actually hold live ammunition, so Andrew was released. As he was leaving the police station, Andrew was asked if he wanted the gun back, he declined.

As 1983 slipped by, my relationship with my parents became a little strained as I increasingly came home at midnight after nights out with my colleagues at work down at BB's and the increasingly rare trip to Hopkinson House to visit Sue Eason.

BB's was a revelation to the city. Five branches of BB's opened up simultaneously around the square mile in April 1983. BB's was a cocktail bar-come-restaurant during the day but was a bar during the night.

Each BB's had a large floor space with booths offering tables around the periphery. It was new, fresh, different and had the added benefit of young staff, the majority of which were attractive young ladies clad in the BB's uniforms. These were black dresses cut well above the knee and complimented with brilliant white aprons, the ensemble resembled a Maids outfit.

Our local branch of BB's was in the basement of Dunster house directly opposite our office in Mark lane.

My problem with the parents culminated one night in late September when a group of us, including Scooter, went down to BB's. Scooter rarely came out with us drinking after hours. We lost track of Scooter early on and assumed he had gone home to Dartford.

As usual, Rowland and I stayed until the manager Colin called time at 10.30. Rowland and I went into the gents toilet to see Colin talking to someone behind the door of one of the cubicles. As we stood at the urinals, we watched as Colin went down onto his hands and knees, talking under the door, saying he was locking up and whoever was behind the door had to leave, to which Rowland and I just burst out laughing.

Our smiles quickly vanished when we recognised this weak voice from behind the toilet door. 'Kev, is that you?'

It was Scooter's voice, and before I could react, Rowland had rushed for the exit saying, 'This one's yours, Kev.'

The toilet door opened, and a very green Steve Robertson staggered out of the cubical. Colin looked at me and said, 'You know him?' I nodded, wondering what I was supposed to do with Scooter – he was in no condition to see himself off to Dartford. Now that my 'mate' Rowland had departed, it left one unattractive option: namely, taking Scooter home with me. And with the clock ticking, it was not going to be easy.

Scooter and I staggered out into Mark Lane as Colin quickly shut the doors behind us. I half carried, half dragged Scooter down into Great Tower Street and attempted to flag down a black cab. Taking one look at Scooter all the black cabs with the "for hire" light illuminated just ignored us and drove past.

In desperation, I propped Scooter up in a doorway out of sight, stepped back to the roadside, managed to stop a cab and then with the rear door held open, demanded Scooter emerge from the doorway and get in.

I remember the cab driver looking horrified. 'He's not going to be sick in my cab, is he?'

I shook my head as Scooter promptly plonked himself in the seat next to me, closed his eyes and tried to fall asleep. I asked for Baker Street Tube station, and we set off, both the cab driver and I watching Scooter carefully. I did not fancy being covered in vomit any more than the cab driver wanted Scooter to be sick in his cab.

Luckily, we made it all the way to Baker Street Tube station, and I dragged Scooter out into the station. I propelled him towards the ticket office, bought him a ticket and headed for platform one of the Metropolitan Line, where the Uxbridge train traditionally waited.

We climbed on as near to the front of the train as I dare go, and once again, the moment Scooter found a double seat, he promptly curled up and went to sleep. The painful job of waking him up as the Tube train started to slow down for Eastcote station was compounded by having to half drag and half carry him out onto the platform and then propel him up the concrete stairs to the street-level ticket hall.

Once out of the station, we then made the long trek down Field End Road towards my parents' house. It took forever, and it was well past midnight by the time I managed to prop Steve against the wall and pull out the front door keys that let us into the dark house.

As quietly as I could, I planted Scooter on the sofa in the lounge and fetched pillows and blankets from Robin's unused bed. I figured this was the safer option rather than trying to drag a reluctant body up the stairs and wake my parents. I gave him a bottle of water and placed the washing bowl on the floor, just in case, but by now he had the blanket wrapped around him and was dead to the world, still fully dressed in his suit and shoes.

I was too tired to worry, and I just took myself up the stairs and went to bed, promptly dropping into a deep sleep forgetting all about the drunkard on the sofa.

That was until early next morning when my panicked mother came into my bedroom, demanding to know who was dead to the world on her sofa.

Scooter looked a complete mess; his hair was all over the place, his suit, which he had slept in, was creased all over, and he looked ill.

Thankfully, he had not been sick during the night. My mother demanded I give him one of my shirts, underpants, and socks to change into, and like any mother then shepherded Scooter into the bathroom to freshen himself up.

When Scooter resurfaced, he looked a little more human, holding his dirty washing, which was promptly deposited into a carrier bag. Mother insisted he sit, and she fed him tea and toast, as my father looked on with a big knowing grin.

Mother then demanded that Scooter call his own parents to let them know he was well, something that had not occurred to me or Scooter until she suggested it. So off he went to the phone in the hallway, and soon after he had finished, we left the house to set off for the reverse journey back to the office.

As we sat on the Metropolitan train, a very bashful Scooter thanked me for looking after him, and he asked if I thought Paul Thompson might let him have the day off.

Rowland in the meantime had taken great pleasure in letting everyone in the office know how bad Scooter had been. As we walked into the back office, we were greeted with a big knowing smile from Paul Thompson, who made Scooter work for an hour to make a point, before relenting and sending him home.

In the summer of 1983, my brother Robin came home on leave from the Army. As usual, he planted himself in his bedroom at Cardinal Road and just relaxed. Relaxed for Robin meant emptying the contents of his kit bag all over the floor, eating Heinz potato salad from the can and then putting the empty can under his bed, and degenerating into a slob! Understandably, he was enjoying not having his bed space and uniform inspected regularly, having been regimented from the age of sixteen.

Mother eventually could contain herself no longer and went into Robin's room, armed with rubber gloves, and cleaned up one day when he was out.

On his return, Robin was livid, and he told her he liked things just the way they were. I kept my head down, but then it turned really ugly when Robin came out of his room and demanded to know where his Army shirt was that had been on the floor. Mum calmly said she had washed all his dirty clothes and they were going to be ironed.

Robin was furious and walked out to find the shirt. Opening the top pocket of his Army shirt, he pulled out some shredded paper and shouted at Mum that this was what was left of his 'NATO travel pass.' Mum was incredibly quiet as Robin told her that this was Army property, that he would be jailed when he returned without it, and that he was in real trouble. He then stormed out of the house.

Mum was beside herself with worry and tried to iron the mangled pieces of paper. Then, armed with a huge roll of Sellotape, she set about trying to piece the NATO travel pass back together. When she finished, there were bits missing and it was barely legible, so she decided that if anyone was going to take the blame it would be her.

Digging into the paperwork my parents had received when Robin first joined the army, she found the phone number of the Arborfield Army base where Robin had done his training, and promptly phoned them. Being passed to the duty sergeant, Mum explained what had happened and was told that although Robin would be reprimanded, it was not a 'jailing' offence. One can only guess at the amusement the sergeant would have taken from the phone call.

When Robin finally came home, Mum told him not to worry – he was not going to jail. The look on Robin's face was absolutely brilliant, and he replied in slow, measured tones, 'What have you done, mother?'

Mum didn't miss a beat. 'I phoned the Army and spoke to a nice sergeant.'

It was a real 'light the blue touchpaper and stand well back' moment.

Robin was fuming. 'I bet you gave him my name as well didn't you!' Mum told him that she had not, but Robin went into his room, slammed the door, and didn't come out for a few hours.

It has to be said that after that, mum never went into Robin's room while he was home on leave, although she did indulge in a deep clean every time he had left home after his spells of leave.

In September 1983, my grandad passed away after a brief spell in Southampton General. This was my very first experience of a bereavement and my first funeral.

Grandad was a good man, and I had got to know him a lot better during my spell alone in Froghall, as I replaced my dad as Grandad's Sunday drinking buddy.

Inevitably, as gran started cooking Sunday dinner, grandad would drive round to our house in Froghall and pick me and Chipper up, and we would head to the Royal Oak just outside Beaulieu.

Here, Grandad was a noted regular with his own pint mug on a hook. The pub was a favourite with tourists in the summer, but the landlord never forgot about his locals who turned up all year round. No matter how many people were at the bar, if a regular walked in, they got served first.

During our Sunday lunchtimes, we chatted about football, his time as an accountant at Smiths Industries, and current news events, on which grandad always had a view. Grandad was a staunch Labour supporter, which reflected his life post WW2.

I have to say that grandad's proudest moment, in his retirement years anyway, was in 1982 when he was invited to Arborfield Army base to watch my brother Robin's passing-out parade. As a WW2 veteran himself, it must have brought back many memories. Robin had not only joined the Army, but he had also joined the Royal Electrical and Mechanical Engineers, grandad's old regiment. We all missed him.

Robin was unable to attend grandads funeral as at this time, having completed a riot driving course at RAF Leconfield in the UK, he had been posted with this unit on Operation Banner to Moscow Camp in Belfast, Northern Ireland. There, he was maintaining vehicles at the army patrol bases as well as RUC stations in Belfast. This was because local garages and mechanics could not maintain RUC vehicles without becoming IRA targets.

In addition, Robin flew into Crossmaglen by helicopter to do similar work. Sometimes he travelled to RUC stations in plain clothes, armed with an automatic handgun in unmarked cars. This was what two Army corporals were doing on 19th March 1988 when they unwittingly drove into an IRA funeral procession and were promptly executed.

Because units posted to Northern Ireland spent a huge amount of time in their bases, locked behind fences, Robin often volunteered for patrols in Belfast, where he would travel in Humber Pigs in uniform, armed with a rifle.

Back in the City, my relationship with the new BB's at Dunster House was improved further when in October 1983, Lesley Neenan and I decided, in the absence of any formal company Christmas party, to arrange an informal one ourselves.

Lesley & Me at BBs

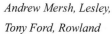

Andrew Mersh, Lesley,
Tony Ford, Rowland

Putting notices on the noticeboards on each floor, we asked for people to sign up. We had a huge response – almost all the staff were up for an evening out and were happy to contribute towards the hire costs and food.

We set off to Dunster Court BB's to see Colin, who was delighted for us to be the first official Christmas booking he had taken. With the numbers of people who had expressed an interest, we were able to hire the entire venue for the evening.

This cemented our place as not just regulars, but important clients. We agreed a date for the party and a buffet menu, and Colin offered us the services of the resident DJ as part of the deal. After a complimentary drink to seal the deal, Lesley and I went back to the office to put up the official notifications on the noticeboards, and we started collecting the money.

Our initiative actually embarrassed the senior management of Czarnikow due to the sheer number of staff who happily signed and paid up. Czarnikow now felt obligated to do something thereafter every year.

However, the company was not happy with arranging one big Christmas party in the way Lesley and I had. Instead, annually thereafter, managers were told to organise department functions, preferably an evening meal, for which the company would pick up the tab.

Christmas of 1983 was marked by our informal company-wide disco at BB's and my first and only experience with a strip-o-gram. Unbeknown to me, Lesley had secretly organised this 'treat' while collecting money for the party and had seen plenty of willing donors contributing to this additional cause.

At the party I had been more than a little surprised when this slim lady, who I had never seen before, came straight up to me and said she wanted a dance. As we headed onto the dance floor, it cleared and everyone ringed us. I knew immediately I had been set up, and as the lady concerned started to strip, I could hear Lesley's laugh.

In perfect time to the music, this young lady just kept on going, shedding clothing until she was clad in only a black lacy bra and knickers. At this stage, she insisted on me removing the final garments.

Once I had embarrassingly fumbled with her bra clasp and removed her knickers, I was pulled back to my feet by the now totally naked young lady as she continued dancing with me. The moment the music stopped, a huge round of applause followed, and I helped the young lady collect her clothing from the dance floor and we headed off to the bar to buy her a well-earned drink.

The party was a huge hit, and Lesley and I followed up with a summer version the next year, which was equally successful in terms of numbers. At this function we convinced Czarnikow to pay for staff from the ICCH, Drexel and EF Hutton to attend, as a cheap form of corporate entertainment.

1984

1984 was a year of political turmoil, and it started with a national miners' strike.

On the 12th of March 1984, Arthur Scargill, president of the National Union of Mineworkers (NUM), called a national strike against pit closures. The decision to strike was technically illegal, as there had been no national ballot of NUM members. This was despite the best efforts of the Nottinghamshire and Midlands coalfields who had called for a national ballot. This miners' strike was to be one of the most bitter industrial disputes Britain had ever seen.

Also in March 1984, I received in the post an official invitation to the wedding of Sue Eason and Nigel Carlton, to be held in Hythe in June of that year, with a reception in Dibden Purlieu village.

At what turned out to be a muted 22nd birthday meal in the Fulham Road for Sue, Steve Dickinson and I told Mark and Bev we were declining the invitation to the wedding. This upset Bev, and an argument ensued. Things got a little heated, and it resulted in Mark and Steve falling out as friends.

I maintained that it simply was not in Nigel Carlton's DNA to stay faithful, and I did not give the marriage a year. I argued that it would be highly hypocritical of me to attend the wedding. Steve did not know Nigel well enough to form the same opinion, but he was happy to defend my position.

I did not realise at the time that my prediction would be way off.

At the end of 1984, on my pre-Christmas visit to Dibden Purlieu, I bumped into an old school friend, Trudi Tulley, and we started chatting about friends from school. Sue Eason cropped up in conversation, and I explained I had missed the wedding. I really did not want to go into too much detail, and so I just told her that I had never got on with Nigel and I did not think he was good enough for Sue.

Trudi then told that the marriage had lasted only a matter of weeks!

Nigel had come home two weeks after their return from honeymoon and told Sue he had made a huge mistake and that marriage was not for him. He had packed his bags and left her in their new home. Sue was now living with some other nurses in a rented house in Marchwood village.

As tempted as I was, I never did get back in contact with Sue Eason.

Firstly, I thought it was going to be exceedingly difficult with me in London and Sue now living in the New Forest.

Also, when I did have time to travel down, I was already struggling to find enough time to get around to see my old college mates.

I was not convinced Sue would want to see me. I felt incredibly sad for her, but I figured she would always associate me with Nigel and Waitrose, and she knew how hard I had tried to warn her about Nigel.

I expected that Sue was probably still friends with Bev and Mark, it was all too messy.

Further developments occurred at Czarnikow in 1984, with a major restructuring of our oil and financial futures departments.

Czarnikow formed a partnership with Schroders on the oil markets, and the department had a new and very dynamic head in Tony Lessor, who joined us from Schroders as part of the deal.

Tony Lessor was a huge asset in the oil department and was able to secure quality clearing accounts, including a few airlines, who had been convinced that hedging their oil use was a smart move due to the volatility of the oil price. In addition, large oil companies and shipping companies were signed up.

Tony eventually went on to become the chairman of the IPE exchange itself.

On the financial futures business, and in recognition of the increased volumes Czarnikow were doing in Chicago, a formal partnership was created with our American broker Transmarket.

Both of these developments increased the number of trades and ultimately oil deliveries the back office had to manage.

The new partnership on financials and the resulting competitive clearing rates in Chicago helped Czarnikow attract some quality institutional client business. In addition, London-based, high-net-worth traders opened clearing accounts clearing trades on the London and Chicago markets.

Just as we were starting to struggle in central operations with the increased workload, we lost Scooter. He had been offered a chance to trade on the floor of the London Traded Options Market with a company called Smith Newcourt.

Scooter's departure and the increased trading paved the way for two new faces in the back office: Sue Bright and Russell Edwards.

The LIFFE exchange was now engaged in a war of words with the ICCH.

The LIFFE exchange felt that it was being significantly overcharged for the central counterparty services provided by the ICCH. The vast majority of the exchange fee that LIFFE charged per trade was being paid over to the ICCH.

LIFFE also wanted improvements to clearing system, in particular to INTERCOM. These complaints seemed to be ignored and so LIFFE announced it would investigate setting up its own clearing house and develop a new clearing and settlement system.

Another change was forced onto the central operations department, and this one was political.

Paul Thompson had been advised by our line director, Nick Grason, to move John Brown off of the LIFFE reconciliations.

As a result, I was taken off of the soft commodities and moved onto the LIFFE reconciliations, John Brown was moved onto oil, and Gavin Brodie took over the soft commodities.

Paul Thompson was at great pains to explain to me that this was not a demotion or reflective that I had done anything wrong. The change was purely political as Nick Grason had decided he was not happy with John Brown, and he had demanded that I be given the role.

This actually meant less work for me initially because there were no 'deliveries' on financial contracts which were cash settled. There were also fewer clearing clients at that time. However, the positions were larger, and this meant a lot more interaction with the financial trading desk, and in particular Dave Peart and Wayne Holloway.

I was a little disappointed with this change as I was extremely comfortable with the soft commodities and had made some good friends among the clients and clearing companies I spoke to daily.

In particular the team at EF Hutton. Linda Booth was the department manager, and her deputy, Nadia Bellows, led an all-female back office. Their office was based just down the road, in a building called Peninsular House, on Lower Thames Street.

We had recently started to mix with them at lunchtimes and in the evenings.

Along with the internal changes, there was a physical move for our department, as we were shifted off the fourth floor and dropped down to the second floor where we were sandwiched in between the oil and financial futures desks. This reflected the new internal dynamic, as most of our work was now coming from these departments.

In addition, this put us on the same floor as our line director Nick Grason.

Our evening social gatherings were at this stage exclusively taking place at BB's Dunster House which I was incredibly happy about. The reason I was happy to keep going back to BB's at lunchtimes and in the evenings was that I had my eye on a very sexy Essex girl by the name of Sue Holland. Sue was one of the waitresses and had an infectious smile. I had formed an instant crush on her, but as usual I was lost as to how to make any sort of move on her.

Andrew Mersh was not so shy. He had taken a shine to one of Sue's colleagues, a very Amazonian blonde called Catherine, and had wasted little time in asking her out and had been given a yes.

Meanwhile, my good friend Rowland had his eye on Virginia Adams, who worked as an usher/till operator in BB's restaurant.

All three of the ladies concerned were decked out in the racy BB's uniforms and seemed very friendly to us as regulars. We were down at BB's until closing time so often that Colin, the manager, tended to leave us to help the girls lock up at night.

Andrew was totally smitten, and we all secretly thought that he had done exceptionally well for himself with Catherine. He was soon seeing her at weekends and even staying at her house with her parents' blessing. Unfortunately, his joy was to last a matter of months.

I was working away in the office when Lesley Neenan came into the back office to say she had just met with a terribly upset Andrew Mersh, who had been banned from BB's, and that Catherine had finished with him.

Puzzled as to what could have happened, I had to wait until after work to meet Andrew back in our old haunt of the City Yeoman. Here, Rowland and I learned that at lunchtime Andrew had witnessed a trader from the IPE floor 'molesting' Catherine, to quote Andrew exactly. When Andrew had intervened to protect his girlfriend, fists had flown and both Andrew and the IPE trader concerned had been banned from BB's.

It was then that Colin had 'asked' Catherine to end her relationship with Andrew, and the other BB's staff were discouraged from getting romantically involved with customers.

Lesley was adamant that we stay away from BB's, but Rowland and I were not ready to admit defeat with Sue Holland and Virginia Adams just yet.

We hit on a happy compromise of lunchtimes in the City Yeoman with Andrew and evenings in BB's. The next day, when Rowland and I appeared in BB's, Colin came over immediately to explain his decision.

After a few nights out with the EF Hutton crowd, I had a surprise invitation for Sunday dinner from the deputy manageress, Nadia Bellows. Nadia was a bubbly, chatty lady of French extraction who had started her career at the ICCH.

While working at the ICCH, she had met and married a colleague, but things had not gone well, and in the resulting messy divorce she had moved from the ICCH to EF Hutton.

Nadia owned a two-bedroom flat above a furniture shop, a stone's throw from Goodmayes train station, which in turn was two stops on the main train line from Rowland Dunn's flat in Ilford.

A couple of years older than me, and a little insecure, Nadia was nonetheless good company. I got the impression that she was lonely, and she tried to fill her spare time with friends and colleagues to limit the amount of time she had to spend alone.

I agreed to her invitation for Sunday dinner and arranged to stay at Rowland's that night and to head into the office together the following Monday. Sunday lunch with Nadia was very enjoyable; we drank a few bottles of wine, and she was a great cook. We spent a lot of time chatting about ICCH and work before we started to get to know each other better.

Nadia's mother was divorced, and her father was not mentioned. She had two brothers, one older and one younger. Our Sunday lunch ended with a pledge to follow up with an evening out in the West End that week. This was the first of many invitations that followed.

I started to include Nadia in evenings out with Rowland, and this increased the frequency of my nights in Ilford and Goodmayes. In fact, we started to spend so much time together that Nadia's colleagues at EF Hutton started to assume we were a couple.

On 18 June 1984, an already ugly political battle turned uglier with a confrontation between striking miners and police in what would become known as the Battle of Orgreave.

Changes in the financial markets in London picked up pace with the announcement of a new government-backed regulator for the derivatives market. The Association of Brokers and Dealers (AFBD) was an attempt at 'self-regulation.'

Primarily, the AFBD established a framework to which brokers and dealers on futures exchanges were expected to conform. Each company had to employ at least one person to act for and on behalf of the AFBD to set and maintain internal standards. It was the start of a process that would result in the FCA in the years ahead.

Personally, a huge event occurred in the spring of 1984. My father told me that we should go for a Sunday pint, which in itself was ominous. We climbed into his car, drove down Field End Road and pulled up at The Ascot public house. We went in, and as I grabbed an empty table, Dad returned with two pints of lager and lime.

Dad cleared his throat and said, 'Son, your mum and I have decided that we may well be leaving London. We're looking at buying ourselves a little business somewhere. But before we do anything, we want to see you settled, and so …' He reached into his coat and pulled out a stack of property details – flats and apartments in the Eastcote, Harrow, and Kenton area.

I was horrified, with my salary at the time I really couldn't see how I could afford a mortgage!

My dad had this covered. 'Your Grandmother has agreed to provide you with a deposit of £6,000 which should be more than enough, and we'll help you with anything that needs doing.'

I started to look at the property details Dad had placed on the table. Still in a state of shock as I flicked through, I was trying to absorb the information. My parents buying their own business was also a huge leap. How far away were they going to move and when?

Over the next couple of weeks, we looked at all sorts of properties in the £30,000 price bracket. Most were run-down or in very dodgy areas.

Finally, we came across a one-bedroomed 1930s-style flat in Central Parade, Kingsbury High Street, priced at £28,000. Above a row of shops and Midland Bank were two floors of flats, all of which had been rented out for generations. The landlord had started selling the flats offering 90-year leases, and this was one of them.

The flat we looked at was in serious need of modernisation. The windows were all contemporary glazed metal. The two huge windows to the front of the property that overlooked Kingsbury High Street were rusted, and a couple of the vented windows would not even close.

There was a large, open fireplace in the lounge, and the kitchen was very 1930s and looked untouched. But it was a good size, with four large, square rooms. To the front, facing the high street, were the lounge and bedroom, and to the rear were the kitchen and bathroom, with a hallway leading from the front door down the middle of the rooms.

It was obvious that the windows were all in need of replacement and that was urgent, as the noise of the traffic passing down Kingsbury High Street was loud. That said, this flat was much better than anything we had seen before and bigger than most. It had great potential, and the other bonus was that from the front windows I could see Kingsbury Tube station diagonally across the road, this meant it was very convenient for the commute to work.

We made an offer, subject to confirmation from the landlord that we could change all the windows, and it was accepted. Even with gran's deposit the result was that I was going to have a £22,000 mortgage!

With a straight purchase from the landlord things went through very quickly on the flat.

Dad and I spent the next month totally stripping the place.

We started by knocking out the fireplace in the lounge, which assumed a huge amount of space and was an ugly utilitarian concrete monstrosity, clad in brown square tiles.

We had driven from Eastcote to Kingsbury on the Sunday following the completion of the purchase. Armed with hammers and a large black sack, we set about the brick mantelpiece. We smashed off the offending tiles and started on the bricks behind them, collecting the debris as we went along.

After we had been at it for an hour, we were about halfway through, both covered in dust and sweat. I had just brought a couple of cups of tea into the lounge when there was a loud knock on the door.

Expecting the neighbours, I went to the front door to see five uniformed policemen standing menacingly outside on the landing. I opened the door and the uniformed police sergeant asked if they could come in. They trooped into the hall and demanded to know what we were up to.

Thinking it was a bit overkill for a bit of hammering, I led them into the lounge as dad was removing another chunk of brickwork in a cloud of dust.

The police sergeant then explained that our demolition of the fireplace had triggered vibration alarms in the branch of Midland Bank directly below us and that the police had been called out by the bank manager, who was convinced someone was trying to tunnel into the bank!

The police explained that they couldn't leave until we stopped the hammering. Seeing that we did not have much more to do, the five police officers sat in the kitchen, drinking tea, and there they stayed until we finally had the fireplace removed. Once we completed the demolition, they promptly left, and dad and I moved on to sealing up the open chimney stack.

Once the double glazing was installed and the flat was redecorated, I moved in.

My parents gave me a lot of kitchenware, and I bought a new gas oven and fridge freezer.

The only item I could not install was a washing machine – the drainage in the flats was simply not up to it. So, playing a guilt card for as long as I could, I quickly got into the routine of driving back to my parents in Eastcote on Sundays. I enjoyed a cooked Sunday diner, and I was getting all my washing done. This left me to collect the washing that I had dropped off the previous weekend, mum was even ironing my shirts for work.

Having my own place gave me a huge amount of freedom, but paying a mortgage, gas, electric, domestic rates and all the other bills made a profoundly serious dent in my disposable income.

Temporarily, my days of drinking every lunchtime and evening were over. To start my new budget, lunchtimes seemed the easiest to economise on, and so I started grabbing a sandwich and heading down to the basement at Czarnikow. Once there, I frequently joined the computer development team in their daily lunchtime card games.

Evenings and weekends quickly became a routine of heading off to Ilford with Andrew and crashing out at Rowland's with an Indian or Chinese takeaway. We still managed an odd Thursday or Friday night, which was now Disco night, at BB's with Tony Ford, Nadia Bellows, and some of their colleagues from Bache and EF Hutton.

The other sacrifice was my beloved Opel Mantar. The insurance and running costs were now too expensive to justify.

Due to the great condition of the car, added to its rareness and novelty, I made a tidy £200 profit on it. I was then able to ask gran for grandad's old gold-coloured Vauxhall Viva, which she was delighted to agree to. It had been sitting on the driveway since grandad had passed away, and she had been reluctant to get it scrapped.

I caught a train down to the New Forest to collect it, and as gran gave me the keys she said that grandad would have been happy to see me have it. But it was a shock to go from a two-litre sports coupe to a very modest aging 1300cc family saloon.

My new economy budget meant that while I was still seeing the lovely Sue

Holland at BB's on a semi-regular basis, I still had not plucked up the courage to ask her out – post Andrew/Catherine, I figured I would get a no anyway.

In August 1984, I had another trip back to the New Forest for a wedding.

This time, my ex-Waitrose colleagues Debbie Frazer and Ian Shrive were getting married. I was delighted to see a number of my old workmates, but sadly the event was marked by a number of key absences, with Debbie's ex-deli colleagues not in attendance.

At this stage, I did not know about the demise of Sue Eason and Nigel Carlton's marriage, and I was relieved they were not there. But I was disappointed not to see Jane Whatney and Josie Smart.

When I finally got a chance to talk to Debbie, she told me that she had lost all contact with Jane after she left for university and that Josie no longer worked at Waitrose. But the day was joyful – Debbie and Ian just belonged together, and I am pleased to report that they are still together and seem to be just as happy.

Back in the City, an opportunity for me to ask out Sue Holland at BB's finally came my way when Eddie Simonds, in the sugar document department, posted a notice on the Czarnikow noticeboard announcing that he and his 'housemates' were having a Halloween fancy dress party. I knew my brother Robin had lots of Army gear back at my parents' house, enough for me to go to the party dressed as a soldier.

I decided I had nothing to lose and plucked up the courage to ask Sue Holland to join me at Eddie's party. I walked down to BB's that lunchtime, watched Sue serving in the restaurant and waited for my chance to grab a few moments with her. As I watched Sue, I spotted a new member of BB's staff, a very young-looking petite blonde girl.

Catherine came over to say hello and introduced the new staff member. Her name was Lucy, and Catherine introduced me to Lucy as one of the valued 'regulars.'

Lucy hailed from Bethnal Green and was just seventeen. Catherine explained that she was training Lucy, but as she was not eighteen yet, Lucy couldn't serve alcohol. Lucy was taking food and drink orders under Catherine's watchful eye and was able to deliver the food while Catherine delivered the drink orders from the bar.

Catherine could see, as we chatted, that I was watching Sue for a chance to talk to her. 'I will let her know,' she said, and she marched into the restaurant to whisper in Sue's ear.

Soon after, Sue headed towards me, and I could feel my heart beating like mad, my mouth going dry. This was it – no backing out now.

Sue smiled as she approached and then said hello. I immediately stumbled on my words. 'Sue ... I ... err ... wondered, if you're not doing anything on Halloween night, do you fancy going to a party with me?'

Sue looked about; I assume for any sign of Colin. 'Where is this party?' I could see a smile. She had not turned me down flat, not yet, so I ploughed on.

'Wanstead. A guy at work and his mates rent a big Victorian house.'

Sue nodded. 'Sounds nice ... Yes, why not. Let me know the address and the time it starts. But yes, it sounds good.'

I was a little taken aback. I felt elated. This had gone exactly the way I hoped, but there was something I needed to tell her, and as Sue turned to head back to the restaurant, it came to me. 'Oh, Sue ... I should tell you, the party, its fancy dress.' I started to panic – what if this additional nugget of information turned the yes into a no??

Sue turned to face me once more, and with that devilish smile she glanced down at her provocative BB's uniform. 'French Maid do?' I nodded vigorously, and with a smile and wink she returned to the restaurant.

Result! I was going to be the envy of everyone at the party. 'Oh yes,' I muttered to myself as I left to head back to the office with a spring in my step.

As elated as I was, I didn't dare mention my date to anyone.

Not Andrew, as I knew he was still hurting over Catherine.

Not Rowland, as I didn't want him making any comments to any of the others at BB's. The more people who knew, the more likely Colin would hear about it and put a stop to it.

I certainly did not mention my date to Lesley, who had not forgiven anyone at BB's for Andrew's banishment and may have given me an ear full.

The following week, in the run up to Eddie's party, I went across to BB's with the address of Eddie's place in Wanstead. Sue and I agreed to meet up in the ticket hall of Wanstead Tube station at 7.00 on the Saturday.

I drove over to my parents on the Friday to collect the Army gear. Robin had full spare sets of uniform, and he was not that different to me in build, so everything fitted, even the boots which took forever to lace up. I looked very authentic.

Early that Saturday evening I set off dressed in full Army attire, including a beret with the REME badge, and crossed the road into Kingsbury Tube station and onto the train heading for Bond Street.

From Bond Street, I boarded the Central Line to Wanstead. The uniform drew lots of glances, and as I got off at Wanstead a quick look at my wristwatch told me I was early.

Luckily, I was not the only one to arrive early, as ten minutes later I saw Sue appear at the top of the escalator. But she was not alone – clad in an identical BB's uniform was Lucy. I was not sure if I was disappointed, angry, or just surprised as Sue grabbed one of my arms and Lucy grabbed the other.

'I hope you don't mind,' Sue explained, 'but Lucy was at a loose end, and she needs to make friends, so I brought her along.'

There was not much I could say, but as we were early, we headed to the nearby George Hotel for a few drinks.

The moment I walked into the pub in full Army gear with two young ladies dressed as they were in the BB's uniforms, the pub fell quiet. I could feel all the eyes of the male customers focus on Sue and Lucy. I walked up to the bar while Sue and Lucy found a table and sat down.

I am sure that the Army uniform I was wearing discouraged the guys in the bar from heading straight over to the table to talk to the girls. I took a number of photographs that night, including a couple of the girls in the pub. After a couple of 'warm up' drinks, we headed off for the short walk to the party.

Sue, me and Lucy on our
way to Eddies party

Lucy and Sue on our way
to Eddies Party

We were not the only ones heading towards the large Victorian detached house As we approached, a number of people were ahead of us, going in through the large wooden front door and into the spacious hallway. We followed in behind as a man dressed as Frankenstein's monster held the door open. As we entered, he asked, 'Who are you with?'

'Eddie Simonds,' I replied.

Frankenstein nodded and said, 'Head up to the top floor. Door to the right is Eddie's.'

We went up the big winding staircase as the music played in the lounge, and on the second floor we were presented with three doors, one to the left, one to the right and in front a bathroom. I knocked on the door to the right, and Eddie, dressed as a vampire, complete with fake blood, opened the door.

'Kevin …' He looked at Lucy and Sue in. 'With two dates!' He stepped aside. 'Come in.'

Four people were already in Eddie's large bedroom. I didn't recognise any of them. Eddie explained he was going to lock the door when we all headed downstairs. There were stacks of food in the kitchen, including burgers, hot dogs, a chilli, salads, and quiche, and to just help ourselves.

Eddie said that although he was locking his bedroom, if we wanted to stay for the night that was fine. There was plenty of room in the chairs and on the sofa in his room and failing that the floor, we just had to find him to get the key. But he stressed that we must stay off of his bed, that was his.

With that, we all headed off downstairs to join the fun.

The party involved plenty of drinking, eating, and dancing, and at its peak the house was so full that some headed off to the George for a while, while others strayed out into the large back garden. Any romantic notions that I may have hoped to enjoy with Sue Holland vanished when Lucy quickly became a little drunk and I was forced into protection mode.

As the evening drifted into the early hours on Sunday morning I ended up sitting on the sofa in the vast lounge with Lucy asleep on my shoulder. Sue danced away with a series of guys, always within eyesight. Despite my disappointment, we still had a good time.

At two in the morning, the party had started to wind down, and with Sue back with Lucy and me, I located Eddie, who told me his bedroom was already unlocked. We headed off up the stairs to the top floor and Eddie's bedroom. A couple were already stretched out on the sofa and so, against previous instructions, the three of us climbed onto Eddie's bed and quickly fell asleep with me in the middle, with an arm secured around each of my dates.

In the morning, I found Eddie asleep in the chair and another body stretched out on the floor alongside the bed. We struggled downstairs to find a cup of tea or coffee. The house was a mess, as you would expect, and after a cup of tea, and with Eddie still not in sight, we left the house to head for home.

In the fresh air, we walked towards the George public house when Sue spotted a black cab with its light on. With a quick peck on the cheek and a promise I would look after Lucy, Sue jumped into the cab and headed off. I escorted Lucy down to Wanstead station and onto a Tube to Bethnal Green, where she assured me she was fine to make her own way. I stayed on the tube and headed off back home to Kingsbury.

A couple of weeks later, mum was travelling to the West End to do some shopping, so I offered to take her to lunch. I decided to take her for a meal at BB's as she had heard so much about it. I booked a table the day before with Virginia, and she asked who I was entertaining. When I told her it was my mum, she winked and said that they would 'look after us.' I wasn't sure what that meant, but the next day as I escorted Mum down into the bar, I quickly realised.

Virginia had shuffled the tables and made sure it was Sue Holland who was serving us. All of the serving waitresses, including Lucy and Catherine, made a point of coming over and saying hello and introducing themselves. I had not told mum anything about Sue, but for a very enjoyable hour and a half, Sue was very chatty and attentive, and we had a great lunch. I left a tip, and as we left, mum said she could see why I spent so much time down at BB's.

I never got another date with Sue Holland; I think the fact she had invited Lucy along to our date told me all I needed to know. Then there were the potential problems with her manager, Colin. Given time, I might have been tempted to give it another go, but once again fate was about to take me in another direction.

In October, Nadia Bellows held a big party at her Goodmayes flat to celebrate her birthday. Andrew Mersh declined, but Rowland was up for it, and this meant I could relax and crash at Rowland's overnight afterwards.

Lots of Nadia's colleagues from EF Hutton and a few of her ex-colleagues from the ICCH were there, and by the time Rowland and I arrived, armed with lager and cider, the party was in full swing with the majority of the guests dancing in the lounge.

Rowland headed straight into the kitchen, cutting his way through all the dancers in the middle of the lounge. I stopped halfway and said hello to Nadia and having done my good deed I followed Rowland into the kitchen, where a group of guys were in conference.

In the kitchen was Roger from EF Hutton, a couple of guys from the metals desk at Shearson and another guy who was talking about his job as a spot welder – he was Katie's date for the night. Katie was a petite young girl from Nadia's department who had been out with us a couple of times.

We were on our second or third drink when a female visitor entered the kitchen, stilting the conversation. She made her way over to the bottles of spirits on the counter behind Katie's boyfriend and started to pour herself a very generous glass of vodka. 'Don't mind me, boys,' she said with a slight lilt in her voice. The guys quickly went back to talking about football, and West Ham United in particular.

I could see this young lady, with drink in hand, standing with her back to the kitchen worktop, scanning the room and looking at each of the males in the kitchen in turn as the conversation continued around her. With a gentle smile fixed to her face, I eventually felt her eyes on me, so I looked her straight in the eye and smiled back.

I took the opportunity to have a good look at her. She was pretty but not the sort of girl I would normally be attracted to. She was petite, just over five foot with short, cropped light-brown hair. Now that I had been able to study her, I was drawn to her eyes, they reminded me of my old flame Lisa Davis. She was wearing baby-blue coloured blouse and dark-blue denim trousers that looked new and clung to her legs.

As her eyes scanned around the males in the kitchen again, she seemed to be taking in the conversation and made no attempt to leave and re-join the people in the lounge. I had been a little bit of a spectator since she arrived, taking more interest in our female guest than the conversation about West Ham.

When her eyes came back to look in my direction, she caught me looking back at her. We held each other's gaze for a few moments. The conversation went on unabated as she took another sip of her drink, and then she seemed to arrive at a decision and set off meaningfully across the kitchen floor.

Once again, the moment she moved away from the kitchen worktop, the conversation in the kitchen faltered. I was more than a little surprised as she walked straight across the kitchen, still holding my gaze and took my hand. 'Excuse me, boys,' she went on, 'but I'm going to borrow this young man.' And with that, she gently tugged my hand and led me out of the kitchen.

I could hear the calls from the guys left behind, particularly Rowland, as I resigned myself to a few dances with this young lady.

We entered the crowded lounge where 'Can You Feel It' by the Jackson Five was blaring, but I was led this way and that, weaving between the dancers, and to my surprise we went out of the lounge, into the hallway and then turned left, heading for the front door. My guide turned to face me, with a playful grin fixed to her face looked me in the eye as she opened the front door, careful to leave it on the latch.

With a gentle tug on my arm, we passed out into the hallway. She stopped briefly to pull the front door to, and then she led me down the stairs to the communal front door, out to the left and into the car park behind the flats.

We came to a halt, and with her back to the wall, she let go of my hand and pulled a packet of cigarettes out of her jeans pocket and a lighter from the cigarette box. She offered me one, and I shook my head. With that, she lit the cigarette, took a quick puff, gentling exhaling the smoke in a very ladylike way, and then held out her hand. 'My name is Dianne,' she said.

I took her soft hand and gave it a gentle shake. 'Kevin,' I said.

'How do you know Nadia,' she said with a soft lilt that I still could not place.

I explained the connection, and her eyes never left mine as she carefully nursed her cigarette. 'And you?' I asked. 'How do you know Nadia?'

She laughed. 'I don't. I know Paul Swain and his girlfriend Laura. Paul used to work with Nadia at the ICCH.'

Dianne carefully put out her cigarette and stayed very still against the wall with a look that reminded me immediately of Lisa Davis backed against the oak tree waiting for me to … I leaned forward, slowly bringing my lips to hers. If I had misread this, I was about to get a slap or worse, but I had to find out.

My lips slowly touched hers, and with no resistance her hands circled my neck.

A very gentle exploratory kiss quickly turned into a passionate kiss. As I pulled her in close, I could taste the tobacco and vodka, and to me it tasted wonderful. My arms circled her tighter, and she felt so good. The kiss became more passionate the longer it went on. It had been so long since I had enjoyed an experience like this, and I wasn't about to let her go quickly.

When our lips finally parted, Dianne looked up into my eyes. 'I don't live far away from here, but sadly I think your friends and mine would miss us if we vanished, so maybe we should go back up.'

I was surprised at her forwardness. We had only just met and only just kissed – was she really contemplating taking me back to her place?

Before I could think further, Dianne once again took my hand and guided me back to the communal door and the stairs back up to Nadia's flat. With a gentle push, the front door opened, but before we went back into view of the lounge, Dianne kissed my lips and with a big smile asked, 'See you later?'

It was a question to which I nodded eagerly, and with that and a little shimmy she went back into the crowded front room, leaving me to head back into the kitchen.

My head was spinning as I tried to work out what the hell had just happened. I felt great, elated, but when I got back to the kitchen, Rowland was waiting anxiously. 'Parker you idiot,' he said, pulling me deeper into the kitchen and out of eyesight of the lounge. 'Don't you look before you leap?' He was waggling the fingers of his left hand under my nose.

It took a moment, and then it hit me. 'No, of course I don't check for rings. Why would I? Is she married?' I said this more to myself than Rowland.

My friend nodded. 'Her husband came in looking for her about ten minutes after you had both gone, but I wouldn't worry too much.'

He propelled me towards the kitchen door and pointed in the direction of the sofa at the other end of the lounge. I had to look hard, waiting for bodies to sway temporarily out of the way, and I could just make out a guy with shoulder-length brown hair with his arms around two ladies sitting either side of him, neither of which was Dianne.

'That's him?' I asked.

Rowland nodded. 'I think he wants to have his cake and eat it,' he added.

I wondered just what it was I had been dragged into. But I kept watching for Dianne, and I could see her dancing with a pretty blonde lady, then with some of the other ladies at the party. She looked like she was intent on having a great time.

Rowland and I moved from kitchen to lounge and back again, chatting, dancing, eating, and drinking. All of the time I could see Dianne in and around the lounge. We exchanged the odd glance and smile as the evening went on.

Eventually, people started to leave, and just when I thought she had forgotten about me, Dianne came back into the kitchen, took me by the hand and headed back into the lounge, this time for a few dances.

We did not say a word as we started to dance. I looked into her eyes, and she looked right back, holding my gaze. I asked if she was having a good time which she said she was and we slowly got closer, and just as I slipped an arm around her to pull her even closer, Rowland coughed from the kitchen doorway and pointed to his watch.

Dianne looked at me. 'You have to go?'

I looked at my watch – it was 2 am and the lounge was emptying. I could see Dianne's husband chatting with the pretty blonde I had seen dancing with Dianne earlier and a guy with curly black hair. 'Yes,' I said, 'I'm crashing round my mates, as I don't live locally.'

'Oh,' she said, casting her eyes down in disappointment. And with that, once the dance had finished, she slipped away.

I gathered my coat and said goodbye to Nadia, and then Rowland and I headed into the hallway.

Just as I thought my strange evening had ended, Dianne appeared in the hallway. Ignoring Nadia and Rowland and with complete abandon, she kissed me full on the lips, and her hand discreetly pushed a piece of paper into mine. With that, she whispered into my ear, 'I know you won't call me.' And then she spun away, heading back into the lounge.

I resisted the urge to open my hand until Rowland and I had walked out the front door. The moment we were the other side of the front door and heading down the stairs, I opened the heavily folded paper in my hand, and there was a telephone number with 'Call me at work … please' and four 'X's.

For the rest of the weekend, I could not think about anything else but the events of the party, Dianne, and calling the phone number she had given me. When I got home to Kingsbury, I just paced around with butterflies in my stomach.

When I arrived at 66 Mark Lane on the Monday, I decided to wait until 10 o'clock, not wanting to appear too keen, nor disinterested. As I worked on my reconciliations, my eyes kept flicking up to the clock. At 10 o'clock exactly, I picked up the phone and dialled. The phone rang a few times, and then I heard her unmistakable voice.

'Hello Dianne, it's Kevin … from the party.'

She replied, 'I know who you are … I was really hoping you would call, but I really wasn't sure you would.'

That eased my nerves a little. I asked if we could meet up and she immediately suggested that lunchtime. Dianne explained that she worked just across the river in Bankside Power Station and suggested a local pub overlooking the Thames.

I quickly jotted down the name of the pub and the address, and we agreed on 12.30.

I asked Paul Thompson if I could have a slightly extended lunchtime, as I was meeting a friend, and then I sprinted down to the ground floor to ask the messengers the best way to the pub I was meeting Dianne in. These guys were our equivalent of black cab drivers – there was nowhere in City that our messengers had not been to at some time or another, and the City was always navigated via pubs.

Armed with a detailed description of how to get there, I returned to the office and work, my eyes flicking constantly up to the clock. The time crept painfully slowly towards 12 o'clock.

The moment the clock hit twelve, I was off, out the door, quickly down to Tower Hill Tube station to catch the train to Blackfriars, across the bridge and down the Thames-side path to find the pub we had agreed to meet in.

I was early and queued at the bar. Just as the barman came over to serve me I saw Dianne enter. She looked different, dressed in a long coat that was open to reveal a formal brown dress and a black belt. Her face was framed by a large pair of glasses. To me, she looked even more attractive than I remembered.

Dianne came straight over, and I asked her what she would like to drink. She ordered a Red wine and then suggested we order our food at the same time, which we did.

We took a table by the window looking out over the Thames. Dianne took the seat opposite, and as we sat. She took a deep breath then looked into my eyes and told me how happy she was that I was there, she looked incredibly nervous and so I reached out and placed my hand on top of hers.

Dianne left of her hand on the table as I gave it a gentle squeeze, I took that as a good sign. Her smile faltered slightly as a serious tone came into her soft voice and she told me that she was married. I replied I knew, but only because my mate Rowland had pointed out the rings on her finger and that I had been oblivious to them. Dianne went on to explain that she had been married for five years and was very unhappy.

I guessed Dianne was older than me, but I didn't know how much older. She explained that her husband, George, was rarely home. George worked for the Ministry of Defence with Paul Swain's girlfriend, Laura, and often worked late. When he was not working, he was in a 'band;' they spent several nights a week rehearsing, and at weekends they were usually playing gigs or doing even more rehearsing.

On the rare occasions he was about, he would usually arrange for them to be in company, and more often than not that company was his workmate, Laura, and her boyfriend, Paul Swain. In short, he spent as little time alone with Dianne as he could, and as I looked at her, I simply could not work out why anyone would do that to her.

As the food arrived, Dianne just chatted, telling me she was Welsh, which explained the lilt and provided yet another connection in my mind with Lisa Davis. Dianne's parents lived close to Chester on the Welsh side of the border. She had two cats that she loved and had a close friend called Sandra who lived in Ilford. Sandra had been in a bad relationship and did not have much time for 'men.'

Once Dianne had started, she just unloaded. It was as if she was simply happy to be able to talk with someone outside her social circle and had been storing all this up for some time.

I could see at times she was coming close to tears, and as a waiter appeared to clear away our plates she suddenly panicked as she looked at her watch. 'I have to go,' she said. 'My boss is a bit strict on lunch hours.' She reached out and took my hand again. 'Sorry, I have done nothing but talk. You will probably never want to see me again.'

I replied immediately 'Dianne, of course I want to see you again, but next time let's meet after work, so we don't have to rush.'

The smile returned. 'How about this Wednesday? That's one of George's band nights.'

I agreed, and with that we got up and left the pub. I managed to give her a quick kiss on the cheek before she rushed off in the direction of the imposing Bankside Power Station.

That Wednesday was the first of a series of twice-weekly evening meetings. We met every Wednesday and Friday night during November and December, which were band nights for George. On these nights, we would head into the West End to have a few drinks or go for a meal in a restaurant.

We were regulars at TGI Friday's in Covent Garden. After each meeting, I would escort Dianne back to her road in Seven Kings. We would hide in an alleyway within sight of her front door and say goodnight to each other, and then I would watch her walk down the road and go into their house, after which I would head back to Rowland's to crash for the night.

Christmas was soon upon us, and I was due to spend it with my parents in Eastcote.

I had mixed feelings about Christmas that year; it meant I would not see

Dianne for a week, and by this time I was totally besotted with her.

Our meetings had got more intimate as we both quickly relaxed in each other's company. I would catch the Circle Line to Blackfriars, jump off the Tube and wait for her on the platform. When she appeared, we would kiss and hug on the platform before jumping onto the West End-bound train and going out for the evening.

In the early days of our relationship, Dianne would clock watch, and we would head back to Seven Kings early, so she was always indoors before George. Later, she relaxed and started to use her friend Sandra as cover. Sandra lived locally and was no fan of George. Dianne had quickly confided in her about our relationship, and Sandra seemed to be more than happy to cover for us.

Every time we met, the bond between us got stronger, the conversation flowed, and I felt totally at ease in Dianne's company. We just had fun. I never felt the need to be anything other than myself. Whatever I said or did always seem to be the right thing, and we just gelled.

There was a distraction in early December with an unusual Christmas party invitation – the BB's staff Christmas party, which Rowland and I were officially invited to. This was due to Rowland, and I having spent so much time down at BB's helping out where we could, we were now considered part of the BB's family. It was yet another fancy dress party and held at the Ship and Compass pub, just outside Fenchurch Station, on 14th December.

As Sue Holland and Lucy were going, it did not seem a good idea to borrow Robin's Army gear again, so I decided to go back to my punk roots. I used sugar water to recreate the shape of the Mohican hairdo that Lisa had produced many years before. My hair was much shorter now, so it was not as good, but with black shoe polish as eyeliner, the faithful donkey jacket still in the back of the wardrobe, ripped jeans, and Dr Martens boots, I managed to pull it off. Rowland went as John McEnroe, which suited him.

It was a great party, and the staff made a huge effort with their fancy dress. There were a lot of kitchen staff we did not usually come into contact with, but it was all good natured and it felt like Christmas by the time we left.

The Czarnikow 1984 Xmas party was a week later and held at The Five Lamps wine bar close to Fenchurch Street station. This party was unusual insofar as the company asked the staff to organise it and they paid for it. Lesley had a big hand in organising it, and we had another great turnout, including Victor Dowell, the director of our New York office, who always came home for

Christmas and was more than happy to attend.

Also in attendance was Nadia Bellows, who I managed to invite on the back of the work connection with EF Hutton. Another non-staff attendee was Paul Thompson's wife, Gwen. Paul had asked us if anyone had an issue with her coming along, nobody did and Gwen proved to be great fun, very cheeky and mischievous. It was Paul who had the reservations thereafter. But every year after this party we all insisted that Paul invite Gwen.

Dianne's birthday was on 20 December. I had been able to grab a few hours with her that night and learned she had just turned thirty, but neither of us was concerned about the eight-year age gap. It was a bittersweet night as we knew we would not see each other again until the new year.

I repeated my twice-weekly routine of walking her close to her house, ducking in a secluded driveway for a goodnight kiss, and then watching her walk to the door of her house and go in. Then I had the walk back to Seven Kings station, the short train ride to Ilford and a walk to Rowlands's place.

We observed the usual Czarnikow traditions on Friday 21st, starting with our champagne breakfast in The Ship public house and, as the markets shut for half a day, the usual post-work drinks, and the walk home, armed with a modest turkey and bottles of whisky and wine from clients. But this Christmas lacked the usual festive spirit for me, as I kept thinking about Dianne.

That night as I sat in my Kingsbury flat, wrapping presents and preparing for the trip to my parents the next day, the phone rang. My heart leapt, and sure enough Dianne was on the phone, but she was terribly upset. Through the sobs and tears, I heard that Dianne and George had been to a pub having Christmas drinks in Seven Kings with Paul Swain and Laura. After lots of drinks, George had declared loudly to the entire pub that Laura was the most beautiful woman in the world, and he was totally in love with her. This was in front of not just his wife, Dianne, and Laura's fiancée, Paul Swain, but anyone else who was within earshot.

Dianne was mortified at being so publicly humiliated. I asked if she wanted me to get her, but she declined. We talked, and at the end of the conversation she asked me to promise her that I would see her early in the new year. I was not happy to wait that long, so I told Dianne that the Thompson Twins were playing Wembley Arena on 28th of December and asked if she wanted to go. Dianne quickly took me up on the offer, saying that having something in the diary to look forward to would get her through Christmas, and so I secured the tickets and we agreed to meet up at Liverpool Street after work on Friday 28th December.

With this cloud hanging over me, I went to my parents for Christmas.

When I finally met up with Dianne on the 28th for the Thompson Twins concert I was overjoyed. I was surprised at just how much I had been worrying about her after her pre-Christmas phone call. We kissed passionately and then headed for the Circle Line Tube. Once again. I had managed to get Rowland to agree to me crashing at his place, and this meant I could do my usual and escort Dianne back to her house.

The Thompson Twins were really good live, and although not as 'full on' as my recent Jam gig, we were all dancing at the end as they went through their hits, 'Doctor Doctor,' 'Hold Me Now' and 'Love on Your Side.'

I had an amazing night. We sat on the Tube back to Liverpool Street, chatting and laughing, and as always, the nearer we got to Seven Kings, the quieter we became.

As I walked Dianne towards her house, we ducked into the alley as always and enjoyed our moments together before she made her way to the house. I watched her go inside and started to walk back to the station, wondering what 1985 had in store for us.

1985

Dianne and I went to see the blockbuster film *Dune* in Leicester Square early after the New Year break.

Dune was a film we both wanted to see, and it was a particularly long film. I held Dianne in my arms during the entire performance, and as we arrived at Liverpool Street station, we kissed as never before. Then she asked me not to travel back with her to Seven Kings. I was mighty confused and worried at this turn of events as I watched her go.

Lesley Neenan had a wicked sixth sense, and she always knew when I had lady issues – it was an uncanny knack that repeated several times over the years. She sat me down and demanded to know what was troubling me, and so I told her.

Lesley listened intently as I explained how hard it was getting to take Dianne back to their house night after night and how upset she had been on Christmas Eve due to George's announcement. Now, after the trip to the cinema, Dianne had stopped me at Liverpool Street station instead of letting me see her home as we had done every time previously.

Lesley was not known for her subtlety, and she just looked me in the eye and with her usual style said, 'Parker are you telling me you haven't invited Dianne back to your flat yet?'

I was stunned into silence and did not reply, 'For heaven's sake, Kevin,' Lesley went on, 'you're an idiot. The poor girl is probably wondering if you're gay at this stage.'

Before I could defend myself, Lesley held up a hand. 'I know exactly what you're going to say – she's married, she's not like that, right?'

I nodded.

Lesley sighed and looked at me with an element of frustration and pity. 'Right, Kevin, this is what you're going to do. You're going to buy a really nice bottle of wine, and next time you see Dianne you're going to give her the option of coming back to your flat.'

My head was all over the place. Of course, I wanted to take Dianne back to my flat, but I had convinced myself it was not an option as long as she was rushing back to her husband George every night.

But now that I thought about it, Dianne had made that hint about going back to her house right back when we first met at Nadia's.

Plus, you didn't say no to Lesley – she had given me the look that said,

'Lesley knows best,' and if there was even an outside chance Dianne would say yes, then I had to give it a go, and so I nodded.

The following Wednesday, I was on the bench at Barbican station, armed with an expensive bottle of red wine. Dianne arrived, looking lovely as always, and asked what I had planned for the evening. I said simply, 'We can go to Covent Garden or ...' I produced the bottle from the bag, and without taking a breath continued, 'We could go back to my flat and enjoy a night in with this.'

Dianne beamed at me. 'Let's go back to your flat.'

I was happy, surprised, and now kicking myself. How long ago should I have made this suggestion?

We chatted as usual as we travelled in the direction of Kingsbury, but as the train pulled into Kingsbury station there was this sense of expectation, that we were crossing a boundary, taking everything to a new, different, exciting level.

When we got to my flat, Dianne took the bottle of wine from me, put it on the table, took my hand and headed down the short corridor, looking for the bedroom. As we entered, she immediately started undressing. I stopped and watched – this was something that had been going on in my head for an exceedingly long time, and now it was really happening.

There was an urgency in Dianne, and I simply did not have time to think about anything. I was swept away with the passion of the moment, and in my mind I thanked the heavens for Lisa Davis ensuring I was not a total novice.

As we lay in bed afterwards, Dianne in my arms, she looked at me with a wry smile and said in her soft Welsh lilt, 'I was beginning to wonder if I would ever get invited to your flat.' Then she explained that I had inadvertently had such an effect on her while I was gently caressing her at the cinema while we had been watching *Dune* that she felt she was going to burst into tears if I had taken her back to Seven Kings and let her to go home to George.

I felt a complete moron for not noticing the signs as usual.

With the added travel time that went with the trip to Kingsbury, one glance at her watch and Dianne looked at me and said she had to go. I told her I was escorting her and was not going to take no for an answer. After a quick call to Rowland to make sure I could sleep at his, we set off for Seven Kings together.

The long journey back was mostly in silence. I had my arm around Dianne, but I started to wonder if she was regretting coming back to my flat. But as we walked from Seven Kings station, holding hands, Dianne looked at me as if she was reading my mind. She told me not to worry, because after the events on Christmas Eve she had told George that she was not interested in sex with him anymore.

That evening, watching Dianne walk back to their house was a little less painful than it had been previously.

The next day, I walked into 66 Mark Lane with a large bunch of flowers, marched down to the cable room and, without saying a word, handed them to Lesley. Lesley accepted the flowers and as the rest of her department looked on bemused, she burst out laughing and said in her typical fashion, 'I told you, Parker, didn't I?'

Dianne called me in the office that lunchtime to say that she had spent the morning walking around with a permanent smile on her face. It was a small thing, but it meant so much to me.

I felt like I was now on firmly a path that would lead to us to getting together.

This was further reinforced when Dianne surprised me soon after by asking to be introduced to my parents. I had not seen that coming, and it meant I was going to have a difficult conversation with my mother in particular.

On the plus side, I took this to be a serious step towards Dianne leaving George. But first it was time to tell my parents everything, and I was nervous.

My answer was to drive around to Kenton, where long-time friends of my parents, June and Irvin Levitt, lived with their two children, David, and Sian. Kenton was just down the road from Kingsbury and a stop-off en route to Eastcote, so I had decided to do a trial run with June.

Irvin let me in, expecting me to be there to see David or Sian, and he was more than a little surprised when I explained I wanted a quick chat with June. I was after a mother's opinion, and June was equally surprised I had chosen her to talk too. June reassured me that if I was happy then my parents would be happy, and so I set off to talk to them with renewed confidence.

I arrived at Cardinal Road where a 'Sold' sign had been erected.

The parents had finally found a business to buy in Yeovil and would soon to be on their way. I asked mum if I could have a word, and then I sat down and explained as best I could about my relationship with Dianne.

To my surprise, mum took it all in her stride – older by eight years, married, wants to come to dinner the following weekend to meet them. The last bit was the obvious clincher.

I knew this meeting would be crucial, and as it happens, I was not the only one who was nervous.

Dianne told me she would meet me at Kingsbury and when she arrived she was wearing a very formal black dress. Once again Sandra was covering for us. If George did take it upon himself to call Sandra, they were having Sunday dinner in Ilford. But Dianne considered it to be highly unlikely he would call, as George was very aware Sandra disliked him.

I tried my best to make Dianne feel at ease as we drove over from Kingsbury to Eastcote in my car.

Once we arrived, dad opened the door and I introduced them, and mother was not far behind. Dad said dinner would be ready in half an hour and I should get Dianne a drink.

Mum escorted Dianne into the lounge, and by the time I returned they were in a deep conversation. I handed Dianne the glass, and she asked me to give her and my mum a few moments, so I promptly left the lounge and headed back into the kitchen, concerned as to what was being said and how it was going.

Dad and I spent what seemed an eternity in the kitchen before I felt a hand slip into mine, and a smiling Dianne appeared beside me. I was more than a little relieved and gave her hand a squeeze as dad carved the Sunday roast, asking Dianne how much she wanted.

I never found out what they discussed. All I do know is that mum said she was extremely impressed, and that Dianne would be good for me.

Mum also told me that she had noted something that, once again, I had not – Dianne was no longer wearing her wedding and engagement rings.

After that weekend, everything Dianne and I did together centred on trips back to Kingsbury. With Sandra covering for us, we went to the theatre, the cinema, and concerts. I even took her to a BB's staff party, where she was made to feel at home.

On the 7th March, Simon Cullen and I were off again to see another concert – my second Stranglers concert, this one being at the Rainbow Theatre in Finsbury Park.

The theatre was built in 1930 as a cinema, and it later became a music venue and was famous for its pitched floor. All they had really done was remove the cinema seats, which meant in the frenzied atmosphere that accompanied a Stranglers gig and the inevitable 'pogo' dance that was mandatory with new wave or punk bands, you all ended up piling forward towards the stage.

Once again, we had a great evening and ended up tired and very sweaty before dashing for the last Tube home.

Later in March, the miners' strike ended with a bitter defeat for Arthur Scargill and the miners.

In the same month, my parents finally moved away from Eastcote having purchased a sweet shop in Yeovil, Somerset. Situated in a new shopping arcade off the bus station, it was an old-fashioned style shop with jars of sweets weighed into bags. It was also a specialist tobacconist that sold smoking pipes and tobacco.

As a going concern, it was perfect for them and had lots of potential for development. The cost of their new venture forced them to downsize to a bungalow in a village just outside the town, and overall, they were excited at the prospect of working for themselves.

For me, it meant no more Sunday dinners and having to go to the local launderette to get my clothes washed, as the plumbing in my flat still wasn't up to accommodating a washing machine.

On 28 May, I had a phone call in the office – it was Nadia asking to meet me at lunchtime. I could see immediately she had something on her mind, and she explained she had got herself into a bit of an uncomfortable position.

One of her male work colleagues had taken a shine to her. His name was Roger, and he was an office-based metal broker. He had asked her out, and she had clumsily accepted, but in a panicked attempt to try and extract herself from the date, she had asked if they could go out in Goodmayes and had somehow inferred that he could stay the night at her flat.

Linda Booth, her boss, had overheard the conversation and asked Nadia if she realised just how high she had stoked Roger's expectations. Horrified that she had more or less invited Roger to sleep with her, she asked if I would help.

'What can I do?' I asked, puzzled as to what she was asking me to do.

Nadia said, 'If I give you the spare key, can you be at my flat when we come back?' She looked at me pleadingly.

'Nadia … you do realise he could go mad? He could even end up hitting me.' I was putting myself in Roger's shoes – I would be very unhappy if I found him sitting there if the roles were reversed.

Due to her panic, I felt I could not turn her down. On the plus side, there was a European football final on TV that night – Liverpool versus Juventus – so I agreed.

On the 29th May, I headed off from the office to Nadia's flat and let myself in. The fridge was well stocked as always, and a curry had been left out for me to throw into the microwave. Armed with my curry and beer, I sat down on the sofa and turned on the TV.

I was only watching the build-up to the match for a few moments when the crowd trouble started at the Heysel Stadium. Like TV viewers all around Europe, I watched in horror as things got worse, leading to the collapse of a wall and reports of people being gravely injured and even killed.

Despite the teams being removed from the pitch, the trouble seemed to continue until the two team captains appealed to the crowd for calm and the game eventually kicked off extremely late.

When Nadia and Roger finally turned up, the game was still on. Roger looked more than a little surprised and upset to see me, but as I explained about what had been going on in Belgium, the ill feeling drained, and in disbelief the three of us sat in quietly watching a pretty meaningless game of football play out.

Nadia retired to her bedroom, leaving Roger on the sofa bed in the lounge and me on an inflatable mattress. Needless to say, Roger never asked Nadia out again.

As always, I was thinking of ways to push Dianne a little further along, and when I found out my grandmother was going away for a couple of weeks, I asked her if I could bring some friends down to the New Forest to stay in her bungalow, she agreed.

On my next date with Dianne, I asked if she would come away with me down to the New Forrest for a couple of days. After what seemed an age in silent thought, Dianne suggested that it was a little risky but, if I talked Nadia into going as well, she would come along.

I was not about to let this opportunity go, and so I called Nadia from a payphone. Nadia agreed to make the trip but, on the basis that she didn't want to be an odd one out, only if she could bring Lucy, one her EF Hutton colleagues. I eagerly agreed.

I drove round to Nadia's the evening before the trip, and with Dianne in my car, and Lucy in Nadia's Citroen, we headed off for the New Forest early the next morning.

The weather played ball and we had a great couple of days and nights. We visited Beaulieu, Calshot beach and Bucklers Hard. With Dianne and I using the spare bedroom, and Lucy and Nadia in gran's room, I felt like I was making real progress.

I did everything I could to make sure the trip was a huge success, and as we headed back towards London, I could see Dianne was deep in thought. As we approached Goodmayes, she held my hand whenever she could. Parting was even more painful that day, but luckily I had agreed to stay at Nadia's that night. I am not sure I could have driven home safely with all the thoughts buzzing around my head.

Dianne and me at Beaulieu

Dianne & Me

After such a great trip, I decided I wanted to do something to impress Dianne, to make a statement, something I hoped would finally push her over the line. I wanted to get two tickets to the hottest concert ever, a concert that had just been announced to the world – I was going to take Dianne to Live Aid.

The problem was everyone wanted to go to Live Aid – it was billed as the concert to end all concerts. The who's who of current music greats were going to be there, and there was a rumour that the remaining Beatles, complemented by Sean Lennon taking the place of his father, would be taking part.

The tickets went on sale midweek in late June, and people started queuing at Wembley Stadium days before they officially went on sale. Despite Wembley being just down the road from my Kingsbury flat, I could not get the required time off work to queue for tickets, and they sold out before I could do anything about it.

But I had a secret weapon: Sue Bright.

Sue was a bubbly Essex girl who since joining our department had quickly settled in proven to be a great addition to the team. Sue's mother just happened to work for a ticketing agency. Just as I was losing any hope of getting tickets,

Sue said she would ask her mother if she could secure two of the coveted tickets.

The next day in the office, I got a call from Sue's mum directly saying she could get me two tickets at face value under a friends-and-family booking. I was delighted, as I feared that I would end up paying multiples of the £25 face value. (The tickets were actually £5.00 with a charitable donation to the cause of £20.00 each.) There were already reports in the media of tickets changing hands for vast sums.

As agreed, I went to the bank that day and gave Sue Bright the cash to take home to her mum. I decided to wait until I had the tickets in my hand before surprising Dianne.

The next day, Sue told me that the tickets would take a week or so to arrive, but not to worry as they were secured. I was due to meet Dianne the next day, and so I toyed with the idea of telling her, but I thought just producing the tickets when I had them would be much better.

As a pre-Live Aid warm up, I took Dianne to see Foreigner at Wembley Arena on Friday 14 June. Foreigner had recently enjoyed a smash hit with 'I Want to Know What Love Is,' and as a finale it was amazing as a vast choir took to the stage. We had planned to grab an hour back at my flat, but the clock went against us.

As Dianne and I headed back towards Seven Kings on the mainline train out of Liverpool Street, she curled up, resting her head on my lap. The walk back to her house was getting more painful for us both again. I had a feeling that things were coming to a head. I hoped my secret Live Aid plan would be sufficient to push her over the line.

The following Monday, Sue Bright finally produced my Live Aid tickets, and I just grabbed her and gave her a huge hug.

This was it – all I needed to do was get a date in the diary with Dianne and produce the tickets.

That afternoon, Monday 17th of June, as I was typing away on the keyboard with the other central operations team members, Gavin Brodie interrupted me. 'Kevin, Sid says you have a young lady downstairs asking for you.'

I was a little confused but completed the input sheet and headed for the lift.

As the lift hit ground and the door opened, there, in a seat facing me, was Dianne, her usual smile missing. As I approached, I could see she was upset, and she quickly asked if we could go outside. I could feel the eyes of the messengers on us as we walked past reception and out into Mark Lane.

Dianne looked at me for a moment. There were tears rolling down her cheeks, and then she said in her quiet Welsh lilt, 'I have decided that I need to leave George.'

My heart soared. At that moment, I realised just how much I had been hoping to hear those words.

But before I could react, she continued, 'I cannot see you anymore.'

It was as if someone had punched me hard in the stomach. I even doubted that I had heard her correctly.

Dianne could see the confusion in my expression as she tried to explain. 'I have to do this for me. I can't leave George for anyone else. It has to be for the right reasons, and so I need you out my life … just for now.'

I was rooted to the spot, fighting an overwhelming wave of emotions, and trying desperately not to dissolve into an emotional mess.

I had been playing scenarios in my head for months – George leaves Dianne for Laura, Dianne leaves George and turns up on my doorstep with her bags, things continue as they are – but never, not for a second, did I consider Dianne needing me out the way in order to actually leave George.

Dianne wiped away her tears, took my hand and looked me in the eye. 'Thank you, Kevin. I would never have been able to do this if it wasn't for you … maybe in six months, maybe twelve, when all this it is over, I'll be able to get in touch … but please, don't wait.'

I wanted to tell her I would wait for as long as it took, that I loved her, but in those precious seconds, I simply could not get my brain to unscramble. The words wouldn't form, and in the end all that came out of my mouth was, 'I've got us Live Aid tickets.'

Dianne gave me a weak smile; I could see her eyes tearing up again. She just said 'goodbye' and turned away and walked down Mark Lane, heading for Liverpool Street. She did not look back.

I watched her go and then finally vanish amongst the other people heading for the stations.

I had work to do. I have no idea how long I stood there on the pavement in Mark Lane, fighting back the tears and this overwhelming frustration, hurt and anger. But finally, somehow, I managed to will my feet to move and headed back to the office.

I walked like a zombie to the lifts and back into my department. John Brown looked up as I walked to my chair opposite him. John was worldly wise enough to see how close I was to a full meltdown. Without saying a word, he took a box from the desk and offered me a cigarette, I just took it as he offered a light.

Nobody had ever seen me smoke in the office before, and I received more than a few looks from the others, but nobody said a word.

I managed to get through the remainder of the day and was on my way out the office front door to head back to Kingsbury when I saw a familiar face outside. Nadia Bellows, she walked up to me with a look of pity and said simply, 'I was told you might need a friend tonight, so you're coming home with me.'

Dianne had obviously called Nadia, and so I went in a semi trance to Goodmayes, where I promptly got supplied with wine and scotch. A good meal was cooked for me, although I couldn't eat, then I collapsed on Nadia's sofa bed and promptly fell asleep.

From that point on, Nadia was like a mother hen. My free time was organised, and she insisted I bring some spare clothes over to her Goodmayes flat, so I always had the option of crashing there.

After finding out about Dianne, Lesley and Rowland rallied, and between them all I was given little time to dwell on things and feel sorry for myself. Despite all this, I had trouble thinking I would ever be genuinely happy ever again.

Everyone thinks the same – that was the one, I will never feel like that again and never have a relationship like that again.

Having people trying to cheer you up and drag you out the pit of self-pity just makes you angry. I wanted to feel upset; I wanted to hurt because I felt I should. But with Rowland and Lesley, I was not allowed feel sorry for myself, and I certainly could not be angry with them for long.

Nadia was grateful for the company and was more inclined to let me mope. She just kept saying that if Dianne felt the same way, then it would be when, not if, I heard from her. At the end of the day, if she did not get in touch, then I had my answer.

But the plot thickened when it turned out that soon after Dianne had left George, Paul Swain and his fiancée Laura had split up. Whether this was directly or indirectly due to George and Dianne, or the events of Christmas Eve, I could only guess. But Laura did not move on to a relationship with George, as I am sure he always wanted, and so it was just a big mess all around.

With my parents living in Yeovil, I spent most weekends in east London. Usually, Friday nights and Saturdays were spent with Andrew Mersh and Rowland in Ilford or round Lesley's in Peckham. Sunday was with Nadia in Goodmayes where Sunday roasts became a regular feature.

Given all the attention I was getting, and how good Nadia had been, I offered her the now spare Live Aid ticket. Nadia was overjoyed and desperate for me to take the money for it, which I politely refused.

Live Aid was held on Saturday, 13 July 1985 at Wembley Stadium. It was agreed that Nadia would crash at my flat straight from work on the Friday. The moment we arrived we set off for Sainsbury's in Kingsbury High Street to buy the food and drink that we planned to take with us in our respective rucksacks.

We knew that we would be sitting on the Wembley 'pitch' area and that people were already queuing at the turnstiles outside Wembley Stadium. But with the concert due to start at midday and the turnstiles opening at 10.30, we had plenty of time to make our short trip from Kingsbury to the stadium. Even so, we were up early the next morning, and we set off at nine, climbing onto the Wembley-bound Jubilee Line train.

As we started the walk down Wembley Way from the station to the nearby stadium, you could already feel the anticipation building. You could sense that this was going to be a once-in-a-lifetime event.

Nadia and I quickly purchased two programmes outside the stadium, with plans for keeping them safe as souvenirs, along with a free 'running order' pamphlet. We looked for our allotted gate and once there found a surprisingly short queue in front of us.

Once inside Wembley Stadium, the 72,000 people quickly dispersed onto the pitch area with plenty of room to lay out blankets and make a base for the duration. We had plenty of time to kill before the show actually started, so we relaxed and stretched out.

Most of the people who charged to the front to be near the large stage soon changed their minds, as everyone had a good view. People were keen on seeing different acts, and so once the Live Aid concert was in full swing, people just rotated, going forward towards the stage for acts they were enthusiastic about and staying further back, or at their base, to watch those they were indifferent about.

There was a real shot of adrenalin when the Coldstream Guards opened the event with a brief version of the National Anthem. Status Quo then kicked off Live Aid proper with 'Rocking All Over the World.' The entire audience were up, singing along and dancing.

The Live Aid Stage

The tickets

The crowd at Wembley were amazing but choreographed to a point.

When TV coverage was due to be broadcast from the stadium, we were given prompts to get up and cheer.

This happened when Noel Edmonds was due to fly Phil Collins, who had finished his set at Wembley, in Noel's helicopter to Heathrow Airport for a flight to Philadelphia, where Phil would perform at the US version of Live Aid.

The idea was that Noel Edmonds was going to fly over Wembley Stadium and we, the crowd, were encouraged to all stand and wave … except that he missed the stadium altogether on his first attempt and, much to our amusement, had to circle round and try again.

I found out later that the concert we saw in the stadium was a little different to the one seen on TV.

After the initial novelty wore off, we did not pay much attention to the huge screens broadcasting the live TV coverage, only getting up for the acts as and when they appeared on the Wembley stage.

We had additional fun with DJ's and commentators on stage that was never actually broadcast on TV.

We also amused ourselves; for example, someone had brought along a huge teddy bear – I have no idea why – and when the acts performed on stage, the bear was tossed around by the crowd and travelled all around the stadium.

We all laughed when Mel Smith and Griff Rhys Jones dressed up as policemen, appearing on stage to tell us the neighbours had complained about the noise and could we keep it down.

The camaraderie and atmosphere was unique, and everyone just got along sharing food and drink. In between acts, we chatted with the people around us discussing the acts we had seen and those still to come. There was a real sense that we were part of history being made and that we were all humbled to be there.

As and when you wanted to go forward to the stage to watch an act, there was no pushing or shoving, and I don't remember any bad behaviour or rudeness.

With the pop royalty of the time all performing, we were treated to performances by the Style Council, Spandau Ballet, Elvis Costello, Nick Kershaw, Sade, Sting, Phil Collins, Howard Jones, Bryan Ferry, Paul Young, U2, Dire Straits, Queen, David Bowie, The Who, Elton John, and finishing with Paul McCartney. It was a truly magical event.

It was also an exceptionally long day, but the time just seemed to evaporate once Live Aid started, with act after act interspersed with the social interaction with those around us.

Nadia and I were emotionally, as well as physically, drained when the show ended. We got swept along with the departing crowd down Wembley Way, most people heading for Wembley Park Tube station.

Our original plan had been to head for Nadia's Goodmayes flat after the concert, but we abandoned that idea when we saw the size of the queue waiting for the London-bound Tubes, whereas the northbound platforms were quiet. That made it an easy decision, and so we headed back to my Kingsbury flat for the night.

When we got back, we collapsed onto the sofa to watch the news and a few of the after-show recaps and then we just headed for bed.

With my enforced return to the bachelor life, I once again rededicated myself to work.

Things at Czarnikow had been going well; I was secure and in my comfort zone with my daily reconciliation role on the financial futures. With the Czarnikow–Transmarket joint venture adding to the growing success of Czarnikow's participation on the LIFFE market, we had taken on a number of new desk brokers.

Barry Fontera was a very colourful American trader who was a Transmarket representative in London. He traded the 'TED spread' which was an interest rate strategy that hedged the US T-bill future against the Eurodollar contract. It was a complicated position as the Eurodollar was traded around the clock in London, Chicago, and Singapore, while the US Treasury bill contract did most of its trading in Chicago.

Barry was a noticeably confident, loud, and sometimes verbally aggressive trader, and his additional volumes meant that I had a full day once more.

My friend Andrew Mersh left Czarnikow for a job at ACLI Commodities, which meant a change of drinking venues and more contact with Tony Ford.

Tony worked at Bache, and he was usually accompanied by Rob 'Dodger' Briton, who ran the Bache metals desk, and Terry Guymer, known as the 'General,' who ran the Bache back office and was Paul Thompson's opposite number.

Over a few drinks one lunchtime, Terry asked me if I would be interested in a move to Bache. He enquired what I was earning, which at the time was £9,100 per annum plus bonus which usually came in at ten per cent of basic. Terry quickly suggested he could get me £11,000, which he then left with me to think over.

I really did not want to leave Czarnikow, but with a mortgage I had to take a 21 per cent pay rise seriously, so I decided to book a lunch with Dave Ritchings to have a chat.

As always, Dave was more than happy to accommodate me, and so over a meal I explained my predicament, and armed with Dave's advice I went back to talk to Paul Thompson.

The next day, I had my second audience with Nick Grason, my line director. Paul Thompson and I walked up to Jennette, who ushered us into Nick's office, and we took our seats.

Nick gave me a look and then started. 'Well, Mr Parker, I understand from Mr Thompson that you have been made an impressive offer for your services by Bache.' I nodded, and Nick leaned back in his chair. 'Ordinarily, if someone puts a gun to my head, I get them to pull the trigger.' I could hear Paul attempting to intercede immediately, but once again he got the hand, and Nick continued. 'If Mr Thompson will let me finish, I was about to say that I understand that is not what you have done. You have quite correctly mentioned the offer and stated you were considering it.' I nodded again. 'So,' Nick fixed me with a look, 'having considered the matter myself, I have decided to match the Bache offer, and in addition I have decided to allow you access to the management dining room.'

This was a rare honour indeed. The dining room served hot food daily, had a free bar and, if rumours were true, free cigars! The senior traders from all the desks and the likes of Dave Peart ate there. Even Gavin Brodie had not been invited, and he was Paul Thompson's deputy!

Nick gave me one of his knowing smiles and leaned a little towards me. 'However,' he added, 'don't get too excited as its closing down in four months' time. We need the space.'

I left Nick's office with a big smile on my face.

Once I had told Terry Guymer the bad news, I set about my job at Czarnikow with renewed vigour.

My decision not to join the Met Police seemed to be even more vindicated when another serious riot broke out on 6th October 1985, and PC Keith Blakelock became the first police officer since 1833 to be killed in a riot in Britain.

LIFFE continued to bring new contracts onto the floor, and volumes continued to expand. At the same time, the Czarnikow computer department continued to develop the internal clearing system, which negated some of the increased workload, with improved functionality and time-saving improvements.

The financial futures department employed a new 'double act' on the office trading desk. They had one significant new clearing client called the 'Rainbow Fund.' A generous clearing commission was agreed, and trading commenced.

This new client quickly started to stretch our clearing services and new computer functionality as it built a remarkably diverse portfolio of derivatives contracts.

Most of the new contracts the Rainbow Fund established positions on we had never dealt in before: live cattle, orange juice, live hogs, lumber, wheat, and a vast range of agricultural contracts.

Each time we had a new contract we had not traded before, it required us to consult our CBOT and CME exchange directories and to sit with the head of the IT department, Ken Maloney, to get the pricing convention, contract size, delivery dates and exchange margins set up correctly before we could input the trade.

The problem was that these contracts were deliverable contracts, and the client would always run positions into the delivery cycle. This usually meant we had panicked phone calls from EF Hutton asking, for example, where we wanted our live cattle delivered!

I would head into the desk traders responsible for the Rainbow Fund, and they in turn would phone the Rainbow Fund to advise them. This phone call usually resulted in the Fund issuing instructions to 'roll' its position, which meant selling its prompt deliverable long position and buying the same position in a later delivery month. This, in turn, resulted in another bumper commission income for Czarnikow.

After a couple of these scares, I asked the back-office staff at EF Hutton to warn me in advance when we were approaching any delivery cycle on these Chicago-based commodity contracts.

The second half of 1985 saw a regular return to BB's.

My new post-Bache salary meant the financial constraints had been lifted a little, and so Rowland and I spent increasing numbers of nights down there. On Fridays, Nadia and fellow EF Hutton teammates would inevitably join us.

Friday nights down at BB's was disco night, and Erol, the resident DJ, was brilliant and had all the tools of the trade, including huge speakers, a great sound system, dry ice, and strobe lights.

Due to its increasing popularity, there was now security on the door of BB's on a Friday night, and they occasionally had to turn people away as the place was packed. But from time to time, these large security guys also had to evict troublemakers.

Erol had a secret weapon he could deploy at the start of his Friday evening sets when he decided it was time to get people onto the dance floor: his girlfriend, Francesca.

Francesca, or 'Frankie' as Erol called her, was a mix of European and African descent, with braided hair. She was stunning but very shy. Despite our absolute best efforts, all Rowland and I could elicit from her was a smile, the occasional wave, and a thanks when we inevitably fetched drinks for her and Erol on disco night.

Whenever Erol wanted to get the dancing started or the dance floor had gone quiet, he would send Frankie out to dance. Frankies appearance on the dance floor would always be accompanied by the 12-inch version of 'Blue Monday' by New Order.

Once she was on the dance floor, all Frankie's shyness evaporated, and like John Travolta in *Saturday Night Fever*, she would quickly grab the attention of the crowd, especially the males.

Frankie was mesmerising as she glided and shimmied around, and it was never long before a guy, or a few guys, would go onto the floor to try and dance with her. With a huge smile and silky-smooth moves, she would rise to the occasion, and it never failed. More people would drift onto the dance floor, and after a few tracks Frankie would usually get a nod from Erol and retreat to behind the safety of the DJ decks.

Of all the acts that I had enjoyed at the legendary Live Aid event, there were two I had made a point of wanting to see again live.

I definitely wanted to see Queen; Freddie Mercury had stolen the show at Live Aid. Prior to Live Aid, I had not been a huge fan of the group. Unlike many, I had not been impressed by 'Bohemian Rhapsody,' but everyone who had been at Live Aid walked away a huge fan.

The other act I wanted to see again live was Elton John – another brilliant live performer and someone who I had liked before Live Aid.

The opportunity arrived to see Elton at Wembley Arena on 11 December 1985. I asked Nadia if she was up for another concert, and she immediately said yes, so I bought two tickets.

The concert was brilliant, and Elton was every bit as good live as he was a recording artist. His flamboyant nature and endless string of hits meant we walked down Wembley Way on another high. We headed back to Goodmayes, and being a Wednesday, by the time we got back to Nadia's flat we just went to bed and headed back into the City the following day.

Late in 1985, we heard that Robin would once again not be home for Christmas as he was being posted to the Far East and to Brunei with the 2nd Battalion Gurkha Rifles, REME Light Aid Detachment. The Sultan had asked for some British soldiers to remain and protect the country from being invaded.

As 1985 passed and Christmas approached, I could not stop thinking about Dianne, wondering what was going on. The moment six months was up, I decided that I had to contact her. But how?

Christmas, as always, was busy; I had the usual turkey to collect and deliver to my parents in Yeovil, where I was spending Christmas, so I ordered a modest sized bird and waited for delivery.

The Czarnikow staff Christmas party of 1984 had been the very last company-wide party. The 1985 Christmas parties were organised on a departmental basis, although still funded by the company.

Paul Thompson booked us into The Five Lamps restaurant, and at the request of the staff his wife Gwen was invited to join us. It was a chance for everyone to let their hair down and for a good bit of team bonding. This set the template for the Christmas company events thereafter.

Before heading off to Yeovil to join my parents for Christmas, I decided that the right thing to do about Dianne was to let Christmas pass and to get in touch in January 1986. I decided I would head for her place of work, Bankside Power Station (now the Tate Modern), and leave a bunch of flowers as a late birthday gift.

Upon my return to the City after the Christmas and New Year's break, and armed with a huge bunch of roses, I walked up to the reception desk of Bankside House and left the flowers and a large card with the bemused security guard and then dashed to Mark Lane for work.

I had a nervous day. Each time the phone rang, I hoped it was her and was disappointed. By the end of the day, I figured that was it, I was not going to hear anything.

One evening a few days later, the phone in my flat rang, and I heard that unmistakable gentle Welsh lilt. Dianne thanked me for the flowers but asked me not to do anything like that again. Then she added that she would meet me in a month or so, but to just give her a little more time.

1986

One of the benefits of working in the financial markets was that on all the office-based trading floors there were televisions scattered around on wall-mounted brackets. These television sets kept the news flowing 24/7, and when things were quiet enough, they could also be switched to major sporting events.

On 28 January 1986, all trading stopped, and we all gathered in the financial trading room and watched in horror as the news channels showed the destruction of the Space Shuttle Challenger. None of us could comprehend that what was expected to be a routine piece of television coverage of the launch would turn into such a horrifying spectacle.

In March, I finally gave up with waiting and wondering, and I picked up the phone and called Dianne at Bankside House. We had a brief discussion, and I managed to convince her to meet me. We agreed to meet in Covent Garden Saturday lunchtime.

I decided to drive and park up close to Mark Lane in the City, as parking was easy at weekends. That way, I hoped I could offer Dianne a lift home, spend as much time with her as I could and then head for Rowland's.

Saturday could not come quickly enough, and that morning I drove from Kingsbury into the City via the Westway and parked up in Seething Lane.

I was nervous as hell on the Tube journey from Tower Hill to Embankment. I walked up The Strand and stood outside TGI Friday's, waiting for Dianne to appear. When I finally spotted her walking towards me, she looked as beautiful as always, but the usual smile was missing. I kissed her on the cheek, and we exchanged small talk as we went into the restaurant and were taken to a table.

As always, the waiter pounced as soon as we sat down, took a drink order, and promised to come back for our food order. Dianne and I exchanged a few pleasantries, and once we had taken a sip of our cocktails, she started to explain what had gone on back on that fateful day back in June, when she turned up at the Czarnikow.

After leaving me distraught on the pavement outside Czarnikow's reception, Dianne had gone back to her house in Seven Kings, packed her bags and left George. In what was obviously a pre-arranged contingency, she had moved in with her friend Sandra in Ilford.

I was a little confused, but she went on to say that it was Sandra who had convinced her that she needed to put distance between us and to leave her house in Seven Kings. The idea had been to step away from George and to take time out before making any decisions about her future. Knowing a little about Sandra's past and her attitude to men my concern grew.

The more Dianne spoke about George, Paul Swain, Laura, and the events leading up to her walking out, the more apparent it was that despite nine months passing by it was all still very raw.

George had, predictably, been shocked and surprised about Dianne's departure. He had not taken the split well and had constantly made a nuisance of himself.

Dianne told me that she appreciated my compliance with her 'stay away' request, and that was the main reason she had agreed to meet me. The real message was that she needed more time and made it clear she would contact me as and when she had decided to move on with her life.

Currently, she was in the midst of divorcing George and did not want any other complications.

After the meal, as we stepped out into the street outside TGI Friday's, I told Dianne I was off to Rowland's in Ilford, and I had my car in the City so I could drop her at Sandra's. Dianne agreed to a lift to Ilford, but not to Sandra's – she asked to be dropped off at Ilford station. The obvious conclusion was that she did not want me to know where Sandra lived and where she was staying.

As we travelled via the tube to Tower Bridge and then in my car to Ilford, we continued chatting about work, people, and current news events. By the time approached Ilford station, we seemed to be getting back to something like our usual relaxed banter.

I pulled up outside the station, I got quick kiss on the cheek, and Dianne once again said, 'Thank you for everything.' Then she closed the car door and walked away.

I went back to Rowlands, and we just went down the pub, where I got very drunk.

I never saw or heard from Dianne ever again.

I found out many years later, at a chance business meeting with Paul Swain, that Dianne had taken Sandra's advice on a clean slate to a different level. Once her divorce was complete, Dianne quit her job, left London, and cut communications with everyone connected to her past life. Paul told me that he had heard Dianne had moved to Reading.

Just as I started to think life could not get any stranger, a few weeks after my meeting with Dianne, I was sitting on the Jubilee Line heading from Wembley

Park to Kingsbury when I heard a remarkably familiar laugh. I looked around and could not see anyone I recognised, then looked back at the *Evening Standard*, assuming I was hearing things.

As the Tube train approached Kingsbury station, I heard the laugh again. I looked about the train carriage and again could not see anyone I knew, but it nagged at me as it was so familiar, and I desperately tried to place it in my mind.

The train gently pulled into the platform at Kingsbury, and I stepped out of the train and onto the crowded platform. I heard a voice up ahead and stopped in my tracks. It could not be! Not in London, not in Kingsbury of all places!

I scanned the heads of the commuters in front of me heading up the concrete stairs towards the ticket hall and spotted the back of a tall young lady's head that fitted the description. Could it be? No, surely I was imagining things. I speeded up, attempting to weave through the crowd, and as I arrived at the ticket hall I was rewarded with a side view of the lady concerned. My heart skipped a beat. It was her!

Jane Whatney, from Hardley village, from the deli at Waitrose, my date at Nick and Carol's engagement party. A big part of me still refused to believe it, but I sped up as she turned left into the high street.

Jane was chatting with another shorter young lady and a tall, thin, dark-haired guy. I was scared that if she crossed the busy road, I would lose her and so I shouted, 'Jane.' Jane paused and looked around. Certain now, I called again, 'Jane, here.' I waved, and she looked straight at me.

For a few seconds she was confused and then her mouth fell open in total amazement. She shouted back, 'Parky!!' I could not help myself as I ran up to her and totally enveloped her in my arms.

We were both laughing at the absurdity of bumping into each other this far from the New Forest. As I finally let her go, we both started talking at once.

To prove the world is ridiculously small, it turned out that after university, Jane had taken a job at an American software development company, and they had a company flat in Kingsbury High Street. When I pointed above Midland Bank and told Jane that was my flat, we both fell about laughing again. We agreed to meet up the following evening at the local pub.

Jane and I met up as planned the following evening, and after a few drinks we went on for a meal at the local Chinese. It turned out that she was now based in New York and was only in Kingsbury for a week, after which she was then heading back to the USA.

I updated her on Sue Eason and Nigel Carlton and told her she had been missed at Debbie Frazer and Ian Shrive's wedding, at which point Jane held out her ring finger. Once again, I had not checked. Jane was engaged to an American colleague and had every intention of taking American citizenship once she was married. I ducked conversations about my love life – Dianne was still very raw with me – but we had a great evening catching up and promised each other we would meet up again next time she was back in the UK.

On 1 June 1986, I was off to another large event. This time it was the last day of the *Evening Standard* Four Stars International Pro-Celebrity golf tournament at Moore Park golf course. I had applied for my ticket via the newspaper, and the weather was perfect on the day.

I set off for Moore Park, which was on the Watford-bound Metropolitan Tube line. Armed with my rucksack, complete with lunch, drinks, and my trusty camera, I set off to see the who's who of UK celebrities at the time.

The guest list of participants was enormous and included top golfers, Hollywood A-listers and the great and good of UK sports at the time. Among them were golfers Nick Faldo, Ian Woosnam and Jose Rivero, singer Johnny Mathis, ex-footballers Ian St John, Kevin Keegan, Bob Wilson and Kenny Daglish, comedians Russ Abbot, Des O'Connor, Bernie Winters, Eddie Large, Jimmy Tarbuck and Ronnie Corbet, ex-boxing European champion Henry Cooper, broadcaster Terry Wogan, entertainer Bruce Forsyth, singer Frankie Vaughn and actor Patrick Mower.

The main interest was in Hollywood A-lister Telly Savalas and ex-US president Gerald Ford.

There were lots of spectators and having arrived an hour before the first foursome were due to tee off. I selected the tee for the seventh hole as my place for the day. I sat myself down at the front of the roped-off area and waited for all of the playing quartets to pass through, before joining the gathering masses as we followed the final players around the rest of the course.

I got a lot of pictures, but the funniest moment of the day involved a golf buggy containing four of Gerald Ford's personal protection team. They were travelling ahead of the ex-president to position themselves at the next golf hole before he got there. They were driving flat out and didn't see a deep bunker ahead of them before ploughing into it and being thrown in all directions.

The only damage was their pride and a slightly dented buggy that needed to be manhandled out of the bunker, with the help of a contingent of the spectators. Discreet they were not.

On 11 July 1986, I got my wish to see pop giants Queen play live once more. I also had the double pleasure of watching Status Quo again, as they were the support band for the 'It's a Kind of Magic' tour. The concert was held once again at Wembley Stadium, but this was a vastly different experience. The crowd was much bigger and packed in, meaning no sitting down before the gig in the way we did for Live Aid.

Status Quo belted out all their hits and were a really good warm up for the main event. With the heat and all the dancing and shouting, Quo was a gig in itself.

Then came the wait and building anticipation for Queen themselves. As the lights came on and the opening cords of the opening track 'It's a Kind of Magic' started up, four giant balloon figures of the band – duplicates of the characters on the cover of the album – started to inflate at the four corners of the stadium. The only problem was they were supposed to inflate and slowly rise above the stadium, but one didn't inflate properly, and it descended into the fans who promptly shredded it.

Freddie was at his best, and the concert really was a tour de force with all their hits and of course the traditional 'God Save the Queen' finale, with Freddie strutting across the stage in his crown and cape.

I was incredibly pleased to have seen Queen play live at Wembley once again, and it turned out to be one of the last times the band ever played live.

We didn't know Freddie had AIDS at the time, and just a month later, on 9 August 1986, Queen played their last ever live gig at Knebworth Park in England and drew an attendance estimated as high as 160,000.

It was a fitting last concert for the best live band ever. It was also the last time I attended a stadium concert; nothing was ever going to top seeing Queen at their very peak.

In October 1986, a political event took place that accelerated change in the City and increased volumes on all the exchanges. Known as 'Big Bang,' on 27 October 1986 the City experienced the deregulation of the financial markets. Perversely, just as the markets deregulated, Czarnikow was 'encouraged' to close the door on its big fund client.

The 'Rainbow Fund,' the client who traded anything and everything in good size, had once again run a little low on funds. When I had issued the fund with a margin call, I had confirmed our banking instructions but instead of sending the money by way of an inter-bank transfer, a representative of the fund turned up at Czarnikow's branch of Barclays Bank with a suitcase full of cash.

Senior management at Czarnikow had received a phone call from the bank manager to suggest that this may not be the type of client we should be clearing for, and so the fund was promptly given notice. But the volume and income provided by the Rainbow Fund was not hugely missed, as business for the financial futures department was booming.

Changes occurred in the central operations department. Once again, the call of the trading floor had lured away Russell Edwards, who moved down to the coffee market to join Rowland Dunn. Paul Thompson's niece Paula had also left us, and this meant two new faces: Karen Loftus and, making a move from the telex department, Martin Finn.

LIFFE and the ICCH's fall out over the amount the ICCH was charging for its clearing services finally came to a head. LIFFE announced they had decided to go it alone and embark upon an ambitious project to develop and introduce their Trade Registration System (TRS) to support the current and predicted volume growth.

We were all shocked in November when we heard that all of BB's bars were being closed down. It turned out that they were just too successful. While they had been entertaining City workers, the City police tolerated them, even if they stayed open longer than the local pubs had previously.

But their successful disco nights had encouraged people from east London and Essex to head for the City instead of the West End on Friday nights. This was not a trend the City police wanted to encourage and so when BB's licences came up for renewal, they were politely declined.

Over time, other City bars started to offer later drinking and dancing on a Friday night, including the Mithras wine bar. The Mithras became a popular venue for LIFFE floor workers, but they avoided falling into the trap of attracting too many people from outside the Square Mile.

Paul Thompson and I had another of our periodic meetings with Nick Grason just before Christmas. Nick said that there were going to be a few important changes coming in the new year. Although he would not go into any details at this meeting, he cryptically asked if I had a passport, which I did not. Nick then told me to talk to his secretary, Jennette, and she would apply for one on my behalf through the company.

He also told me I would not be disappointed with my pay rise and bonus, and that 1987 was going to be a big year for Czarnikow.

The 1986 back office Christmas party was held at the Good Friends restaurant. As usual, it was staff only plus Gwen Thompson, and it was another hugely enjoyable evening.

Xmas Party, Me, Ron Wallis, Paul Thompson (standing) Sue Bright, Martin Finn, Kim, John Brown, Karen Disley

1987

Little did I know just how big 1987 would be for me, and it started as early as January when my brother Robin arrived at my Kingsbury flat.

The previous year, Robin had been attached to the Royal Regiment Of Wales, British Forces Germany in Lemgo, West Germany. This was a mechanised infantry battalion with armoured personnel carriers and reconnaissance vehicles, part of the 4th Armoured Brigade.

Shortly after arriving back from Germany, he had his second tour of Northern Ireland. He was attached to the Reconnaissance Platoon of the Royal Regiment of Wales. He was the only REME soldier attached to them and was based at Fort George, Londonderry, Northern Ireland from late 1986 to spring 1987. The job his unit had been given was to assist the Royal Anglian Regiment, who were on a two-year tour but needed reinforcements. This operation was called 'Cara.'

On 4 November 1986, Robin had been part of the eight-man patrol split into two Land Rovers. That evening, they saw a suspicious van and discovered the three occupants were actually heavily armed IRA terrorists. The IRA operatives lay down their weapons and surrendered without firing a shot.

Robin told me that during his previous posting to Brunei, the Sultan, who was very pro-British, allowed UK troops to use his personal jet if he was not using it, and so Robin had made used the Sultan's jet for several trips to Thailand.

When Robin heard I was close to getting a passport, he insisted he was going to take me on my very first flight and international holiday to Thailand. Sure enough, my blue UK passport arrived on 26 January 1987, and on 12 February I boarded a plane for Thailand with Robin.

The first thing to say was that Robin was a seasoned traveller, and this turned out to be his third trip to Pattaya, which at the time was just transitioning from a sleepy fishing village and not the notorious destination it is now. Our holiday took place before the package holidays to Thailand had started and the country was just starting to gear up to become the major tourist destination it is now.

My trip to Thailand is a story for another day. It was a revelation in many ways and was just what I needed at the time. This alien environment distracted me with sights, smells, tastes, and experiences that just opened my eyes to the world, international travel, and the possibilities.

This trip also allowed me to bond with my little brother, who, having left for the Army at sixteen, had changed hugely.

By the time he left the army he had completed three tours of Northern Ireland during the Troubles, some of which he still cannot talk about. Added to that his spell in the Falklands, helping with the post-war clear up of the minefields and debris left by the conflict, his posting to Brunei and more mundane tours of West Germany. His Army experiences had all had a profound impact on him. Robin was a vastly different person from the brother I remembered back in the New Forest.

On 5 May 1987, I was pleased to join a huge number of Czarnikow staff as we headed to Peckham and the biggest wedding of the year: Lesley Neenan, my good friend from the cable department, married John Baxter.

John lived with his son Jay in the Peckham area, he worked for the Post Office, and he was a particularly good footballer. John had played for a number of semi-professional non-league teams before he had trouble with his knee which stopped him achieving more.

It was at a chance invitation from friends to a football match that Lesley saw John playing. Lesley pointed to John on the pitch and told her friends that she was going to marry that guy. Sure enough, and with typical Lesley determination, she got her date and eventually got her man.

With Sandra Larwood and her old friend Lorraine from Peckham as a brides maid's, Rowland, Andrew Mersh, and I joined almost half the staff from Czarnikow to celebrate the event. As you would expect with lots of John's colleagues from the Post Office and his non-league football teams mixing with the great and good of Czarnikow, it turned into a huge London knees-up.

In June 1987, I came home to a nasty shock. As I opened the door of my Kingsbury flat, I found an unexpected letter from the landlord. I opened the windowed envelope and read in horror – the letter turned out to be a demand for £7,000 as a contribution to extensive building work they had scheduled.

The works included rebuilding the three concrete staircases to the rear of the flats and a complete overhaul of the roof. Since I had moved in, the landlord had been replacing renting tenants with leasehold owners. Having achieved a situation where just over half the flats were now owned, they had decided to spring this upon us.

The owners of the flats quickly formed a 'tenants committee,' and luckily amongst our number was a young lady who worked at a top law firm in Fleet Street. When she told her company about the landlord's demand, they quickly agreed to work for us for free.

The first thing our legal team did was ask us to supply copies of our leases and armed with these they quickly deduced that the landlord had deliberately not included the retail properties on the ground floor in their calculations – this included Midland Bank below my flat.

Based on the calculations they should have made, the lawyers acting on our behalf challenged the landlord. In the weeks that followed, the landlord admitted the demands they had made were not in line with our obligations under the terms of our leases and so the bills were reduced by 50 per cent.

I had no choice but to get a mortgage extension to cover the resulting £3,500 bill, and I promised myself that once the work was completed at the end of the year, I would immediately sell, get out of leasehold property, and find myself a small house.

Back in the City, changes occurred in June 1987 as Czarnikow took the decision to sever a very one sided relationship with Transmarket. Czarnikow had introduced huge amounts of clearing to Transmarket in Chicago, but extraordinarily little had come back the other way into London.

Barry Fontera, our colourful American desk trader, who had joined us from Transmarket, did not want to go back to the USA, having moved his family over to the UK. He agreed to stay with us at Czarnikow in London. As a consequence of this decision, Czarnikow transferred its Chicago clearing business to a new clearing partner, Harris Futures, a division of Harris Trust & Savings Bank.

This meant a new clearing relationship, and due to the impact on my role in reconciliations, I was included in conference calls with the head of clearing at Harris Futures, Jennifer Johnson. Jennifer told me that my day-to-day contacts for trade queries and fund transfers were Denni Machi and Rose Dimenza-Meo in her clearing team. Together with Denni and Rose, we co-ordinated the transfer of our positions and funds from Transmarket to Harris.

This change of clearer coincided with the addition of a new broker joining the Financial trade desk, Roy McDermott.

Czarnikow was, as I mentioned previously, a very 'public schoolboy' dominated company. We had a half dozen directors all from top public schools, including Michael Denys Chataway, who was related to the famous British runner Christopher Chataway.

Our floor manager on the LIFFE exchange was the Right Honourable Daniel Beckett, reputed to be the Queen Mother's favourite dance partner and often seen with her in the carriage at Royal Ascot.

Another notable ex-public schoolboy learning his trade at the company was William Knottenbelt, who would, in later years, become the head of European business operations at the CME.

Roy McDermott arrived straight from a Guards Division in the British Army under a little bit of a cloud. We learned that he and the Army had agreed to part ways after an exercise on Salisbury Plain.

At the time, Roy had been a tank commander, and during an exercise had been told to go out deep into Salisbury Plain, find a wooded area and camouflage his tank. His mission was to remain undiscovered for 48 hours.

Armed with his map, Roy set off with his crew into a wooded area, set about camouflaging his tank and then waited. But after 24 hours, his crew got bored and so they decided to head off and find a local pub to kill a few hours, which they duly did.

The problem was when they returned, they couldn't find the tank!

Hunting for hours to no avail, eventually Roy had to report in, and the entire military exercise was stopped as everyone was tasked with finding Roy's tank, which they eventually did.

With Roy out of the Army and out of work, he had a discussion with a few friends based at pension funds and City institutions, and it was decided that he should take a job in the City.

After a few phone calls to friends and family, he ended up at Czarnikow.

Roy was supported by a couple of good friends who were in a position to open institutional clearing accounts at Czarnikow, meaning his salary was more or less already covered with commission income. Now, Roy set about using his personal contacts to try and bring in additional business. In turn, all this meant more work for me on reconciliations.

In September 1987, LIFFE started to roll out the first implementation of its much-anticipated TRS, and on 3 September 1987 the system was finally online, processing all LIFFE's option contracts.

It was the beginning of a huge change for the better in our trade processing. For the very first time, 'give-up' trades, which were trades executed for one exchange member for and on behalf of another exchange member, could be processed on a screen, rather than the old way of writing on a printout and taking it to the ICCH for processing.

On 19 October 1987, I experienced my first significant market crash, on what would later become known as Black Monday. This notorious stock market crash represented the greatest one-day percentage decline in US stock market history.

This culminated in a bear market after a more than 20 per cent plunge in the S&P 500 and Dow Jones Industrial Average. The primary causes of the chaos were program trading and illiquidity, both of which fuelled the vicious decline in stock prices.

The volume of trading on the LIFFE market was huge, but in the US the CBOT and CME Markets had a fire break called a 'limit move.' This meant that if the prices moved too far in one trading session, the markets would close for the day to let things cool down.

LIFFE had no such rules, and our biggest casualty was Barry Fontera, who dropped over £975,000 in a day, which, at the time, was an eye-watering amount.

Barry quickly put on some option trades to draw a line under his potential losses, but David Peart quickly spotted that the loss would have doubled before these option trades stopped the loss. Nick Grason and senior management quickly decided that they would take over the positions and manage the losses from that point.

Volumes and volatility continued for the rest of the week, by the end of which we were all exhausted. In the aftermath, there was an increased focus and urgency in Dave Peart's development of a risk department.

Czarnikow management managed to recover some of Barry's losses, but it was agreed he needed to diversify his trading portfolio, and so it was decided that we would start to investigate allowing him to trade the physical bond market.

This was a new area of reconciliations for the company and unsupported by our clearing system. Barry wanted to trade the physical bond market and hedge it against the T-bond futures market.

The problem was that the futures markets enabled you to trade while only funding a percentage of the face value of the contract you were trading. The physical bond market was a delivery versus payment (DVP) market, meaning you had to fund the entire face value of the physical bonds. To negate this, Barry would 'borrow' or 'lend' his physical bond exposure on the 'repo' (reposition) market.

For example, if Barry had a short futures position, he would offset this with a long physical bond position which he would pay for in full. Barry could then lend the resulting physical bond position to a US-based bond repo desk at an agreed price, and the resulting cash would finance his physical position. While the US Company held our bond, they would charge us interest at an agreed rate on the cash they had 'lent' us against the bond.

Our computer system was simply not up to this type of trade, and so with Dave Peart's help we designed a few simple programs on his PC which required me to spend an hour or two a day in the financial futures department, keying in the trades and positions in order to calculate a profit-and-loss calculation. This calculation was required in order for me to agree our bond and cash position with Harris Futures.

We started with a few test trades, and it was very labour intensive and meant me spending a lot of time on the phone to Jennifer Johnson and Denni Machi at our new American Clearer.

Not long after we started testing with some modest T-bond trading, Nick Grason called a meeting with Barry Fontera, Paul Thompson and David Peart to discuss the new business.

At this meeting, it was explained that Barry wanted to scale up his trading, and it had been agreed that Prashant Laud would transfer from the coffee trading desk to the financial futures desk to learn from Barry, and to function as his deputy. The idea was that while Barry was trading bonds, Prash would watch his TED positions.

In a total surprise, Nick Grason asked me to confirm I was now in the possession of a passport. I told him I was, and he then told me I would need it, as in the new year I was going to be sent to Chicago to meet with our new Chicago based clearers Harris Futures.

My primary objective for the trip was to learn more about the new physical T-bond trading from the traders out there. I was both incredibly surprised and a little shocked – I was going solo to Chicago to represent Czarnikow.

In November 1987, I had a phone call from Nadia Bellows. She told me she was a little depressed and wondered if I would accompany her on a weekend trip to Nottingham to visit Goose Fair.

The Nottingham Goose Fair is an end-of-season gathering of fair operators, who converge for this one evening each year. The event is held at the Forest Recreation Ground in Nottingham.

Nadia said she had already booked a hotel room, but one of her colleagues from work had let her down, and she didn't want to go alone. I agreed to go with her, and on the Friday I headed straight from work to Goodmayes and Nadia's flat.

We set off early on the Saturday in her car and arrived midday.

Having quickly checked in to the modest hotel, we headed off to the fair, which was huge. Nadia told me that her brother lived in the area and had told her about it. I did wonder why, if Nadia's brother lived locally, we were in a hotel, but I did not ask. We busied ourselves on various rides and stalls, had hot dogs and spent some time in the pub to recuperate before setting off again.

When we finally decided to retire back to the hotel, I suddenly realised that there was only one double bed. I had not really noticed when we dumped our bags on checking in. Nadia did not miss a beat, and she went into the bathroom to get ready for bed while I turned on the TV.

When Nadia came out in knickers and T-shirt. I headed into the bathroom, wondering what was going on but deciding to just play it casual. When I came out, Nadia was under the covers, and I climbed in next to her in just my pyjama bottoms. Nothing was said, and as I lay on my back, she just rolled over towards me, cuddled close and fell asleep.

The next morning, we woke up next to each other. Once again, nothing was mentioned about the sleeping arrangement. Nadia just got up and showered, and we just continued as if nothing had happened.

On the Monday back in the office, and in the aftermath of the market crash, plans went into action to prepare for Barry's increased bond trading. I was told that my trip to Chicago was pencilled in for late January 1988.

I was asked to bring my passport into the office, and I handed it to Jennette, who promptly sent it off to the US Embassy in London, where it was stamped with an Indefinite Work Visa.

This sought-after visa was a benefit of having a US Office in New York, and it allowed free movement of staff between London and New York.

The central operations departmental Christmas party in 1987 was held at the 'Good Friends' Chinese restaurant in Shoreditch. At our request, Paul Thompson invited his wife Gwen along once again, and the usual good-natured time was enjoyed by all.

Karen Loftus's fiancée Paul turned up just as the meal finished and we started on the customary Flaming Sambucas, which had become another annual tradition. The department had managed to get through a year without any staff changes, and we looked forward to 1988; especially me, with my pending trip to the US.

1988

On my return from the Christmas holiday, plans were progressing at a pace for my trip. I was flying out on a Saturday and staying at the Palmer House Hilton, which sat on East Munro Street just round the corner from West Jackson Boulevard.

Harris Futures was halfway down West Jackson Boulevard, and at the other end of the street was the Chicago Board of Trade. My itinerary included several days at Harris and a visit to the Chicago Mercantile Exchange, which Barry had arranged with Anne Meyer and Len McConnel, who were his main brokers on the floor and traded his Eurodollars and T-bills.

A gentleman by the name of Geoff Swainson was co-ordinating my trip with the staff at Harris Futures and was making sure I had time with Jennifer Johnson and her team, as well as key traders on the bond trading desk at Harris. I told Geoff about my trip to the CME floor, and he indicated he would make sure there was time in my schedule for some sightseeing.

I was then informed of a change to my itinerary by Nick Grason, who had decided that it would be a missed opportunity for me to be in the US and not spend time with the Czarnikow team in New York. So, I was now flying into Chicago on the Saturday and leaving midday Thursday for an internal flight to New York, where I would spend Friday at the New York office, have an evening out with the team and then fly home on the Saturday.

I chatted with Denni and Rose at Harris and told them I would soon be coming out to see them. They promised to look after me when I got there. Before I knew it, everything was booked, and I was ready to go.

I had a final meeting with Nick prior to my departure for a pep talk. I was given a company Amex to use for all expenses while I was in the US. Nick told me to make sure I kept the receipts as I had to account for the spending. I was expected to entertain key people while I was in Chicago, although the New York office was picking up the tab for my stay at the UN Plaza Hotel during my brief stop there.

Then, Nick slapped a wad of dollar bills in my hand, and he explained it was 'confetti' that I did not have to account for. Nick told me that porters, doormen, waiters, bar staff, etc. all expected tips and that I was to just slap the dollar bills into any/all hands. He also suggested there was enough there for cabs as well, but that limousines had been booked and paid for to take me to and from the airports.

Lastly, Nick told me to make notes at the end of every day: who I met, what was discussed, and any important points that cropped up during my stay. I would have a full debrief upon my return. At the end of our meeting, he looked at me and said, 'Most importantly, Mr Parker, enjoy yourself, and do you have a thick coat?'

I looked at him quizzically.

'Chicago in January,' he continued. 'The wind off the lakes will freeze you in no time. Get a good coat.'

Armed with my instructions from Mr Grason, I prepared for my first ever business trip and my first visit to the USA.

My colleagues from all the departments were not shy in giving advice. Dicky Gibbs, our main foreign exchange trader, told me that he had stayed in the Palmer House Hilton in Chicago and that I had to make sure I had at least one meal at Trader Vic's restaurant based in the hotel.

Barry Fontera, who was a native, told me that I had to go to the viewing gallery at the top of the Sears Tower, and that because it was January, I should walk a block and then jump into a building to defrost, then walk another block and so on. Harris Futures was seven blocks away from the Palmer House Hilton where I was staying, so I made a mental note of that, and guessed Nick had not been joking about that coat.

Dave Peart, who had made a few visits to our New York office off Battery Park, told me that he had spoken to his good friend Victor Dowell, the director in charge of our New York office, and that Vic was going to take me to a famous steak restaurant. I was also told the younger lads in the New York office, most of whom I knew from their days in the Mark Lane office, were going to take me for a night on the town afterwards, which sounded ominous.

I was excited, I was nervous, and I felt a weight of expectation and responsibility on my shoulders, but as I dragged my bag into the ticket hall of Heathrow Airport, I was in for another surprise.

I had arrived incredibly early for my 11.50 British Airways flight, which was scheduled to land at mid-afternoon at Chicago's O'Hare airport. Lots of people were in front of me at the check-in, and I took my place behind them, fishing out my tickets and passport from my coat pocket.

A lady in British Airways uniform was walking around behind us and spotted me. I was wearing my three-piece suit in an attempt to stop it getting too creased, and I was holding my tickets in the BA envelope I had been given by Czarnikow. Spotting the envelope in my hand the lady walked straight up with a big smile and asked if she could see my tickets. Having quickly looked at them she gave them back and stated, 'You're in the wrong queue, sir.'

I was confused – the board above the desk definitely had my flight number, but she continued, 'This is economy, sir. You're booked onto business class.' She pointed at an empty desk further down.

'Business class!' I had not noticed, and nobody had said anything to me at Czarnikow. 'Oh,' I said.

The lady gestured for me to follow her down to the empty desk and called to her colleague, 'This young man is one of yours.'

I was beckoned forward by the young lady behind the empty check-in desk, and I handed over my new passport and flight tickets. Her perfectly manicured hand took them, and she looked back at me. 'First time, sir?'

'Oh yes ... first time in business class,' I replied.

She put a tag on my bag and looked back at me. 'Well, you're all done here. As a business-class passenger you can wait in our executive lounge once you are airside.' I liked the sound of that, and as my bag vanished, she handed back my ticket envelope, boarding card, and passport, wished me a good flight, and off I went.

Once through passport control and security, I spotted a big sign that directed me to the British Airways Executive Lounge. It was very posh, and as I walked in I was immediately offered complimentary drinks and nibbles. I figured with a good hour plus to wait, I had better pace myself, and sat down with my book.

Flying business class, and on a 747, was a significant improvement on my previous flight to Thailand which had been with GulfAir. That flight had been a much smaller plane and had also involved a change of flight in Dakar.

The business-class seat and service were amazing, and the experience put me in a great mindset when the plane finally touched down in Chicago. The other benefit of business class was that my luggage was handed to me when I got off the plane, and I was rushed to the US immigration desk.

Anyone who has experienced US immigration agents knows that they are at best grumpy and at worst rude. Being a business-class passenger does not change this but armed with my shiny new passport and my all-important indefinite US work visa stamped inside, I was quickly though and on my way.

Once in the airport arrivals hall, I scanned the numerous drivers holding up signs for the disembarking passengers. I spotted a very dapper suited man who was holding up a sign that read 'Mr Kevin Parker, Palmer House Hilton.' I walked over to him, and in his very thick Chicago accent, he asked, 'Mr Parker?' I nodded and he immediately took my bag. 'This way, sir.'

We weaved in and out of the other people and out a side door. After a short walk in the cold but clear weather, we arrived at the 'executive parking' bay, where a big black limousine was parked, and we were quickly on our way. The journey was short, 30 minutes along one road, but I had lots to see – the huge cars, the big buildings. The driver attempted to engage me in banter, but he quickly realised I just wanted to take it all in.

As we pulled up outside the main entrance of the Palmer House Hilton, a doorman was quickly alongside the cab, opening the door, as another was already unloading my bag from the boot. I looked to the driver, but he waved me off. 'All paid for, sir. Have a wonderful time in Chicago,' and off he went.

Remembering Nick Grason's advice, I was quickly slapping dollar bills in the hands of the porters and doormen as I was ushered up to the reception desk.

The Palmer House Hilton is one of the older buildings in Chicago. The hotel was proud to tell guests that it has been trading for over 120 years. As you would expect of a Hilton, it was very plush and grandiose.

Everything about the hotel was impressive – the period theme was maintained throughout, and the reception desk was no exception. The gentleman behind the desk quickly processed me, confirming my booking, and I was soon on my way towards the lifts, with a porter insisting on bringing my bag and showing me the way.

I was not sure what to expect in terms of the room but this being a Hilton, and having been impressed so far, I really didn't think there would be anything ordinary about it.

I was not disappointed. The room was huge and very Victorian in style, with big windows and curtains. The bed was a double, and there was a large ornate writing desk and chair, free-standing wardrobes, a TV, and a minibar.

Having slapped yet another dollar bill in the hand of the porter, I dropped onto the bed and looked at the hotel information booklet.

There were two restaurants; one was a Trader Vic's as mentioned by Dicky Gibbs. Both looked good, although expensive, so I decided that it would be best not to eat in them every night. The room service was very comprehensive, and I was shattered by that stage, so I decided to stick to room service for my first evening meal.

I spent Sunday in the hotel, not confident enough to venture out, and I figured Chicago was like the City of London in that nothing would be happening in the financial district on a Sunday.

I had room service for all the meals and tried to comprehend American television, which was wall-to-wall adverts – much worse than ITV back home. They didn't even warn you when the adverts were coming; it just seemed to switch from programme to advert and then back again.

There were a lot of US police shows on, and then I saw something unexpected, a show called *Tour of Duty* about the Vietnam War. I had thought the Americans were a little sensitive about that, but it seemed to have taken the recent big-screen movie *Platoon* and turned it into a weekly show.

By the time Monday came along, I was keen to start. I showered, changed, had breakfast in my room and then set off, armed with my suitcase, which I had purchased especially for the trip.

The doorman asked me if I wanted a cab, and I shook my head, explaining I was off to Harris Futures in West Jackson Boulevard. He took a look at my scarf and coat, and decided I was sufficiently attired. He told me to take a left at the next junction, then first right, and it was seven blocks further down.

So, I set off taking in the sights as I went – plenty of fast-food restaurants, traffic, and noise as you would expect. I went past a street vendor who was just starting to cook American chilli dogs, and I made a mental note to give that a go before I left.

Nick Grason had not been wrong about the wind that whistled down the streets, funnelled by all the tall buildings. As you hit an intersection, the wind really hit you until you got to the shelter of the next block of buildings.

After a healthy walk I saw a large retail bank with Harris Trust and Savings blazed across it. I couldn't see any other way in, so I entered, passing a bemused security guard who looked me up and down. As I was obviously looking lost he asked if I needed help, and I told him I was looking for the offices of Harris Futures. He gestured that I go back out into the street, walk past the retail bank section, and look for a set of double doors further down the street.

I headed back out into the cold and quickly found the doors.

Once I was into a warm, wide reception area, I could see a desk with three reception staff, so I walked up. As I arrived at the desk, a lady immediately asked if she could help me, and I explained I was meeting Geoff Swainson. She picked up a phone and called Geoff. Having put the handset down she asked me to take a seat as Geoff was on his way.

Geoff Swainson was a short, slightly balding gentlemen, I guessed to be in his mid-forties, dressed in a navy two-piece suit, crisp white shirt, and narrow patterned tie. Like all the Americans I had met thus far, he had an enthusiastic tone to his voice, 'Welcome to Chicago.'

He gestured for me to follow him towards the bank of lifts behind the reception desk. Geoff told me I would be provided with a guest pass, which would allow me to head straight for the lifts from now on. We went up to the seventh floor and out into a large corridor.

The first thing I noticed was that everything was bigger – the corridors were huge, as were all the offices, and space was obviously not in short supply. We walked down to, and through, a fire door, after which large glass offices lay to the left and right, we continued on down.

Finally, we arrived at Geoff's office, and he gestured for me to take a seat. He immediately picked the phone. 'Jennifer, its Geoff. Kevin Parker is here. I'll run through his schedule, explain a few things, and bring him to you about 10.30 if that's OK?' He got an affirmative, finished the call, and then explained to me that he had booked all my meetings but had left an afternoon for sightseeing. He added that Jennifer had 'assigned' someone to look after me during my stay in Chicago.

I was to spend the morning with Jennifer in the back office. In the afternoon, Geoff was going to show me around all the other departments, and he said that he would be taking me out for a bite to eat after work.

I would be spending Tuesday morning with the bond desk and a trader called Eric Callion. Tuesday afternoon had been left clear to enable me to get out and see the sights. I mentally pencilled in a trip to Sears Tower.

On Wednesday morning, I would be back with Jennifer Johnson and the back office. At 11.00 I was scheduled to visit the Chicago Mercantile Exchange floor to meet Anne Meyer, followed by lunch with her. On Wednesday afternoon I had a meeting scheduled with Geoff and Jennifer to wrap up and cover any outstanding issues or questions, and then on Thursday I was off to New York.

It looked like a relaxed schedule, and with that Geoff stood and said he would walk me around to meet Jennifer Johnson and her team.

The Harris Futures back office was on the fifth floor, so a quick ride in the lifts took us down to another very generous corridor. We turned left this time, through another set of fire doors and into a large open-plan office with internal room dividers and sectioned areas that I expected most big clearing banks would have.

We continued into a large working space with four banks of four desks, at the far end was one exceptionally large desk where a lady in her mid-fifties sat. This was Jennifer Johnson, a rotund, matronly lady with a big, warm persona. She was truly knowledgeable and a derivatives clearing veteran.

Geoff introduced me to her, a hush fell around the clearing and settlements area, which I noted was all female. Jennifer encouraged me to take a seat next to her. Geoff said he would see me after lunch, and he then vanished back the way he had come.

Jennifer gave me a brief overview of what her department did, which was much the same as our central operations department at Czarnikow. The main difference being that Harris used the extremely popular GMI clearing system instead of an internal computer system.

With a big grin, she said, 'Let me introduce you to the team.' We went through the first three desks, where I met the ladies working in accounts, treasury, foreign exchange settlements, a commodities settlement team, and an exchange reconciliations team. Lastly, we arrived at a desk where two young ladies were sitting – these were the same two ladies I had been chatting with daily since the transfer from Transmarket.

Jennifer told me that this was the customer relations team. Gesturing to a striking young blue-eyed blonde, who struck me as very much the American cheerleader type. 'This,' Jennifer said, 'Is Rose Dimenza-Meo, Ro to her friends.' Jennifer then gestured to the young lady sitting opposite Ro. 'And this shy young lady is your guide during your stay with us, Denni Machi.'

Denni was an Italian American, and you could see her Italian heritage. She was very pretty with shoulder-length, jet-black straight hair, and deep brown eyes. I gathered by the muted laughter around the office that Denni was anything but shy.

Jennifer indicated that I should sit with Denni and Ro to get acquainted. Ro offered me the chair next to her, and I sat down. 'Would you like a coffee, Kevin? I was just about to fetch one for Denni and myself.'

Denni immediately jumped in, 'He's English, Ro – he only drinks tea.'

I could see she was teasing, and I immediately got a feel for the way things were going to go during my stay.

I faced Ro. 'Ro, I would love a coffee, because I have to say, based on the tea I've had in the hotel, you guys don't know anything about making real tea.'

With that, Ro set off, leaving me with Denni, who looked me in the eye from the other side of the desk.

Denni checked over her shoulder that Ro was not within earshot and then she leaned towards me and said, 'You don't have to stay on that side of the desk. I understand that you men all love Ro because she's blonde and gorgeous.' I heard the others around us tittering as they listened to our conversation. 'But you can, if you want to, move over to my side of the desk. Remember, I'm the one looking after you while you're here.'

Denni could see I was hesitating, she shot me a dazzling smile as she said, 'I promise you Ro won't mind.'

I got up and moved round the desk and into the seat next to Denni.

'And' she whispered loudly, 'Just in case you are interested, Ro is married.'

I had no idea what that meant, but I was to learn quickly that Denni had a mischievous sense of humour.

When Ro returned with the coffees, she burst out laughing and said, 'Well that didn't take you long, Denni.' And she left it at that.

Denni went through the derivatives processing at Harris Futures and showed me the GMI clearing system and its programs that enabled her to book the physical bonds I had been sent to learn more about.

Before I knew it, lunchtime was upon us, and Denni explained that she was taking me out to a local restaurant. I said a temporary goodbye to Jennifer, Ro and the others and followed Denni to the lifts.

We went to a local version of TGI Friday's, and Denni explained that if I ordered one of the meals on offer, I would struggle to eat it. So, when the waitress came over to take our order, I followed Denni's example and ordered the club sandwich, the waitress paused next to me, 'Sorry, sir,' she said, 'can you say that again?'

I repeated my order, and the waitress looked at me with a smile and leaned in close. 'Sorry darlin,' I just love that accent. I just had to get you to say it all again.' And with that she went.

Denni giggled, 'You're going to get a lot of that.'

When the plate arrived, I realised just how right Denni was. My club sandwich was held together with a large wooden cocktail stick and was heaving with chicken, ham, lettuce, and tomato, and it came with a huge pile of fries (chips to us Brits), and a huge mound of coleslaw and salad.

As I chatted with Denni, I discovered that she was from Milwaukee, which became the source of an ongoing joke between us as I teased her about the TV programme *Happy Days*, which was based in the same town. She insisted she always ate in Arnold's restaurant when she was home.

Denni told me that she was giving me the tour on Tuesday afternoon and asked if I had anywhere in mind. I explained that our local American, Barry Fontera, had suggested the viewing gallery at the top of the Sears Tower, which Denni agreed would be a good start.

Then Denni asked if Barry had mentioned the 'walk of faith.' I told her that he had not, and that just bought a worrying smile to her face. 'Good,' she said. I sensed trouble brewing.

I offered to pick up the bill, but Denni refused, saying Jennifer had already said she would put our lunch bill through expenses.

As we walked out and headed back to the office, I spotted a couple of Chicago police officers getting out of a patrol car. I whispered to Denni, 'All your police officers tend to be overweight from what I've seen.'

She nodded. 'They do like their food.'

'So,' I replied, 'if you're a mugger, all you have to do is run away, and they'll never catch you.'

Denni leaned in and said, 'Chicago police don't chase anyone – they're all excellent shots!'

I realised I would be enjoying Denni's company over the coming days, and so I decided that I should take the opportunity to get at least one evening's entertainment on my new shiny company American Express card. I asked Denni if she would like to join me for an evening meal at the hotel at the Trader Vic's restaurant.

Denni seemed to be shocked, and she stopped in her tracks in the middle of the pavement and looked at me indignantly. 'Mr Parker, I only met you a few hours ago and you're already inviting me back to your hotel!'

I was horrified that she had misinterpreted my invitation, but then she burst out laughing before saying, ' I accept.' Then she gave me another look. 'The invite to Trader Vic's, Mr Parker, nothing more!'

As we continued our walk, Denni actually seemed extremely excited about the invite, as she had never set foot in the Palmer House Hilton. We agreed on Wednesday night, which I figured, even at this early stage, was going to be a wonderful way to spend my last night in Chicago.

When I arrived back at the office, Denni walked me to Geoff Swainson's office. He immediately handed me my temporary security pass and then proceeded to show me around the rest of the office.

Harris occupied the entire building. The trading room took up the entire sixth floor. The huge open-plan trading floor was full of desks, with traders and brokers sitting in front of banks of screens. They all had key and lamp dealer boards with multiple phone handsets and mics.

The noise and vibe that comes from an active dealing room is difficult to explain in words. It's unlike the frenetic wall of noise and colour you get from an exchange trading floor, like LIFFE.

A bank dealing floor is still a charged atmosphere, with traders and brokers calling to colleagues and dashing around the desks. There is a hum of constant phone conversations and orders being taken and executed as well as an unrelenting background noise from microphones relaying prices from the trading floors and news services on televisions screens.

Harris had a desk for each contract on the floor of the Chicago Board of Trade and the Chicago Mercantile Exchange, which covered the US Treasury contracts, the US Treasury bills, bonds and notes, as well as the Eurodollar, multiple foreign exchange contracts, the S&P and Dow Jones indices, and numerous commodity contracts, including wheat and corn.

Geoff pointed out the bond desk and Eric Callion, who I would be spending Tuesday morning with.

We travelled down to another floor and walked through the Treasury department and the bank administration departments, which were huge, as Harris Trust & Savings Bank was a major retail bank in both the US and Canada.

My first day was ending. Geoff walked me back to the lifts and we returned to the derivatives back office on the fifth floor. He said he would pick me up from the hotel at 7 pm for our evening meal.

As I took my seat next to Denni, she immediately began taking the mickey out of my accent by asking me periodically to repeat what I was saying, before replying in a very exaggerated American accent, 'Sorry darlin' but I love that accent. I just gotta get you to say it again.'

Jennifer Johnson came over to join in the 'bash the Brit fun' by pretending to be offended that she had paid for my lunch and yet it was Denni I had invited to Trader Vic's. I was relieved when I realised it was mock offence, as she added she would have suggested taking Denni anyway.

With that, everyone finished for the day, grabbing their coats and bags, saying goodnight, and heading for the lifts. I said goodbye and headed to the lifts myself.

As I stepped out onto the pavement, I could feel the temperature had dropped considerably but luckily the wind seemed to have eased as well, and so I headed south for the hotel.

I considered my first day at Harris to be a success, and upon my return to my hotel bedroom I sat at the writing desk and started writing the days notes for my ultimate report back to Nick Grason.

Geoff arrived at the hotel reception at 7 pm, and we jumped into a cab and went to an Italian restaurant that was a 20-minute drive away.

Once seated at the restaurant, Geoff hit me with the news that he was coming to London to establish a European hub for Harris Futures. Geoff hoped to be working closely with Dave Peart and myself once he arrived in the UK. Harris were intent on finding their own office space, independent of Czarnikow, although at this stage he didn't know much about the location.

Geoff apologised to me, saying that he had hoped to take me to see one of the big Chicago-based sporting teams. He had wanted to get tickets for us to watch either the Chicago Bears American football team or one of the two big Chicago baseball teams, but that sadly there were no matches scheduled during my brief stay.

We chatted about the LIFFE market, Barry Fontera and our previous Transmarket relationship, and then back to Geoff's imminent transfer to London and how much he was looking forward to it. Geoff said that initially he would be coming over by himself, but that once he had found a home to rent, his wife would be joining him.

We had a great meal, but I made the mistake of ordering an Italian sausage dish as a starter, which looked like a main course when it arrived at the table. When the huge lasagne turned up that I had ordered, I hardly made a dent in it before admitting defeat. This was a real shame as I kept seeing this dessert trolley passing our table with amazing-looking dishes.

By the time I returned to the hotel, splashing out the dollar bills again as I went, I just jumped into the shower and went to bed.

On Tuesday morning, I had my usual breakfast via room service and then set off for my walk to Harris's office.

The weather was much milder on the Tuesday, and so it was a pleasant walk down West Jackson Boulevard. I walked directly to the large double doors and passed the reception desk using my new visitor's pass. I entered the lift with a group of other Harris staff and headed for Geoff's office.

On arrival, Geoff suggested I leave my coat and briefcase in his office, and we set off for the trading floor and my meeting with bond trader Eric Callion.

Eric, like all American traders, was a larger-than-life character. He was short and slim in stature, but very flamboyant, with shoulder-length hair. He wore brown trousers with a red check pattern, an open-necked cream shirt, black braces, and an immensely powerful aftershave.

As Geoff introduced me, Eric gripped my hand in a very firm handshake. I took the empty seat next to Eric, and Geoff left the trading floor, telling me he would return after lunch at 2 o'clock.

Eric introduced me to the bond team, which was eight guys scattered around the desk handling futures, options, physical bonds, and the all-important 'repo' trades. In between phone calls and actual trading, Eric took me through the basics of what his desk did, before going into more depth about repos.

Most of the big American banks had repo desks that lent and borrowed physical bonds. If Barry Fontera had a bond he needed to loan out, he could call Eric and his team, and they would agree a price. This price was usually based on the current futures 'spot month' price, the spot month being the nearest to delivery.

Once the price was confirmed, they would then agree a rate of interest on the cash leg of the trade. This was how a repo desk made money – they took the bonds and 'lent' you the face value in US dollars on the bond, based on the price you had agreed, and then charged you interest on the resulting cash.

Likewise, if Barry Fontera was short of physical cash bonds, he could borrow them from Eric and his team, and the trade would work in the same way. The repo team would lend Barry the bonds, take the agreed cash in exchange, based on the spot price, and deduct daily interest for the duration of the loan.

I watched as Eric and his team took orders and arranged repo trades, and I studiously took notes about the process as they went along. I recorded the way they processed each of the trades and then filled in trade tickets for processing. This was similar to how Czarnikow worked, these tickets went into a tray which was periodically cleared by members of an input desk located on the trading floor itself.

On the Harris input desk, a dozen clerks were busy processing the entire floor's trading tickets directly into the GMI clearing system. This was the clearing system I had seen demonstrated by Denni and Jennifer in the back office.

The way the Harris trading floor worked was much the same way I expected Czarnikow would have worked if we had been able to accommodate all the various trade desks onto one big trading floor. Paul Thompson and his team would have managed the central input desk.

It was difficult not to be impressed with the volume of trades that Eric and his team were doing and the way they managed the portfolio of Bonds they were lending and borrowing. It was also very apparent that all the physical bond trades were executed over the phone with a number of American banks and trading companies.

Eric explained that each of his team had their own market relationships with counterparties, and this involved frequent evenings out to keep the relationships ticking over.

Eric confirmed what Geoff had intimated the previous day during our evening meal: that Harris Futures had corporate seats at all the major Chicago sporting teams, and these were used for this corporate entertainment.

Before I knew it, lunchtime was upon us, and I noticed that all around the trading floor, traders were heading off and returning with trays of food and drink.

Eric explained that lunches out, away from the building, were frowned upon.

He walked me off the trading floor and through a set of double doors that opened into a large restaurant area that had three separate kitchens. Each of these kitchens offered a different menu, as well as shelves containing salads, sandwiches, wraps, drinks, and confectionery.

Eric handed me a tray and told me to get what I wanted and meet him at the 'tills.' I had already spotted one of the kitchens advertising a chilli dog, so I quickly went over and ordered.

Like everything in America, my chilli dog was huge. It contained the biggest frankfurter I had ever seen, slapped into a family-sized baguette. This was accompanied by a generous amount of fried onions and then a large spoonful of chilli sauce poured all over the frankfurter. My chilli dog was served with the compulsory side of French fries and a token salad. I grabbed a juice and joined the waiting Eric, who had gone for a tuna salad.

Eric was surprised by my unhealthy choice of lunch. The kitchen was heavily subsidised, and Eric handed over his staff pass, explaining that the costs were deducted straight from his payslip, but he was hugely better off buying lunch here than he would be if he went out for lunch.

Although the restaurant had lots of tables where we could have sat, they were mostly empty, and like the majority of the other traders, Eric headed back onto the trading floor with his tray, and I followed.

As we ate at the bond trade desk, the other guys fielded Eric's calls, and occasional questions would be put his way, but he was mostly able to eat in peace.

I felt stuffed as I finished my lunch, and Eric gathered up the trays and placed them on the end of the desk, pointing out that a couple of people with trollies were constantly circling the trading floor, gathering up the trays and returning them to the restaurant.

Before I knew it, my time with Eric and the guys had passed and Geoff had appeared. I thanked Eric and the other members of the bond desk, and just as I was about to head off, Eric asked where I was off to next.

Before I could answer, Geoff replied for me, telling the bond desk that I had a 'date' with Denni Machi. This was immediately the cause of real excitement, with all the guys grinning. They finished by wishing me 'luck.'

We returned to Geoff's office, and Denni was already there in her coat, waiting. I gathered up my coat and briefcase, thanked Geoff and told him I would see him the following morning.

Denni and I headed down to the ground floor and out into West Jackson Boulevard where we flagged down a cab for our trip to the Sears Tower.

The Sears Tower dominated the Chicago skyline. With 109 stories, it was, at that time, the tallest building in the world, a record it held until 1999. It remained the tallest building in America until 2013 when One World Trade Centre in New York took the title.

As we headed off, Denni explained that we were going to the Sears Tower's Skydeck, which was located on the 103rd floor. Denni seemed to take an element of local pride in telling me that to get to the 103rd floor, we would be travelling in the fastest lifts in the world. These lifts went from street level to the 'Skydeck' in 60 seconds.

The entrance for the Skydeck was on the south side of the Sears Tower. I told Denni I was paying the entrance fee, as I was determined to get as much use as I could out of my American Express card.

Armed with our tickets, we boarded these fast lifts. About a dozen people boarded behind us, and Denni whispered to me to hold on to the silver handrail that ringed the lift car. It was slightly disturbing just how quickly the lift got up to full speed, and you could almost feel your stomach being left behind and a slight feeling of nausea, but it was an exceptionally smooth ride.

I had no idea why I was hanging on to the handrail. The inevitable slowing of the lift started very quickly, and with a gentle bounce we stopped as the illuminated floor counter, which had been a blur for most of the ride, read 103. Then the doors opened.

Denni took my arm and held me back a second as we let the other passengers get out the lift first. That was when I heard a semi scream from one of the ladies who had stepped out, mixed with laughter.

The noise was coming from a middle-aged lady who had just stepped out of the lift and was struggling to get her skirt back down, as it flapped around her midriff. It looked exactly like the famous Marilyn Monroe scene in *The Seven Year Itch* – her skirt kept being propelled upwards until her other half pulled her further onto the Skydeck.

Denni chuckled, let my arm go and firmly grabbed the hem of her skirt as we stepped out of the lift. A huge updraft blasted out from the small gap between the lift and the floor of the Skydeck. I had little doubt that had Denni not maintained such a determined grip on the hem of her skirt, she would have had the same problem as the embarrassed lady who was now laughing with her partner.

Denni explained that on her first visit she had been equally embarrassed at having her skirt blasted upwards, except that Denni's skirt had gone right up to chest level. The problem was a side effect of the speeds at which the lifts travelled up and down the lift shafts.

Denni gestured to a group of guys all watching avidly from the glass viewing panels opposite the lifts. Watching unsuspecting ladies getting out the lifts appeared to be a recognised spectator sport. 'My fans will be disappointed today,.'

Denni couldn't understand why the ground-floor reception staff didn't warn ladies in skirts and dresses before they got into the lifts.

As I looked around us, all I could see was a wall of glass giving the most spectacular views of Chicago. The sky was thankfully clear, and we walked over to take in the stunning view immediately in front of us. I grabbed my camera and started snapping as we slowly walked around the Skydeck.

View from Sears Tower

From one side of the building, you could see Lake Michigan, and Denni explained that from the Skydeck on a cloudless day like today, we would be able see into the neighbouring states of Indiana, Michigan, and Wisconsin. She pointed out various sites as we slowly worked our way around the Skydeck: Soldier Field stadium, home of the Chicago Bears American football team; the famous Wrigley Field, home of the Chicago Cubs baseball team; and Comiskey Park, home of the Chicago White Sox baseball team.

Then there was Chicago O'Hare Airport, where you could clearly see the planes taking off and landing, as well as the queue of planes in the sky waiting to land or heading off.

As we slowly continued around the viewing gallery, I kept hearing the 'ping' as the lift doors opened, and each and every time, I could see Denni looking at me, expecting me to succumb and join the craning-neck brigade. Even when I did hear a screech or exclamation, I made a point of looking right back at Denni, showing I had no interest in joining in. Each and every time, I was rewarded with a smile, and Denni would say, 'Good boy, Mr Parker.'

Finally, we arrived at the 'walk of faith' as Denni called it.

This was a glass box that projected out from the Skydeck four feet or so. A group of people were clustered in front of it. Individuals, couples, and sometimes a group of three or four, would walk out onto the clean glass floor, 103 floors above street level.

'You can't tell who will step out and who won't,' Denni explained. 'Last time I was here, I saw full-grown men freeze, unable to walk out and little old ladies step out without a second thought. I love people watching.'

We joined the informal queue, and as we got closer to the glass box, I could see what Denni meant. People would freeze as their eyes and brain said, 'What are you doing?! There's nothing there. You're going to fall.' It was obviously a defence reflex action; the brain was totally convinced death was imminent.

This glass box was immaculate, and it was surprising how many people just could not bring themselves to step out onto it. As we got closer, I realised Denni was holding my hand. 'So, Mr Parker,' she said. 'I couldn't do this last time I was here. But I'm here with an English gentleman this time, so if you will, I will.'

I looked into those brown eyes of hers. She had given me a challenge with a patriotic spin.

As we got ever closer to the front of the queue, the people in front of us either stepped out or baulked. The closer we got, the more the doubts grew in my mind. That glass box had vanished, and now all I could see was the edge of the Skydeck floor. I was doubting myself increasingly the closer we got.

Then we were there, standing on what looked like the very edge of the 103rd floor, looking down at the minuscule cars and dots that were obviously people below.

The box was empty, and it was our turn, but my eyes were telling me that we were about to step off the 103rd floor and plunge. We went to step forward, but my feet refused to go any further. Denni kept going, releasing my hand, and walking right up to the glass panel four feet out from the edge of the floor.

Denni turned slowly to face me, as people hovered behind me. She now had this very scared look on her face, as if a wave of fear and realisation seemed to have suddenly hit her. Denni stood at the far end and looked at me with those deep brown eyes. I was convinced she was about to burst into tears. 'Kevin,' she almost whispered, 'I can't move ... please come and get me.' She held out her hands in my direction.

I felt a lump in my throat. A large lady behind me gave me a slight shove, which really did not help. 'Go get your girl, son,' she demanded in a deep southern American accent.

Bugger ... I just looked straight at Denni. I thought about how I would be ridiculed back at Harris's offices if I did not rescue her. In my head, I could see Ro and Jennifer Johnson giving me a really tough time. I just did not have any option – I had to live up to my English gentleman persona and rescue Denni. I had to step out and get my feet to move. I sensed the impatient people behind me.

Not looking down, left or right, but concentrating solely on Denni and her outstretched arms, I stepped forward.

My brain told me I was about to beat those fast lifts back to the ground floor, but my hesitant foot found the glass surface. The next step was easier, as was the one after that, and then I was able to reach out and take Denni's hand.

The moment I reached her, the distressed facial expression was instantly replaced with a huge grin, and she said, 'I knew you could do it, Mr Parker.' And with that, she walked past me with no trouble at all.

The large lady who had given me a shove in the back looked at Denni in horror, and as Denni passed her, I heard the lady say in her loud, thick accent, 'You're wicked girl!'

I practically jumped back onto the safety of the floor of the Skydeck, as Denni walked ahead laughing about her little trick. All I got was a very sympathetic look of apology from the large lady as I walked past her and those queuing to take their turn at the walk of faith.

I chased after Denni, and we did one more quick circuit of the Skydeck before jumping the upblast into an open lift for the trip back down to the ground floor.

As we exited the building, Denni quickly hailed a cab, and I followed her and climbed into the back seat. She told the driver to take us to the Art Institute of Chicago and then explained to me that it was her favourite place to visit in Chicago, after the shops of course.

The Art Institute, as I would learn, is one of the oldest in America and has a vast and varied collection of all forms of art, from classical to pop art and statues. It even has mythological pieces from South America and varied art from all over the world, including fashion items.

We quickly skipped through the exhibits, as we were aware time was against us, and Denni was determined to show me her favourite pieces, some of which surprised me. As a person of Italian heritage, she seemed particularly taken with the Roman artefacts, of which they had plenty.

Before we realised it, it was six o'clock, so we stepped back out of the Art Institute and into the Chicago dusk. Denni told me that she was heading in the opposite direction to me. I thanked her for the tour, kissed her on the cheek and we climbed into separate cabs.

I was still not that hungry when I arrived back at the Palmer House. My huge chilli dog from lunchtime continued curbing any hunger, and so once back in my room I set about writing up my notes for the day and watching a bit of TV. After that, I ordered a light meal from room service before settling down for the night.

I woke up the next morning with mixed emotions. This was my last full day in Chicago, and I felt a little sad. I did have my evening meal at Trader Vic's booked with Denni to look forward to, so that took the edge off my disappointment a little.

I ordered breakfast from room service, going for the eggs benedict, which was amazing and so I made a mental note to have the same the next day.

I walked out of the hotel doors and into sleet. The doorman gave me a glance, but I pulled the collar of my coat up and headed down the now familiar path to Harris.

This was a major mistake – each block, as I hit the intersection, was like walking into a blizzard, and I had six more blocks to walk. I followed a few of the hardy locals who stayed in the shade of the buildings until the pedestrian lights on the road crossings were green and then sprinted over and into the shelter of the next batch of buildings on the other side of the street.

Three blocks down, I was freezing, and my right side was coated in snow. I brushed myself off and kept going.

By the time I arrived at Harris's office, my teeth were chattering. I got the 'stupid tourist' looks as I flashed my temporary pass and headed up to the fifth floor and the derivatives back office. I took my coat off, draped it over my arm and attempted to sort my snow-blizzard hair into a semblance of normality before stepping out onto the floor.

Jennifer spotted me first, smiling as I made my way towards my seat next to Denni. Both Denni and Ro spotted me at the same time, and we exchanged pleasantries as I took my seat.

Jennifer walked over. 'Did Denni look after you yesterday, Kevin?' she asked.

I nodded. 'Denni was the perfect hostess, Jennifer.'

Ro leaned forward and, looking me straight in the eye with her flashing blue eyes, said, 'Would you have rescued me, Kevin.' There was general laughter from all the other girls in the office. Obviously, Denni had told them all about her trick at the 'walk of faith.'

Before I could answer Ro, Denni jumped in once again. 'Oh, Ro, behave. Mr Parker here would have been trampled in the rush of rampant jocks and he-men if you had shown the slightest sign of fear and called for help.' This caused louder laughter all around the back office.

But I was not going to get side-lined. 'Of course, I would have saved you, Ro.'

'Thank you,' Ro replied with a smug look at Denni. 'A true English gentleman.'

'So,' Jennifer interrupted the girl's fun, 'you're off to the CME floor for a visit with Anne Meyer at 11, that only gives as a couple of hours before you have to go. If you would like to come over to my desk, I'm sure Denni would be more than happy to make her English gentleman, and the rest of us, a coffee.'

Jennifer grinned at Denni, who pretended fake horror while the rest of the girls shouted their orders at her. And with that, I followed Jennifer to her desk.

Harris had started clearing their LIFFE business through Czarnikow, and so I explained a little about our reports and systems to Jennifer. We went through the overnight reports she had received from London. Jennifer explained that once Geoff was in London, they planned to switch more business our way, as the Harris Futures commodities desk would start to use us to hedge more of their US positions through London.

I explained the ICCH delivery process and grading to her, although Jennifer felt it unlikely that Harris would run any positions through to delivery in London.

Then it was 10.30 and time to think about heading off to the CME, which was at 30 South Wacker Drive. I grabbed my coat, leaving my bag with Jennifer, and headed down to the ground floor.

The short cab ride took me to a large modern tower block with a vast glass reception that was bustling with people going in and out. I headed to the reception desk and advised one of the receptionists that I had a meeting with Anne Meyer on the CME floor. I was provided with a visitors pass while the receptionist phoned to tell Anne I was here.

I could see brightly coloured trading jackets all around the reception area, moving around in the same way they did at London's Royal Exchange. But this was America – everything was bigger, brighter, more in your face. The jackets were more varied and flamboyant, and I even saw one that resembled a Dalmatian dog's coat – white with uneven black blotches.

I was advised to take a seat amongst the collection of leather sofas that sat just to the right of the reception desk.

I had no idea what Anne would look like, and I had not asked Barry or Geoff for a description, so when I saw a lady in a bright orange trading jacket walk up to the reception desk to be pointed in my direction, I was surprised. Anne was medium height and build with shoulder length mousey brown hair, freckles and large round glasses that made her look more like a librarian than a CME floor trader.

I stood, and Anne offered her hand, which I shook formally. In a strong New York accent, she asked me to follow her.

Anne asked how I was enjoying my time in Chicago, and at Harris. We chatted as we went up an escalator bank and then proceeded to go up another flight of escalators before she led me to a security door. Once there, she deftly keyed in the four-digit combination and was rewarded with a beep. We then proceeded onto a balcony that looked down on a huge trading floor.

Just like walking onto the LIFFE floor, a wall of noise hit us as we passed through the doors, and below us was a huge open trading floor. There were banks of desks and phones all around the outer wall. About twenty-five feet above floor level was a complete wall of Ferranti screens that circulated to all four corners of the market, with prices flashing and changing. In the middle section of the trading floor there were various trading pits of differing sizes and milling below were hundreds of traders in their brightly coloured jackets.

The admin staff were dressed in the same yellow jackets used on LIFFE, and I assumed this was another aspect of the Chicago floors that LIFFE had adopted.

There were banks of admin booths flanking the far walls, under the Ferranti pricing screens and facing in towards the trading pits; they were the centre of frantic activity as admin staff and traders rushed about.

Apart from LIFFE being housed in its historic Royal Exchange home and cramped compared to this vast modern hanger-style trading floor, there were plenty of similarities. I guessed the founders of LIFFE had spent time visiting and borrowing ideas from their Chicago-based cousins.

I spotted something different, however – scattered around the various pits were people dressed in black jackets who appeared to be observing. I asked Anne who they were, and she explained that they were CME pit officials. They looked like football referees, and Anne explained they could, and did, issue on-the-spot fines for breaches of rules, and in extreme cases could remove someone's trading rights or even shut a pit if it became 'disorderly.'

Anne told me an anecdote about two Eurodollar pit traders who were having an argument and then got into a fistfight in the pit, with one knocking the other out. One of the black-jacketed pit officials issued an on-the-spot $2,000 fine to the standing trader, who promptly pulled out his chequebook, wrote out a cheque and handed it over to the official. On looking at the cheque, the pit official said, 'I said two thousand dollars, not four thousand.' The trader is reported to have replied, 'It's right, because if he gets up, I'm knocking him out again!'

Anne pointed over to where her 'booth' was. It gave her a view over the Eurodollar and T-bill pits. She told me that the entire expanse of the trading floor was 'floating' and on rollers, and that it could all be reconfigured overnight by jacking it up and changing the size of any/all pits. It was a remarkable piece of engineering and inventive thinking.

The CME floor utilised its much larger space to accommodate far more trading pits than its LIFFE cousin, but some were not even active on a daily basis. Anne pointed to a far corner where there was a CME 'butter' pit which she indicated was active and trading a couple of days a week, and even then only for a matter of hours.

Most of the other contracts I recognised from the short spell we had cleared the Rainbow Fund, which had been trading everything and anything.

We walked slowly down the long viewing gallery as Anne continued pointing out the options pits and the characters who worked on the trading floor. As we reached the end of the gallery, she asked if I was ready for lunch, and we walked the long way back down the gallery, out the doors and departed from the CME floor.

The Rivers restaurant was just downstairs in the lobby, overlooking the river that flows into Lake Michigan.

The food was good, and we chatted about the CME trading floor and LIFFE, as Anne was extremely interested in what I saw as the differences.

Then she asked if I was interested in moving down to the LIFFE floor to trade or take an admin position. I explained about my earlier experiences on the commodities floor and told her I was more than happy in the office and that the trading floor held no attraction for me. Anne told me that the LIFFE and CME floors sounded quite different in culture, and I would be more at home on the CME floor.

We chatted about Barry Fontera, and Anne's view was that he was, 'a big teddy bear' with a bark that was far worse than his bite. I explained that we were all scared of him in the back office, which she found funny.

We chatted about my visit and the fact I was heading back via New York. Then our time was up, and Anne told me she had to get back to the trading floor. I thanked her for her time, and I headed for West Jackson Boulevard.

I made my way back to Geoff Swainson's office, and he waved me in as he finished a phone call. Once he was off the phone, he asked me how the trip to the CME floor had gone and then called Jennifer, who made her way up to join us.

The final meeting was very relaxed. I had no real questions to ask them – I felt I had made comprehensive notes back at the hotel and had covered everything. I thanked them both for their time and for making my visit to Harris interesting and enjoyable.

We chatted about my trip to New York. Geoff explained that if it was clear, I was going to be flying into LaGuardia, which was in the river and involved an 'interesting' descent into New York's skyline.

As we wrapped up, the question of my evening meal with Denni cropped up. Once again, Jennifer Johnson feigned offence but finished by suggesting to Geoff that the relationship with Czarnikow should be cemented with an arranged marriage between myself and Denni! Geoff found this highly amusing.

I shook Geoff's hand and asked him to let me know when he was in London and available for a lunch and that I would be happy to show him around Czarnikow and the LIFFE floor.

I walked with Jennifer back to the fifth floor and said goodbye to the team, especially Ro who insisted on a hug and kiss. Right on cue, I heard Denni say, 'Put her down, Mr Parker, she's a married woman.'

I thanked Jennifer and had planned well in advance exactly what my parting line was going to be.

I turned to Denni and told her I was looking forward to seeing her at my hotel later on. For the only time since my arrival, it was Denni blushing and lost for words.

I beat a hasty retreat with the laughter from all her colleagues ringing in my ears, and before Denni could think of a comeback line, I was out the door.

With that, I said a sad goodbye to Harris Futures and took my last walk back down West Jackson Boulevard, heading to the Palmer House Hilton.

When I got back to my room, I had a shower and I changed out of my three-piece suit and into a formal shirt and trousers. I had decided on a collar and tie as Trader Vic's was a Hilton restaurant and I expected there would be a dress code. With a healthy amount of my rarely-used Kouros aftershave on, I sat on the bed and waited.

It did occur to me as I waited in the hotel room that, after my parting comment to Denni, I could be stood up.

At exactly the agreed 7.30, my room phone rang, and I was told that a young lady was waiting for me in the hotel lobby. With a quick check in the mirror, I headed down to reception desk.

As I approached the hotel reception, I could see Denni waiting in a buttoned long winter coat, she had styled her hair, wore bright red lipstick with black eye shadow. She looked lovely. As I got closer, she spotted me and gave me a cheeky grin. 'Mr Parker,' she said formally.

'Ms Machi,' I replied with equal formality, and I took her offered arm and walked her towards the stairs that led down to Trader Vic's.

Dicky Gibbs had been completely accurate; the restaurant was dotted with mystical nick-nacks and artefacts and had a great ambience. We walked up to the concierge who checked my booking from his list before grabbing a couple of menus and leading us to a table.

It was still relatively early, so very few tables were occupied.

The waiter walked us to an immaculate table for two that was slightly out the way and to one side of the main dining area. He put the two food menus on the table and offered to take Denni's coat, which she accepted, unbuttoning the knee-length coat to reveal her black satin dress.

As the coat slipped from her shoulder, I got a better look, the dress was conservative with a collar-height neckline and short sleeves. It was cut just above the knee and fitted her figure perfectly.

Spotting me taking in the view, Denni's grin broadened, and she did a little twirl. 'Like what you see, Mr Parker?' The waiter took this as his que to run off with Denni's coat.

'You look lovely, Ms Machi,' I replied, offering to help her with her seat, which again she accepted, making a comment about an 'English gentleman.'

As I sat down opposite Denni, she put her matching satin black clutch bag on the table. With her usual effortless switch from 'formal Denni' to 'naughty Denni,' she caught me out once again by saying, 'If you wanted to see boobs and lots of flesh, you should have invited Ro. That girl has some outrageous dresses.'

I looked into her eyes and replied with her own line, 'But Ro is a married woman.'

Denni nodded. 'Yes she is, and her husband is a football jock. You would be dead long before you got to the dessert menu.'

The waiter returned, asking if we were ready to order a drink while we looked at the menu. I ordered a Budweiser, and Denni a ordered a glass of the house red wine.

The menu was extremely broad in scope, with Asian, European, and American sections, and so the waiter delivered the drinks and retreated as we worked our way through it. We compared notes as we went through and having agreed to not ruin the main course with a starter, we signalled to the waiter and ordered.

We chatted about London and my trip to Harris, and as the drinks flowed, so did the conversation.

Denni wanted me to put in a good word with Geoff when he arrived in London, saying it would be a clever idea for her to come to London to see Czarnikow and meet the back office. I liked that idea – the thought of not seeing Denni again left me with a hollow feeling.

I really didn't know what to make of Denni; on the one hand she was great company, on the other she had this dangerous ability to keep me on the back foot. She could charm one moment and shock the next. I liked her sense of humour and unpredictability, but I suspected underneath she was really a sweet girl. Plus, she was attractive and growing on me by the minute.

Like a lot of Americans, Denni did not travel much. She had not even been to New York, although it was on her 'to do' list. Denni's parents and younger sister lived back in Milwaukee, and she explained that the Machi family had always lived in the Chicago area ever since arriving in America from Italy.

As we finished another drink and the main course arrived, Denni explained that her family originated from the Italian region of Tuscany. Interestingly, her surname Machi was a truncated American version of Machiavelli, and her ancestors had arrived in the US in the early 1900s.

The food, service and company were excellent. As we finished the main course and the plates were cleared, we were given the dessert menu. I was full, but I spotted a cheesecake on the menu, and something told me American cheesecake was going to be amazing. Denni was not interested in dessert, having set her heart on an Irish coffee.

As I explained my love of cheesecake, Denni became interested and suggested that as we were both full, we should take a slice of the cheesecake 'to go.'

I wasn't sure if a Hilton restaurant was going to do 'doggy bags,' When the waiter came back, Denni explained that we both wanted an Irish coffee and the cheesecake to go, and the waiter didn't bat an eye.

As we finished our Irish coffees, I looked at my watch – it was 9.30, and I really didn't want to let Denni go yet.

The waiter returned with two paper bags containing boxes of cheesecake. I showed him my room card and slapped a five-dollar tip on the table. He thanked us and headed off to fetch Denni's coat.

I turned to Denni and said, 'How about we head up to the b …'

Denni jumped in. 'Mr Parker, I thought you were an English gentleman.'

I went very red. 'I was going to say bar.' The waiter arrived with Denni's coat to save me from further embarrassment.

Denni maintained eye contact as she confessed, 'I know, but I couldn't resist.' She offered me her arm once again, and we walked up the stairs to the ground-floor cocktail bar.

We both had extravagant and expensive cocktails and chatted happily, but as the glasses emptied, Denni looked at her watch and said, 'Mr Parker, I have to go. Some of us have to work tomorrow.'

I had arrived at the moment I had been increasingly dreading. I nodded and escorted Denni to the main doors, where the ever-eager doorman was waiting to let her out and flag a waiting cab to pull forward.

I thanked Denni for a fabulous time and told her I would speak to her upon my return to Czarnikow on the Monday.

I pulled her close and kissed her on the cheek. As I held her, Denni whispered, 'Don't forget to get Geoff to invite me to London. I'm relying on you, Mr Parker.'

I promised, and with that I got a return kiss on the cheek and a gentle squeeze of my hand. Then Denni pulled away.

I watched her walk through the hotel doorway, carrying her clutch bag in one hand and takeaway cheesecake in the other. She turned to give me a wave as she climbed into the cab door, opened by the eager hotel doorman, and I watched the cab pull away.

I had a restless night; I was so sad to be leaving Chicago, and after an hour of tossing and turning, I gave up. I turned the lights on and set about updating my notes while eating my delicious cheesecake.

Eventually, I dropped off asleep, and my alarm went off as normal at eight, although I did not have to check in at O'Hare until 11.30 for my 12.15 flight to New York – it was an internal flight so there was none of the usual security and passport control.

I decided to head down to the restaurant for a leisurely breakfast instead of my normal room service.

I knew that just down the road, my Harris Futures colleagues would be turning up for work, and I had this surreal feeling that I was missing something, and something was not right. I ordered the eggs benedict again, as I had promised myself I would, and I enjoyed it just as much the second time around.

I returned to the room for the last time, packed my bag and ambled down to reception. It occurred to me how unlikely it was that I would ever stay in a Hilton again (I was wrong), and I checked out using my company Amex and very carefully stored away the receipt with my growing collection in my wallet.

I did not have to wait long for a doorman to come in and advise reception a limo was outside to collect me, so I headed for the door, handing the doorman his final dollar bill before getting into the black stretch limousine.

It was the same driver who had picked me up from O'Hare on my arrival just six days beforehand, although it felt much longer.

We exchanged pleasantries, and I watched the Palmer House Hilton, the Sears Tower and Chicago quickly vanish behind me and into the skyline.

My flight to New York was on an American Airlines plane, so I had to make my way to Terminal 3 rather than the international terminal I had arrived at.

As this was an internal flight, it was on a much smaller Boeing 737. I had time to kill, and the vast airport had plenty of distractions. Internal flights didn't have class differences; they were all cattle class, and the only benefit of a business-class passenger was priority boarding, so I was the first passenger to board the plane.

The flight time was 1 hour 55 minutes, and my first experience on a narrow-bodied plane was not great.

We hit turbulence midway, and it felt like being a leaf on the wind. I was pleased I was at the front; some of my fellow passengers looked too big for the seats, and I was grateful I had not been seated next to one of the 'larger' ones.

As Geoff Swainson had indicated to me in our final meeting, when the plane descended for landing at New York, it did seem as if we were going to set down in the river. The New York skyline loomed on either side of the plane as we were on final approach, and I was almost grateful when the plane finally touched down with a bump onto the runway.

With no passport and security checks on an internal flight, the only wait in the terminal was for the luggage to appear on the carousel. There was no priority bag handling this time, but to be fair my bag was the first to appear, and then I was out on the concourse.

The New York office didn't let me down. As I came out of the airport and into reception, a large guy was holding up a board with 'Parker. Czarnikow' on it. I nodded and walked over, he grabbed my bag and asked me to follow him out the terminal.

To my surprise, there was no limousine, just a standard yellow American taxicab, and the reason became very apparent as we set off. The drive from the airport took just twenty minutes, and then we pulled up outside the UN Plaza Hotel.

As you would expect, the UN Plaza Hotel was just around the corner from the UN headquarters and was used heavily by foreign diplomats. Accordingly, the hotel had armed security in the reception lobby.

I continued the practice of slapping dollar bills into the hands of the cab driver as he unloaded my bag and the doorman who then carried it up to the reception desk.

The UN Plaza was a total change from the Palmer House. It was a brash modern skyscraper, and the room was much smaller than the one I stayed in at the Palmer House. But with a king size bed and a view from the eighth floor, it was good enough.

I quickly booked myself into the Hotel restaurant for an evening meal. I then set about going through the notes I had written for Nick Grayson.

I was due at Czarnikow's New York office the following afternoon, so my morning was clear, giving me the chance to do a bit of exploring. I decided on a trip to the Empire State Building and Macy's department store. I had contemplated a trip on the New York subway but decided against it.

The hotel offered a complimentary local map, and I decided to stick to using Taxi cabs, as I still had lots of dollar bills.

After a satisfying meal in the hotel restaurant, I retired for the night.

On Friday morning, I ordered breakfast and then set off. The porter called over another of the big yellow taxis, and I headed off for the Empire State Building. The roads were horrendous and choked with traffic, and the driver cut this way and that until eventually we arrived.

I was not overly impressed with the Empire State Building. Unlike the Sears' Skydeck, you couldn't get to the viewing gallery in one elevator trip, instead having to change lifts midway. Once at the top, the view wasn't great, with fences stopping potential suicides. Macy's was like a New York combination of Fortnum & Mason and Harrods and had its own museum inside. Having ticked them off the list, I jumped into another yellow cab and headed off to Battery Park.

I located the Czarnikow office and then backtracked to a local restaurant for a bite to eat.

For the second time, I found communicating my order was a struggle, but instead of the flattering comments the waitress in Chicago had given me, I had my first experience of the New York attitude. Having finally ordered, I had my light lunch and then set off on the short walk back to the office.

Czarnikow's New York office was surprisingly compact compared to the vast amounts of space I had seen at Harris.

It took the top floor of a six-storey office block and had around two dozen staff, with both a sugar and energy desk. As well as my host for my short visit, Victor Dowell, I recognised three of the younger lads – Peter Hadsley and Guy Morrison on the oil desk and Alan Good on the sugar desk, all of whom had been seconded from London to the New York office.

Victor gave me the office tour, and I was introduced to everyone.

Taking a chair at the sugar desk, I could hear the open phone lines to the familiar voices from London, as orders and trade data were communicated between the desks.

The London markets were already closed for the day, and the orders flowed from London to the US office and then down to the New York trading floors. The atmosphere was a lot more relaxed in the New York office.

Victor Dowell was a big bear of a man with a big character to match his build.

His wife lived back in the UK, and he had been in New York for a number of years, taking his summer holidays and Christmas back in the UK with his wife. Their relationship did not seem to be negatively affected by his spending the vast majority of each year away in the US.

Victor had an apartment in New Jersey, and his significant expat remuneration, and the fact he had no children back in the UK, meant that he could indulge his love of every modern electronic gadget that came on the market.

Victor explained that he was taking me to his favourite steak restaurant, Keens, located in Midtown.

Keens boasted it was 120 years old and had provided steaks to JP Morgan, Babe Ruth, and Teddy Roosevelt. After my scheduled evening meal, he told me that I would head off to Greenwich Village where the company had rented flats and I would meet the 'boys' who were going to take me clubbing. I had visions of *Saturday Night Fever*; I guessed my three-piece pinstriped suit would have to do.

Once the New York markets had closed, Vic and I jumped into his huge American car for the short drive to Keens.

Once we were seated in this compact restaurant, I made the mistake of letting Vic order. Nothing could have prepared me prepared me for the steak – it was huge and came with all the trimmings, French fries, and salad.

I was defeated just looking at the mass of food piled onto my plate. My steak was half the size of Vic's, which looked to me like it was an entire cow with the legs and head chopped off. The steak itself was very tender and tasted amazing, but I only got through a third of it before I just couldn't eat another bite.

All this food I had consumed really wasn't the best preparation for a night out dancing. I refused the dessert menu, and with that Victor paid the bill and we walked out into the street. Victor called over a cab and told the driver where to take me in Greenwich Village and gave me the address on a piece of paper.

Greenwich Village was the typical picture I had of New York from all the US television shows – full of 1920/30s-style red brick apartment buildings with the metal fire escapes. The cab turned down a narrow street and pulled up outside a four-storied building that had the number I was looking for.

I paid the driver, walked up the concrete steps and rang the bell. Guy Morrison answered the door. Dressed in a white open-neck shirt, his trademark red braces and black trousers, his hair slicked back with hair cream, he called me in and said the other guys were ready.

A big staircase stretched in front, with a door to the left which Guy had vanished back into. Each of them occupied a self-contained flat from the little I could see.

Peter Hadsley came down the steps, followed by Alan Good and an American colleague called Vince, who I had met briefly at the office.

We went out into the street, Guy securing the door behind us, and after a short walk, we flagged down another yellow cab and all piled in. Guy told the driver the name of the club, and we headed towards Midtown.

In the back of the taxi, Peter advised to me to become ultra-English for the evening. Guy explained that the New York girls loved the accent, and he told me the posher I sounded, the more they would love it.

Peter explained further that they were regulars at the club we were heading for and that the staff were convinced Guy was related to the Royal Family, which upset Peter a little, as technically his family was much closer to the aristocracy than Guy's. But Guy was full of self-confidence, and with his ginger hair and freckles, he just oozed aristocracy, whereas Peter was a little shyer by nature.

Although Alan Good had been to a public school, he considered his background to be modest, but even he was sounding more like Prince Charles by the second. This was all highly amusing to Vince, who told me he came along to the club and was popular with the girls just by being associated with his 'Royal' companions. Vince being a native New Yorker.

We pulled up outside what looked like just a door in the wall of an unremarkable office block. The pavement area in front of the door was roped off, and behind it were stairs that descended down. The moment we climbed out of the cab, the three huge bouncers enthusiastically waved us in, greeting my four hosts like family.

We walked down a wide staircase and descended into a vast basement club.

The nightclub was very functional, the roof contained visible pipes and sprinklers, and the walls were all bare painted brick. Along the entire far wall, furthest from the stairs we had just descended down, was an exceedingly long bar with a dozen bar staff. All the bar staff wore white shirts or blouses, black trousers or skirts and black waistcoats.

The dance floor itself was vast, illuminated from above with bank after bank of flashing coloured lights, strobes and spinning glitter balls. To the right was a huge, elevated DJ setup and sound system, with hundreds of lights all pulsating. The other two walls contained booths, tables, and chairs.

Guy led the way up to the bar where a stocky blonde man greeted him like a long-lost brother. Guy introduced me to Danny the bartender, who turned out to be Australian. Guy opened a bar tab and explained to Danny that I was visiting New York and I was good to join the other four on the tab he had just opened. I was handed what looked like a raffle ticket, which I needed to show to the bar staff whenever ordering drinks.

At that time of the night the club was relatively empty, but a steady stream of people were soon filtering down the stairs and taking seats at the tables and booths. We occupied a booth with eight seats, which Guy announced would soon be full of his 'ladies.' He then slapped me on the back and told me I was in for a good night.

The drinks kept flowing, with the four guys taking it in turns to run up to the bar and come back with beers. I soon realised that if I didn't pace myself, I was never going to survive the night, so I started taking a few sips now and again as I watched my drinks pile up on the table.

It did not take Guy long to spot a group of girls, all dressed up to the nines, that he was obviously expecting. With a wave of his hand, the girls came over and joined us.

Guy told the young ladies I was a colleague from work and having taken on board the advice I was trying to speak very posh English, much to Alan Good's amusement.

I was introduced to each of the six young ladies in turn, but I was struggling to remember their names. The young lady who had taken the seat next to me was a ridiculously cute African American girl wearing a gold sequined top and short black skirt.

Although there were six girls and five of us, they didn't seem to mind the odds not being equal – Guy just put his arm around two of them and that seemed to be everything sorted. The others all knew each other and just paired up naturally, leaving me with the young lady I had started talking to.

I explained to her that I was here for just the one night and I was flying back to the UK the next day. By virtue of being with Guy, Peter, Alan and Vince, my new lady friend told me that she had hoped I was a new recruit to the New York office.

We spent the rest of the evening drinking, chatting, and dancing, and before I knew it the club was packed with the loud hum of conversation and the music ramped up to a point where you had to speak into each other's ears to stand a chance of being heard.

Whenever we struggled to the bar, Danny seemed to appear, as if by magic, and we never waited long to get served. At some stage in the evening, the beer suddenly turned into spirits, and I knew I was in trouble.

Our numbers in the booth fluctuated, with the people alternating between the table and dance floor. My new best friend stuck with me, and I have to say she was great company and a real mover on the dance floor.

Guy Morrison by now seemed to be swapping girls every dance, and even Peter had let his hair down and was dancing with a couple of girls. I have no idea what time it was when I realised I was totally drunk, but we stayed until the early hours and closing time.

I was offered the chance to go back to the company's Greenwich Village home to continue partying, but I declined.

As we stood on the pavement outside the club, Guy whistled loudly at a passing yellow taxi, slapped dollar bills into the driver's hand and said, 'Take this man to the UN Plaza Hotel please, and make sure he gets there safely.' The driver nodded, and I shook hands with the lads and said goodbye to the ladies who were all heading back to Greenwich Village.

My companion for the evening seemed to be a bit upset I was not going back with them, I thanked her for her company, said farewell, climbed into the cab and off I went.

The driver pulled up, I unsteadily climbed out of his cab and staggered over to the building in front of me. Struggling to find my room key, I waved at the gentlemen on the reception desk and walked into the lift and hit eight. The lift set off, and when the doors opened, the hallway in front of me was pitch black – not a single light was on.

Confused, I hit the button for the ground floor, and as the lift opened the security man was waiting outside the lift doors. 'Can I help you, sir?' he said in his deep American accent.

'UN Plaza Hotel?' I asked.

He gestured and said, 'Next door, sir.'

I lurched back out into the street, turned right in the direction I had been sent, went into the building next door, passed the hotel reception, and entered the hotel lift.

I hit eight and this time made it back to my room. Once the door closed behind me, I staggered the short distance to my freshly made bed where I just pitched face first and fell immediately into an alcohol-induced sleep.

The phone was ringing. My head hurt. I dragged myself into a sitting position and picked the bedside phone up.

'Mr Parker?' a female American voice said.

'Yes,' I replied.

'Your limousine is here to take you to the airport.'

Holy cow! I looked at the clock in horror. I had not packed, I was still in the crumpled suit and shirt I had been wearing yesterday, and my car was here!

'I'll be right down.' I quickly hung up the phone, started to pull a clean shirt and underpants out of my suitcase, changed as fast as I could and quickly shoved everything into my bag.

I doused myself in aftershave and rushed off, my head pounding, my mouth dry and my teeth unbrushed. I rushed to the lifts, and when I got to the ground floor I dashed over to the reception desk to hand my room key over.

A quick check, and the lady behind the desk smiled. 'You're all done, Mr Parker. Enjoy your flight.' That was one thing I was definitely not going to do!

The big stretch limousine was waiting out front, and the driver held the door open as the porter grabbed my bag. 'Mr Parker?' the driver asked. I nodded. It was all coming back to me – this flight was from JFK Airport to Heathrow. I climbed in, feeling deeply sorry for myself.

I desperately needed a drink of water, and water was the one thing that was not in the mini bar the car offered. My stomach growled as I looked at the beers and spirits arrayed before me. I felt even more sick now the car was moving, and the only non-alcoholic drink in amongst the bottles was a small tonic water, so I opened that. The drive from the UN Plaza to JFK Airport took around 30 minutes, and I didn't feel good for any of it.

We arrived at JFK Airport, and I left the limo, slapping dollar notes into the driver's hand, and headed into the international terminal. All the noise and hubbub around me was not doing anything for my throbbing head. I looked around at all the signage and spotted an arrow for the British Airways check-in.

This time I made straight for the empty business-class check-in desk, and with my bag checked in, the lady told me I could use the business-class lounge while I waited airside. I headed for the passport control and cleared security on my way to the lounge.

Even the business-class seat and service on the plane didn't make me feel any better.

I had picked up a pack of aspirin and managed to drink copious amounts of water during my wait in the business lounge, but my head was still throbbing, and I just couldn't settle. The flight time was eight hours, and then I had the tortuous Tube journey to Kingsbury, so I figured I would be home a shade before 11 pm if all went well.

We landed a little before 8 pm, and once again I was thankful that I didn't have to hang around for my bag. I cleared customs and headed down for the Tube. As it was a Saturday night, the Tube trains seemed to be running frequently, and I was so happy when I finally sat on the Kingsbury-bound Jubilee Line train.

The following Monday, I felt deflated, my adventure over. I just couldn't slip back into the old routine. It felt wrong. It was as if my horizons had been broadened, my expectations expanded, and now I was being expected to return to my 'old' life. This feeling of anti-climax stayed with me for the days following my return.

As I arrived back to 66 Mark Lane and headed for the back office, armed with my notes, receipts and Amex card, I was greeted with a barrage of questions about my trip. Paul Thompson asked me to sit down with him a little later to give him a quick review, and then he stated that Dave Peart and Nick Grason would want me to see them later in the day to discuss the bond clearing.

In my absence, Gavin had been covering my reconciliations and margin calls. He was more than happy to hand the financial markets reconciliation back to me. I discovered later, after speaking to Gavin, that he had not enjoyed dealing with Barry Fontera. Remembering Anne Meyer's 'big teddy bear' analogy, I hoped I could tame the bear a little in my future dealings with him.

I got back to the 'day job,' my eye on the clock and looking forward to my daily call to Harris Futures.

I spotted Nick Grason enter the department on one of his rare visits. 'Mr Parker,' he said, 'good to have you back. When you've settled in, come and see me, and you can tell me all about your trip.'

I had a quick chat with Paul and then gathered myself up and headed for Nick's office.

Jennette gave me her usual warm greeting, and as I went into Nick's office, he bellowed out to Jennette to get David Peart to join us. I sat down and gave Nick my remaining handful of dollar bills and my very carefully detailed list of expenses.

Nick leaned back in his chair as he looked at the spreadsheet I had given him, onto which I had carefully accounted for everything I had used the credit card for.

As David Peart entered Nick's office, I attempted to hand over the Amex card. Nick put my spreadsheet down and shook his head. 'No, no, no, Mr Parker, this will never do.'

I was panicked. Had I overspent?

'Not only have you returned with ghastly dollar bills, you also appear to have only entertained once and purchased no duty-free?'

Nick looked at me. 'If the company knows it can send someone out to America for a week, and they only spend this much, we're all in trouble.'

He handed me the Amex card back. 'Go and buy your lady or your mother some perfume and treat your friends to an expensive lunch, and be creative with the dates, then hand me the card back with a revised spreadsheet.'

With a prompt from Nick, and with David Peart now seated next to me, I went over my notes from my trip.

I explained what I had learned about the bond trading and processing, and the systems Harris Futures deployed for clearing and settlement. I did a quick recap of my trip to the CME floor with Anne and my trip to the New York office, which prompted a smile from David.

Nick spotted Dave's smile and questioned me further.

It seemed obvious that the boys at the New York office had told Victor I was more than a little worse for wear when they had loaded me into the cab. Victor had passed this information on to David.

I put my hands up and told Nick and David that I had been taken out and consumed far too much alcohol. I explained about my trip to the building next to the UN Plaza and that I had collapsed onto my hotel bed and was still that way when my limousine turned up. Nick, in particular, thought this was very funny and considered the boys in New York had done an excellent job of 'entertaining me.'

I gave Nick a copy of my detailed notes from the meetings, and I returned to the back office.

That lunchtime, I set off to buy perfume for mum, thinking I could put it aside and give it to her for her birthday.

Then I told Rowland and Andrew to invite Tony Ford out for a meal the next day, and we booked a table at a local Indian restaurant in nearby Rood Lane.

Post lunch, I prepared myself for my daily call to Chicago. I phoned and recognised Ro's voice as she recited her usual 'Harris Futures, Ro Dimenza here.'

I smiled to myself. 'Hello Ro, how are you?'

'Kevin!' I heard her shout. I heard Denni's voice in the background, demanding the phone, but before passing it over, Ro managed to stir the pot by saying, 'Someone is missing you.'

Denni's voice quickly followed. 'Don't believe a word that girl says to you, Mr Parker, but thank you for a lovely evening.' I could hear the girls from the back office in the background, all calling out and giving Denni good-natured abuse.

From that moment on, our flirting banter became part of my daily routine.

That week, we heard that EF Hutton was being sold to Shearson. Luckily, our friends all kept their jobs. The merger just involved a rebadging in London, so Linda Booth remained as the manager of the back office, and Nadia Bellows remained as her deputy.

Weeks after my return to the UK, I had a phone call from Nadia, asking to meet me for a drink that evening. I was still a little unsettled after my trip, and a couple of weekends alone at Kingsbury had not helped much. I agreed, assuming she had an issue of some kind.

That evening, we met up in City wine bar, and Nadia told me that she had made a new year's resolution to put her previous marriage and life firmly behind her. She had appreciated that I was there for her when needed – with Roger on the night of the Heysel Stadium tragedy for example, but also weekends and evenings whenever she called.

I returned the compliment, reminding her that she had been there for me to help me deal with the fallout over Dianne.

Nadia then told me she wanted to cook a special meal for me, and could we book a weekend so that I could come over on a Saturday and stay over. We agreed on a Saturday towards the middle of February.

When the day came, I set off from my Kingsbury flat, armed with an overnight bag, and headed for Goodmayes.

Nadia, who always had seemed to be full of life and energy, was even more ebullient and attentive than normal. She asked me about my trip to the US and about work, and we enjoyed a Dover sole dinner and then settled down in front

of the TV. Nadia pulled out a bottle of champagne, and she told me it was a late
New Year's Eve celebration.

The alcohol flowed, and Nadia told me for the very first time more
information about her marriage. At the end of the tale, she was a little tearful
and so I put my arm around her.

We watched the television in silence for a while and then she told me she
felt safe with me. Nadia qualified that by saying she appreciated that I had never
tried it on with her, especially when we had shared the bed in the Nottingham
hotel months earlier. I told her I valued our friendship, but then she asked the
inevitable follow up question: did I find her attractive?

Nadia was a statuesque lady at six foot tall and with a full curvaceous figure.
I had never looked at her as anything other than a friend. Of course, I had noticed
when she was wearing anything dressy or slightly revealing, but I had never
viewed her as 'girlfriend' material.

I was a little thrown by what she was asking me. I had a split second to
answer – too much hesitation wasn't going to go down well, especially with
someone I knew to be insecure and attempting to move on.

Everything she had told me about her previous marriage had explained her
fear of being lonely and her insecurity. What had occurred had been years of
mental abuse; her ex had undermined her confidence, told her she was ugly, fat,
unattractive, and he never shown much affection.

Knowing all that, I responded in the only way I felt I could: 'Of course
you're attractive.'

Nothing more was said, and she just cuddled up on the sofa, and we watched
TV and drank.

When the time came to go to bed, I went to set up the sofa bed in the lounge I
had used previously, but Nadia stopped me, saying that after Nottingham it wasn't
necessary, and I should join her in her double bed. She moved to take the glasses into
the kitchen and told me to use the bathroom first and that she would be in shortly.

I did just that, stripping down to my boxers and getting under the duvet on
her metal-framed double bed.

I heard her go into the bathroom, and I settled back.

After what seemed an age, Nadia came in wearing a plum silk nightdress
that seemed to be glued to her and left little to the imagination. With a shy smile,
she walked over and stopped just as she was about to get under the duvet.

Then, taking a step back and she said, 'Thank you for being you.' With that,
she swept the two straps from her shoulders, and her silk nightdress seemed

to slowly glide down her ample bust, and then it quickly slipped to the floor, leaving her naked.

For a few seconds, she stood still, letting me take in the view, before reaching forward, slipping under the duvet, and immediately moving over towards me. I may have been slow to notice signals from the fairer sex normally, but there was no potential for misreading things this time.

From that day onwards, bed at Nadia's inevitably meant more than just a night's sleep.

We never officially became a couple, but we spent an increasing amount of time together, and more of my wardrobe slowly made its way to Goodmayes

At Kingsbury, with all the landlord's work done on the roof and three new staircases to the rear, a rush of flats in the block went on the market. I hesitated a little, not wishing to join the first wave of sellers. But as the 'For Sale' boards were replaced with 'Sold' boards, I put my flat on the market and started to consider where I should look for a freehold house or bungalow.

Northwest London was not an option – the houses in Eastcote, Ruislip, Harrow, and Kingsbury were well out of my price range – so I switched my search along the train lines, looking east towards Essex and south of the river into Kent.

My brother parted company with the Army, moved into my flat in Kingsbury for a brief while, and then started working with my Uncle Walter Becker or "Wally" as we knew him.

Wally was running a team of tradesmen who were replacing sash windows for the council in the St John's Wood area, so Robin alternated between living with me and Wally, who lived with his long-suffering partner, Julia, just outside Croydon in Purley.

The previous summer, the three LCE commodity markets moved from their traditional separate homes in Plantation House to a new bespoke trading floor in St Katharine Docks.

This state-of-the-art trading floor was a statement of intent, and this was followed by a rebranding exercise as the London Commodity Exchange was rechristened the London FOX (Futures & Options Exchange).

The three commodity markets were quickly joined by the IPE exchange, which moved from its old Dunster House location to a separate bespoke floorspace in the same St Katharine's Dock building.

The local pubs in and around St Katherines Dock welcomed the influx of highly paid traders. The biggest local pub the Dickens Inn, and the Indian restaurant next door, the Mala, were overjoyed with their affluent new neighbours.

Dunster House, directly opposite Czarnikow's building, soon became a building site as demolition started and the planned Minster Court development commenced.

On 18th February 1988, LIFFE started listing its futures trades on its new TRS clearing system. The system was a huge improvement on the old ICCH system, INTERCOM, but the clearing staff needed to learn both because the commodity and oil markets continued to be serviced by INTERCOM.

The central operations department was as busy as ever, and the days just seemed to speed by.

In May, I had another of my meetings with Nick Grason and Paul Thompson. My reconciliations on the growing bond portfolio had meant I was spending increasing amounts of time with David Peart in the financial futures department. This in turn coincided with Wayne Holloway asking for a transfer down to the LIFFE trading floor.

It was agreed in the meeting that Paul Thompson would take on a new member of staff. I would start to teach Martin Finn to cover my role in central operations. Once Martin was up to speed, I would officially move from central operations to the financial futures department.

However, as part of the deal, I would take the bond reconciliation, clearing and settlement with me.

Paul 'Ollie' Collister would step up to cover Wayne, and I would cover Ollie and assist David with his increasing risk function. Before that could happen, Paul Thompson had to find a replacement, and he had decided he ideally wanted another young lady to join the team.

Things became more complicated when Martin Finn was diagnosed with HIV.

Little was known about the condition at this stage, other than its seriousness. In these less than enlightened times, our HR department suggested to Paul that he have a bucket with bleach on standby in case Martin cut himself or had a nosebleed.

Martin was provided with his own mug and cutlery for lunches.

All the departments were invited to a meeting to discuss Martin's condition and were advised that they were not at risk and that they should continue to collaborate with him as they had before his diagnosis. We did have a couple of staff saying they were not happy to continue working with Martin, but after a series of internal discussions these issues were resolved, and we all continued as normally as we could.

Geoff Swainson arrived in London and commenced the job of establishing a Harris Futures London office. Harris had taken office space at Bucklesbury House opposite Cannon Street station.

I was keen to reciprocate Geoff's hospitality in Chicago and gave him a tour of Czarnikow's offices at 66 Mark Lane. Dave Peart then escorted Geoff for a visit to the LIFFE market at the Royal exchange, after which the three of us went to a Teppanyaki restaurant in Bucklesbury House.

Geoff had seen the Teppanyaki restaurant on the ground floor of Bucklesbury house and wanted to try it out.

It was the first time I had experienced a restaurant where the chef cooks the food in front of you.

Teppanyaki is a style of Japanese dining where a chef cooks the food on an iron griddle, known in Japan as a 'teppan.'

The chef who cooked at our table was also an entertainer, flicking the food around with the ease and style of the cocktail waiters down at TGI Friday's. He could cut meat and vegetables with amazing speed and the accuracy of an artist, and he had a few party tricks up his sleeve as well.

The show was as enjoyable as the resulting food, and Geoff was impressed.

When the time was right, I asked Geoff when he was going to invite Denni over to London, to which he burst out laughing. He told me that Jennifer Johnson had been listening to Denni's frequent reminders to me over the phone and that she wondered if I would raise it with Geoff the first chance I got. Armed with Jennifer's warning, Geoff said he was sure I would raise it at lunch.

Geoff then explained in great detail to David Peart the events that I had subtly avoided mentioning about my time in Chicago.

Geoff was more than happy to tell David that Ro Dimenza-Meo was acting as a matchmaker-in-chief and that he would never be able to return home to Chicago if he didn't advise the authorities at Harris Futures about the benefits of letting Denni come over to London on a visit.

Geoff said that it would be a while before he would be in a position to recommend the trip to Chicago, but he would take great delight in getting back to Jennifer and telling her I had done 'as I was told.'

Content that I had done my bit, but a little embarrassed, I was happy to return to the office and let Denni know the good news. I phoned her and told her that her trip to London was on, but she would have to wait a while for Geoff to get established, I got my customary 'Good boy, Mr Parker.'

The search for the new member of staff in central operations was more or less immediate.

Paul had met two of the three young ladies scheduled for interview when he received an unexpected phone call from the ground-floor reception telling him the third young lady was downstairs waiting.

As he got up from his desk to head for the lifts, he was chuckling and told us that the messenger department had told Paul that, if the young lady waiting downstairs did not get the job, he could deliver all his own post from now on.

'So,' Paul said, 'she must be rather attractive.'

As he went to collect her, a heated debate went on between the existing team members, and when Paul walked in with the young lady concerned, silence descended.

At this point in history, the 'Page 3' daily topless pin up in *The Sun* newspaper was still very much a thing. The more popular Page 3 girls went on to become media celebrities. The biggest of these at the time was a busty blonde called Samantha Fox.

The young lady who walked into central operations with Paul Thompson was a young Samantha Fox clone, and so it was obvious why the messenger department had decided to cast a pre-emptive vote. The lady concerned was Amelia Kennett.

Needless to say, Amelia got the job, starting the following Monday, and she was immediately taken under the wing of the other ladies in the department, Sue Bright, Karen Loftus, and Kim Harris. The four young ladies were quickly christened as 'Paul's Angels' by all the trade desks, a mickey take based on *Charlie's Angels*, a big American TV show.

Amelia's start enabled me to complete my training of Martin Finn and move to my new role in the financial futures department.

My first task was to get up to speed on the daily trade blotter for financial futures and cover Ollie on the office/LIFFE floor liaison.

Just as Linda Hicks was doing on sugar and Katherine Ferrato on oil, this involved diligently writing up all the trades executed via the office-based financial futures traders and brokers and recording all the trades delivered to the back office for processing. At the end of the day, all the trades were then verbally cross-checked back to the admin staff on the LIFFE floor.

David Peart then started teaching me how he managed the profit-share calculations for all the floor traders, the biggest of which was Cliff Donovan in the LIFFE Eurodollar pit. At this stage, Cliff was making over £1m annually.

At the month end, the profit-and-loss figures calculated by David were agreed with the individual traders and brokers, and then they were paid – usually in cash, the larger payments via cheque – all of which Paul Collister delivered in person.

This delivery was a monthly event in the Cock and Woolpack public house in Finch Lane, just a short walk away from the LIFFE market itself. Invariably, Mr Collister would be bought copious amounts of alcohol during this delivery. For that reason, on this day each month, Paul was told not to return to the office, and he was usually in no state to do so anyway.

Barry Fontera was included in David's P&L calculations, and my daily calculations of the T-bond and repo trades provided a piece of that puzzle. Barry was still trading his TED spread (Eurodollar/T-bill futures) and Barry's assistant, Prash, now had his own trading account.

My work on the T-bond and repos meant that I did not lose my daily communications with Harris Futures, so I continued my banter with Ro and Denni.

I also had frequent calls to Eric Callion on the Harris bond desk, but we were also using Manufacturers Hannover Trust and Bank of New York for our repos, so I was spending increasing amounts of time on the phone, checking trades and settlements.

As part of the deal for my transfer from central operations, I had to train David Peart and Paul Collister to cover for me on the bond reconciliation and daily profit-and-loss calculation.

Another Czarnikow staff get-together occurred that summer and became a biannual event – Linda Hicks from the sugar desk hosted a party at her flat in Islington.

Linda and her husband, Chris, were a very friendly couple of Londoners who would have been at home on the streets of Walford in the popular TV soap *EastEnders*. Linda was always the life and soul of any party. They lived in a 1970s block of flats in Islington and had a large group of friends and family around them, all ready and willing to pitch in and help on party night.

This particular party was themed fancy dress, and as usual my dear friend

Lesley Neenan decided to push the boundaries and hired a costume that only she could select. Leslie's choice of costume would definitely be described as not Politically correct in this day and age.

Having totally changed into her fancy dress outfit at her flat in Peckham, Lesley then proceeded to drive through the streets of Peckham and Islington in her Mini Clubman car. Lesley and I still laugh about that costume!

As always with Linda and Chris's parties, the drink flowed, and we were all supplied mountains of home-cooked food. You never went hungry at one of Linda's parties. Eventually, the contemporary dance music was always switched off and then Chas & Dave came on and everyone of all ages joined in with the dancing and singing.

It was every bit the traditional family-and-friends London knees-up, and we always had a really enjoyable time.

I received an invitation to my old friend Steve Dickinson's stag party on a Saturday night in late March 1988. Steve had met his fiancée at the Met Police when she was a uniformed WPC. At this stage, Steve's fiancée was no longer a serving police officer, having taken a career change and become an air flight attendant for British Airways.

The stag started in Covent Garden, and it was the first time since secondary school that I had seen Steve's elder brother Keith, also a serving Met Police officer.

I was very much the odd one out, not being a police officer, and by the time we headed off for a nightclub I was in the company of a dozen policemen. We went to a nightclub in Charing Cross Road, and Steve and his colleagues used the old warrant card trick to get in for free. This was something Steve had done before when the two of us had gone clubbing.

Night clubs liked having off-duty officers in the club in case of trouble, but I doubt they had ever had a dozen or so in one go. Anyway, due to the number of warrant cards shown at the door, and as an obvious member of the party, I was able to get in without paying.

In what was obviously a pre-arranged meeting point, off-duty WPCs and lady friends joined us. Steve was eventually a mess – it was obvious to me that various members of the group had been lacing his drinks from an early stage – and as he collapsed on a chair, the drinking and dancing continued into the early hours.

In April 1988, the then chancellor of the exchequer, Nigel Lawson, announced the end of double tax relief for unmarried couples buying property.

This meant that couples could no longer both claim 30 per cent relief on their first £60,000 mortgage. From the 1st August they could only claim 10 per cent.

This led to a surge in house prices as couples stampeded into the housing market to avoid the 1st August deadline. I had a very unusual discussion with my estate agent who, despite having supplied plenty of viewings had received no offers, and now encouraged me to put the price up!

My flat, which I had bought just years earlier for £28,000, was now on the market for £61,000.

I decided that if I eventually accepted an offer on the flat that I would concentrate my search for a house in the Plumstead/Abbey Wood area of London. This was an area where I could afford a house and still have reasonable access to the City via either the Woolwich or Bexleyheath train lines.

Following the chancellor's announcement, I didn't have to wait long to sell my flat. I received a firm offer at the full asking price, subject to the sale completing before the 1st August deadline.

I immediately started spending weekends in southeast London looking at properties, my hopes plummeting as the choice of houses on the market seemed to be limited. The houses I had seen were either in bad areas or in poor condition.

I was starting to get despondent, then one night I got home from work, and waiting was an envelope of house particulars from local estate agent Jacksons. In amongst other properties, I found a three-bedroom Victorian mid-terrace in Abbey Wood. It was priced at £71,500, listed as in need of 'modernisation' and painted in an unfortunate dark green. It looked promising, and I made an appointment to see it.

Woodbrook Road in Abbey Wood was actually on the border of Welling in Kent. The road was crescent-shaped, leading to and from the busy Wickham Lane, which connected Plumstead to Welling.

The house ticked all the boxes. It was a solid mid-terrace Victorian house, bay fronted on a quiet road, and a bus ride away from Woolwich station or a 25-minute walk away from Welling station. Behind the house was a large, wooded area, and although the house needed work, including a new boiler, a new kitchen, and an overhaul of the roof, it was by far the best I had seen. I had the budget to do the work that the property desperately needed, and so I made an offer of £69,000, and we agreed on £70,000.

I was excited at the prospect of owning a house and I rushed home to Kingsbury, phoned my parents and then rang Nadia, who immediately invited me over to Goodmayes. I had endured enough train travel at that stage and so we agreed to meet up later during the week.

When I finally got to spend time with Nadia later in the week, there was the ritualistic meal, followed by drinks, then the move to the bedroom for a passionate encounter. The more time we spent together, the more relaxed and uninhibited she had become. Her entire wardrobe had changed in terms of underwear and nightwear.

That night I could see something was on her mind, when I enquired, she told me that her French cousin was coming to stay with her. Her cousin Frederick had set his heart on becoming a commercial airline pilot. A prerequisite for any airline pilot was good English, and his was simply not good enough.

The 'family' had decided that what he needed to get his English up to the standard required was to live and work in England for a while.

Nadia told me that Frederick was in his mid-twenties, and she hardly knew him. She had managed to secure Frederick a temporary position at Shearson Hutton.

Nadia's main concern was that he was moving into the flat with her. This created a big issue for her, Nadia did not want her family to know she had a 'boyfriend,' and that meant if I came to stay, I would be sleeping back in the spare bed.

While Frederick was living with Nadia, there could be no overt signs we were anything other than just friends. I could see she was torn and so I suggested that we make more use of my flat during Frederick's stay, which she happily accepted.

Upon Frederick's arrival, Nadia came over to my flat in Kingsbury a couple of nights a week, but that quickly became once a week and then even that stopped. Frederick did not want to be left alone in the Goodmayes flat, and under increasing pressure from him and Nadia's mother, Nadia stopped leaving her flat.

Nadia simply did not want to explain anything about us to her mother, and so giving in to Frederick was the easiest option for her.

The one and only time I did go over to Goodmayes while Frederick was there, I was resigned to having to sleep on a beanbag bed in the lounge, which was where Frederick was sleeping on the sofa bed. Somehow that night, Frederick convinced Nadia that he didn't want to be in the same room as a 'stranger' and so he ended up in Nadia's bed with her. Nadia wasn't happy about that at all, so I just did not bother visiting again.

I did meet Nadia subsequently one lunchtime, but by this time it was apparent that Frederick was going to be around for much longer than either of us had anticipated and our relationship just ended.

My flat sale was completed just before the August deadline, and I moved to Abbey Wood.

My move was not without problems. I headed off in my car in advance of the removal lorry to collect the keys from the estate agents in Welling High Street. I was half an hour early and so walked up and down, getting a feel for the local high street.

When I was finally in possession of the keys, I drove back the short distance to Woodbrook Road, and as I pulled up outside I could see one of large glass panels of the front ground-floor bay was covered with a sheet of hardboard.

When I entered the house, things got worse, with the main bedroom contained a very manky double bed and soiled mattress and the kitchen was a mess.

I called the estate agent, just as the lorry with all my furniture pulled up. The removal guys were great, helping me put the offending bed and mattress into the back garden.

The estate agent called the seller, who apologised for the window, saying his son had thrown a stone through it just as they were leaving, and he agreed to pay for the repair. As for the double bed, he said he thought I would want it!

Luckily, one of my new neighbours, who was fireman by trade, owned a van and was happy to help me load the bed and mattress into it and deposit them at the local dump. By the end of the day, I was exhausted.

Once settled into my new Abbey Wood house, I quickly recruited tradesmen to fit a new kitchen, new carpets and to overhaul the roof.

I made a major mistake in not checking the loft space before the builders started replacing the roof.

Once they had finished, I went up into the large loft space and found a cardboard box filled with 78 rpm records. On top was a large tile that had fallen directly into the box, smashing every single one of the stacked records. Amongst them were original Glen Miller and Bill Haley records, and I was cursing myself as I consigned them to the dustbin.

My two new neighbours were genuinely nice. To the left was a young couple who had a large Doberman who, if I ventured into the garden, growled at me every time. I quickly added the erection of a new fence to the list of early jobs.

On the other side was my hero on moving day, Fireman Laurie, his wife Janice and their first child who was a babe in arms. Laurie was a part-time

WoodBrook Road after the roof repair

builder as well as a firefighter. He had built his own ground-floor extension and was happily offering to do the same for me. But a three-bedroom house was more than adequate for my needs.

I tried walking to Welling station on my first commute to the City. I was exhausted by the time I got to the station, and I figured that in anything other than mild weather, it was going to be a bit too much. Instead, I started getting on the 96 bus from Wickham Lane and travelling down Plumstead High Street to Woolwich. The train service from Woolwich station was excellent, and so I decided to do my daily commute from there.

Spurred on in part by Nigel Lawson cutting taxes, 1988 had seen a return of high inflation to the UK economy. To combat this, Lawson started a hike in interest rates which would double from 7.5 per cent to 15 per cent in 1989.

On one memorable occasion when Nigel Lawson was on the BBC news announcing a hike in interest rates, Barry Fontera, in frustration, stood at his desk and shouted over to Prash, 'Prash, get my hat and coat.'

Prash jumped up and dashed to the nearby coat stand, handing the garments to Barry as a hush fell around the trading room. Barry pointed excitedly at the TV and said, 'Prash, you see the fat man on the telly.' Prash nodded. 'Well, the fat man is going down!' With that, Barry walked out of the office.

For the rest of the day, we watched the TV, avidly waiting for news that the chancellor had been attacked by a mad American. It never happened, but it was a typical example of Barry's often flamboyant nature.

In November, I had my official housewarming party, which I combined as a Halloween party. Lesley, Rowland, Linda Hicks, and her husband Chris, as well as a dozen or so of my work colleagues attended. So did my new neighbours.

Sadly, not attending were David Peart and Paul Collister. David lived in Bedford, so it was a bit too much of a journey, while Ollie was at this stage heavily involved with a young lady called Denna who he seemed reluctant to introduce to us.

Ollie's nickname for Denna was 'Mogwai' after the cute cuddly creature in the *Gremlins* film that mutated into a beast if you got it wet. Ollie said that Denna looked cute on the outside but often mutated into something less friendly. Knowing Ollie, we felt safe in assuming that the cause of this mutation was him.

One famous story about Paul Collister and Denna came soon after they were married.

Ollie played Sunday league football, and a couple of his teammates had a housewarming party scheduled. They told Ollie that lots of his ex-school friends would be attending, and he was invited to come along. Ollie told them he didn't think he would be allowed out and he certainly didn't want Denna mixing with his football mates, who she had already classed as a bunch of juvenile idiots.

Having taken abuse from his friends about having to ask permission, Ollie hit upon an idea. Denna had been nagging him to do jobs around the house, including cutting the grass, so on the Saturday of the party he got up early and got cracking.

Having done all the jobs Denna had been asking him to do Denna handed Ollie a cold beer and was full of praise for his endeavours. Deciding now was the time, Ollie asked Denna if she would mind him going to his friends housewarming party. Denna relented but told Ollie he must come home at a reasonable time that night, to make sure he was not falling down drunk and to behave.

Ollie set off for the party, promptly got completely drunk and fell asleep on the lounge floor.

The next morning, waking up with a hangover amongst party debris and a group of fellow party goers. Ollie realised what he had done and in a complete panic, he went to the bathroom to freshen up, wondering what he was going to say to Denna.

As he combed his hair, he thought something did not look quite right, and then staring intently into the mirror he realised what it was – he had no eyebrows. He went back into the lounge to demand an explanation, wanting to know which one of his ex-school friends had shaved his eyebrows off. The culprit identified himself and reminded Ollie that he had done the same to him two years earlier.

As the host of the party came down to see what the fuss was about, Ollie announced he would be moving in because Denna would kick him out anyway. He told his mates that he had not only failed to return at a reasonable time, as he had promised, he had got drunk and now had no eyebrows, he was 'dead.'

His mates refused to believe that Denna would be that tough on him, and so the host and the friend responsible for his lack of eyebrows volunteered to explain to Denna in person. They loaded Ollie into the car, and all headed off for his house.

As they approached the house, Ollie completely lost his nerve, telling his two mates he was not going to get any closer.

They all got out of the car, but Ollie elected to hide behind a large tree at the bottom of his drive as his laughing friends walked up the door to explain to Denna what had happened.

Ollie said he heard the front door open, and his two friends begin to explain. Then he saw his friends running past his position behind the tree shouting 'RUN OLLIE RUN,' causing Ollie to break into a sprint alongside them as Denna pursued all three down the road, wielding a broom above her head.

I have never been able to confirm the validity of this story but knowing Ollie it should be divided by two – he did like to exaggerate.

My solo house living at 87 Woodbrook Road did not last long, as my brother Robin moved in, having finished his association with my Uncle Wally.

Robin was taking time out, having successfully applied to the Metropolitan Police, who were more than happy to take him being ex-forces. He had to wait for the next intake to the Hendon Police Academy.

Meanwhile, he got a job at a local garage in Welling, putting his Army vehicle mechanic training to effective use. He moved into 87 Woodbrook Road in early December, although he was spending most weekends back in Dibden Purlieu, staying with school friends in the village.

The central operations Christmas party was once again at the Good Friends restaurant in Spitalfields. Dave Peart and I were invited along as honorary members of the back-office team. As usual, Gwen Thompson came along to keep us all on our toes, and it was the usual goodhearted evening that we had all come to expect.

Just before we broke up for the Christmas festivities, I had an early present when Geoff Swainson advised me that Denni Machi had permission from Harris Futures for a trip to London in the first half of 1989.

I wasted little time picking up the phone to talk to her, and we discussed what she wanted to do while she was in London. I convinced her that we should have an evening meal in Chinatown, but Denni also wanted to see a West End show. I told her to leave that with me and that I would get us tickets to a good show.

1989

On the 21st March 1989, I had my only ever stay in hospital thus far.

I have a deep dislike of anything medical, known as 'white coat' syndrome. This includes dentists, and my mother also has had a huge dislike of dentists. Just the sound of that dentist's drill is enough to give me palpitations.

During the period that my mother had worked as the deputy manager of Horne Brothers' Duke Street branch, just off the Strand, one of her colleagues suggested a private dentist to her.

The dentist was called Linda Goldman, and she was based just down the road from the shop in Covent Garden. Linda registered the bare minimum number of NHS patients required by law at that time, and she agreed to take mother on as an NHS patient. They became friends, and so when an NHS slot became available, mother signed me up.

I had huge tonsils; they had plagued me throughout my childhood with frequent sore throats. If I got a cold, it always went straight for my tonsils, making it difficult to swallow. My college dabble with smoking had made things much worse. My tonsils became 'pitted,' and not long after I started seeing Linda Goldman she said she didn't like the look of them.

After one nasty infection, which was treated with a medical dose of prescription mouthwash called Oraldene, I suffered a mild blood poisoning. The doctor kept renewing my prescription, and according to Linda I should have been off the Oraldene after just one bottle. This episode proved to be the end of Linda's patience with my tonsils, and she told me a good friend of hers was the ear, nose, and throat specialist at St Bartholomew's Hospital, and she would get me a consultation.

I went to see Linda's friend, and the doctor took one look at my huge tonsils and said, 'They need to come out. You'll get Quinsy. It's not a matter of if, it is when, and Quinsy is nasty.' He then told me I had two choices: either I could get an NHS appointment which would be 48 hours' notice and I would be off for a week, two if an infection set in, or I could go private and be treated when it suited me.

The doctor had been advised by Linda Goldman that I worked in the financial services industry, and he asked who my boss was. I knew this was going to lead to another of my chats with Nick Grason, and so I gave him Nick's name. The next day, a letter arrived at my home, addressed to Nick Grason, and I went to see him armed with the letter.

Nick read the letter and gave it back to me. 'Well, Mr Parker, we cannot afford to lose you at such short notice, so based on the price indicated in the letter, I agree to fund you going private.'

My operation was booked for the 21st March 1989 at the St John & St Elizabeth Hospital in Grove Road, where the doctor did his non-NHS work. I had a private room, and once I arrived I changed into a hospital gown and was told I had an hour wait. Before long I was on the trolley, anesthetised and wheeled in.

When I woke, my tonsils were in a glass container on my bedside table. My bed and room were strewn with open men's magazines showing naked ladies, and there were two huge bags of crisps on the guest chair next to my bed.

I had a very sore throat. It felt like I had swallowed a cup of glass. I reached for a drink of water and, as I sat up, a nurse came into my room to help me and to give me a quick once over.

My voice was incredibly quiet as talking hurt my throat, but I gestured to the magazines and the nurse laughed. 'That was your friends. They came earlier when you were still asleep. They watched some television and then said they had to go, but they left you the crisps and your reading material.'

I found out afterwards that Rowland Dunn and Andrew Mersh had come to see me.

I was asleep, recovering in the room, but they were allowed in. Obviously they had to work the next day, so giving up on me waking, they had left. I had finally woken at 11 pm.

The next day, I was allowed to go home. Robin came to collect me in my car. The doctor said it was 50/50 as to whether an infection would set in, as it was a big wound. If I experienced any significant bleeding, I was to go straight to my GP.

To my mind, it was never 'if' I got an infection – I knew my tonsils would have the last laugh, and they did. Three days after I returned home, I started bleeding and rushed to my GP to get antibiotics.

What didn't help was waking up the morning after my return home to find a sweet jar next to my bed with a field mouse looking at me from the inside.

My lovely brother had found the tell-tail signs that a mouse was in the kitchen at 87 Woodbrook Road. He looked for where the mouse may have managed to get in and found an air brick missing at the rear of the house.

Having sorted the air brick, he rigged a trap, balancing one of the sweet jars my parents had given me from their sweet shop and using a Cadburys chocolate bar as bait. It turned out the mouse couldn't resist, and as it went into the sweet jar after the chocolate, the jar tipped back onto its base, trapping the mouse inside. Instead of turning the mouse out, Robin stuck it next to my bed in the sweet jar as a surprise for when I woke up. It was certainly that!

The next day, we went out into the woods behind the house and released the mouse back into the wild!

♪♪♪

I had to wait patiently until May 1989 for Denni Machi's visit to London to finally arrive.

Denni would be in England for just under a week, arriving on a Sunday and scheduled to leave the following Friday. It was agreed that she would stay with Geoff Swainson and his wife in their central London apartment, something she was more than happy to do.

For someone who had spent little time away from her native Chicago, her first trip abroad was a huge adventure. Staying with people she knew made the trip significantly less daunting.

On the Monday after her arrival, Denni was due to spend a day with Geoff in the Harris London office, and he and his wife would be taking Denni out for a meal that evening.

I had agreed with Geoff that I would manage all the arrangements at Czarnikow. I would personally give her a tour of the 66 Mark Lane office and make sure Denni met everyone she needed to see.

I told Geoff that on the Tuesday I planned to introduce Denni to Ollie and David and show her around the various trading desks at the Czarnikow office. Then I would escort her to central operations, where I would introduce her to Paul Thompson and his team.

Once that was done, I would then take her for lunch. I had cleared it with Dave Peart that after lunch I would take Denni to see Tower Bridge and the Tower of London for the remainder of the afternoon.

Denni would be back to 66 Mark Lane on Wednesday morning for me to introduce her to Nick Grason and the traders on the financial trading desk and,

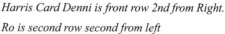

Harris Card Denni is front row 2nd from Right.
Ro is second row second from left

Harris futures team. Denni black and white top near centre. Ro left. Jennifer Johnson to the right of centre behind the girl in red

in particular, Denni would spend time with Barry Fontera and Prash Laud.

David Peart had arranged with Geoff Swainson to take Geoff and Denni down to see the LIFFE floor on the Wednesday afternoon. David had taken Geoff previously, but Geoff was happy to accompany Denni on another visit.

I was scheduled to take Denni out on the Wednesday evening to Chinatown, and for the Thursday evening I had secured two tickets to see *Return to the Forbidden planet* at the Cambridge Theatre, which was advertised as 'Shakespeare's forgotten rock and roll masterpiece.' I had heard good things about the play – it was another cult hit in the way that *The Rocky Horror Picture Show* had been, and I had my fingers crossed that Denni would like it.

On the Sunday of Denni's arrival in the UK, I started to get butterflies in my stomach. It was the only time I can remember actually wanting the weekend out of the way and to be on that train heading from Woolwich to London Bridge.

The Monday was even more un-settling, knowing Denni was just down the road in London and the anticipation of the week ahead building.

I had no idea what may have changed during the long gap following my trip to Chicago. I was hoping that our continued banter on the phone meant we would simply pick up where we had left off.

I made my daily call to Harris Futures to agree the bond positions with Ro Dimenza-Meo. Ro wasn't interested in the figures; she was extremely excited about Denni's visit to London.

Ro insisted I went through the full itinerary that we had planned for Denni during her stay. I could hear her relaying it to the others in her office, and she made me pledge to give her a daily update on how things were going.

That Tuesday morning, I sat on the train wearing my best shirt-and-tie combo and had a bottle of aftershave in my pocket. I headed to the second floor as usual and took my seat, watching the clock, much to the amusement of Paul Collister.

At 9.30 on the dot, I got the call from ground-floor reception, and I headed for the lifts. I was growing increasingly concerned about the reaction we were going to get when I walked Denni back onto the financial trading floor.

As the lift door opened on the ground floor, I could see Denni sitting demurely on the sofa in an unbuttoned white coat, crisp white blouse, and black trousers. As I walked over from the lifts, I spotted no less than three of the messengers leaning on the reception counter, looking at me with beaming smiles.

Seeing me step out of the lift, Denni stood, picked up a small bag and walked toward me with her usual cheeky grin. 'Hello Mr Parker,' she said in her familiar accent.

I gave her a hug and kiss on the cheek and then I escorted her to the lift.

'Not as big as Harris, Denni,' I said to her as the lift doors closed.

'No,' she replied, 'and Czarnikow is in a very disappointing modern building. I haven't seen much of the City of London yet, but from the bit I have seen there are so many lovely old buildings.'

The lift door opened, and I took a deep breath before leading her to the left, towards the double doors that took us straight onto the financial trading floor.

As I held one of the double doors open for her, I could see all the eyes of the traders and brokers focus on Denni, but they all stayed thankfully quiet. We walked to the coat stand and I offered to take Denni's coat.

I slipped the coat from her shoulders and hung it up on the coat stand, gesturing quickly towards the other end of the floor away from the trading desk, to where David Peart and Paul Collister sat waiting. I walked her down and introduced her to David and then to Ollie and then offered her the seat next to mine.

We had a quick chat and got Denni settled a little before I started the tour. We walked around the various floors showing her the commodity desks including coffee, cocoa, and the all-important sugar desk on the fourth floor.

Then we headed back to the second floor and into the Oil trading room before taking the short walk to the central operations department. There, I introduced Denni to Paul Thompson and Gavin Brodie, and I left her in their company, telling Denni that I would be back to collect her for lunch.

Denni spent the morning with Paul and his team, and when I came back at 12.30 she was sitting with Sue Bright and Karen Loftus who were showing her the LIFFE Trade Registration System.

TRS was a more advanced exchange-matching engine than anything currently on offer by the CME and CBOT, so Denni was fascinated.

When she noticed me, Denni smiled and said to the girls, 'Mr Parker is taking me to lunch, and then we are having a tour of some of the historical sights. Isn't that right, Mr Parker?'

'That is the plan,' I replied. As Denni stood to say goodbye, Sue silently mouthed to me, 'She is lovely.'

We collected Denni's coat from the coat stand, and I managed to get us off the financial trading floor without any comment.

I took Denni to the George and Vulture at 3 Castle Court, but I made a point of walking her past the Jamaica Inn first.

The Jamaica Inn was acknowledged by some people as the real home of the futures markets. In one of its street-facing windows sat an incredibly old book which was purported to record the very first futures trades.

The 'Jampot' as we called it, actually dates from 1869, and its origins go back to Samuel Pepys' day, when it was London's first coffee house.

Our venue for lunch, the George and Vulture, was just a short walk on from the Jamaica Inn. There has been an inn on the same site since 1142, and it is mentioned in the 1837 novel *The Pickwick Papers* by Charles Dickens, who frequently went there himself for a drink.

Having done a little homework beforehand, I was able to impress Denni with these facts as we entered the wooden panelled entrance and waited to be seated.

The George and Vulture was a little dark due to the old oak panelling on all the walls and the closeness of the nearby buildings, but it was full of atmosphere. We were escorted by the waiter to a table with two wooden benches on either side. Denni slid into one side of the table next to the window, and I slipped in opposite her.

It felt good to finally have her to myself and to be able to really catch up.

I pointed out a picture of Charles Dickens that hung on the old walls of the George and Vulture. Denni absolutely loved the historic start to her tour. She was eagerly taking in the ambience and loving the very traditional English menu when it was presented to her.

I explained that she would have to get used to UK-sized food portions, and so a starter would be worthwhile. She shook her head, saying she was saving herself for dessert and ordered the steak with bubble and squeak and then couldn't resist the 'spotted dick and custard' for dessert, all of which she washed down with generous glasses of red wine.

I could not resist asking Denni how the food compared with the food at Arnold's from *Happy Days* and was rewarded with a playful kick in the shins under the table and told to 'behave.'

As the weather was clear, I asked Denni if she would prefer to walk to the Tower of London so we could take in some more of the sights, which she was more than happy to do, despite her heels.

I took the opportunity to walk via Leadenhall Market, down Fenchurch Street, and then on towards the Tower of London via Crutched Friars, showing her the home of the ICCH.

Denni was having fun, taking lots of photos as we went. As we arrived at Trinity Square, Denni was particularly taken with the gothic arch outside number ten (used on the opening credits of tv show *the Professionals)* and asked me to pose in front of the building, saying Ro would never forgive her if she didn't bring at least one picture of me back to Chicago.

We walked on towards the Tower of London, and as we approached, Denni took my arm and said to me, 'Are you having fun with the American tourist?' I laughed and said I was, and then added that it was great to see her again.

Denni was keen to go straight into the Tower of London, but I told her to be patient, and we walked around and down to the riverfront where she saw clearly, for the first time, Tower Bridge, and that was it – she went snap happy, taking numerous photos.

I asked her to pose in front of Tower Bridge, taking a couple of paces back and waiting for a suitable gap in the passing crowd.

Having taken a picture, she held up her hand, took off her coat and, handing it to me, started to pose again.

Then, in typical tourist fashion, she managed to flag down a passer-by and asked her to take one of the two of us together. Not to be outdone, I took off my jacket before we posed together.

Denni thanked the photographer and recovered her coat from the railings, putting it on before taking my arm, smiling at me, and saying, 'Onward, Mr Parker.'

On we went, heading into the Tower of London, passing the two Beefeaters at the entrance. I managed to get us past without Denni wanting to pose with one or both of them. By now, Denni was into her full playful mode and enjoying being both the American tourist and my guest.

We had to stop at the gift shop so she could buy a new roll of film, and then we completed the entire tour of the Tower, including the Crown Jewels. By the time we walked out the Tower of London, it was late. I flagged down a black cab for the short return to Bucklesbury House to deliver Denni back to Geoff Swainson.

We walked into the compact Harris Futures office, where Geoff was waiting patiently for us. Geoff explained that the plan had changed and that they were now going to have a quiet meal at his new home that evening. This was on the basis I was taking Denni out for the next two evenings before her return flight.

This reminded Denni to enquire where I was taking her on the Thursday. I had told her it was a West End show but refused to give her any details – I merely smiled and said she would have to wait, which prompted a pout in response. With that, I wished them both goodnight and made my way to the nearby Cannon Street station for my train home.

On Wednesday morning, Denni was back at 66 Mark Lane nice and early. This time, she wasn't waiting on the sofa but was at the reception desk, getting the full attention of the messenger department. As I walked up to rescue her, I got my usual smile, and we headed up to the financial trading floor.

This time, the traders were a little less attentive, until I took her coat for her.

Denni was in a short black skirt and powder-blue buttoned blouse – even I did a double-take as I held her coat. I hesitated a second too long and got a playful dig in the ribs. 'Behave, Mr Parker,' she whispered but with a smile which I took to mean she was happy with my reaction.

I quickly walked Denni towards Nick Grason's office. Jennette, held up her hand and said, 'Nick is on a call at the moment, Kevin. I don't think he'll be long. I'll get you when he's free.'

With that, we made our way back towards David and Ollie, but we didn't have to wait long before Jennette was gesturing for us to head for Nick's office.

Nick Grason had, what would be considered to be, a 'posh' voice, and as we walked in and I introduced them, I could see that Denni was fascinated by his accent. My mind went back to the boys in New York and Guy Morrison holding court in the nightclub, and a wry smile crossed my face.

'Denni,' Nick repeated after we had sat down. 'Is that short for Denise?' he enquired.

Denni nodded. 'That's what my birth certificate says, Nick, but I have always been called Denni. If my mother calls me Denise, I know I'm in whole lot of trouble.'

Nick chuckled and he gestured towards me. 'Is Mr Parker looking after you?'

Denni didn't answer immediately, looking at me with a look of mischievous pleasure. 'Mr Parker has been the perfect gentleman so far, although he won't tell me where he's taking me tomorrow night.'

I could see that Nick had taken an instant liking to our American guest. He looked at me and said, 'Is that right, Mr Parker? Well, I'm sure it'll be somewhere nice, Denni. If not, let me know.'

With a look of victory on her face, she replied, 'I will do that, Nick.'

We chatted about Harris Futures and the new London office, and Nick enquired about the plans for the rest of her stay. I explained that Denni was to be formerly introduced to the financial desk traders once we left his office, and that Denni would be spending some time with Barry and Prash. Later in the afternoon, David Peart was taking Denni to the LIFFE floor, accompanied by Geoff Swainson. Then I told Nick that I was taking Denni to Chinatown for a meal after work.

Denni explained that Geoff Swainson was giving her a big tourist tour on Thursday to see Buckingham Palace, the Houses of Parliament, Westminster Abbey and finishing at St Paul's Cathedral on her way back to Geoff's flat in Dalston, to get ready for my mysterious trip to the theatre.

With that, we left Nick, and I introduced Denni to the financial futures desk, starting with Roy McDermott, Philip Plumber, Richard 'Dicky' Gibbs, Andrew Todd, Adam Chapman and of course Barry Fontera and Prashant 'Prash' Laud.

Barry was delighted to have a fellow American and Chicago native in the office, and he quickly sat her down and started to explain what he was doing. Barry was an entertainer and a lady's man, and he was soon charming Denni.

I left them to it and retreated back to my desk with Dave and Ollie to get on with my work.

As lunchtime approached, Denni said goodbye to the trade desk and came over to say goodbye to us, as she was heading off to the Harris office for a business lunch. David said he would see Geoff and Denni at 2.00 outside the Royal Exchange for their LIFFE floor visit, and I told her I would see her at 6.00 at their office for our trip to Chinatown.

I walked with her to the coat stand and held the coat for her. As she slipped her arms into the sleeves, she said in her loud American voice, 'Good boy, Mr Parker.' I should have expected it, I could see Dicky Gibbs' shoulders moving up and down as he stifled a laugh, and I sensed the others trying not to laugh aloud.

I escorted Denni to the lift, and as she was about to get in, she gave me a quick peck on the cheek and said, 'See you later, Mr Parker.' And with that, the lift doors closed.

As I walked back onto the trading floor, the guys could contain themselves no longer, and the laughter roared.

For the next couple of months, they used that line whenever they could – if I made coffee, delivered information or reports, I always got 'Good boy, Mr Parker' in a fake American accents.

At 5:45 precisely, I made my way over to Bucklesbury House in Walbrook and Harris's office to collect Denni.

We headed down Cannon Street Tube station and made our way to Embankment on the Circle line.

Once out of Embankment tube we walked up to Charing Cross then on to Trafalgar Square to enable Denni to see Nelson's Column, Admiralty Arch, and the National Gallery. Then we made our way to Charing Cross Road before cutting down Little Newport Street into Chinatown.

I had booked us a table into the Golden Dragon, a restaurant I had been to before and knew to be good.

Once sat at a table I suggested a set meal with several courses. The one I suggested included dumplings to start, followed by shredded duck and then a multitude of different dishes for the main. Denni handed me back her menu and said she was more than happy to go with my suggestion.

Once our drinks arrived, Denni immediately tried to get me to divulge what I had planned for the following evening, even using the excuse that she needed to know so she could dress appropriately, but I held my ground.

We chatted happily about her visit so far, her time with Geoff and his wife, and how sad she was that her trip would soon be over. I confided that I had felt exactly the same on my trip to Chicago, it all went by far too quickly.

Denni, like most Americans, loved London and all the history, and she was looking forward to her planned tour with Geoff the next day. She told me that she was under instructions from Ro to get as many pictures as she could, and with that she pulled her camera out of her handbag. When the waitress came back with our starter, Denni asked her to take a picture of us both.

As always with Denni, the time just slipped by.

We finished in the restaurant at 9.00, so I suggested the short walk to Covent Garden. We walked around, taking in all the old buildings, and when we discovered a couple of buskers, Denni insisted on stopping and listening to them play.

We stopped at a couple of different drinking establishments, and then I noticed the time was approaching 11.00, we dashed down to Fleet Street and grabbed a black cab to head back to Dalston.

As we climbed into the back seat, panting a little, Denni rested her head on my shoulder, and so I naturally put my arm around her. We sat like that silently as Denni looked out the window at all the sights. Even the red double decker buses held an interest for her, and as we passed St Paul's Cathedral she was entranced.

When we eventually pulled up outside Geoff's rented house, Denni told me that she would make sure to be at Mark Lane at five o'clock to say goodbye to everyone before we set off for the theatre.

For the very first time, things felt awkward. I wanted to kiss her, but I was desperate not to overstep the mark. I really couldn't work out where we were relationship wise. Denni made the decision for me, kissing me on the lips quickly before getting out of the cab.

I watched her walk up to the door and knock, and I waited the few seconds for Geoff to open the door, before telling the cab driver to get me to London Bridge station as fast as he could.

As I boarded the train at Woolwich the next morning, I started fretting over whether I had made a huge mistake with my choice of play. Why hadn't I gone for a safe option like *Les Miserable* or *Phantom of the Opera*?

What if this was a huge disappointment for Denni?

This could be her one and only trip to London, and instead of playing safe and going for one of the big headline shows I had gone for a cult musical version of a 1950s Lesley Nielson B movie! Yet in my gut, I felt Denni was more of a rock chick and that seeing something a little more unusual would be her thing.

My doubts kept growing throughout the day. There was nothing I could do about it.

Ollie noticed I was distracted, but he decided it was because Denni was leaving, so I let him continue digging me– after all, I had to admit it was a factor. I wanted her to leave on a high and look back fondly on her trip to London, and me!

The clock seemed to be static, the day dragged, then at last I got a call at five o'clock from Sid at reception. I quickly headed to the lifts and down to reception. As the lift door opened, there was Denni in her white coat which was unbuttoned to reveal a deep-blue dress.

I gestured for her to come into the lift, with my hand on the lift door to keep it open. As the doors closed behind Denni and the lift started to move, she immediately looked me in the eye and said, 'Mr Parker, you've had your fun.

You can tell me where we're going now.' I just smiled as the lift stopped, and when the doors opened and we made our way onto the financial trading floor, I left the question hanging.

As usual, I offered to take her coat, and once again I was surprised as the coat slipped from her shoulders and the dress was revealed. It was formal, cut just above the knee in length, with short sleeves, but as she turned, I realised the dress was low cut.

This was the first time I had seen Denni in anything that I would classify as overtly sexual and the very first time she had revealed any cleavage. She looked amazing, and I realised from the unusual hush that descended around the trading floor that I was not the only one who was admiring the dress.

Denni looked at me. 'Do you like it? I bought it today. I decided that the one I had travelled over with was not good enough for a trip to a top London theatre.'

'You look amazing,' I said. Suddenly, guilt piled on top of the growing doubts. Top London theatre! What had I done?

I couldn't help looking her up and down, taking in the nylon-clad legs and the extremely high heels. Then I realised I was staring in front of the entire trading desk.

I quickly walked Denni into central operations where Sue, Karen, Kim, and Amelia quickly surrounded her, telling her she looked great and inevitably turning on me to ask where I was taking her. I kept fending the question off, saying it was a surprise.

Denni then said goodbye to the four girls, and we went around Paul Thompson, Gavin Brodie, and the rest of the guys before heading for Nick Grason's office.

Denni made a point of reminding Nick she would be reporting back on where we went.

We did the rounds of the trading floor to Barry, Prash and the rest of the desk traders before finishing with Ollie and David. Then it was time to head for the coat stand.

As I slipped her coat off the peg and held it up for Denni to put on, I heard Barry's deep American voice shout from behind his trading desk, 'Good boy, Mr Parker.' Once again, the office, including Denni, burst into laughter.

I grabbed my coat and we set off for the lifts down to the ground floor. As the lift doors closed and we were alone briefly, Denni was still laughing and then she looked over at me and said, 'Sorry.'

I replied, 'Don't worry, the novelty will wear off … in ten years or so.'

We went to the Fenchurch Colony wine bar at the back of Czarnikow's office and had a couple of drinks and ate some food before setting off. We grabbed a black cab from Eastcheap, and I said, 'Cambridge Theatre please.' As I sat back, I thought, 'Here we go' and crossed my fingers

Denni took my hand and looked me in the eye. 'Cambridge Theatre?' she said. 'At least I know where we're going!'

As the cab travelled towards the West End, Denni told me how much she had enjoyed her tour of London with Geoff earlier in the day. Denni had taken pictures of Buckingham Palace and all the other sites and had managed to get through five rolls of film. But her trip inside St Paul's Cathedral had made the biggest impression on her.

The Cambridge Theatre is on the corner of Earlham Street in Covent Garden, and as we pulled up outside and I paid the cab driver, the huge billboard above the entrance was unmissable.

Denni looked up at the huge picture of a spaceman running from a green tentacled monster, in large yellow writing, was *Return to the Forbidden Planet*. There was no hiding it now.

I looked for a reaction, but I just got a wry smile.

We went into the foyer of the theatre, and I bought a couple of glossy programmes from the vendor. We checked in our coats, and then we entered the auditorium.

As we entered the aisle into the stalls, a female cast member in a bright red uniform and huge beehive hairdo greeted us and, after checking our tickets, showed us to our seats. We were in row H in the middle, with a splendid view of the stage. Denni looked about as other cast members showed people to their seats and around the historic theatre.

As we settled into our seats and Denni started to consult the programme. It was very obvious from the pictures that it was a rock musical. The programme listed all the well-known musical numbers that would feature in the production from the 1950s and 1960s. She silently flipped the pages and finally leaned into me and said, 'I feel a little overdressed.'

I shook my head and said, 'No, you're fine.'

Denni smirked at me. 'You're only saying that because I'm flashing my boobs.' Before I could think of a reply, she continued, 'Is this the same *Forbidden Planet* that Lesley Nielson starred in?'

I nodded. Denni frowned a little and said, 'I don't remember that being a musical.'

I laughed and gestured to the programme, flipping past the pictures of the cast in action and the list of the songs and music to a brief explanation about the origins of the show which referred to the film.

I knew that the jury was still out, but Denni hadn't walked out of the theatre or hit me yet, so I figured she was prepared to give me the benefit of the doubt.

The theatre filled quickly – the show was a sell-out – and as I looked around, I noted that our fellow audience members were a very mixed bag in terms of attire. Some people were formally dressed like us. Others were more casually dressed, but many wore *Return to the Forbidden Planet* T-shirts, and I guessed they had been to see the show before. That boded well.

Finally, the curtain went up, a huge screen descended, and Sir Patrick Moore appeared on the screen to narrate the start of the play. The screen retracted and the curtain opened fully to reveal the main stage set featuring a spaceship control room with several levels, and actors all in the same red space suits we had seen cast members wearing earlier.

After moments of initial dialogue, the entire stage erupted with the opening tune of 'Wipe Out' with pounding on multiple drum sets that had been well hidden amongst the spaceship interior. Then cast members equipped with electric guitars joined in, and the growing wall of noise was followed by a couple of cast members playing trumpets.

The sound was amazing, and the cast revealed that they were not only good actors and singers but also expert musicians. The wave of music was bringing me out in goosebumps.

I felt Denni squeeze my hand, and in those opening first few minutes, any and all doubts vanished. I had made the right choice.

The songs kept coming – 'Great Balls of Fire,' 'Don't Let Me Be Misunderstood,' 'Good Vibrations,' 'Young Girl,' 'Only the Lonely' – and by the intermission, we were both ecstatic at the pure quality of the show.

Denni leaned in close and whispered in my ear, 'I love it.'

We joined the huge queue for a drink during the intermission and then settled back into our seats. Before long, the second half of the show had started.

The musical hits and pace of the show never stopped, and early in the second act people started standing and dancing, and then a real party atmosphere set in.

As the second act finished, we joined the shouts for more, and I noted nobody moved for the exits.

The encore was a musical treat as the cast relaxed by starting off the encore with 'Monster Mash.' Everyone was dancing in the aisles and wherever they could.

Denni kicked off her heels and we danced and sang, and then she pulled me into the central aisle, and we continued dancing together as best we could.

When the final musical notes sounded and everyone was cheering and applauding, the cast took another bow before retreating behind the curtain as it came down for the last time.

I turned to Denni, and she just leapt into my arms. Caught up in the moment, our lips met, and a full-on enthusiastic kiss followed. How long we were there, I don't know. People filed out, leaving us where we were.

As we finally let go of each other, I glanced at my watch and nearly fainted – it was 11.00. I had to work the next day, and Denni had to pack for her flight back home to Chicago.

Some of the cast on stage at Cambridge Theatre

We dashed out of the theatre and hunted for an available black cab, which seemed to take forever as we competed with all the other people filing out of theatres. Finally, I spotted one for hire and we piled into it, and I told the driver to go to London Bridge station via Dalston.

As we rested back into the seat, I put my arm around a sweaty Denni, and she angled herself so that she was leaning back into my arms. I silently cursed myself. Why did I keep falling for the impossible – married or living half a world away?

Return to Forbidden Planet

We sat quietly as the cab headed down Fleet Street, then I said to her softly, 'What are the chances of you moving to the London office?'

Denni looked up at me for a moment before replying, 'None I'm afraid, Mr Parker. There's not enough going on in London, and even if there was, my family are all in Chicago.' I nodded sadly, and she reached back and brushed my cheek with her finger. 'It's a lovely thought though, Mr Parker.'

All too quickly, we arrived outside Geoff's for the last time. Denni thanked me for looking after her and quickly kissed me on the lips and in a flash, she was gone. I watched her go inside the house and then the cab raced off for London Bridge.

I had to sprint through the station and down the platform to catch the last Woolwich train.

As the train left the platform, I was in an emotional turmoil. I had this euphoria that the evening had gone so well and yet this crushing depression that Denni was heading back to Chicago, and I may never see her again.

On Friday as I sat on the Cannon Street-bound train, in my head I played around with a dozen scenarios, including my "An Officer and a Gentleman" scenario of turning up at Heathrow, snatching Denni up into my arms and heading off into the sunset.

I went through the motions in the office. I was exhausted, mentally, and physically. I made my daily call to Ro and told her that Denni and I had enjoyed a great evening at the theatre. Ro said she was really looking forward to Denni coming back on the Monday and hearing all about her trip and seeing the pictures.

As Friday came and went, I headed back to Abbey Wood feeling deeply sorry for myself.

Post Denni's trip, things slowly returned to normal. I spoke to Denni every day, and Ro told me she had seen the pictures and that Denni had had an amazing time.

Not long after, Martin Finn fell extremely ill with full-blown AIDS. Paul Thompson was forced back into the staff market, taking on David Trudeau as cover, although Martin never returned to the office and passed away soon after.

For the staff, it was a shock – he was in his early thirties, and from the initial

HIV diagnosis to full-blown AIDS, it had all happened very quickly.

In May 1989, my brother Robin joined the Metropolitan Police, moving to Hendon for his training, so I had 87 Woodbrook Road to myself again.

In June I was still a little down and so Lesley decided to invite me along to a riverboat shuffle she was going along to with John, Chris, and Linda Hicks. But there was a snag, Lesley told me it was for couples only, so in order to accept I had to find a date for the evening.

I really didn't think I had any realistic options, so I kept my head down and hoped Lesley would forget about me. I should have known better.

Two days after the initial invitation, Lesley was back, looking to collect the money for the tickets. I explained I didn't have a date, and in typical fashion she said, 'Leave that with me, Parks.' And off she went.

Now I was very afraid. Fifteen minutes later, Lesley was back with a broad grin. 'Sorted. So that's £25 please.'

I looked at Lesley. She was enjoying her moment as I pulled the notes from my wallet. 'Can I ask who I'm taking?'

Lesley winked. 'You owe me big time, Mr Parker. I've got you a date with Nicki Lane.'

Nicki was a simply stunning young lady who worked on the Czarnikow reception desk. All the guys had a crush on young Nicki.

That was Lesley for you – I had made a comment that Nicki was attractive, and Lesley had stored, processed, and then acted, which was something I would never have done.

The ball had been firmly planted in my court; I could not wait until the day of the dance itself to talk to Nicki. I now had to make a move, and so I walked around to the reception desk to ask Nicki if she fancied a lunch the next day.

Nicki and I went out for lunch, and it was agreed that on the Saturday of the riverboat shuffle I would drive out to Essex to pick her up. Armed with an overnight bag, we would head back to my place so Nicki could change. Then we would jump into a car with Lesley and John for the drive down to the Thames for the Saturday night boat trip up.

A full sit-down meal was included in the price of the tickets, but we would not get back to Welling until extremely late. We agreed that Nicki would stay the night with me at Abbey Wood and that her dad was going to drive round and pick her up from my place on the Sunday morning.

Early on the Saturday of the riverboat shuffle, I set off and drove down the A2 via the Dartford Crossing to Thurrock and on to Nicki's house. I met Nicki's parents, and after a cup of tea and a chat, we loaded up my car and headed back to Abbey Wood.

Nicki looked amazing on the night. But sadly, things didn't go quite according to plan as Nicki started to go down with a virus and was not feeling at all well an hour into the boat trip. I spent the latter part of the evening sitting with Nicki at the back of the boat. The downside of a riverboat shuffle is you are stuck there for the night.

When I got Nicki home and onto the prepared sofa bed, she just curled up, and I was concerned about her. The next morning, although still off colour, Nicki felt a little better and her dad arrived promptly to take her home.

Nicki and I enjoyed plenty of lunch times together after that, and we become good friends, but she was engaged in an on/off relationship at the time and so sadly no further dates ensued.

On Friday, 13th October 1989, the financial markets experienced their second serious crash. This one was noticeably short in comparison to the previous one. It was caused by a failed leveraged buyout of United Airlines, and on this occasion Barry was on the right side of the market and there were no problems.

On 9th November 1989, the Berlin Wall came down. News coverage showed people from East and West knocking chunks off the wall under the glare of television coverage. We had a sense of big political change being in the air as we watched the end of the Cold War.

In November of that year, I had a chance meeting with Linda Booth of Shearson Hutton, Nadia's boss. We were attending a CBOT market seminar on their grains contracts. Linda told me that Nadia had gone through, what Linda considered to be, a bit of a mental breakdown.

It turned out that Frederick, her French cousin, had opened multiple bank accounts and got himself into debt. This had put him in further trouble with Shearson as previously he had given the work address to the banks for statements. All of this had reflected badly on Nadia. I told Linda I had not heard from Nadia, but I was there if she wanted to contact me. I never heard from her.

In October 1989, LIFFE introduced a new concept in trading financial futures: the Automated PIT Trading System (APT). This was a screen-based trading system that replicated, as best it could, the open outcry method of floor trading on a screen.

APT was introduced onto the financial futures trading desk at Mark Lane and was utilized to extend the trading day for the major futures contracts traded on LIFFE. As the day's trading ended on the LIFFE floor, orders would be

Me, Dave Peart, John Brown, Paul Thompson and Karen Disley (Loftus)

passed back to the office and the trading continued on the APT system.

This also provided LIFFE with a platform to start launching new contracts cheaply, and in later years it would provide a daytime trading environment for non-floor-based derivatives contracts.

It was also a partial answer to the Frankfurt-based Deutsche Terminbörse (DTB), which was a fully screen-based market. Launched in 1987, the DTB had not managed to get much traction in the market, and the sentiment at this time was that it would never rival the established floor-based open outcry markets.

Philip Plumber and Dicky Gibbs quickly took responsibility for learning the new APT system and established themselves as the primary screen-based traders in the office.

On the 24th of November, the back office Christmas party was held at its now usual venue the Good Friends restaurant. Once again Dave Peart and I were invited to the party. It was the usual fun way to end the year.

Linda & Chris Hicks on the River Boat Dance

The end of 1989 saw the Parker family return to the New Forest and Dibden Purlieu village. My parents, having sold their shop and property in Yeovil, returned to a newly built house in Foxtail Close, which was just off the Butts Ash estate where we had lived previously.

This put them close to gran, who was still living in Wellington Close in her bungalow, so Christmas was spent in familiar surroundings, and gran came to join us in the parents new house for Christmas Day. I was also able to catch up with Charlotte Luke at her partner Dave Freeman's property in Hardley.

My parents' move back to Dibden Purlieu also suited Robin, who on free weekends was spending more time with his old school friends in the village, and that led to him starting a relationship with Victoria Eastman. Vicky had been in Robin's year group at secondary school and was someone he had stayed connected with during his Army years.

On the personal front, I went into another of my barren spells. My life was work, home and monthly trips back to the New Forest. At this stage, my love life was non-existent, and I seemed intent on chasing lost causes. My daily phone calls with Denni were very bittersweet.

1990

During the first week of January 1990, Nick Grason told David Peart that he wanted him to fly to New York for three weeks to assist in finalising the purchase of a company called Mercoil.

Mercoil was a New York-based oil brokerage business with a floor trading presence on the New York Mercantile Exchange (NYMEX). This was a strategic purchase that reflected our oil division's increasing volume of trading on the NYMEX exchange.

David agreed to the trip on the proviso that Czarnikow paid for his wife, Margaret, to fly out for a week afterwards and join him. He pointed out that he would be staying with his good friend Victor Dowell and so saving the company hotel bills for the three weeks he was working in New York. In return David wanted the company to pay for him and Margaret to stay in a New York hotel for the week of her trip.

Nick agreed to this, but this meant that Ollie and I would be picking up all David's work on risk and P&L calculations as well as the LIFFE floor trading board. Nick therefore agreed that due to Dave's trip and the increased work in our area that a new member of staff would be employed.

David had an incredibly small window to get a new member of staff employed. He held interviews after hours, on Thursday 4th and Friday 5th January, and then he called me at home to tell me that he was flying out the following Monday and had offered the job to a Richard Watkins. David said that Richard seemed very keen, and he felt he would be a good addition to the team and would hit the ground running.

On arrival at the office on the Monday, I told Ollie about our new member of staff, and we waited for the call from reception.

When the phone finally rang, Ronnie Hales, the messenger on the other end of the phone, was laughing, and he told me that David had obviously been in a rush and had neglected to tell the new boy about the dress code.

I walked to the lifts with a feeling of trepidation, and as the doors opened at ground floor level I could see a very tall, stocky guy wearing a black leather jacket, white T shirt, and blue jeans. The reception desk was full of grinning messengers.

I walked over and said, 'You must be Richard Watkins.' He nodded, holding out his hand. We shook hands, and I introduced myself. 'Before I take you upstairs Richard, did David mention the dress policy for the office?'

Richard nodded. 'Oh yes, David said suit, shirt and tie, a formal dress code.'

That was not the answer that I was expecting. 'OK, so … did you forget?'

He shook his head. 'Oh no, I have a suit on order. It's being handmade by a Greek tailor. He says it should be ready in a few weeks.'

I was now genuinely concerned. 'Well, look, you cannot wear jeans in the office. You must have some formal trousers you can wear in the meantime and a formal shirt and tie.'

He thought for a moment. 'Yes, I have a couple of buttoned shirts and trousers that are a bit more formal, and I can buy some ties at lunchtime. Sorry, I just went into autopilot. I didn't think it would matter for a few weeks.'

I could picture Nick Grason sending him home for wearing jeans. 'It absolutely does matter. We'll see if we can get away with it today. Anyway, what do you mean autopilot? What job did you do before you got this one?'

Richard smiled. 'I was a motorcycle messenger.'

My heart sank. What had David done to us?

I steered Richard towards the lifts and pressed two, wondering if I should talk to Nick and warn him before he saw Richard. Then there were the traders on the desk – they were about to have a field day.

As the doors opened, I tried to speed him down to the far end where Ollie was waiting, but the moment Richard walked onto the floor he stopped.

He was taking in the screens, the noise of the floor squawks and phone calls, and the ambience of the trading floor. I immediately spotted Barry Fontera's broad grin as he chatted on the phone. Nick Grason was also on the phone and had not looked over yet, so I gave Richard a gentle push to get him moving again.

I walked Richard down to our area, sat him down and introduced him to a very bemused Ollie.

I suggested to Richard that he restrict his movement around the office as much as possible and told him I would introduce him to the traders the following day when he was more suitably attired.

I told Ollie that Richard used to be a motorcycle messenger before joining us, and Ollie explained to Richard that the traders on the desk liked to give everyone nicknames.

Ollie explained that David was known universally on the trade desk as 'Sarge' because they felt he would easily have fitted into the cast of the television programme *Dad's Army*. I was known as the 'Corporal' as Dave's junior, and 'Ollie' was his own nickname.

Ollie suggested we call Richard *'Boon,'* after the then immensely popular television show about a company of motorcycle messengers of the same name starring Michael Elphick. Ollie explained it was always better to get a nickname out there, rather than let the traders pick one, which in all likelihood would be one you really would not want.

Before long, a grinning Barry Fontera walked down the trading floor to our area and asked who Richard was. We introduced Richard as 'Boon' and said that he was a new member of the team. Barry laughed. 'Boon – great name, I take it you didn't get the dress code memo then Boon.'

Richard launched into his Greek tailor story and said he was going to buy a tie at lunchtime. Barry wandered, off his curiosity sated.

We told Boon that Barry was trading the TED spread and the bond arbitrage, and he looked starstruck. As Ollie started to teach Boon the LIFFE trading blotter, I saw Barry chatting with Nick Grason who then gestured for me to head down to his office.

I walked down the trading floor, past a grinning Barry and Prash, past Jennette sat at her desk, and into Nick's office. Nick took his seat and leaned back, looking at me. 'I understand our new member of staff, Boon, is rather casually dressed. According to Barry, he looks ready to round up cattle. Is that correct?'

I nodded. 'Yes, Nick. Richard says he has a suit being made for him, but I have told him he should have formal trousers, a shirt and a tie at least tomorrow.'

Nick shook his head a little, then looked down the trading room at Boon. 'Tell him to sprint from the reception to the lifts when he gets his lunch, and that if I get any comments from any of the other directors, he'll have to go home. Try to keep him out of sight for the day.'

I acknowledged Nick's comments and returned to my desk to let Boon know.

That afternoon David phoned from the New York office and enquired after Richard. 'Boon has made an impression,' I replied.

David immediately got the nickname. 'A good one?' he enquired.

I explained the issue with his dress, and I could hear David was slightly exasperated. 'I told him he would need a suit,' he said.

'Oh,' I replied, 'he has ordered one. It's due to arrive in a few weeks!'

'Why didn't he just go to Marks & Spencer over the weekend?' David said he would call daily, but he was due at Mercoil's office the next day and he would phone when he got back to Czarnikow's office.

The next day, Boon arrived in very loud checked trousers, a navy-blue shirt, and a very wide, unfashionable tie that we assumed he had borrowed from his grandad. As he took off his leather jacket and hung it on the coat stand, Barry just stood and shouted, 'Boon, I can't wait to see the jacket that goes with those trousers.'

Boon looked down at them and was about to explain there wasn't one, when he heard the others laughing and just wandered down to our area. Ollie looked at me and rolled his eyes in exasperation.

'Boon,' I said as he arrived, 'they're not exactly what I would call formal trousers. Don't you have a pair of black or navy trousers you can wear while your suit is being made?'

Boon looked down and shook his head. 'I have navy cords and a pair of white trousers.' This caused Ollie to laugh aloud. 'But this is it really. Everything else is jeans.'

Ollie looked at him. 'Boon, what do you wear when you're trying to impress a lady or when you're going out to a fancy restaurant?'

'My white ones,' he replied. Ollie gave up.

'Boon,' I said to him, 'You need to go out at lunchtime and buy a pair of plain black trousers.'

He nodded, and we got on with the morning work routine. I decided to leave introducing Boon around the office for another day.

Nick Grason was talking with Philip Plumber on the desk, and he looked at Boon's trouser choice in amusement as Boon went off to lunch. I quickly advised Nick he was under orders to buy a pair of plain trousers for work while waiting for his suit.

The next day, Boon finally arrived in plain black trousers, a white shirt and a tie that was of normal size. I was now able to walk him around to the central operations area to introduce him to Paul Thompson and the back office.

Then, the bit Boon had been anxiously waiting for, a formal introduction to the financial trading desk.

When we finally got down to Barry, Boon was almost falling over himself to ask what Barry was doing. Barry went through briefly what he was trading as Boon pulled up a chair next to him.

Barry held up his hand and said, 'Boon, if you want to know what I do, it would be best to wait until the US opens – that's when things really get going.'

Boon nodded, and I led him back down to our area, trying to curb his obvious enthusiasm. But Barry wasn't about to miss a trick, shouting down the length of the trading room, 'Hey, Boon, if you want to help, I would love a coffee.'

Suddenly, all the other traders jumped on board, and Boon hurried off with the tray and the large coffee order, on what would become an almost hourly ritual for him thereafter.

Ollie just rolled his eyes in exasperation. 'Any chance of him doing any work?' he enquired.

As the US markets opened, Boon vanished from our area, taking his seat next to Barry as the 'squawk' to Anne Meyer on the floor of the CME came to life. Boon was mesmerised, and Barry, ever the entertainer, was happy to have such an enthusiastic disciple.

From that moment on, Ollie and I had a battle on our hands to get Boon back in his seat to do any work. He just wanted to be a trader and was simply not interested in what we were doing.

When Dave Peart made his daily phone calls from New York to check in, Ollie and I vented to Dave that Boon just wasn't working out. Dave thought we were being harsh, and that Boon was just 'enthusiastic' about life in a trading room and that he would settle down.

On the fourth day, as the CME opened, Boon was delivering his usual coffee run to all the traders on the desk. Barry told Boon he thought this was going to be a good day, and as usual Boon took a seat next to Barry while Barry got Prash ready.

Whenever Barry was busy, he would get Prash to concentrate on the TED spread and the squawk to Anne while he dealt on the T-bond futures and physical cash with speed-dial phones set up with all his important bond counterparties.

Barry was already building a bond position and shouting over to Prash, 'Prash, get me a price in the Eurodollar.'

Prash got a live price from Anne, as the market sometimes ran ahead of the screen in busy conditions. He then shouted the price over to Barry who was watching multiple screens and with a phone to his ear on the T-bonds.

'OK Prash, watch me now. Concentrate.' Boon watched avidly. 'Bills, Prash.'

Prash got the current T-bill prices from Anne.

'Stay with me, Prash,' Barry demanded. 'Dollars,' he shouted.

Prash got a price on the Eurodollars and told Barry.

'Bills still at ninety-five Prash?'

Prash confirmed.

'OK, OK.' Barry quickly did a bond trade on the phone, and then with his eyes on the screen in front of him, he suddenly shouted, 'Prash, market for fifty.'

Prash relayed to Anne, and both Barry and Boon watched the screen avidly. 'Filled, Barry,' Prash said as Barry watched the screen.

'OK … OK … another fifty, Prash.'

Prash relayed the order to Anne. Seconds passed. 'Filled Barry … Anne is confirming levels.'

Barry cursed, watching the screen. Boon looked at the screen and then Barry. 'What's the problem, Barry?'

'The problem, Boon,' Barry explained, 'is that the price hasn't moved as much as I hoped.' Barry stood, phone still glued to his ear, and he looked over the desk at Prash. 'Prash, another fifty.' Barry sat as Prash relayed his order to Anne, and both Barry and Boon watched the screen.

'Filled, Barry,' Prash shouted. Barry slammed the phone down. 'Goddammit!' he shouted, cupping his hands over his eyes before saying almost quietly, 'Prash … what the fuck have I been buying?'

'T-bills, Barry. That was the last price you asked about.'

Barry cursed, 'I wanted dollars, Prash. I wanted bloody Eurodollars.'

Boon sat rigid as the trading room fell incredibly quiet. Moments later, he appeared back in his seat with us and got on with his work.

With help from Anne, Barry was able to scratch his T-bill position, and Boon waited a couple of days before returning to Barry's side for another lesson in trading.

Dave Peart finally returned to the office in mid-February, and Boon immediately cut his frequent visits to the trading desk to sit with Barry, but he maintained his hourly coffee runs.

Much to Ollie and my annoyance, Boon switched his enthusiastic attention to David, wanting to know all about charting and David's pride and joy – his huge T-bond price chart which he had diligently updated upon his return.

One thing that didn't change was the suit that Boon insisted was coming was still in the hands of his infamous Greek tailor. But with David's return, a semblance of normality returned to the office.

In February 1990, one of our biggest competitors in London, American Wall Street giant Drexel Burnham Lambert, was forced into Chapter 11 bankruptcy, which came as a major shock to everyone.

They had a large office in Winchester House, Old Broad Street, London. The previous year, Drexel had been in trouble with the US regulators and had paid a record fine to the US Government of US$650 million.

Then Drexel had been caught out by an unexpected crash in the junk bond market, in which it had been a major participant. They posted record losses in 1989, and this had caused panicked US banks to cut exposure and credit facilities to the company. This resulted in a knee-jerk reaction from UK banks, with similar constraints being applied to anyone in this financial sector, including Czarnikow.

Rushed meetings were held with Czarnikow's Bankers where it was explained to them that Czarnikow was not active in the junk bond markets and had no cashflow issues.

Nonetheless, for the first quarter of 1990, things were tough, and the company had to restrict a significant amount of its daily activities while they convinced the banks to allow credit facilities to flow once more.

On 3 March 1990, I attended another wedding. This time it was my old school friend Steve Dickinson getting married to his British Airways flight attendant. I was invited to the reception along with my parents and some school friends from Dibden Purlieu. The reception took place in a large hotel in Weybridge.

The Met Police made a special gesture for the big day – as the happy couple left the church in a big, white Rolls Royce, six Met Police motorcyclists came out from their hidden location, two pulling in front, two behind and the other two stopping traffic at every junction on the short run to the reception.

It was an incredibly happy event, and it was good to meet up with Steve's mum and dad as well as his elder brother, Keith, his younger sister, Catherine, as well as old school friends I hadn't seen since college.

On 31 March 1990, the streets of London were swamped with protestors, upset at the government's plans to introduce a poll tax to replace domestic rates.

Starting at Kennington Park, a crowd of just under 200,000 marched on Trafalgar Square with the intention of marching on to Downing Street.

What followed was a riot, and at 4.30, as we watched the news feeds and witnessed the violence on the screens that were dotted around the office, the police started to shut Tube stations.

Staff at Czarnikow were advised to be cautious on their way home, and in particular staff travelling to, or through, the West End of London. We were told to dress down, removing ties or anything that might advertise that we worked in the City. This was the first time, but not the last time, that the City and its workers became potential political targets.

I was heading back towards the New Forest in April, and I did my usual phone around to see who might be available for a get-together. Charlotte was busy with a visit from her partner Dave's parents, and I couldn't get hold of anyone else, so I decided to give Julie Ross a call.

Since her marriage to Keith back in May 1983, our communications had become exceedingly rare, as Keith had made it increasingly clear I was not welcome. I didn't want to cause her trouble, but neither was I prepared to give him the satisfaction of forcing me out of her life altogether – especially now that my parents were living a stone's throw from Julie's parents' house in Partridge Road.

I picked up the phone and dialled Julie's number. As usual it was Keith who picked the phone up, but this time he was aggressive the moment he realized it was me. He snapped, 'She's not here and don't ever ring this number again.' Then he slammed the phone down.

This got me really concerned and so I pulled out my old diary with phone numbers and called her parents. Julie's mother picked up the phone, and I explained about my brief conversation with Keith. Her mum tutted and then said, 'Don't worry, Kevin, she's here. They've split up. Let me get her.'

Julie came to the phone. 'Sorry to hear about you and Keith,' I explained. 'I called because I'm in the village visiting my parents this weekend and wondered if we could catch up. But under the circumstances, I understand if ...'

'No, not at all,' Julie cut in. 'I'd love to see you. I didn't know your parents were back in the village.'

I explained about my parents' move and that it meant I would be down a little more often. Then I decided to step up my invitation and asked Julie if she would like to go for a meal on Saturday night. She agreed immediately and so we were set.

I set off from Abbey Wood the following Saturday morning in the Morris Ital, heading around the M25 on the south loop, round to the M3 and then down, heading for the notorious Winchester bypass.

As explained previously, this notorious stretch went back to a single-lane road. Approaching the hill as always, I could see a coach and five cars trailing with me behind.

As the coach plunged down the long hill, I checked and could see nothing coming down the other way. I pulled out and pushed the accelerator to the floor just as the coach arrived at the bottom of the drop and started the long climb. Previously when I had made this manoeuvre, the Opel Manta had cruised past the traffic, but this was not the Manta.

As I started to pass the coach and hit the incline the revs dropped. I slowly inched alongside the coach and then I saw a lorry crest the hill in the other lane and start to plunge down towards me. I was never going to make it!

My foot was to the floor, and I was still only inching past the coach. I had to chicken out, but the question was would anyone let me back in? I dropped the revs, letting the coach pull away, and I jammed on the indicator.

The oncoming lorry was not slowing and was growing larger in my view. I was crawling along and finally I saw a gap on the inside lane as a car dropped back far enough to give me space. I cut in, my heart beating like mad, as the lorry hammered past me I gratefully held my hand up to my saviour in the rear mirror.

I never, ever, tried that manoeuvre again.

I managed the rest of the drive down to Foxtail Close in Dibden Purlieu without further stress. Once I was in and had completed my greetings, I told my mother I had a 'date' with Julie Ross.

At first, she looked a little concerned – I guessed that she thought her son was getting involved with another married woman. I explained that Julie was separated and back home with her parents. Mother was suddenly incredibly positive about my date, saying that, from what she remembered, Julie was a lovely girl!

At 6 pm, I had a shower, dressed, and applied the Kouros aftershave.

I had booked a table at the Mariner restaurant in Hythe over the phone. I had decided to walk round to Julie's parents, a ten-minute walk, and then order a cab to take us the short run down to Hythe. That way I could drink.

Plus, my hour thirty drive down to the New Forest and near-death experience meant I was glad not to bother about getting behind the wheel of a car again for the evening.

I left my parents' house dressed in a formal shirt and trousers and my thick brown leather jacket, and I was soon in Partridge Road. I walked up the steep drive up to the front door of the semi-detached house that I knew well from my frequent visits in my mid-teens.

I rang the doorbell, and Julie's mum opened it. With a huge grin and hug, she ushered me into the hallway and walked me to the kitchen. Julie's dad and younger brother Mike were playing on the snooker table I had spent so much time on in my teenage years. I said hello to them.

Julie's mum pointed upwards with her finger. 'Julie's getting dressed. She'll be down shortly. She's extremely nervous.'

'Why would she be nervous about going out with me?' I enquired.

Julie's mum got closer and whispered, 'I'm sure she'll tell you all about it. But if it had been anyone else, I really don't think she would have said yes to going out. But I'm so glad she is. She really needs this.'

I listened intently, thinking 'no pressure then.'

When Julie appeared, she looked very formal in a black dress. It was a Chinese style, with a round choker-style neckline, fitting tightly. She wore deep-red lipstick, light-blue eyeshadow, and a pair of sparkly dangling earrings. She gave me a smile and said hello before moving quickly to her mum to give her a hug.

Julie's mum asked me where we were going for the evening, and I explained I had booked the Mariner and was going to order a cab, but before I could finish what I was saying, Julie's dad volunteered to drive us to Hythe. I agreed, as I thought this would relax Julie a little more, although I insisted that we would get a cab back.

We climbed into his Volvo estate, me in the back, and Julie in the passenger seat next to her dad.

By now, she seemed to have relaxed a little, explaining that this was the first time she had been out for a meal in years.

The drive down to Hythe was over very quickly, and we pulled into the large car park I knew exceptionally well.

The Mariner restaurant was next door to Waitrose, where I had worked eight years beforehand. I climbed out of the rear door and opened the door for Julie, and we waved off her dad before walking the short distance to the restaurant.

We had a really satisfying meal, the drink flowed, and as time went on the tension I had sensed in Julie melted away. We seemed to be approaching the easy relationship we had enjoyed during our school and college years.

Keith's name never cropped up, and we tactfully avoided talking about her years of marriage. It was not my place to approach the subject, and from what Julie's mum had said, there was a story there.

I explained what Robin was up to, and we chatted about my parents' move back to the village and what was going on at my work. Then the conversation turned to mutual friends from school, including Steve Dickinson and his police career and new wife.

After we had enjoyed a relaxed dessert, I requested the bill and asked if the restaurant could call us a cab back to the Butts Ash estate. Once the receipt arrived and I had paid we were told the cab was waiting downstairs in the car park.

Julie got into the back of the cab with me, and as the car headed towards Frost Lane, she asked when I was due to head back to London. I explained that

I usually set off after Sunday dinner, around three o'clock. She then asked if she could come around on Sunday morning to see me. I was a little surprised but totally happy to agree – my parents liked Julie, and it would be good to see her before I went back to London.

As the cab arrived back at the bottom of the Ross family's driveway, I paid the driver, and Julie insisted we go back indoors for a little while to relax before I headed back to my parents.

As soon as Julie had opened the front door and we stepped into the hallway, her mum came out to greet us. I guessed both her parents had been waiting anxiously for our return. All this concern for a recently-separated 28-year-old just seemed to increase the mystery surrounding the demise of her marriage. Just how bad had it been?

Julie volunteered to make the coffee, and so I went out into the kitchen with her, her parents tactfully retreating back to the lounge. The barriers were still up. I have never met a more naturally tactile person than Julie, so the fact she had avoided all forms of physical contact screamed a warning at me.

I took her parents' coffee into the lounge; both had taken armchairs, leaving the three-seater sofa as the only other seating option. I took a seat to one side of the sofa as Julie came in with our two coffees. Julie took the middle seat directly next to me. We answered her parent's questions about the meal, and as I put my coffee down on the table, I felt Julie's hand sneak into mine, give a gentle squeeze before taking her hand away again.

We all watched TV for a while, and as the clock ticked to eleven, I explained I should be getting back to my parents' house. As I got up off of the sofa and made to head for the hallway, Julie's mum pointedly said she hoped to see me again soon – the message was unmistakable.

Julie walked me out into the hallway and to the front door, and as I stepped out the house, she thanked me for a lovely evening and said she would be round at 10.30 if that was OK. I said, 'No problem,' and with a little wave she closed the front door. I walked the short way back to my parents with more questions than answers but having a sense that my visit had been a success.

The next morning at 10.30, Julie, dressed in jeans and a T-shirt, was at my parents' front door. My mother gave her an enthusiastic greeting and then left us to it. As I came into the hallway, I asked Julie if she fancied going for a walk so we could have time together and also as it was a nice day.

We walked for a while through the Butts Ash estate, heading for the village. Julie talked to me about her cousin Wendy who I knew from all the family get-togethers back in our school and college days. The last time I had seen her was at Julie's wedding.

As we walked, the conversation moved on naturally from me last seeing Julie at her wedding to Keith himself. Finally, Julie started to tell me a little about her marriage to Keith.

She told me that over the first 12 months of their marriage, Keith had very successfully isolated her from old friends and much of her family. Julie told me that I was one of the few that had persisted in my contact with her despite Keith's obvious annoyance.

She told me that Keith was usually terribly angry after my phone calls and never moved far from the phone in both an attempt to listen to our conversation and also to make her feel uncomfortable. Towards the end of their marriage, his anger had moved on into physical violence.

Julie stopped talking, and I knew she was crying. We halted and I decided to take a chance and put my arms around her. I half expected her to push me away or object, but she just clung tight, crying for what seemed like an age. We stayed still for a while, and then I let her go and we started walking back towards my parents.

By the time we got back, dad was suggesting a drive out to the Royal Oak for a pre-dinner drink. Despite being invited, Julie declined, saying she should head back to her parents.

I walked her back to Partridge Road, and we hugged at the end of her driveway. She asked when I was going to be coming back to Dibden Purlieu. I told her I could be back in a couple of weeks, and we agreed to speak on the phone later that week and finalise plans to meet up again.

Back at Czarnikow, Boon was as enthusiastic as ever, now slowly returning to his spells hovering around Barry the moment he heard Anne on the CME squawk. David could see nothing wrong with his frequent visits. Boon maintained his hourly coffee run, and Ollie and I agreed we had never drunk so much coffee.

One day after Boon had delivered yet another coffee run, David was sitting behind us, working on his PC, when we heard a curse as David spilled the contents of a cup full hot coffee cup over the desk and his lap, steam actually rising from his trousers.

Quick as a flash, Boon was out of his chair, shouting back, 'Don't worry, David,' as he scurried down the trading floor heading for the door. David stood still as Ollie, and I hunted for the few tissues we had around and quickly mopped up the pool of coffee around his desk and keyboard.

'I don't know why you boys are so down on Boon,' David said as we dumped the coffee-covered tissues in the bin.

Time dragged as David stood there with a huge coffee stain drying on his trousers, and even the guys on the trade desk were casting eyes in the direction of the door, wondering why Boon was taking so long with fetching the kitchen towels.

David was starting to get angry, and finally his patience snapped he said, 'Ollie, for crying out loud, go and see what's taking Boon so long.'

Just as Ollie stood up to head down the trading floor to the door, I heard Prash, and Philip Plumber burst out laughing. As we all looked down the office, Boon was walking slowly around the trading desk with a fresh tray of coffees, distributing them to each of the traders.

David was stunned, and Ollie headed out to get him paper towels, although by now the coffee stain on his trousers was dried in. I tried my best not to join in the with the laughter that echoed around the trading floor as Dave muttered, 'Stupid boy.'

Over the next few months, I was back in the New Forest every two weeks, and Julie slowly returned to her old self. We were hugging and kissing, and she was much more like the Julie I knew from college. Keith was never mentioned, and once again I was a member of the Ross family whenever I visited her parents' house.

Finally, Julie accepted my invitation to come to London for the weekend. I suggested she come up by train, but she was keen to drive as she loved driving. Her father part-owned a local garage, so she had been brought up with cars and loved anything to do with them. Her prized possession was a fully restored Austin Healy, and she was a member of the Austin Healy club, taking her car to shows and events all around the New Forest area.

However, her day-to-day car was a Ford Fiesta, and it was this that she drove to Abbey Wood on the Friday evening. I was concerned about her making that drive, especially someone from the New Forest not used to driving in the London madness.

Luckily, the majority was motorway, and only the last 20 minutes was on London roads. Nevertheless, I was relieved when I saw the headlights on the road outside and she got out of her car. I opened the front door, and she was immediately in my arms, demanding a kiss.

I asked if she would like a tea or something stronger, but she just grabbed my hand, headed for the stairs, and said, 'I want to go to bed … now … before

I change my mind.'

We had only kissed by that stage, and I had not wanted to force the pace, not sure where her thinking was post Keith.

Julie was in a rush, and she headed straight upstairs for the front bedroom and was immediately removing her jeans. As she dived naked under the duvet, and I followed, she was trembling, I could see the fear and the determination, so we went very slowly, kissing, touching, slow and gentle, and afterwards she lay quietly in my arms.

With another hurdle over, we started what I considered to be a normal relationship thereafter.

Every two weeks, we alternated between me heading down to Southampton and Julie coming to London. On the Friday night I was due down to the village, I would head for Waterloo station straight from work and take the train to Southampton Central, where Julie would pick me up. Then she would drive me back to the station on the Sunday.

In April, Paul Thompson called me into his new office, having had a glass box built within the central operations area. He asked a little favour because he was concerned about Amelia Kennett.

Amelia had been with him for 18 months, but she didn't seem to be mixing well with the other girls and was not communicating with the male members of the department, although she was competent and performing well workwise. Paul was used to a friendly, inclusive office environment, and he didn't like to see someone unhappy or not mixing well.

He felt Amelia was more comfortable in male company and asked me to take her out one lunchtime to make sure there were no issues. He had chosen me as someone outside the department itself, but familiar and friendly with all of the staff in central operation. Paul thought I was the best person to ask her out to lunch.

Amelia seemed happy to accept my lunchtime invitation, and we went to City Yeoman and chatted. She was a complex character – she was adopted and had insecurities around that. What she did have were her looks and her figure, and she used these to get attention and affection. She didn't have a close relationship with other girls for historical reasons.

Amelia felt other females judged her and were envious or competitive and bitchy. For this reason, she had not tried hard to make friends or get close to the other girls in the department.

Amelia just talked, and as the hour stretched, it was as if she had been waiting for someone to confide in. I told her that Karen, Sue, and Kim in central operations were all really nice girls and they got on very well together. Amelia had to remember that the other girls had been working together for a while, but they were not being intentionally cliquey.

The main problem was that Paul Thompson, Gavin Brodie, John Brown and Ron Wallis, her male co-workers, were all much older and appeared impervious to her charms. The new guy, David Trudeau, was too young for her taste.

As we walked back into the office, Amelia thanked me, and we agreed to do it another time.

Later, I met Paul in the basement and gave him as much information as I was comfortable giving. Paul was relieved there were no serious work issues, and that Amelia was not thinking of leaving. He said he would have a quiet word with Sue Bright to try and include Amelia a little more in the office banter.

In August, Julie and I took our relationship another step, going for a nine-day holiday together to Jersey. We actually took a flight on a small propeller passenger plane from Southampton Airport. Living in Dibden Purlieu, we regularly saw these planes flying over the village, and here I was now sitting on one. The plane could only hold two dozen people, and Southampton Airport was hardly state of the art, having a grass runway.

We stayed in a hotel in St Hellier and spent our time travelling all around the island in a rented car. We had a very relaxing time and enjoyed each other's company.

Having such a long time together, previously it just been weekends, proved that we had the basis of a good relationship. It went further to put the ghost of her relationship with Keith behind her. It was good for me as well, as I stopped thinking about Dianne and Denni and started concentrating on what was in front of me.

On our return to Southampton Airport, after a brief overnight stay with my parents, I headed back to the City of London with renewed energy.

On 2nd of August 1990, Saddam Hussein's Iraq invaded Kuwait, causing turmoil on the oil market. The United Nations immediately demanded Iraq withdraw. Not long after, America issued an ultimatum demanding Iraq withdraw by 15 January 1991 or risk a war.

On 1st November 1990, Margaret Thatcher resigned as prime minister. This event had looked likely for a while, but even so, it was still a shock when it happened. During my time working in the City, Thatcher had been a constant, and it was the end of an era.

Christmas was looming, and once again this meant a trip back down to Dibden Purlieu.

Robin's relationship with Victoria Eastman had progressed to the point that they were seriously talking about setting up home together in London.

I was continuing my relationship with Julie, who was now in the midst of her divorce proceedings from Keith, and we all seemed to be in a good place. We optimistically looked forward to 1991.

1991

Early in 1991, the LIFFE exchange announced that it intended to move from its Royal Exchange home and into a purpose-built floor that was going to be incorporated into the redevelopment of Cannon Street station. The vast new floor would be state of the art and enable LIFFE to continue its expansion and have a trading space that would finally challenge its Chicago rivals.

On the 16th of January, Allied aircraft started the threatened military action against Iraq, targeting military sites and destroying the Iraq Air Force. With the Iraq Air Force neutralised, a ground offensive began in an operation called Desert Storm.

On the 25th February, Kuwait was liberated, and Iraq had lost a vast amount of military hardware. But as agreed with its coalition partners, the Allied forces stopped at the border and did not pursue the Iraqi military into Iraq itself.

In March 1991, Robin and Victoria moved into a house just down the road from me on the 'Poets' estate in Welling. Their new home was 25 Wordsworth Road, and we celebrated in what was to become our mutually favourite haunt, the Thai Dynasty restaurant in Welling High Street.

Robin and Vicki were not the only arrivals in Welling in the first quarter of 1991 – Lesley and John Baxter, along with John's son, Jay, moved into a small semi-detached property a 15-minute walk from my house in Abbey Wood.

Inspired by the prospect of home ownership and also deciding that central London was not the best place for Jay to be growing up, they made the move to join us in the Welling area. This meant the prospect of lots of local parties and regular get-togethers.

It was at one of these parties that I met James Tucker, Leslie's new neighbour. James was a staunch Charlton Athletic supporter and had been an active member of the Valley Party in 1990.

The Valley Party was the first single-issue political force that stood in the local elections in 1990, fighting the local ruling Labour Party, who had opposed Charlton Athletics' return to their Valley home.

Fielding sixty candidates in all the Greenwich Council local election seats, the Valley Party was taking on the political elite. With no political experience, little funding and just a dedicated band of locals, they sought to take on all the major political might mustered against them.

On 3rd May 1990, the Valley Party secured 14,383 votes. They didn't win any seats but took enough Labour votes to displace a host of Labour candidates to other parties. The Labour Party hung on to enough seats to maintain a small majority and hold the council.

The result of this election rocked the Labour Party sufficiently for them to reverse their original decision on letting Charlton Athletic return back home. Immediately, plans were set in motion to secure planning permission and raise the funding for the urgent work required at The Valley stadium.

Charlton Athletic were booked to play the 1991-92 season at West Ham's ground, Upton Park. I had not seen any live football since my season at Southampton FC in the famous 1975-76 season, which had resulted in Laurie McMenemy's side winning the FA Cup Final against Manchester United.

I have always been a 'local' supporter and had no interest in being a token supporter of a big club in the way many were. Football was about going along on a Saturday to watch your team play, and so I decided that I would go to a few of the Charlton Athletic matches in the coming season.

Back at 66 Mark Lane, I was cornered one day by Amelia Kennett who asked if we could have a chat over lunch. Mindful that Paul Thompson had asked me to keep an eye on her, I accepted, and we agreed on a lunch date.

On the day concerned, Amelia arrived in a noticeably short skirt and white buttoned blouse that she seemed to have forgotten to actually button, and a very visible white lacy bra. It was exceedingly difficult to know where to look as we took our seats in the Dickens Inn at St Katharine Docks.

This venue had been my idea, and if I am honest, I had wanted to move well out the way of the usual lunchtime haunts to avoid being seen out with Amelia. The inevitable office banter, had we been spotted, would have made my life a misery.

My choice of venue may have caused Amelia to think my objective was different. She made a point of sitting next to me, giving me an even better view of her ample lace-clad bust.

Amelia started to talk, and after a couple of drinks told me what was really bothering her. She had told me at our previous lunchtime chat that she was adopted, and now her adopted parents had decided to retire to Devon and had suggested that Amelia stay in London and continue her career at Czarnikow. To aid her, they had rented a flat in Homerton near Hackney, but she was conflicted.

All the bravado and brazenness was just a cover – Amelia was actually a very insecure person. I had no idea why she decided I was the best person to confide in, but as stated before, she was always far happier in male company. That fact, together with my previous lunchtime chat with her, appeared to have put me firmly into the 'agony aunt' bracket.

Despite my ongoing relationship with Julie back in the New Forest, temptation was being put my way. As we chatted, the 1987 film *Fatal Attraction* kept popping into my mind. I didn't have a pet rabbit, but I was sure I was having lunch with a potential bunny boiler.

I re-emphasised to Amelia what I had advised her previously, that she needed to network more. I was aware that there was an ideal opportunity for Amelia to mix with a sizeable number of her Czarnikow workmates coming up – Linda Hicks was having another of her Chas & Dave evenings!

I was concerned that had I invited Amelia to Linda and Chris's party, it was going to be misinterpreted, so I didn't mention it that lunchtime.

Upon our return to Mark Lane, I went straight up to the sugar floor and asked Linda if she minded Amelia coming along. Linda, in her typical happy-go-lucky fashion, was totally relaxed about it. Linda was very much a more-the-merrier type person.

I then asked Linda if she wouldn't mind extending the invitation herself, explaining my concern, and so she did, and Amelia was delighted to accept.

As always, Linda and Chris's Chas & Dave evening was an enormous success, and Amelia got on famously with them, so much so that Linda and Chris firmly took her under their wing. A couple of weeks later, Amelia was included in an invite down to Linda and Chris's static caravan based at Hoo in Kent.

My relationship with Julie back in the New Forest ended over the Easter break.

I travelled down to my parents and took Julie for a meal in Southampton. While we chatted, I suggested that I would come down the following weekend. Back-to-back weekends to the New Forest was something I had not done for a while.

Julie then confessed that she was already committed the following weekend and that she was seeing someone from Midland Bank where she worked. She explained that the gaps between us seeing each other were getting to her, but she couldn't bring herself to finish our relationship.

To be fair to Julie, for our relationship to have developed further, she would have had to move in with me in London. That would have isolated her again, and post Keith, nobody could have asked her to do that. We agreed the best thing for us to do was to split up.

I found out later that there other factors behind Julie's decision.

The first was that during the months beforehand, whenever Julie had dropped me off at Southampton Central station, she would spend twenty minutes or so crying before returning home. Julie could not cope with only seeing me every other weekend, she needed more.

The other element was Victoria Eastman, Robin's other half. I had no idea that Julie's mother and Vicky's mother were workmates at the local Hythe hospital, and they disliked each other with a passion. Nothing was ever mentioned by either Julie or Vicky, but Victoria had been planting seeds of doubt in my mother's mind about our relationship.

I found out that Julie had been round to see my mother and to explain her dilemma about her workmate being interested and how serious I might be about her. I have no idea exactly what was said, but Julie walked away with the idea that she had nothing to lose by going out on a date with her workmate.

The end of my relationship with Julie meant I had no reason for my regular weekend trips back to the New Forest, and so I decided to apply to Charlton Athletic for a season ticket.

No sooner had I sent my application into Charlton than the news broke that long-standing manager Lennie Lawrence had quit, and the team would be managed in the new season by playing duo Alan Curbishley and Steve Gritt. Expectations for the season were low, but that was, as I was to find out, par for the course for Charlton.

The priority was for the club to stay in the second tier of English football, the Football League Second Division.

Once the club had returned to its home stadium of The Valley, they would hopefully consolidate and be regular top-half finishers in the table. From there, the club could hopefully push for a place in the play-offs and get to the promised land, which was at this time called the First Division but went on to become the Premier League.

On 18th August 1991, I set off from my Abbey Wood home, drove down Shooter's Hill, across Blackheath, via Lewisham and into the City, where I parked up close to Czarnikow's office. From there, I walked to Tower Hill for the Tube journey to Upton Park for the first game of the season.

At that first game, I found many similarities with my time at Southampton FC – your average Charlton fan is good company and very friendly. They have a gallows humour and expect little on a match day but are always happy to be surprised.

I met a gentleman called Neil Target, who also worked in the City and was involved with the supporters club. He was always keen to recruit fellow volunteers, and it was at this first match that the seeds were sown that would get me increasingly involved with Charlton Athletic FC.

It was also apparent at this first match that the West Ham fans were curious about this new club playing at their home ground. There was another connection now that ex-West Ham player Alan Curbishley managed Charlton. Right from the first game at Upton Park, West Ham fans started to turn up on days when West Ham were not playing themselves, boosting the numbers in the ground and creating a better atmosphere.

The rest of 1991 slipped by uneventfully. The only event of note in the City was the LIFFE market moving from the Royal Exchange onto its new purpose-built trading floor in the new Cannon Bridge building above Cannon Street station.

Christmas prompted an interesting conversation between Boon and Barry. Barry was flying back to his native Chicago for the holiday period, and before he left, he walked down to exchange customary festive good wishes.

When he reached out to shake Boon's hand, he pointed to Boon and declared, 'Boon, when I get back to the UK, I'll have the perfect Christmas gift for you!' Ollie and I looked at each other with surprise as Barry continued, 'I'm going to get you an authentic Davy Crockett hat!' With a big smile and profuse thanks from Boon, Barry left.

Ollie and I looked at each other, puzzled.

It was a week after Christmas that the penny dropped, the film the *Alamo* was on the television. Barry had totally missed the connection between the motorcycle messenger and the TV programme *Boon* and instead had linked the reference to Daniel Boon, the historical American pioneer.

We all waited for Barry to return with the hat, but it never arrived, a bit like Boon's suit!

1992

The start of 1992 saw a new staff member joining the LIFFE trading desk. Simon Young joined with a client account that Czarnikow had been looking to bring on board for some time: ABN Amro, a Dutch domestic bank that was highly active in the derivatives markets.

Despite all the promise of this new account, the volume expected when he joined never quite materialised. Simon was quickly christened 'Scud' by the other traders as a reference to the Scud missiles used in the Gulf War. The idea was they looked great on the launchpads but didn't do much damage in reality and often failed to explode at all.

Another new addition to the financial futures office-based broking team was Graham 'Pinky' Stewart. An ex-partner at Morgan Grenfell, Graham had lots of experience and gravitas and was a valued addition to the team. He was the perfect foil to Barry Fontera, always laid back and relaxed.

There was also a change of staff in our department at this time, as Boon was finally despatched down to the new LIFFE floor to follow his long-stated aim of becoming a trader. Sadly, he didn't last long with Czarnikow.

Boon was sent down to the gilt pit where the Czarnikow gilt's trader, Tim Clark, took him under his wing. His initial role, while he was learning for his floor trading exam, was to communicate between Tim in the trading pit and Ray Lancaster on the gilt order desk.

The new trading floor was designed in such a way that there was a direct line of sight from the order desks into the relevant pit. However, when high numbers of traders were trading in the pit, maintaining that line of sight was often difficult if not impossible. This necessitated a trader or admin clerk to stand on the outer fringes of the trading pit, using the universal trading sign language and maintaining a line of sight between the two to complete the link.

This gave Boon not only a great incentive to learn this unique sign language but also a chance to see one of our best traders in action and to get his face known, which was often essential to progressing on the trading floor.

Boon, as always, was very enthusiastic, and an hour or so into his first time performing this relay function, Tim walked over to give him a pep talk. Tim said, 'Boon, you're a big lad I want to see you and hear you loud and clear. I need you to dominate your space.'

Boon nodded and waited like a coiled spring for the next order to come down from Ray Lancaster on the phones. He did not have to wait long, and very soon after Tim's chat, Ray picked up the phone and signalled to Boon with an order.

Boon spun to face Tim and flung his arm back to start the hand signal, smacking an unfortunate individual standing next to him on the nose, knocking his victim unconscious and laying him flat on the floor.

On seeing this scene unfolding before him, Ray Lancaster immediately relayed the story via the squawk line to the office. Barry and the guys in the office were in tears of laughter.

Luckily, the victim of Boon's enthusiasm was only stunned for a few moments before he recovered. Boon, on the other hand, was beside himself with guilt and apologies.

A month later, Boon left Czarnikow for a competitor. Unfortunately, despite all his enthusiasm, he actually never made a career on the trading floor, and we soon lost track of him.

Boon's departure left a vacancy with us in the office on the trading blotter, and Paul Thompson quickly spoke to David Peart about transferring Amelia Kennett into the position.

Amelia had continued to be an isolated figure in the back office and had blotted her copybook further after the annual departmental Christmas meal. The story was that she had punched David Trudeau on the nose for having the temerity to refuse her offer to accompany her back to her flat for the night.

I judged this story to have the ring of truth, as I expected Amelia was still very lonely now she was living alone and insecure. It was considered by all concerned that a move to the financial futures trading room and in particular putting Amelia under the wing of Dave Peart, Paul Collister and yours truly was just what she needed.

On the 11th of February 1992, the Queen and the Duke of Edinburgh attended the inauguration of LIFFE's new Cannon Bridge trading floor, in recognition of the importance of the LIFFE exchange to London and the international financial markets. The floor community were excited about the visit, and it all went very well.

On 9 April 1992, the UK went to the polls. Following Margaret Thatcher's removal, John Major had been elected leader of the Conservative Party, and in a complete surprise, he went on to win the general election.

The following day, the City of London was rocked by an IRA Bomb at 9.20 pm.

The Baltic Exchange bombing, as it was to become known, was an attack by the Provisional IRA on the City of London. The bomb had been driven into the

City in a large white truck, killing three people, injuring ninety-one others, and severely damaging the Baltic Exchange building and its surroundings.

My old friend Andrew Mersh was working for Mocatta, a member of the London Metal Exchange, which also had an oil division. He and a colleague were covering the close of the oil market. Their office was in Crosby Square, with the CU building opposite facing across a large open courtyard to the Baltic Exchange.

That evening, Andrew was just finishing up and went to turn the radio off. As he reached towards the window ledge, there was this almighty crash which he likened to a really close thunderclap. The building shook, the ventilators units blew out of the floor and the walls, all the lights went out apart from the dim lighting from Reuters screens and the dealer boards.

Andrew was thrown backwards by the blast. The only real source of light after the explosion came from outside the building. The sky outside was a dusty bright orange colour with white flecks. This debris turned out to be bits of shredded paper and window blinds from the CU building, while the orange colour was the dust and dirt dislodged by the blast.

When the main lighting returned, Andrew made his way downstairs to the office reception area. The night security man was in reception, as was a member of the IT team called Pat who worked the late shift for Mocatta. The main entry doors to the building were buckled inwards.

Pat's car, which was parked outside the entrance, had an office window frame buried in the roof and the passenger door.

As they looked out, they could see a gentleman staggering past the CU building and up the steps towards Crosby Square, holding his briefcase over his head. Andrew and the others called him in and took him upstairs to the office where they had phone lines which were working.

This visitor was Japanese, and all Andrew could understand was when he said 'blood' and 'gargle,' asking for water which Andrew supplied. Andrew suggested the visitor call his family while he phoned his manager, Ian Radley, to let him know what was going on.

Having surveyed the damage, Andrew realized how incredibly lucky it was that the bomb had not been detonated during normal working hours.

For example, Andrew said there would have been a good chance his managing director's secretary would have been decapitated. The window glass where she sat looked like it had been punched in, and it had come down on her empty chair in spear-like shards.

Andrew's managing director phoned and told the staff to get out of the building.

Andrew escorted their Japanese guest downstairs and he just walked off.

As Andrew talked to Pat, and the security guard at the front door, they could see torch beams coming from the alley that led to Gracechurch Street. A firefighter came up to them, and Andrew asked if it was OK to leave the building. The reply was 'Yes, but don't go near any tall buildings.'

Andrew left his office for the walk to London Bridge and a train home. He cut across the forecourt between the CU building and the P&O building, walking on about two inches of shattered glass. The emergency services had taped off the area, so he was forced through Leadenhall Market to Fenchurch Street and on to London Bridge.

Andrew had to wear a hard hat to get back into work the following Monday, and there were responders stopping people from going up Gracechurch Street. They told him that the NatWest Tower had grown a couple of inches due to the blast, and that in the CU building a plastic chair and a desk had been impaled together by a shard of glass.

There wasn't a single sheet of paper left intact in the CU building. Andrew was also told that there had been people in a lift on the 20th floor of the CU building when the bomb had been detonated. As the power cut, due to the blast, the elevator had gone into freefall and had plummeted to the fourth floor before the power came back on and the elevator brakes finally kicked in.

At Czarnikow, my old friend Lesley Baxter (formerly Neenan) had been working in the basement cable department on a late shift when the bomb exploded. She remembered the building shaking as the explosion went off, and she thought the building was about to collapse on top of her.

Lesley's colleague Rod Booty had left the office and was approaching Liverpool Street station when the bomb went off, and he was thrown down the stairs at the station.

In mid-1992, Czarnikow made what would become a fatal decision – they acquired a company called VBerg.

VBerg was a cocoa trading company that was fighting a legal action against the Chinese government.

The Chinese were at the time notorious for deviating from contractual agreements. They had completed a huge deal for cocoa via VBerg, and instead of paying the cash as promised, had handed over the title to a warehouse full of edible nuts, which they considered to be of equal value.

This was not the first time the Chinese had moved the goalposts in their international financial dealings. It was at the behest of Czarnikow's all-important Japanese client base that Czarnikow had been convinced to take over VBerg's business and obligations, and to assume the legal case against the Chinese government.

The Japanese client base had promised to support Czarnikow with increased business and commission income to help finance the court case. The takeover resulted in additional traders and brokers in the cocoa and coffee departments and the back office.

John Brown called me to take a walk into my old department where an extremely attractive lady was sitting in Paul Thompson's office. Dressed in a short black skirt, a dark-brown buttoned blouse and light-fawn jacket was an immaculate young Afro Caribbean lady. Her name was Alison Crawford, and she was joining the back office as part of the VBerg deal.

The City saw a change in 1992 as my godfather's company, the ICCH, rebranded itself as the London Clearing House (LCH). The new company sold its clearing software business to SunGard and returned to its principal role as guarantor to the derivatives business traded in London.

Another change was the merger between LIFFE and the London Traded Options Market (LTOM), adding more liquidity and volume to its ever-expanding business and volume at Cannon Bridge.

During the summer of 1992, my line director, Nick Grason, gave me another of his famous 'good news, bad news' talks. David Peart told me that Nick wanted to see me, and I could tell that he knew what was coming, and so I walked down to Nick's office, getting the usual lovely smile from Nick's PA, Jennette, who waved me in.

Nick gestured to the seat in front of his desk and closed the door behind me. 'Well, Mr Parker, I have some news for you.' He sat down and gave me a big grin. 'I'm pleased to tell you that I've decided to give you a company car.'

I was at a loss for words – this was amazing news. My mind raced. Was it a BMW? A Mercedes?

Nick could see from my face I was incredibly happy with the news, and his smile slipped a little. 'Now the bad news,' he said. 'It's what we call the pool car, one we give to staff to use while theirs is being serviced or repaired. I believe Malcolm Hulme had it last, and unfortunately he usually drives automatics. Anyway, the car is in the basement parking lot so ...' He reached into his desk and pulled out two sets of keys and a logbook '... you can take it away at your leisure. Give Jennette your details, and we'll get you on the company insurance.'

I thanked Nick, and as I walked out of his office I took a quick glimpse at the logbook. I was the proud owner of a Volvo 360 hatchback. I walked back to the desk, and David gave me a grin. 'Congratulations. Why don't you head down and take a quick look?' I didn't need a second invitation, and I headed down to the basement and the car bay.

The car was parked in the corner. It was silver and looked immaculate. According to the logbook, it was 18 months old. I used the key and climbed into the driver's seat. The car even smelt new. I pushed the key into the ignition and the panel lit up. The car had just over 19,000 miles on the clock. It was barely run in, and it was a Volvo. They were built like tanks!

The next day, Jennette told me I was on the company insurance, and I was good to go.

That evening, I went down, got behind the wheel and started the car up. It sounded great, no problems. I set off up the steep ramp and stalled. OK, new car, needs a bit more welly. I restarted it, gave more revs and the car slowly climbed up to street level. Once out on the street, it was fine. I drove home, and I couldn't fault it. It was parked outside the house, and I was looking forward to the weekend and taking it for a spin.

That weekend, Charlton had a home game, and so at one o'clock on the Saturday I set off for my drive to the City and the Tube ride to Upton Park.

As I drove to Welling and approached my usual route up Shooter's Hill, I was happily travelling at 50 mph as I started up the hill, but then the revs started dropping, and I went down to third gear, flooring the peddle. The revs kept dropping, and I was forced down to second gear. By now, I had a bus right behind me, dominating the rear-view mirror. This was embarrassing. The speed held at 30 mph to the top of the hill, and then the car finally gathered speed.

Upon my return to the office on the Monday, I told David about the issue with the car, and he suggested finding a local Volvo garage and taking it in for a check-up. I found one in Plumstead and phoned to explain the problem. They agreed to take a look – with only 19,000 miles on the clock, it was still in warranty.

When the garage called, I was in the office, and the guy on the phone was very unsympathetic, wanting to know what I had done to the car. His words were along the lines of, 'It may only say 19,000 on the clock, but based on the compression in the engine it may as well have been 519,000.' He added that it was as if someone had been on the motorway trying to do 60 mph in first gear. Rumour was that was exactly what had happened!

Anyway, the answer was a new engine, and neither I nor the company were about to pay for that, so Nick had been on the money – it was a good news, bad news gift.

On the 11th July 1992 Czarnikow enjoyed another staff wedding. This time it was Sue Bright and fellow staff member David Southgate who were to be married.

David had been a cocoa floor trader and it was here that he was given the nickname of "Hobbit" which I assumed was due to his height, rather than having very hairy feet.

David was now an established and valued member of the Sugar broking desk at 66 Mark Lane. The reception was in Essex and attended by a large Czarnikow contingent including Victor Dowell from our New York office. It was a joyful event.

The biggest market event of 1992 was to come on 16th September in what become known as 'Black Wednesday'.

Soon after John Major's election, and with a looming referendum in Holland on the Maastricht treaty, the European Exchange Rate Mechanism (ERM) was coming under pressure.

French voters were preparing to decide on plans drawn up by the then president of the European Commission, Jacques Delors, for majority voting and closer economic ties. At the time, polls suggested that 58 per cent were against.

The UK had joined the ERM in 1990, many commentators viewed this as a step towards the UK ditching the pound in favour of the euro. The ERM attempted to bench the value of sterling against the other European currencies.

If sterling as a currency moved out of 'range,' the Bank of England and other central banks would intervene in the currency markets to move it back into the range.

Respected market commentators believed that the UK had joined at too high a value, and so it joined a list of the weaker currencies in the ERM and became a target for currency speculators.

George Soros's Quantum Fund led a field of speculators who borrowed UK Gilts only to sell them and buy them back later at cheaper prices. They repeated the trick every few minutes, making a profit each time.

This concerted pressure on the ERM meant that the Bank of England was having to invest heavily in the markets to keep sterling within the ERM range. Despite UK interest rates already being at 10 per cent, a decision was made that a rise to 12 per cent would be sufficient to kill off this concerted attack on sterling.

At 11 am on 16 September 1992, the unexpected hike in interest rates was announced, causing a huge amount of trading activity on the LIFFE floor as the FTSE, UK Gilt and UK short sterling interest futures contracts all reacted to the news.

All eyes were on the Bund futures contract, now one of the biggest traded contracts on the LIFFE floor. If the German Bundesbank started selling the Bund, it would devalue the Deutsch mark and help sterling to stay in relative value against the strongest contract in the ERM.

No help came – the Bundesbank did not step in. In fact, a rumour hit the trading floor that the German authorities felt the UK should devalue sterling, the pressure on sterling was actually increased.

Further turmoil came when it was announced that interest rates in the UK were going up again, this time to an eye-watering 15 per cent. By now, the currency speculators were convinced they had the upper hand, and they did.

At 7.40 that evening, after the biggest trading day Czarnikow had ever seen in terms of volume, the UK government announced it was suspending its membership of the ERM. This proved to be the end of any ideas of the UK joining the euro.

On the 1st of December 1992 I arrived at another landmark – the return of Charlton Athletic to The Valley.

I was on my second season ticket, and the much-delayed return of the club back to their home ground was a game against Portsmouth. The Valley stadium had a vastly reduced capacity with no east stand, while the west stand was a temporary scaffolding arrangement. Only the north and south stands had survived from the original ground.

The return of the football club to its south London home also marked the start of my involvement with the supporters' club.

Charlton managed to win on the day, the winning goal scored by Colin Walsh. I was hooked. I loved my return to live football, and the Charlton fans were like a family. I increasingly looked forward to home games – win, lose or draw, you always had an enjoyable time, but at this stage the club was on the up, both on the field and off it.

The clubs return to The Valley was the start of a short-term plan to re-establish the club within the local community and to increase the number of fans who were attending home games. To this end, the supporters' club, in conjunction with Charlton Athletic, launched 'Target 10,000'.

This joint supporters' club/football club initiative was an attempt to increase the average gates at home matches to 10,000. When the club had left The Valley in 1985, in the wake of the Bradford City stadium fire, its average crowd had been 4,500.

This initiative included targeting local schools and business, and because of my 'financial' experience in the City, I was co-opted onto the Target 10,000 committee.

All of the Target 10,000 committee were provided with the opportunity to offer match day tickets to local companies and schools for selected home matches by the club. This was a concerted attempt to increase the home crowd at the less attractive games.

For example, I contacted Woolwich Barracks and we agreed to give them a hundred free tickets for a couple of home matches. In addition, the club also frequently offered 'kids for a quid' matches to encourage a following from the local children. This went in conjunction with increased community football courses and local events.

To complement Target 10,000, and in an effort to get high-net-worth individuals involved, City Addicks was launched.

Run by Neil Target, Bob Vassey, and myself, we based ourselves at the City Tavern, just off Eastcheap, and hired the upstairs bar once a month. The club helped us by agreeing to send players along for question-and-answer sessions. These players included striker Gary Nelson, player/manager Alan Curbishley and promising youngster Robert Lee.

In these early days, the club engaged with the supporters' club and fans, and even went as far as to offer the fans the ability to vote one of their number into the boardroom of the club as a director on an annual basis.

We even spent evenings outside the main entrance to London Bridge station, handing out football programmes, hats, and flyers to increase interest in the club. All these initiatives seemed to work, with the average gates slowly increasing week on week.

The pinnacle for City Addicks was the appearance of Colin Walsh.

When we started City Addicks and asked the attendees who they wanted the club to send for a question-and-answer session, repeatedly the answer was Colin Walsh. Colin was the player who had scored our historic first, and winning, goal at Charlton Athletics' return to the Valley. But every time we asked Charlton FC, we were given a flat no.

After the Alan Curbishley night, we asked Alan why the club kept saying no. Alan promised he would ask the senior management if they would make an exception for us.

A week later, an extremely excited Neil Target called me to say that we had 'got him.'

At the next meeting, we had a great turnout, and we waited in our usual upstairs room for Colin to show up. We waited and waited, and were starting to get concerned, when someone said they were fairly sure he was downstairs drinking. Sure enough, there he was.

We finally got Colin up to the venue, and he was in fine fettle. He started to tell us very Unpolitically correct stories which had us rolling around with laughter.

Colin had played under the great Brian Clough at Nottingham Forest and had enjoyed a really good career, so he had lots of stories to tell us.

When the question of his goal in that crucial first game back at The Valley came up, Colin started another of his stories.

He told us about the rousing speeches given by Alan Curbishley and Steve Gritt, and back-slapping that was going on before kick-off. Then he said, 'The changing room was this wee portacabin type thing, and it was a little compact, but as we all walked out that day, I can tell you that every one of the team had tears in their eyes.'

We all had lumps in our throats as we remembered watching the team walk out onto the Valley Pitch that day.

Then Colin added, 'It wasn't because we were emotional or anything like that. It was because Stuart Balmer [Charlton's central defender at the time] had come out the loo having had this awful dump, and the smell in such an enclosed space was the reason for us all to have tears in our eyes!'

This one tale should tell you all you need to know about the stories he told us that night, and it explains why he wasn't allowed out much.

1993

I began 1993 in an incredibly happy place. I was settled at work, getting a good wage, and was enjoying the daily banter with Ollie and Amelia.

Ollie and Amelia had developed a love-hate relationship, which meant the banter often was X-rated, with both dishing out barbed comments and put-downs to the other at each and every opportunity. They both gave as good as they got, and I suspected they enjoyed their verbal battles.

Also, I was learning a huge amount from David Peart, especially about the new accounting software we were using, called EXCEL. I even started writing my own programs under David's supervision.

I was enjoying living the bachelor life in Abbey Wood and all the freedom that gave me. If I wanted company, I had my brother and his other half, Vicky, down the road and my old friend Lesley and her husband, John.

I had no distractions to stop my regular visits to The Valley to watch the Charlton Athletic home games. The fans attending home matches had the pleasure of watching work start on preparing the ground for a proposed new east stand.

The vast grass bank onto which the east stand was now being built had been a historic feature of The Valley. Some of the old fans who had visited The Valley back in the days before the club left for Selhurst Park told to me that if the game was boring, they would head to the top of the grass bank, and on a good day you could watch the boats going up and down the Thames.

I had taken to parking up alongside the Thames Barrier and walking to the ground, a tradition I maintained during my 15 years as a season ticket holder.

On Sunday, 24 April 1993, the IRA struck the City again. It was another truck bomb, but this one was set off in Bishopsgate.

Warnings had been delivered, and the police cleared the area around the parked truck. At 10.27 am, the bomb went off, devastating a sizeable area in and around Bishopsgate. The NatWest Tower was significantly damaged.

As it was a Sunday, the resulting one death and forty-four injuries were light compared to what would have happened had it been a normal weekday.

The knock-on effects of the bomb were that a significant area of the City was out of bounds when we went back to work on the Monday. Each gust of wind brought a torrent of sheets of paper floating down from the broken and destroyed windows of the NatWest Tower.

The tower itself was so severely damaged that there was a serious debate about demolishing it, but the cost of doing that was far higher than the cost of the repairs. NatWest Bank itself never moved back into the tower. The blast also destroyed the nearby historic St Ethelburga's church and wrecked part of Liverpool Street station.

After this bomb, the financial markets and the big banks and institutions insisted that security around the City was tightened, and this led to the City police instituting its 'Ring of Steel.' Checkpoints were set up on all the main roads in and out of the City. Lorry traffic was restricted and checked by the armed police who were staffing these new checkpoints.

Numerous bomb warnings and false alarms followed in the wake of the Bishopsgate Bomb. The mainline stations that served the City had all rubbish bins cleared from platforms. The heightened paranoia meant any unaccompanied bags were immediately assumed to be bombs, leading to frequent station closures and travel disruption. Life in the City was never quite the same after the Bishopsgate bomb.

Just before summer 1993, I joined members of Czarnikow staff at a night out dancing in the City and started chatting to the new member of the back-office staff, Alison Crawford. It was the first time we had really chatted one-to-one, and we hit it off more or less immediately.

As we danced, I plucked up the courage to ask her out on a date and was surprised when she said yes. We agreed to a meal in Covent Garden, and that was the first of many dates we enjoyed together that year. Alison was attractive, an Aries like me, and we enjoyed similar tastes and interests and we just clicked.

I invited her along one evening to my favourite venue, the Thai Dynasty in Welling High Street, and she loved the restaurant and food as well. These frequent, weekly, visits to Welling led to a very quick acceleration in our relationship. In November Alison started staying the night and this quickly became a regular event.

At the time, Alison was in rented accommodation in south west London, and it was more convenient for her to come back to Abbey Wood on the nights we went out together. I learned that she had recently ended a long-term relationship, at around the same time she had joined Czarnikow, with a 'gentleman' who I only knew as 'the Turk.' It was obviously a subject that was not up for discussion in those early days.

Czarnikow itself was now heavily damaged by its ongoing battle with the Chinese, leading to financial problems. Redundancies ensued, with my old friend Rowland Dunn being one of the early casualties.

The old laid-back atmosphere had gone, and uncertainty about the future was the main topic of conversation in the staff areas.

In early October 1993, as I walked home from the bus stop, I noticed temporary signs attached to lampposts warning of road closures. This included Wickham Lane, the main road between Plumstead and Welling. Wickham Lane was the only exit from Woodbrook Road where I lived.

On Saturday, 16th of October, I was going to be trapped! A day later Robin told me that the Anti-Nazi League was marching on the British National Party (BNP) headquarters which was based in Welling.

Up to that point, I did not know that the small, innocuous, blue-shuttered building in Upper Wickham Lane was the notorious BNP headquarters. The BNP had opened an office in a bookshop at 154 Upper Wickham Lane in Welling in 1989.

Trouble was expected and Robin told me he was going to be on duty and that there was going to be vans full of anti-riot police in the side streets, some of which would be parked in Woodbrook Road.

The next day, I spoke to Lesley, and we agreed that I would spend the day round her house. In the early hours of Saturday, the barriers went up and roads were closed. I walked round to Lesley's that morning. When the vans full of police parked up in all the side roads it turned out that the van Robin was in was parked remarkably close to Lesley and John's house.

The demonstrators gathered on Winn's Common in Plumstead, co-ordinated by the Anti-Nazi League and Youth Against Racism in Europe. The numbers that gathered were in the region of 20,000.

The protestors left Plumstead at midday and headed towards Welling via Wickham Lane. The march started peacefully with the protestors passing Plumstead Cemetery, heading along Upper Wickham Lane, and passing the lines of police officers blocking them from deviating into the surrounding roads.

The head of the march was stopped from approaching the intended target, the BNP bookshop – riot police completely blocked the road. The police had set up a wide exclusion zone around the bookshop that began at the bottom of the hill in East Wickham, just before the main road entered Welling.

At the time, Lesley had been delivering trays of tea and coffee to Robin and his fellow officers in the vans parked up outside her house, all dressed in riot gear.

As the riot police attempted to divert the march away from the BNP bookshop and into an adjourning road, the protest turned ugly. Large-scale clashes erupted, and news of this quickly fed down the line of protestors to the those near us. Protestors started to knock down brick walls to arm themselves with missiles, at which time Robin and the other Police Officers in the vans were quickly despatched.

During clashes lasting 90 minutes, police used truncheons and horseback charges, which was later criticised as indiscriminate by organisers of the march.

Once the violence was subdued, the protestors quickly dispersed, and that afternoon the police cordon was finally lifted. Robin and his companions went off to Plumstead police station for a debrief.

1994

In early 1994, it was obvious to all of us that Czarnikow in its current form was not going to survive much longer. The company was looking for a home for its energy, cocoa, coffee, and financial futures departments. None of us really knew if they would be successful nor if it was only the traders and brokers that would be found a home.

Nick Grason called a meeting of the financial futures department, telling us that a number of interested parties were being spoken to, including Sheppard's Money Brokers based at 1 London Bridge. The uncertainty meant a nervous few months.

Alison and I started talking seriously about her moving in, it was obvious at this stage that she would be made redundant, and that would make it difficult for her to continue paying her rent.

Paul Thompson caught wind of our discussions and took me to one side. He spoke to me as a friend, which I appreciated. Paul warned me that as I had been a mortgage holder for a while and had built up reasonable equity in my house, that having Alison move in would put me at risk if we later split up. He gave me the name of a lawyer in Blackfriars and suggested I have a chat with him before letting Alison move in.

The following lunchtime I set off to meet James Carter of Carters solicitors. Based in a wonderful pre-war building in Temple Avenue, the closest I can describe the offices of James Carter would be Hogwarts from *Harry Potter*.

James was a gentleman in his early sixties, and his desk was surrounded on all sides by floor-to-ceiling bookcases, filled with books and files. The floor of his office and his large desk were also covered with files, and it was a wonder he knew where anything was.

I explained that I had been given his name and number by Paul Thompson, and spookily James recalled Paul immediately, 'Ahh yes, a messy divorce case. Send him my regards.'

I explained my situation, and James nodded and immediately recovered a blank piece of paper from under a nearby file and started writing. 'Well, Mr Parker, what you need is a legal agreement that guarantees you remain as the sole owner of the property. You will then need to set up a joint bank account with this young lady, into which you must both put the same amount of funds a month to cover all the joint costs. That would include gas, electric, water, phone bills, and the like. You, Mr Parker, must continue to pay the mortgage in full, all building and maintenance and anything to do with the house fabric and decoration. Provided you do that, you will not have any issues.'

James hesitated before continuing with his advice. Then, pointing to his notes, he said, 'However, if you get married or have any children, this will not be worth the paper it's printed on.'

He leaned back in his chair. 'Come back and see me on Monday. I will have the agreement drawn up. You and your partner must then sign the agreement for it to become binding. I can keep it here for you, for safekeeping.'

I walked out of the building wondering just how I was going to explain this to Alison. Here was a young lady I was in a relationship with, and I was somehow going to have to get her to sign this agreement or else potentially, should we split, have her walk away with a chunk of the equity in the house. I felt like I was about to end a relationship before it had really got going.

I decided the best way to give potential unwelcome news was over a delicious meal, so I called the Thai Dynasty and made a reservation. At this stage, we were on first-name terms with the owner, her three sons and daughters-in-law who formed the backbone of the staff at the restaurant.

Alison and I travelled back on the train, by now she didn't need an overnight bag having plenty of clothes at the house. We both changed out of our work clothes and headed off.

As we took a seat at the restaurant, Alison looked me in the eye and said, 'What is it?' It seemed like she knew me too well already. Alison continued, 'Are you finishing with me?'

I shook my head. 'No, the opposite. I want you to move in, it makes sense but ...' I took a deep breath and explained that I had been given advice, without explaining it was Paul Thompson who had tipped me off. When I finished explaining about the legal paperwork, I waited anxiously for the reaction.

'So,' Alison replied, 'you don't want me to pay any rent, just pay half the utility bills and to sign a legal document to say I am not entitled to any equity in the house.' She remained unmoved as she continued, 'You will continue to pay the full mortgage by yourself.' I nodded, and after a moment's hesitation, she smiled. 'Why would I be upset about that?'

Alison moved in the following weekend.

Back in the City, Czarnikow had tried its best to keep its predicament a secret, but one morning our LIFFE floor manager the Right Honourable Daniel

Beckett phoned the office to say that some enterprising joker had nailed estate agent 'For Sale' boards to the Czarnikow LIFFE floor booths.

The badly kept secret was now out in the open.

At this stage, the deal with Sheppard's had fallen through. Although keen to complete the deal in London, Sheppard's was part-owned by a French bank. This Bank was laying off staff in Paris, and it was deemed to be politically unacceptable to be seen to taking on staff in London while that was going on.

In the meantime, a deal had been finalised with Truxo, a German-based commodity company, to take on all the staff and business from Czarnikow's coffee and cocoa departments.

Also, negotiations with Prudential-Bache to take on all our oil staff and business were at an advanced stage.

The plan was for Czarnikow to restructure back to a sugar-only company, and this left only the financial futures department – all the other smaller departments had already closed down.

On 3rd May 1994, I cemented my relationship with Charlton Athletic by becoming a shareholder in the club. At this point in time a considerable number of major football clubs were listing shares as a way of raising funds. Charlton listed on the AIM exchange, and I promptly signed up.

At a home game against Bristol City, shareholders were invited onto the pitch an hour before kick-off to be presented with share certificates and to have a photograph taken with director Martin Simonds.

In the first week of June, the LIFFE floor team was asked to join the office based staff in the office after the market closed. Nick Grason addressed all the Financial Futures staff to say that Czarnikow was in advanced talks with Cater Allen, a London-based discount house to the Bank of England. It was expected that this deal would be concluded quickly.

Discount houses were financial institutions that functioned as money lenders or served as intermediaries between commercial lenders and borrowers. As a discount house to the Bank of England, Cater Allen was an intermediary between the Bank of England and the market on gilt issues.

Gilts being the way the UK government borrows money from the international markets.

Cater Allen was also a private bank. Its high-interest account (HICA) based in Jersey was well established with the rich and famous, offering high interest for those who could afford the £25,000 minimum balance criteria.

The deal ensured that all the staff in the financial futures department would be employed by Cater Allen and given continuity of contracts. It was fantastic news, and although I didn't know the first thing about Cater Allen, it was a huge relief.

There were going to be changes. Firstly, Nick Grason was not joining – he was going to stay with the new Czarnikow sugar company.

Instead under the terms of the deal agreed, two of our staff would become directors at Cater Allen Futures: Graham 'Pinky' Stewart in the office and Daniel Beckett who would become the floor manager of the new combined entity.

Barry Fontera would not be joining us at Cater Allen as he had found himself a trading position at American giant Goldman Sachs during the months of uncertainty.

Another change was that Cater Allen did not employ proprietary traders on the LIFFE floor. That meant our floor traders, the biggest of whom was Cliff Donovan, would have to become local traders on LIFFE and swap their corporate trading jackets for the red jackets of local traders.

The floor brokers like Tim Clark would be employed as corporate brokers by Cater Allen and would wear the Cater Allen floor jackets.

Cater Allen guaranteed a large number of local traders on the LIFFE floor, and the Czarnikow business seemed to be a perfect fit into their existing Futures business.

David Peart told me that our opposite number at Cater Allen was coming over for a chat and to meet us. His name was Trevor Kemp, and although David and I were confident we were onboard, we knew this was going to be a key meeting.

Cater Allen did not trade physical bonds, nor did they execute any significant business in Chicago. It had therefore been agreed that Cater Allen Futures would sign up with our existing Chicago clearer, Harris Futures, to give continuity to our Chicago business.

This was great news for me, it meant continued contact with Denni Machi and Ro Dimenza-Meo.

On Trevor Kemps arrival at 66 Mark Lane, we spent the day explaining to Trevor how we worked and processed the trades. We showed him internal clearing reports, and David explained how we controlled risk and profit incentive schemes.

We were surprised to learn that Cater Allen currently ran clearing and settlement with just two back-office staff – Trevor plus one other. The other existing member of the Cater Allen back-office staff was already working notice, as he was off to join JP Morgan.

Cater Allen also used a third-party clearing and settlement computer system which David and I were going to have to learn. It was not the GMI platform used by most of the market but a bespoke third party system used solely by Cater Allen.

After Trevor returned to the Cater Allen office, we heard that he had advised the senior management that only David and I were required for the new combined entity.

Paul Collister was happy to be accept a role on the LIFFE trading floor, but this meant no job for Amelia Kennett.

Neither David nor I thought this was a clever idea, this meant that three of us would be covering not only the floor liaison, risk and P&L calculations, Chicago reconciliation with Harris Futures and the bond processing and repositioning but also the TRS matching and trade input work that was currently done by Paul Thompson and his team next door. At that stage however we were not in a position to argue.

Soon after Trevor's visit to Mark Lane, David and I were invited to visit Cater Allen Futures at their 7 Birchin Lane office.

The futures department at Cater Allen was on the first floor, tucked away at the end of an exceedingly long corridor next to the toilets. A single long trading desk and back office were contained in the one large room, which gave the office a dynamic feel.

The trading desk at the time was staffed by the CEO, Tony La Roche, who was well respected on the LIFFE market. Alongside him was director Mark 'Tumble' Dyer, who was a quant mathematician.

Mark was always enthusiastic and was well respected by the client base. 'Tumble,' as in tumble dryer, was Mark's nickname on the trade desk.

Jonathan 'Yorkie' York was an office-based broker dealing with an institutional client base that included Dresdner Luxembourg, Republic National Bank, Moscow Narodny Bank, King and Shaxon and JP Morgan Sydney.

The Cater Allen office team were looking forward to Graham Stewart and our desk traders, Philip Plumber, Richard Gibbs, and Prashant Laud, joining them at Cater Allen, substantially increasing the numbers on the office trading desk.

Yorkie in particular was looking forward to Philip Plumber and Dicky Gibbs taking over some of the responsibility for the APT trading.

On the LIFFE floor, Cater Allen had a well-established short sterling business and a respectable number of corporate brokers and local traders in all the main pits.

On Saturday, 2nd July 1994, all the financial futures staff arrived at 66 Mark

Lane to load up cars and trollies, and we moved from our old Czarnikow home to 7 Birchin Lane.

It was a little emotional leaving the place where I had started my career and made lifetime friends and fond memories. But at the same time, it was exciting. Cater Allen seemed like a perfect home for us. Cater Allen had a small family business feel to it, and it looked like the amalgamation of two profitable entities would see us move on to even greater things.

On Monday, 4 July, with the Americans on holiday for Independence Day, I headed off for the new office. It felt strange to be going from Cannon Street to Birchin Lane instead of Mark Lane.

Mark Dyer and Cliff Heally

Cater Allen dealing room L to R Trevor Kemp, Graham Stewart, Yorkie, Mark Dyer and Dicky Gibbs

Cater Allen Office L to R Dicky Gibbs, Graham Stewart, Jon York, Trevor Kemp

David and I were given a crash course in the new clearing system, but as the first day unfolded it became very apparent that we were understaffed.

Within a week, we had a conversation with Tony La Roche and Graham Stewart about taking on a TRS clerk. Trevor conceded he had not realized that Paul Thompson's back office team were processing the trade input and TRS allocations and had assumed our small team at Czarnikow were dealing with everything.

Amelia Kennett had already been employed by Morgan Stanley, and so we quickly contacted a couple of Paul Thompson's ex staff. Both Karen Loftus (now Disley) and Sue Bright (now Southgate) had started families, but both were interested in a job-sharing arrangement.

Karen and Sue arrived at Birchin Lane for a chat with Graham and Tony after which a deal was agreed.

It was good to see both Sue and Karen re-joining us at Cater Allen and taking over the TRS matching and settlement duties. They slotted straight into the team being experienced and highly competent and the job share worked well.

Karen and Sue's inclusion into the Cater Allen back office freed David and I to get back to reconciliations and our customer services role, especially now we had all the Cater Allen locals to look after as well as the institutional clients that Cater Allen serviced.

One local trader in particular was a challenge, a gentleman called Matt Constantine who traded gilt options on the LIFFE trading floor. Mark Dyer, using his quant mathematics skills, had the job of working out Matt's risk profile on a daily basis and monitoring his market exposure.

Our office broking team was quickly complemented with three fresh faces: Cliff 'Tripod' Healy, Andrew 'Smudger' Smith and Reg DeSousa. Cliff Healy was to become a good friend and had a couple of key institutional clients.

At home, Alison had settled in at Woodbrook Road, and I finally met one of her siblings – her sister Hannah, who was a wild child to say the least.

Alison was twenty-eight at the time and the eldest of five siblings. They were Emma, twenty-six, Carla, twenty-four, Hannah, twenty-two and Ryan, nineteen. Alison's mother was a divorcee, and I knew nothing about her father – he was never mentioned throughout the duration of our relationship.

Hannah had a habit of just phoning Alison unexpectedly to meet up in the City. Alison had quickly found work, post Czarnikow, in the back office at Bank of America, so we agreed to meet Hannah close to St Paul's in a small wine bar.

For sisters, the two of them looked quite different and had vastly different personalities, although they both loved clothes, had great and feminine dress sense. Whereas Alison was quiet and reserved in company, Hannah was full on, loud and, as I said, wild. By the end of the evening, I felt exhausted, and I started to wonder what Alison's other siblings were like, but it would be a while before I met any of them.

Life at Cater Allen was full on in the early days as things bedded in. David and I quickly got to grips with the new clearing system. The transfer of our Chicago clearing at Harris Futures from Czarnikow to Cater Allen had been seamless

I was not slow in suggesting to Denni that she should make another trip to London to meet the new Cater Allen team. Denni agreed it was a clever idea, and we both started to plant the idea with Jennifer Johnson and Geoff Swainson.

We felt at home very quickly at Cater Allen and soon started to network with the Cater Allen Bank staff in the discount house and in the HICA banking area. Graham 'Pinky' Stewart was known to the established traders working in the discount house, and this helped us bed in with the senior Cater Allen Bank staff.

The other enforced change was our choice of lunchtime venues. Immediately behind the new office in Birchin Lane was the Jampot, which became our new 'local.' Just a few feet away was the George and Vulture, which was where I had taken to Denni for our lunchtime meal on her visit to London.

Mark Dyer was a character to say the least. He had a broad 'posh' Yorkshire accent. Although he was a director at Cater Allen, Marks's wife was the main breadwinner of the Dyer household, heading up the foreign exchange desk at Credit Suisse. The Dyers lived in Sevenoaks and had a live-in nanny, who was employed to look after their children.

Our initial observation that this amiable and undoubtedly highly intelligent man was that he was somewhat lacking in common sense.

This was confirmed when he came into the office one morning and confessed his wife wasn't talking to him. Most sensible people would not have admitted that much to a bunch of desk traders, but Mark went further and started to elaborate.

He told the entire trading desk that the nanny had been provided with a car for running around with the children, and she had driven this car through a freshly tarmacked road, causing the wheel arches to be stained with tar.

Mark had decided to clean the tar off and was having mixed success with a sponge and hose, so, for reasons unknown, he then decided to try wire wool! The car was parked in the shade, and when he had finished he was so pleased with the result that he set about cleaning his wife's company BMW with the same wire wool.

Once he had finished, he then settled down indoors to watch cricket on television.

When his wife looked out from the house at her car, she started shouting at Mark to stop what he was doing and come out to the driveway. When he joined her outside, he could see that her BMW, now in the direct sunlight, looked like a skating rink, with scratches all over the bodywork.

The result was Mark had to pay for both cars to be totally resprayed. Doing it was dumb enough but coming in and telling the traders in the office was lunacy. The story quickly spread down to the trading floor.

IT and communications at Cater Allen were managed by one gentleman, by the name of Greg Weeks.

Greg grew concerned very quickly when he noticed that the recording of the phone calls on the broking desk was burning through his tapes at an unprecedented rate. The regulator required all phone communications to be recorded, but it was also handy to identify errors or to support a broker in the case of a misunderstanding.

The additional brokers from Czarnikow, now based at the Birchin Lane office and on the LIFFE trading floor, did not account for the rate at which the large recording tapes were being used up. Greg was concerned that a phone line was being left open, and he set about investigating.

It was a painstaking exercise as he had to go through phone line by phone line. However, in the course of his investigation he found that when he came to Graham 'Pinky' Stewart's phone recording, it was full of live broadcasts of the horse racing!

Often, on quiet days, Graham would even commandeer one of the televisions broadcasting the news channels in the office and flick it to Channel 4 to watch the live horse racing. He was quickly giving horse racing tips to the traders on the desk and the local traders on the floor. Often when things were quiet, the locals would come back to the office to watch a big race with him.

This interest in horse racing was compounded by the fact that our LIFFE floor manager, the Right Honourable Daniel Beckett (his full name was Ralph Daniel Beckett, but he hated Ralph and discreetly dropped it), was often attending Royal Ascot as a guest of the Royal Family.

The fixation with horse racing extended to Graham Stewart inviting traders and locals into a syndicate to actually buy a racehorse, many of them were extremely happy to do so. The trainer had tipped Graham off that the horse was destined for wonderful things, and so a number of the local traders chipped in.

It wasn't long before the horse had its inaugural race, which was televised, and so the traders all made their way to the Birchin Lane office. Graham was waiting with bottles of champagne, and they all stood watching the multiple televisions, all now tuned to the horse racing.

As the race started, their horse was up with the front runners and then it raced away to lead, with all the traders cheering loudly. Then, as the runners and riders came to a long turn, the horse started to lose ground, but once back on the straight it quickly regained the lead. At the next corner, the horse dropped back into the chasing pack again, and as the horses started the final run in for the finish line, it started to make up the lost ground but came in fourth.

Graham started celebrating and all the traders looked at him puzzled, pointing out their horse came fourth. Graham looked a little sheepish and said, 'I bet on the winner. You see I was a bit concerned about the turns.' As the traders all looked at each other, Graham explained, 'The horse is lightning on the straights, but it eases up on the corners as it only has one eye!'

Local trader Mike Clarkson looked incredulous. 'We own shares in a one-eyed racehorse!'

It is obvious that the traders didn't invest in any more of Graham's racehorses.

Christmas 1994 was a crunch time for Alison on two fronts. Firstly, she met my parents, something she had avoided because, as always, she was concerned about the colour of her skin. This had never bothered me, and Alison had spoken to my parents on the phone, and nothing had ever been mentioned.

One day, leading up to our Christmas trip, Alison just picked up the phone to Mum and declared, 'Rosemarie, I'm black.' Mum took it in her stride and Alison seemed to calm down hugely after the phone call.

In all the years I was with Alison, the only issue we ever had with overt racism was from other black girls, some of whom would give Alison a tough time, but never me. These girls would walk up to Alison or past us and make a noise by sucking through their teeth. Others would walk up and call her 'Bounty Bar' to her face in reference to the Cadbury coconut chocolate bar, meaning she was black on the outside but white on the inside.

Both Alison and I were working over Christmas 1994, so we went down to the New Forest the weekend before Christmas Day to drop presents and have a weekend with my parents. My parents just accepted Alison, who immediately relaxed and seemed to enjoy the weekend.

However, my dear old grandmother did not meet Alison while we were in the New Forest on this occasion. Being of a different generation, we decided to avoid that confrontation for the time being.

On Christmas Day, I finally got to meet Alison's mum, as we had her and sister Hannah over for dinner. Her mum was noticeably quiet and seemed to be getting the measure of me, but Christmas dinner was a success, as was the visit.

Alison and I were able to relax for the New Year's celebrations with just the two of us at our favourite Welling venue, the Thai Dynasty restaurant.

1995

Entertainment was a massive thing at this point in time in the financial markets.

The vast majority of the corporate entertainment that took place was concentrated on the trade desks and brokers. Large financial institutions tended to have big annual entertainment budgets to make sure their key clients kept providing them with business.

The benefits were often obvious – a good night out with a key client or broker would usually be followed by a big uptick in commission flowing in and usually made the costs of the entertainment insignificant.

Those of us in the back office usually managed to get the occasional lunch with our opposite numbers at key clients. But in 1994, as we started our new roles at Cater Allen, there was a perceptible shift.

Big banks and institutions started to realise that although brokers and traders could, and would, bring new clients to the company, it was the back office and quality of clearing services that kept the business.

An early example of this change of entertainment policy coincided with a change in our key bond repo counterparty. With Barry Fontera having joined Goldman's when we moved to Cater Allen, Prash Laud had a chance to shine as our key bond trader. Prash started to use Manufacturers Hannover Trust, at this stage part of Chemical Bank, as his key repo counterparty.

'Manny Hanny,' as they were known, were famous for having the biggest entertainment budget in the City of London. I was therefore delighted when just months into my new career at Cater Allen, I was invited out by Manny Hanny for an entire day of corporate entertainment.

Called 'Jurassic Lark,' the glossy invitation was for a day of 'fun' at the Hop Farm at Paddock Wood in Kent.

Tony LaRoche was keen for me to accept, as we heard that back-office staff from all the big counterparties would be attending, and it was good advertising for Cater Allen. I eagerly accepted.

The itinerary arrived, and I suddenly understood why a corporate day out with Manny Hanny was so sought after.

I set out from home at an early eight o'clock in the advised jeans and trainers for the drive down the A2 and onto the M20. The Hop Farm was a sprawling venue that hosted big shows during the year but had an onsite museum and children's petting farm.

On arrival, I parked up and walked toward the main complex, following the signs that said, 'Jurassic Lark.' As I reached the reception, I was signed in, given a name badge, and shown into a dining area where other people were already mixing and helping themselves to a buffet breakfast, which included a full English as well as various fruits, cereals, and drinks.

As everyone finished breakfast and started mixing, I could see from the name tags that all the major houses were present: Goldman Sachs, JP Morgan, Credit Suisse, UBS, Bank of America, Merrill Lynch, Shearson Hutton, and others. There was a healthy mix of gender and ages.

Our hosts were a dapper energetic middle-aged man, who looked like an athlete in his green 'Chemical Bank' tracksuit bottoms and sweatshirt, and a very tall blonde lady, who was similarly clad, alongside two event co-ordinators from the Hop Farm. They immediately started handing out Chemical Bank caps to everyone, most of the guests quickly put them on.

A huge flipboard was erected, and we were divided into six teams. The teams were advised that there would be six events, with each team rotating around them, completing three in the morning and three in the afternoon, with a break for lunch.

At the end of the day, we would congregate back at the dining room for prize-giving. A prize would be presented to each individual who scored the most points at each event. Additional prizes would be presented to the team that scored the highest points at each event and for the team that scored the most points on the day.

The events were clay pigeon shooting, off-road driving, archery, carting, reverse driving, and target shooting. Each team had five individuals, and great care had gone into trying the balance the teams based on gender and age.

The day proved to be very enjoyable. My team started with the carting, which were powerful petrol carts. The carting course was on grass with large tractor tyres and

My Jurassic Lark Team

lines marking out the boundary. The event was not a race against each other but five circuits against the clock.

Each driver was introduced to the cart and given a couple of test laps before driving against the clock. Each of the five laps was timed, and we were told points were allocated for the fastest lap and the fastest overall time for the combined five laps, as well as the fastest combined team time.

Next was the bizarre reverse driving which was a four-by-four Land Rover – turn left and the car goes right. A course was mapped out, and it was similar to a driving test. You had to navigate the course, including reversing into a box, and pulling out. This event was scored on a combination of time and penalties for however many traffic cones you hit.

Our last event of the morning was the target shooting, which was, as the name suggests, target shooting with a powerful air pistol firing lead pellets. Four targets were set up of varying sizes and distances. After practise shots, each of us fired twelve shots, three at each target, and scores were taken.

Lunch was a roast with a choice of meat, and a choice of dessert. No alcohol was being served due to the nature of the events we were doing. We were told there was an open bar once the event was over, but most of us, having driven to Paddock Wood, would not accept the offer.

The afternoon started with our team at the archery course. As with the air pistol shooting, four targets were set up at varying distances, and the instructor gave us all a demonstration. As each of us stepped up, we were given three practice shots before stepping up to the targets. Again, each of us fired twelve shots, three at each target, and scores were taken.

Clay pigeon shooting followed – not something I had ever done before. Three stands were set up, one where the clay crossed from left to right, one where the clay was fired away from you, and then a stand where multiple clays were fired. This was my weakest event. Never having done anything like it before, and with the short practice time getting the hang of the shooting and the recoil of the shotgun was difficult, but enjoyable.

Our last event was my favourite – the off-road driving. The large four-by-four Land Rover was driven around a very muddy course – given there had been no rain, I assumed copious amounts of water were being applied between teams.

The course included climbs and plunges into water-filled gullies and along a narrow gully before more climbs and turns. Again, the actual drive was against the clock. Each of us was given a test lap by the instructor riding shotgun, who advised how to tackle each obstacle. The instructor also rode shotgun on the actual drive just in case anyone got stuck or tried to do something silly.

Then it was back to the dining hall for refreshments, and the prize-giving. Needless to say, my team did not win – we came third – but I had met really good people and had a fantastic day at the expense of Manny Hanny.

Another annual back-office event at Cater Allen was entertaining one of its key clearing clients, Republic National Bank (RepNat).

John and Pete were our back-office contacts at RepNat on a daily basis. We agreed trades and positions and, if required, received, or paid funds to keep the account fully funded. We took John and Pete to lunch a couple of times during the year, but every Christmas we took them out for an evening meal at a venue of their choice. Their choice was the same every year: the Golden Dragon Chinese restaurant in Chinatown.

John was my age, in his early thirties, and Pete was in his mid- to late-twenties, and they were both genuine fun.

Given that Trevor Kemp was a teetotaller, he really had no desire to go out for a night on the town, and when David and I joined Cater Allen, he was more than happy to let us get on with the client entertainment.

The Christmas event with John and Peter always started the same – beers in the Jamaica Inn and then a black cab to Chinatown. We had a set meal with more drink and then hit Covent Garden for even more drink.

Pete used to just call it a night and vanish, but John was always in a complete mess by the end of the evening.

John lived in Hastings, so we both had to get to Charing Cross station for what was usually the last train home. As I had to get the Bexleyheath train, my job was always to stick John on his train and preferably tell the guard that he was getting off at the end of the line, before sprinting off to get my train home.

Our honeymoon period at Cater Allen ended in early February 1995 when a trader by the name of Nick Leeson caused a complete meltdown of the financial markets.

On 16th January 1995, Leeson placed a short straddle in the Singapore and Tokyo stock exchanges, betting that the Japanese stock market would not move significantly overnight. Unfortunately for him, the Kobe earthquake hit early in the morning of 17th January, sending Asian markets into a crash. Leeson's trading position went massively into debit.

In a state of panic, Leeson attempted to recoup his losses by making a series of increasingly risky new trades, this time betting that the Nikkei Stock Average would make a rapid recovery from the earthquake. However, the recovery failed to materialise, and the losses kept mounting.

He worked for a long-established and respected bank called Baring Brothers in their Singapore office, and he was in a position of trust so was able to hide these positions and losses from his bosses. But the losses reached a point where he felt he could not keep on hiding them, and so he fled, leaving a note saying, 'I'm sorry.'

The losses eventually topped £827 million, twice Barings' available trading capital. After a failed bailout attempt, Barings, which had been the UK's oldest merchant bank, was declared insolvent on 26th February.

Rumours about the scale of the losses dogged the markets for days before the actual amounts started to feed out.

The impact of Lesson's trading did not stop with market volatility but once again put derivatives themselves under the spotlight. The demise of Barings Bank led to increased political pressure being applied to the market regulators.

The markets were trading so much volume on the back of all this news that on the biggest trading day, David Peart and I were still working at Birchin Lane late into the night, processing trades. We were so late that David missed his last train home and so I made a phone call home to Alison to tell her that he was coming back with me. We found a taxi willing to take us out to Welling, grabbing a couple of kebabs as we passed by.

A more personal event for the Parker family occurred early in 1995 when my brother Robin started divorce proceedings against his wife, Victoria.

Vicky had followed Robin into the Metropolitan Police and while training at Hendon had started an affair with a fellow trainee police constable. Robin had become suspicious and discreetly gathered evidence that confirmed his suspicions. The divorce meant he had to sell his house in Wordsworth Road.

At the same time, Alison was now earning more than she ever had before in her back-office role at Bank of America and wanted to get involved in the mortgage. We agreed a price with Robin for his house, and I put 87 Woodbrook Road on the market.

After another quick visit to my solicitor friend James Carter in Blackfriars, we had a new joint agreement drawn up which confirmed the equity I was putting into the purchase of the property in Wordsworth Road.

The agreement confirmed that a split of any profit on an eventual sale of Wordsworth Road, over and above the amount I was investing, would be 50/50. Once again, James reminded me that marriage or children would make the agreement invalid.

Woodbrook Road sold very quickly, and Alison and I moved into 25

Wordsworth Road in Welling. The house in Wordsworth Road was a 1970s end-of-terrace and came with a garage in a block that we could access via a large wooden gate in the back garden.

The back garden was small with a steep bank into which Robin had constructed an exceptionally large, landscaped pond. This pond was deep and stocked with goldfish and attracted an annual invasion of frogs and toads from the nearby open woodland.

Alison was delighted to now be a homeowner, and she set about planning changes to the décor. We bought new furniture and settled in.

On 28 April 1995, my godfather, Dave Ritchings, was shaken by the news that his good friend and colleague Gilbert Durieux, the chief executive of Matif S.A., the French commodity and financial futures market, died in Cannes.

Gilbert was forty-seven, and his death was totally unexpected. He was a significant figure in the derivatives space and a good friend to the LCH.

OK, confession time: I am a Trekkie. I have always loved *Star Trek* from the original 1960s show and into the *Next Generation* cast. The good thing about being with Alison was that she wasn't averse to it either. I would not classify her as a Trekkie, but she would happily watch it with me.

For my 33rd birthday, Alison bought me tickets to a two-day *Star Trek Generations* convention at the Royal Albert Hall.

I was over the moon. It was timed to coincide with the premiere of the *Star Trek Generations* movie, and the entire cast of *Star Trek: The Next Generation* was to attend, including Patrick Stewart, LeVar Burton, Michael Dorn, Brent Spiner, Jonathan Frakes, Gates McFadden, and Marina Sirtis.

The cast were scheduled to appear on the Albert Hall stage over the two days to talk about their experiences appearing on the show and to field questions from fans.

I booked the two days off work, being incredibly careful not to let on to anybody what I was doing. My life would have been made a misery in the office had anybody found out.

On Thursday, 4th May 1995, I travelled on the Tube to the Albert Hall, sitting next to a couple dressed as Klingons, and all around me were fans in various costumes from the two television shows.

There were lots of vendors in the rooms and corridors surrounding the auditorium, with books, pictures and all manner of *Star Trek* collectables and paraphernalia on sale.

I was seated in the stalls, about ten rows back from the stage. A huge cinema-style screen was suspended from a gantry above the stage showing clips from the shows and films.

When the five-minute warning went out, the hall quickly filled, and Michael Dorn took to the stage to a huge reception.

The format was that each actor would give a monologue for half an hour or so. Each actor's patter and stories had obviously been honed over the years of doing various conventions. This was followed by a half-an-hour question-and-answer session.

In between each of the actors, there would be writers, special effects staff and behind-the-scenes footage shown on the screen.

The running order for the first day was as follows: Michael Dorn (Wharf) at 10.15, a break at 11.30, then Brent Spiner (Data) at 11.45, after which Michelle Nichols (Uhura) was signing books at the balcony-level merchandise area.

At 2 pm, there was a behind-the-scenes presentation given by Eric Stillwell, including previously unseen footage and a Q&A. There was a Trekmaster quiz at 2.25 and the much-anticipated guest talk from director Rick Berman at 3.30.

Another break was followed by the highlight of the first day: the appearance of Patrick Stewart (Captain Jean Luc Picard) who started at 5.15. As a Shakespearean stage actor, he had a stage presence that was awe inspiring, and overall, I had an amazing time. The first day finished at 6.30 pm.

Day two started with Gates McFadden (Doctor Crusher) at 10.15, LeVar Burton (Jordie) at 11.45, followed by a break for lunch.

The special effects team appeared at 2 pm, and there was a charity auction of items and props at 2.45. At 4 pm, Marina Sirtis (Troi) took to the stage, and at 5.15 it was Johnathan Frakes (William Riker), with the show closing at 6.30 pm.

I had an amazing time and came away from the Albert Hall buzzing. The event made me even more of a Trekkie than ever.

With Alison and I secure in good jobs, we started to talk about a big holiday.

Neither of us were into beach holidays, and we both realised we had an unfulfilled itch to get out and see the world. We had the money and freedom that would allow us to indulge in a bit of foreign travel.

After a long chat, and me talking about my business trip to the US, we settled on an idea to go on a trip to America and see New England in the fall.

One lunchtime, I set off to specialist travel agent Kuoni and found just what I was looking for. It was an escorted coach trip starting in New York and then travelling north via Providence and Boston then into Canada and back. Called simply 'New England in the Fall,' it ticked all the boxes.

I returned home that night with the brochure, and Alison was extremely excited by the New England tour as well as a few of the other tours listed in the brochure.

We agreed to stick with the New England tour for this year, and I was back at Kuoni the next day armed with my credit card to make the booking.

The coach tour had lots of sights along the way, including Salem, Niagara Falls, Fort Henry, and the Thousand Islands, which constitute a North American archipelago of 1,864 islands straddling the Canada–US border in the Saint Lawrence River as it emerges from the northeast corner of Lake Ontario. This was all in addition to our stops at New York, Boston Toronto, and Montreal.

When our late-September departure date arrived, we set off for Heathrow Airport and our flight direct to New York.

I had obviously been to New York, but my short overnight stay to meet the guys at the Czarnikow New York office had not given me much of a chance to explore. This was Alison's first trip to America, and she was excited by all the large cars and sights in the same way I had been on my first visit.

We had a central hotel in New York, and by the time we had cleared the airport and settled into the hotel, it was evening, but Alison was determined to get out and explore a little.

We were close to Broadway, New York's theatreland, so we set off for a walk and settled on the 'Harley Davidson' restaurant for a meal before heading back.

The next day, we had to meet up with the tour, and they had booked a large breakfast table where we met our guides and fellow travellers.

Our fellow companions for the trip were a rum mix of Australians, New Zealanders, and South Africans, with only one other couple from the UK. Our tour guides were both New Englanders, and they were both keen to show us their native state and Canada.

Once breakfast finished, we went off on a guided walk around New York, including Wall Street, Times Square, the Statue of Liberty, and the Empire State Building. That evening, we had the first of our 'tour meals' in the Roof Garden restaurant. This gave views over Central Park, which we then visited after the meal, before returning to the hotel.

The next morning, we boarded a vast luxury coach for the first leg of our trip north towards the Canadian border.

Like everything in America, the coaches were bigger and super comfortable, and the seats were like sofas. We set off, heading north towards New England via Rhode Island.

The initial stages of our trip was dominated by visits to historical sites related to America's War of Independence and early settlement. We took in a full day of stops and sites as we made our way into Boston.

We were booked into good hotels throughout the tour and had a full day and night in Boston before the tour set off again. This gave us time to explore the city and in particular the opportunity to visit the '*Cheers*' bar made famous by the American TV show.

Of all the American cities I visited, Boston remains my favourite. Our hotel there was the Hyatt Regency, which had views over the Charles River. The room was great, and once we had settled, we headed off to the restaurant and had a delicious meal before settling down for the evening.

With the next day being free, we headed straight off into town, as Alison had decided she wanted to buy clothes. Once we had the shopping out of the way, we headed off to Beacon Hill, home of the '*Cheers*' bar.

The first thing to note is the outside is exactly as it is in the credits of the show, but that's it. The inside is totally different, being a small, long bar, unlike the vast basement in the show. That said, we did the tourist photos outside and bought our *Cheers* glasses to bring home.

The next morning, I headed off to breakfast, looking forward to my US vice, which I picked up in Chicago – the eggs benedict breakfast. I had totally convinced Alison to give it a go, and what was good in Chicago was superb in Boston, courtesy, so the waiter said, of the Canadian ham.

With breakfast done, it was time to bring our packed bags down to the coach, and we re-boarded for our trip towards the Canadian border. There were lots of statues of 'Minutemen,' but the real star was the colours of the trees in their Autumn splendour.

We were blessed with clear weather on every day but one, and that was the day when we really wanted good weather. On that day, the coach pulled alongside Niagara Falls.

We were staying in a hotel that overlooked the falls and were booked on a trip on the Maid of the Mist, a boat that takes you to the very bottom of the falls. It was dark, gloomy, and raining heavily.

In actuality, Niagara is a group of three waterfalls, the largest of which is the Horseshoe Falls.

The Maid of the Mist boat tour had been running for over 150 years. Obviously, it was not the same boat, and it was now a large, sleek double-decked vessel. Everyone was provided with a plastic poncho to cover their clothes, ordinarily for the spray that comes off from the falls, but on the day we were there it also protected us from the rain.

The Maid of the Mist leaves from the Observation Tower, and the thirty-minute trip takes you right up to the Bridal Veil Falls and American Falls, before riding into the dramatic thick mist of spray inside the bend of the Horseshoe Falls.

The thing you remember is the sound of the water, which is more dramatic when you are told that the volume of water is much lower now than it was historically. The poor weather could not take away from the breath taking sights and sounds of what was a highlight of the tour.

The journey onwards and into Canada included another boat trip, this time in sunshine, around the Thousand Islands and then on to Fort Henry, an ancient British fort dating back before the American War of Independence. From there, we pushed on into Canada itself, taking in Montreal and Toronto before a full-on drive back into the US for the return to Boston.

Once in Boston, the tour broke up, with all of us going in different directions from Boston Airport.

Alison and I headed for our optional trip to Las Vegas. Our hotel there was the Golden Nugget, located in Fremont Street, the 'old' strip made famous by the cowboy tipping his hat in lights and the view shown in most movies.

The new strip housed all the new, huge hotels, including Caesars Palace, the MGM Grand, Circus Circus and Bellagio. As we were to find out, the old and new strips are separated by a none-too-savoury residential area, forcing you into cabs to go from one to the other.

The Golden Nugget had old-world charm, but by the time we arrived and checked in, Alison was too tired to do anything other than order room service. Once we had eaten, she was insistent that I go out and explore without her, so I headed down to the lobby area.

As I walked towards the main doors, I heard the unmistakable sound of Scouse!

Two lads in their early twenties were desperately trying to cash up traveller's cheques, but they were a little the worse for wear. The poor girl on the reception desk couldn't understand a word the guys were saying.

The thick Scouse accent made it difficult even for me, but I could not just walk past, so I decided to help and function as an interpreter. I translated for the receptionist and then these two drunk and overfriendly Scousers, complete with their Liverpool FC shirts, adopted me.

Both lads took it in turns to shake me firmly by the hand and asked where I was from. I told them I lived in southeast London and that was it – I was christened 'London' for the night and informed I was going on the town with them.

We headed out of the hotel into Fremont Street. The Scousers introduced themselves as Duncan and Larry. They were busy chatting away about football, girls, and drink, and they were overly excited and enthusiastic about everything.

Then I felt my arm being pulled as the guys made a dash for a dark entrance into what looked like a bar. Having missed the sign outside, I figured it was a bar, which it was, but a bar with a significant difference.

As we entered, two huge bouncers nodded, and as my eyes adjusted to the light, I saw two bar-level runways and various scantily clad ladies dancing at various points around the bar. This was my first experience of a lap dance club.

The Scousers propelled me to the bar, looking around and chatting eagerly. 'This is going to be fun, London,' one said. I wasn't sure it would be fun if word of this got back to Alison, but the guys were not taking no for an answer.

Duncan had two attempts at ordering a lager before giving up. To be honest, the alcohol had made their accents extremely broad and even I was struggling. The lads pushed me forward to the young lady serving. 'Three Budweiser's please.'

Already I could see various scantily clad girls hovering around us as I looked around the vast space. I could see only a dozen or so 'customers,' vastly outnumbered by the ladies, who were dotted about and dancing on the runways. I had no idea what was going on.

Drinks in hand, I was propelled towards three stools alongside a runway where a very pretty blonde girl was dancing around a pole.

As we seated ourselves, the blonde smiled and introduced herself as 'Bonnie' and she started to gyrate, smiling back at the two beaming Scousers. 'Where are you from, boys?' she asked in a deep southern American accent.

Duncan pointed to Larry. 'Me and Laz are from Liverpool in England, and this is London … because, well he's from London.'

Bonnie gave me a grin as I replied quietly, 'Kevin.'

The boys then noticed that the large guy nearest to us was busy tucking dollar bills into the knickers of the girl dancing in front of him. Quick as a flash, Duncan and Larry pulled dollar bills from their trouser pockets and started slipping them into Bonnie's knickers. Bonnie quickly responded by going topless.

I noticed that the girls who had been hovering around us at the bar had multiplied, but obviously a form of etiquette kept them from approaching directly. I guessed they were waiting for Bonnie to finish her stint.

One young lady caught my eye and gave me a smile. She was dusky, willowy, and incredibly pretty, not as busty, or as tall as some of those around her, she was more demurely attired in a short dress with brown sequins, which looked like a showgirl-style outfit.

Some of the others might as well have not been wearing anything. The girls were all shapes, sizes, and nationalities, all pretty, and varying in ages from teens to late thirties.

My attention was drawn back to the guys as Duncan shouted in my ear, 'Oi London, I think Bonnie just asked me for a dance.' I was as confused as my inebriated Scouse mate. There was nobody else dancing anywhere that I could see.

Bonnie had finished her stint on the runway and was assisted down from it by the two eager Liverpudlians. She then took a stool between Duncan and myself.

I asked Bonnie what she had said, and she repeated what she had said to Duncan, 'Did he want a dance?' At seeing my puzzled expression, Bonnie laughed. 'Don't you have lap dance bars in England?'

I shook my head and replied, 'If we do, I have not been to any.'

Bonnie took this in her stride and started to explain. 'A dance is like a private strip. We head over to one of the booths.' Bonnie pointed to the seating areas around the outer edges of the bar. 'You sit in one of the comfortable seats, and I strip and dance for you for five minutes or so.'

As Bonnie was speaking, the other girls had decided to close in. One brunette was running her hands through Larry's hair, and another had moved in on Duncan, assuming that I was with Bonnie. I leaned over to Duncan and explained what Bonnie had told me.

His face lit up. 'How much does it cost, London?'

Bonnie clearly understood that. 'Fifteen dollars, young man. You will not regret it.'

Duncan quickly pulled out the money, causing Bonnie to giggle and say, 'Not now, love, when I'm finished.'

Bonnie then looked back at me and said, 'Got your eye on anyone, Kevin?' I nodded, looking again for the young lady who had caught my eye earlier, but

I couldn't see her. I described her to Bonnie, and she knew immediately who I was looking for. She sent one of the other girls off to find her.

Duncan was led over to a booth by Bonnie, and Larry was giving him plenty of verbal encouragement. Bonnie started the dance, gyrating, stripping, and never moving more than a few inches from Duncan seated in front of her.

Then the young lady in the sequined dress appeared next to me. I was once again dazzled by her good looks. She smiled and introduced herself as Tabitha. I offered to buy her a drink.

By now, Bonnie was naked and practically sitting in Duncan's lap as she gyrated. Larry, in the meantime, had been led over to another booth by one of the ladies waiting for the next music track to start.

Tabitha told me she was from Mexico, which explained the dusky looks, and that she had been in Las Vegas for two years. I told her I was on holiday and that I had only met the other two lads an hour ago, and I explained a little about their accent.

By now, Duncan was back on the seat next to me, buying Bonnie a drink and calling out to Larry, who was in the midst of his 'dance' in the other booth.

Tabitha then asked if I was ready for a dance, and I agreed.

She led me by the hand over to the booths and sat next to me while we waited for the next music track. The 'dance' itself was very memorable. Tabitha was stunning and an excellent dancer. It was a tease, and the beautifully choreographed moves had been perfected over the years.

As I got up from the booth to return to the table, both the boys were already back at the booths enjoying more dances with different girls. Tabitha asked if I wanted her to make room for someone else, but I declined and spent the next hour in her company buying drinks and having another dance along the way.

Larry and Duncan were back and forth, on one occasion getting a rebuke from one of the large bouncers for getting a little 'hands on' with one of the dancers.

By the time I decided to call it a night, I promised Tabitha I would visit if I ever came back to Las Vegas. I said goodbye to Larry and Duncan and got a raucous 'Bye London' as I headed off back to the Golden Nugget hotel.

The next day, Alison and I went to the new Vegas strip to witness a scene you would only get in Las Vegas, namely two full-sized rigged sailing ships fighting a historical battle in the reception of the Treasure Island hotel, complete with actors, cannons, and explosions. The pirate vessel and its adversary fought it out several times a day.

Alison was keen to head off to Caesars Palace and its huge shopping arcade.

I was keen to don my Trekkie credentials and head off to the MGM hotel for the 'Star Trek Experience.'

We worked our way down the Strip before heading off to the MGM, where I was happy to have a drink with a Ferengi in Quarks bar and bag myself a glass from the gift shop.

Then I had my picture taken with 'Seven of Nine' from *Star Trek Voyager*. (Simulated of course – the lovely Jerri Ryan was sadly not there in person.) With picture in hand, I was then doing the actual 'Experience' which was an immersive 'play' with actors and a simulated 'ride' in a shuttle craft.

Alison was a reluctant attendee at the Experience, but she secretly enjoyed herself despite her lack of enthusiasm. Then it was back to the Golden Nugget Hotel and our last night in America before heading home to the UK.

We arrived back in Welling, exhausted but totally determined to head back to America on a different tour the following year.

In October 1995, I caught wind of a follow-up to the Stargazer Generations *Star Trek* convention that I had attended earlier. Scheduled for April 1996, another event was taking place at the Albert Hall, and this one was called unimaginatively 'Generations 2'.

For the first time in Europe, the majority of the surviving original *Star Trek* cast would be attending over the three days.

Leonard Nimoy (Spock), Walter Koenig (Chekov), George Takei (Sulu) and James Doohan (Scotty) would be there, as well as actors from the other shows, including Avery Brooks, who played Captain Sisko in *Deep Space Nine*, and Ethan Philips and Robert Picardo from the new show called *Voyager*. Also scheduled to attend was director Rick Berman and 'more guests to be announced.'

Having had such an enjoyable time at the previous two-day convention, I quickly set off one lunchtime for the Albert Hall box office to secure my seat for all three days. I splashed out on a front-row seat in one of the executive boxes which would be my seat for the entire event. I was already looking forward to it. The remainder of 1995 passed with little in the way of incident.

1996

1996 was a good year for Cater Allen. With little in the way of changes in the marketplace, I finally got confirmation that Denni Machi was on her way back to the UK for another visit. Denni had finally convinced Jennifer Johnson and Geoff Swainson that she should meet the new Cater Allen team.

I phoned her to ask her what she wanted to do while she was back in London, and she did not miss a beat: she wanted to go back to the Cambridge Theatre and see *Return to the Forbidden Planet* again. I offered her *Cats* and *Les Miserable*, but no, she wanted to go back to the show we had seen together on her first visit.

I wasn't even sure it was still playing, but it was, and I so one lunchtime I went off to the Cambridge Theatre and secured us two tickets.

It was now eight years since I had first met Denni in Chicago, and she still had the ability to both captivate me and keep me off balance. I couldn't help but get excited about her impending visit.

It was Monday, 4th of March when Denni arrived in the UK. As she did on her previous visit, Denni stayed with Geoff Swainson and his wife, and they picked her up from Heathrow Airport.

The following Tuesday morning, she arrived at Birchin Lane, and I eagerly went down to the ground-floor reception to meet her.

It was a sunny day, and Denni stood with her jacket in her hand. She was wearing a tight black-and-white horizontally striped dress that clung to her, showing off her figure. I stopped in my tracks; my heart was beating like mad.

Despite the vivid pictures that stayed in my mind from previous meetings, time seemed to have made Denni even more attractive to me.

With a beaming smile, this vision from Milwaukee propelled herself over into my arms to give me a huge hug. As my arms folded around her, Denni kissed my cheek and whispered, 'Good boy, Mr Parker.' We stayed quietly in this warm embrace before she demanded that I 'lead on.'

We stepped into the lift, and once on the first floor we walked down the long corridor to the financial futures office. David Peart said hello, and I introduced Trevor Kemp.

The downside of having the trading desk and the back office in one room was that I had to introduce Denni to everyone at once. Poor Denni was shaking hands and saying hello to each and every person as I went down one side of the trading desk and up the other.

Denni recognised the Czarnikow traders and was delighted to see Sue Southgate, who was working that day on the TRS.

We had scheduled a lunch for Denni's first day at Cater Allen, and I was due to take her out on the Wednesday evening and then I had tickets for *Return to the Forbidden Planet* for the Thursday evening.

This was much the same schedule as Denni had experienced on her previous visit, she was flying back to Chicago on the Friday.

David had tactfully declined lunch, and I had avoided including Trevor. In the back of my mind, I kept thinking about the 'kiss' on her last visit, we instantly picked up from where we left off with an amazingly easy, flirty banter.

Denni updated me on events in Chicago. Ro was a mother now and had been away from work on maternity leave for a while. Denni told me Ro was already pregnant with baby number two and she was unsure if Ro would be back to work after her second baby.

I gave Denni a brief update of events in London, including my relationship with Alison. Denni asked if marriage was on the horizon, but I said no.

I was feeling very conflicted – on the one hand, things were going well with Alison, and yet the feelings Denni generated in me were hugely different.

Alison was safe, comfortable and our life together cruised along, while Denni was unpredictable, a challenge, which made her exciting, but she was unattainable, living so far away. When I was with Denni, I had to up my game, the banter, the flirting; it was as if we both knew our time together was going to be short and we just went with the moment.

Lunch this time was at Sweetings in Queen Victoria street, and it was here that Denni expressed an interest in me taking her to see the new LIFFE floor. Having visited the previous Royal Exchange floor on her last trip to London, she had heard a great deal about the new LIFFE trading floor at Cannon Street, and a number of the big American houses now had a presence there.

One thing you never really wanted to do was to take an attractive young lady down onto the LIFFE floor itself. The LIFFE floor may have moved to glossy, new, bespoke premises, but the traders were the same politically incorrect people they had always been.

I suggested the idea of going to the viewing gallery instead of the actual floor, in the same way Anne had shown me the CME trading floor. But Denni was not the sort of lady to back down, and she stubbornly preferred to experience the trading floor in person.

I conceded but decided to reduce the odds of getting totally embarrassed by asking if she had something in her suitcase that was a little less revealing.

Denni gave me 'the' smile – I was in deep trouble. 'So, Mr Parker, are you telling me that my dress is too revealing?'

'Well not for me, no,' I replied. 'I like it, but for the trading floor, a nun's habit would be better.'

Denni seemed to arch her back a little, highlighting her figure even more as she looked me in the straight in the eye. 'What exactly am I revealing? I mean the neckline is around my neck, no cleavage on display this time, and it's just above the knee, so it's not too short. Why is this not acceptable for a visit to the LIFFE floor?' She leaned closer and semi whispered. 'What if I told you I had the same outfit in blue and black lined up for tomorrow?'

I felt my cheeks burning as I maintained eye contact, our noses nearly touching closer, 'Then, Denni Machi, I would tell you that I was unable to arrange a LIFFE floor visit at such short notice.'

Denni laughed and pulled away slightly as I continued, 'As for your dress, it may be up to your neck and just above the knee, but it looks like it's been sprayed on.'

Denni gave me a fake indignant look. ' Mr Parker, are you saying I look slutty?'

I could not help but laugh out loud at her pout. 'No, Miss Machi, you look gorgeous, as always, but for the trading floor ...'

Denni jumped in. 'I know, a nun's habit. I'll see if I have something baggy and frumpy if you promise to arrange the visit.'

I gestured to the waitress for the bill as Denni, who always had to have the last word, added, 'I guess I can save the blue and black dress for our Thursday trip to the theatre as you obviously like it so much!'

I said goodbye to Denni as she headed off back the short distance to the Harris office and I returned to Birchin Lane, hoping that she would not actually turn up in a nun's habit. I definitely would never have put anything past her.

I phoned down to the LIFFE floor and spoke with the Right Honourable Daniel Beckett to explain the situation. Danny told me he would get us signed in for 12.30 the next day and would meet us and take us around.

That eased my concerns a little – with Danny as my guide, we may just get around without the usual catcalls, innuendos, and crude remarks.

The next day at 12.00, Denni arrived in a modest deep-purple jacket-and-skirt set with a white blouse, buttoned high enough for me to be relieved.

With a mischievous grin, she opened her jacket wide and said, 'Will I do,

Mr Parker?' I nodded – at least it wasn't a nun's habit. Then we set off towards Lower Thames Street and the entrance to the LIFFE floor.

I must have been slightly more quiet than usual as Denni enquired if I was concerned at having to take her onto the floor. It was a tongue-in-cheek question I am sure, but I just replied that I was worried about taking an attractive lady into the lion's den. Denni looked suitably flattered, and once again I had succeeded in making her blush.

We arrived at the small Lower Thames Street LIFFE floor reception, conveniently within sight of the Thames-side 'Bouncing Banker' public house.

We walked up to the ladies on the reception desk, and I explained we were there to meet with Daniel Beckett for a floor visit. The lady gave us a quick up-and-down and sorted out two floor passes which you clipped onto your jacket and loudly pronounced 'Visitor.'

Armed with our passes, we walked over to the airport-style security based at the bottom of the four long escalators that led up to the new trading floor.

When we arrived up at trading floor level, we walked to the main entrance onto the LIFFE floor, with traders walking around in their multicoloured trading jackets, local traders in their red jackets and the admin staff in their yellow jackets.

I spotted Danny talking to another trader, and as we approached, he saw us and cut short his chat.

I introduced Denni, and Danny was charming as always. I had explained to Denni that he was a Right Honourable, and she asked if she should curtsy. Danny didn't hesitate and replied only if she wanted to.

Danny then led us through the turnstile security gates and into a corridor that ran behind the admin booths before walking us onto the trading floor itself.

As always, the sheer volume of noise hit you and the adrenaline started pumping. We walked round to the gilt booths that looked into the gilt trading pit.

Ray Lancaster was the Cater Allen gilt booth manager and a safe pair of hands, as he was one of the senior admin clerks on the trading floor and an absolute gentleman. Danny hovered, ready to take us on to the other pits and away from the relative security of the gilt pit, which was widely acknowledged as the 'gentleman's pit.'

Ray pointed out our traders in the gilt pit to Denni; there was Tim Clark in his blue-and-white striped jacket that denoted a Cater Allen corporate trader and Richard Taylor and John Arnold, our two local traders in their red jackets.

Thankfully, things were busy with trades flowing, and a couple of times Ray was interrupted by orders coming through on the phones. This was good because Denni was standing right next to Ray and could watch him in action, using hand signals to communicate the orders to Tim in the pit.

However, on the third order, Ray's view of Tim was obscured, so he gave the order to Danny who strode into the gilt pit and was immediately given a loud reception.

Five or six of the traders had seen Denni and me standing beside Ray, and on spotting Danny walking into the gilt pit with an order, they started shouting 'Get Orrrfff my land' at him.

Ray laughed and explained to Denni that Danny, being 'titled,' was always greeted in this way whenever he stepped into the gilt pit, which Denni thought was extremely funny.

As Danny came back with a trading card and Ray's order completed, he suggested we move on and head for the BTP pit.

The new LIFFE trading floor had a considerable number of young ladies working on it. Most were deployed as admin clerks in yellow jackets, but any new or unfamiliar young lady elicited the sort of responses that ladies in the 1960s and 70s might have expected on a building site.

Usually, this started with a trader or clerk spotting a new face and shouting, 'Oi.' This immediately made all the traders and clerks in earshot focus on the lady concerned. It was usually followed by other calls, such as 'Alright darling!,' 'What are you doing tonight?' and 'Come and join us over here!' etc.

Our walk from the gilt pit meant moving from the outskirts of the trading floor onto the trading floor proper, and for the first time Denni started to attract looks and the calls and comments. She ignored them as we walked onwards.

The BTP was the Italian government bond contract, and at the time it was the home to what was known on the LIFFE floor as the 'South London Mafia.' This reflected the fact that the majority of the traders in the BTP hailed from South London.

The Cater Allen booth manager on the BTP was none other than Paul Collister, my old colleague from Czarnikow and someone Denni knew from her previous trip. I got the usual winks and gentle elbow in the ribs from Ollie as Danny chatted with Denni.

We slowly worked our way around the other trading pits and admin booths until we arrived at the short sterling pit where Ian 'Burger' Hughes was our booth manager. Danny, in a slip of the tongue, introduced Ian as 'Burger' which meant Ian then had to explain to Denni why he had that nickname.

It had derived from a challenge issued by other floor staff and involved Ian eating four McDonald's cheeseburgers in under four minutes. Denni gave Ian the look, and he nodded and said, 'I succeeded, hence my nickname.'

Danny was required back in the gilt pit as Tim Clark was off to lunch, so our head admin clerk, Angela Marsh, replaced Danny as our guide.

Denni seemed happy to have a female escort for the remainder of her visit. Angela's presence also quelled any further male chauvinistic comments, which I was relieved about.

The rest of the visit went by without incident, and I was finally able to escort Denni off the LIFFE floor and into the pub nearby, the Bouncing Banker, for a quick drink.

Denni had enjoyed her LIFFE floor visit and meeting some of the key floor staff. Having experienced a similar male mentality on the vast trading floor at Harris Futures, Denni had taken the banter and comments with good humour.

We happily chatted, and, as always in Denni's company, the time evaporated and then she was due back at Bucklesbury House.

I walked Denni back to the Harris Futures office. We agreed to meet up at the Cater Allen office at 6.00pm for our evening meal.

When Denni had first told me that she was coming back to London and wanted to return to the Cambridge theatre to see *Return to the Forbidden Planet* on the Thursday night, I had been in a quandary as to what to do on the Wednesday night. I wanted to surprise her with something different. This time I elected to avoid the usual panicked trip back to Dalston by looking for a City restaurant.

Denni arrived promptly and contented herself watching 'Yorkie' who was happy to demonstrate the APT trading system to her. Once I finished work, we said goodnight to those still in the office and went for a drink in the Jampot before heading off towards Liverpool street.

We enjoyed another couple of drinks in the Magpie, a pub in New Street frequented by staff from nearby Bache Securities.

Denni had been very patient about my plans for the evening, but as we left the Magpie she took my arm and asked if we were now going for something to eat. I smiled and said "Maybe" which elicited her usual pout.

We walked a little further down Bishopsgate before turning into Artillery lane. We arrived at the "Eat and Drink" a Chinese restaurant that provided reasonable food but was renowned for something that was not immediately apparent to Denni as we sat at the table and studied the menu.

After a quick consultation we elected a four course set meal and ordered drinks.

As the drinks arrived, the owner of the establishment started his party piece by murdering Elvis's "Blue Suede Shoes" over the karaoke machine. Denni along with our fellow diners were laughing as he finished, but it was a tried and tested method of ensuring that customers started to take turns singing, if only to keep the owner off the machine.

After finishing our first course Denni took my hand and dragged me out to the reception area where the karaoke screen and microphone were located. Grabbing the folder containing the list of tracks that were available Denni deliberately shielded her selection from me as she handed it to the gentleman behind the counter who set her track up.

It wasn't until the tune started and the words hit the screen that I knew that Denni had selected "Islands in the stream" by Dolly Parton and Kenny Rogers. We had to share the mic and Denni gave it her all and the truth is she had a good voice.

We secured a polite round of applause as we returned to our table where our next course of shredded Duck was waiting.

We returned to the mic to sing "I got you babe" by Sonny and Cher in between courses and after a round of Irish Coffee's we returned once more to sing karaoke favourite "Daydream Believer" by the Monkees before leaving.

As we walked out into the street Denni took my arm kissed my cheek and told me that she had really enjoyed her evening. As we arrived back at Bishopsgate, it made sense for me to head towards London Bridge and for Denni to get a cab back to Geoff's but neither of us wanted to say the words.

I asked Denni what Geoff had planned for her the next day. It was a series of meetings with London based clients including lunch at Marble Arch.

We agreed Denni would return to Birch lane at 3:30 the next day for a tour of Cater Allen followed by our trip to the West End and our second viewing of *Return to the Forbidden Planet*. I managed to secure another quick kiss on the cheek from her before she finally climbed into a cab, and I set off for the station.

The next day, and on schedule, Denni arrived and was escorted down to our office by the always-bubbly blonde receptionist Sophia Hunter.

Denni had not been joking about her dress – it was indeed a navy-blue-and-black version of the dress she had worn to the office on Tuesday. Denni was delight to see Karen Loftus managing the TRS allocations that day and once they had greeted each other, Denni sat down with Trevor Kemp who demonstrated the bespoke clearing system that we used at Cater Allen.

Following this Mark Dyer had volunteered to take Denni round to the discount house and the HICA areas of the Bank.

As the clock reached 5 o'clock I started clearing up to get out the office.

The desk traders were hanging around Philip Plumber as he was trading on the APT. Dave Peart could see I was keen to get out the office, and he told me that he and Trevor would finish up. I slipped beside Denni and suggested we go.

As this was her last scheduled visit to Cater Allen, before returning back to Chicago, she did the rounds saying goodbye to everyone, and then we headed out of the office.

I had booked a table at the Ivy restaurant, which was a short walk away from the Cambridge Theatre.

We grabbed a black cab, and as it pulled away, Denni asked if we would have time to do a little shopping before we went in to see the show.

I gave her a quizzical look. 'Shopping?'

'In the theatre, Mr Parker. I want to get some T-shirts and the CD from the show.'

I told her we would, and the penny started to drop – Denni was not expecting to be back to London.

I felt my stomach knot. Of course, this could be the last time I ever get to spend with her. My enthusiasm for the evening was replaced with a sick feeling and a sense of impending loss, which just didn't make sense. How can you lose something you never had?

We pulled up outside the Ivy, and I told Denni that this was one of the London celebrity haunts and that we should keep our eyes open, although we didn't see anybody famous during our meal. The food was excellent, and as a restaurant used to pre-theatre venues bookings, the service was swift, and we finished with plenty of time to spare.

Denni and I walked the short distance to the theatre, I felt her hand slip into mine.

As always, the reception area of the Cambridge Theatre was packed, and I could see a number of the audience wearing their *Return to the Forbidden Planet* T-shirts. The number of people returning now seemed to outnumber people seeing the play for the first time.

Denni bought a glossy programme and quickly joined the queue at the gift shop to secure two T-shirts and the CD. I joined in, buying a T-shirt and CD for myself, and then we headed into the auditorium.

We were in row D of the stalls, alongside the central aisle, closer to the stage than we had been last time.

In a repeat of our first visit, fully costumed actors were showing people to their seats and explaining the actions they wanted the audience to complete when the captain demanded audience help the ship's crew 'reverse polarity.'

Denni was quick to explain to the actress who approached us that we had been before. The actress, on hearing Denni's American accent, asked where she was from, and before I knew it a camera was thrust into my hand as Denni posed with the actress. Then I was posing with Denni as the actress took the camera to take a picture of us in return.

The theatre filled quickly, and once again a big cinema screen came down in front of the main curtain and Sir Patrick Moore was into the narrator's dialogue.

The show was as brilliant second time around, but this time, knowing what was coming and joining in with abandon with all the songs and dance moves made it an even more enjoyable. We both threw ourselves headlong into the experience, and as we were alongside the centre aisle when the encore started, Denni and I were quickly out into the space beside us dancing.

As the final notes of music faded and the curtain came down for the last time, both of us were sweating profusely. Denni turned to face me, and for one of the only times in my life, I ceased the moment, pulling her into my arms and kissing her passionately.

I have no idea how long we embraced each other, but I could sense the theatre emptying and the unfortunate people next to us giving up on exiting via the central aisle and heading off in the other direction. I didn't care.

When we finally came up for air, I had this real déjà-vu moment as Denni pressed her forehead to mine, noses touching, staring directly into each other's eyes – she didn't let me down. She whispered, 'Good boy, Mr Parker.'

We grabbed a black cab and headed off to Dalston and Geoff Swainson's house. We hardly spoke during the journey, holding hands, tired and yet still riding the wave of a surreal high that follows a perfect experience. We were coming down into that deep depressing feeling you get, knowing the evening was ending and reality was returning.

I have never had a holiday romance, but I imagine it is much the same feeling, knowing you are back to work the next day and returning to your routine, and this moment of 'magic' is ending.

We had been here before, having this same cab ride after watching the same show, and yet this felt much worse.

As we pulled up outside, Denni gave me a weak smile and said thank you. I wished her a safe flight back to Chicago, and we kissed briefly like parting friends. Then she was gone.

I travelled in the cab back to London Bridge and then on the train back to Welling in a daze. I walked slowly back to Wordsworth Road. I couldn't bring myself to walk upstairs to where Alison was sleeping; it didn't feel right. So, I slumped on the sofa, and at some stage fell asleep.

That morning, a none-too-impressed Alison asked what time I had arrived and why I was sleeping in my work clothes on the sofa. I showered, changed, and headed into the City.

On Saturday 6 April, which was the Easter weekend, I once again set off for the Albert Hall and the *Star Trek* convention.

We had been told that Leonard Nimoy (Spock) was no longer attending as he was directing a stage show on Broadway that was opening at the same time. Instead, on the last day, Monday the eighth, none other than William Shatner (Captain Kirk) was replacing him, and Michelle Nichols (Uhura) was added to the line-up.

Once again as I got onto the Tube, I was surrounded by people in *Star Trek* outfits, dressed as all types of crew members and aliens, and a carnival atmosphere ensued.

On this occasion I had let slip to Trevor Kemp what I was up to, in the mistaken belief that, being a God-fearing man, he would not tell the others. A silly mistake.

On the first day of the event, I took my seat in the box and realised that the other seats in the box had been taken by one party, a very excitable group from Holland.

As I was to discover, the success of the first Generations event at the Albert Hall meant that this time people had travelled from all around the globe.

It was assumed that due to the age of the original cast members, that this was likely to be the very last time the majority of the original 1960s cast would be attending an event like this.

The group from Holland occupied the other nine seats in the box and included two couples and five single ladies, all dressed in original 1960s style costumes. I was the odd one out, not being a member of their party and not being dressed up. I was quickly adopted and introduced to each of them in turn. Once I confirmed that I was there for all three days, I was part of their family.

What followed over the next couple of days was Trekkie heaven.

The show started at 10.20 on Saturday, 6 April with an amazing musical on-screen introduction that featured clips from all the shows – *Star Trek*, *Next Generation* and *Deep Space Nine* – put to an upbeat score created especially for the event, and subsequently auctioned off later in the show.

The fast pace began at 10.30 , the first guest was none other than James Doohan (Scotty) who appeared in *Star Trek* and almost all the movies. He started his speech by telling us that he had been incredibly lucky to even get into acting as he had been with the Canadian forces on D-Day.

After a quick break at 11.45, Walter Koenig (Chekov), who had also stared in a recent television show *Babylon 5*, appeared on stage. Walter regaled us with a funny story about how, after doing his first year in the original *Star Trek*, he and a group of fellow actors had been sitting in a restaurant and attracted the attention of young ladies seated nearby. He told his fellow actors that he had been recognised and their meal may be interrupted by a request for autographs.

Sure, enough, a couple of the ladies got up and approached him, one of them saying, 'Excuse me, are you …' Walter stopped her mid-flow, saying, 'Yes, it's me. What can I do for you ladies?' They asked , 'Would you sing the chorus to "Hey, Hey, We're The Monkees"?' This caused his friends to fall around laughing. Walter had been mistaken for Davy Jones, the lead singer of the pop group The Monkees.

After a break for lunch, for which I had brought sandwiches, we went into a two o'clock behind-the-scenes presentation. At 3.15, it was Robert Picardo, who was the doctor in the new *Star Trek* show *Voyager*, followed at 16.15 by Ethan Philips, who was also in *Voyager*. After another break, Avery Brooks (Captain Sisko from *Deep Space Nine*) took to the stage, and this closed out day one.

On day two, we kicked off with another musical and visual film, and then George Takei (Sulu) took to the stage. One of the key questions put to all the original actors, thus far during the question-and-answer sessions, had concerned the widely rumoured antagonism between William Shatner and the rest of the cast.

James Doohan had said he didn't have any issues, while Walter Koenig said he was aware of it but did not go into any details. George Takei was less reticent, saying that the show was a collective success and that a certain individual thought the success was his alone.

The next actor on stage at 11.45 was Wil Wheaton, who played Doctor Crusher's son in *Next Generation*. The rest of the day was taken up with special effects guys and scriptwriters from the various shows and films.

On the last day of the event, I arrived at my seat to see a Star Trek uniform from *Deep Space Nine* on my seat.

My Dutch friends in the box had decided I was not going to be the odd one out for the last day of the event, and they had clubbed together and bought me the uniform. I had no choice but to unbutton my shirt, pull on the uniform and spend the rest of the day wearing it.

The day was full of events, including the much-anticipated speech from director Rick Berman.

But the climax of the show was the hugely anticipated arrival of William Shatner.

William was very polished, and his speech was interesting and funny, with lots of anecdotes about the show and subsequent films.

When the question-and-answer started, the first question was inevitably, 'Why do the rest of the original *Star Trek* cast dislike you?' William took it in his stride, saying that he had no idea. It was rumoured that he had leaned on the writers to give him more lines and indeed other people's lines, and that he had expected preferential treatment, all of which he denied.

But then he said he understood why one member of the cast may still have had a grudge against him.

The auditorium fell incredibly quiet. 'DeForest Kelley,' William said.

He went on to explain that of all the cast in the original series of *Star Trek*, DeForest was the only really established actor, having had parts in a string of 1950s westerns.

After DeForest was cast as Doctor McCoy in the series and they started talking, William explained that he was looking for a house in Beverly Hills. DeForest told William that the house opposite his in Hollywood was up for sale, and so William took a look, liked the house, bought it, and they became neighbours.

After that, they became good friends and socialised regularly, but they had a difference of opinion when it came to dogs – William believed that a real dog should be at knee level or higher, and anything at ankle level was a 'rat.'

One day, DeForest knocked on William's door and, as they chatted, DeForest's small dog started to play with William's Doberman. William was concerned his dog would injure DeForest's, and so he started throwing a ball to distract his dog.

He said that as his dog returned the ball William threw it again, DeForest's dog was increasingly joining in.

On the third or fourth throw, so determined was DeForest's dog to beat William's to the ball that it ran like the wind in the direction of the throw. Fully concentrating on the ball and running full pelt, DeForest's dog crashed into a garden sprinkler sticking up from the grass and promptly dropped dead.

A laugh went up around the auditorium. William pointed and said, 'That's exactly what I did – and he never spoke to me socially ever again!'

The next day, I returned to the Cater Allen office and was duly given endless 'Beam me up, Scotty' and 'Klingons' references. I kept the fact I spent the last day in uniform to myself in fear of even more sustained abuse.

Sophia Hunter had started working on the Cater Allen reception desk shortly after Czarnikow and Cater Allen's financial futures departments merged in July 1994. She was the perfect receptionist – bright, bubbly, full of charm and enthusiasm, although at times she did fit into the 'blonde' stereotype.

Sophia did not want to spend the rest of her days on a reception desk but desired a job as an admin clerk on the LIFFE floor.

Having set her heart on being a yellow jacket, she actively pursued Tony La Roche and Mark Dyer, asking them to give her a chance. In turn, Tony and Mark applied pressure on Danny Beckett. Danny in turn was applying pressure on Angela Marsh, who managed our LIFFE floor admin team.

Having missed a couple of vacancies already, when Sophia was advised by her good friend Gill Hyde, a member of the Cater Allen LIFFE floor team, that another position was coming up, she was immediately on the case.

Sophia asked Tony La Roche and Mark Dyer to be considered for the position. Danny finally told Angela that if she wasn't going to give Sophia a chance, she needed to explain the reason to Sophia in person.

Angela came up to the office and arranged a lunch date with Sophia for the following day. Sophia was both excited and apprehensive, being concerned that Angela had an issue with her personally.

Angela and Sophia met for lunch and Angela explained that she had real reservations about letting Sophia join the team, but these concerns were for Sophia's welfare.

Angela explained that the LIFFE floor remained a very male, testosterone-driven environment and that there were plenty of men on the trading floor who would happily target any naive or vulnerable young ladies.

Angela then went on to explain that in the main men's toilets on the trading floor was a list that was regularly updated onto which the names of female members of the LIFFE floor community were recorded. This was a list of ladies who had supposedly succumbed to the dubious advances of some predatory members of the male trading-floor population.

Angela sent a male member of her team into this men's toilet every month to copy the list and give it back to her. Angela explained to Sophia that none of her girls had ever appeared on the list, and she intended to keep it that way.

Sophia was shocked by the implication, but Angela went on to say that she considered Sophia to be 'too friendly.' However, she was prepared to give her a chance on the strict understanding that Sophia went down to the LIFFE floor with her eyes open and never appeared on the notorious list.

Sophia started her life as a Yellow Jacket on the LIFFE floor and enjoyed her time there and managed to avoid getting into Angela's bad books and the notorious list.

Mark Dyer serviced a number of Japanese corporate clients, and soon after my LIFFE floor visit with Denni Machi, he had to arrange a floor visit for one of his best clients who was on a business trip from Tokyo to London.

Mark phoned the LIFFE reception desk to explain that he had an institutional client who wanted to see the trading floor. However, LIFFE told him that the viewing galleries were fully booked. This meant that if Mark wanted to take his client to see the trading floor, he would have to run the gauntlet of taking the client onto the actual trading floor in the same way I had.

When the client arrived at Birchin Lane, Mark went out to meet him at the reception desk and then escorted him into the office, flanked by two surprise additions. These were the client's teenage daughters, resplendent in their school uniform, navy-blue skirts, matching blazers, and crisp white blouses, complete with white ankle socks.

The office fell incredibly quiet as a flustered Mark was trying to explain to his client that he was not sure he would be able to take his daughters down onto the trading floor. I could see the desk traders trying not to laugh as Mark looked pleadingly at Tony La Roche.

Tony suggested Mark phone LIFFE to check the 'dress code' required for a floor visit. Mark was cherry red as he dialled the LIFFE reception. He did not have a quiet voice, but the usual hubbub of the trading desk went remarkably quiet anyway as he started to talk to the LIFFE reception desk.

Mark explained he had a floor visit booked but he needed to increase the numbers; however, the additional two guests were schoolgirls dressed in 'SCHOOL UNIFORM' – he practically shouted the words down the phone. He continued saying he knew the trading floor had a strict dress code and he assumed this excluded 'SCHOOL UNIFORM.'

All eyes were on Mark as he ran his fingers nervously through his hair. The crestfallen look of sheer panic on his face told us all we needed to know. He put the phone down and looked at Tony as he explained that according to the LIFFE reception desk, school uniform was acceptable.

Mark headed off out the office with his client and two daughters like a man heading to the gallows.

He had barely set foot outside the office when Yorkie was on the phone to his mate Burger on the short sterling booth. 'You'll never guess what Tumble is bringing down onto the LIFFE floor.'

I have no idea what occurred, but I can guarantee that Burger had told as many of the floor community as he could, and that Mark and his guests were given a huge reception.

When Mark finally reappeared in the office, he was beside himself, and in his posh Yorkshire accent all he managed to say to Tony La Roche was, 'They're animals, Tony, a pack of wild animals.'

The misconception of the public away from the City that the LIFFE floor was a haven of public schoolboys stretched to a short ill-fated period during which 'work experience' students were allowed onto it.

It seemed madness at the time, and even more bonkers in hindsight for anyone to think that it was a clever idea to send any schoolchildren down to a trading floor.

Cater Allen was no different. We assisted with placing a schoolboy onto the LIFFE floor for work experience.

He was there for a day and after the market close invited out for the evening by a group of the traders and brokers.

The next morning, Tony La Roche took a call from the irate mother saying her son had been delivered home at 9 pm, propped up against her front door with the doorbell ringing. When she opened the door, her son duly collapsed into her hallway, inebriated, and was promptly sick all over the carpet.

Tony was very apologetic as the mother explained that when she sent her son for work experience, getting him drunk was not the sort of experience that she had in mind.

Cater Allen immediately stopped all work experience on the trading floor, but the LIFFE market itself took a little longer to arrive at the same conclusion.

This finally happened when a director of American broker Refco sent his schoolboy son onto the LIFFE floor for work experience.

The boy returned to his dad's office traumatised after one of the LIFFE floor traders was rumoured to have crept up behind him and whispered, 'What's this noise?' while gently slapping his hands together. When the boy said he didn't know, the trader concerned whispered that it was the sound of a particular sex act that he would perform on the boy later.

The boy fled from the LIFFE trading floor, and the irate father immediately called the senior management of the LIFFE market, demanding that the trader concerned be identified and suspended. This did not happen, but LIFFE did ban all work experience on the trading floor.

A new member of staff joined the trading desk in the Cater Allen office – a bespectacled studious looking man in his early forties called Ray Heseldine, otherwise known as 'Skip'.

Skip was American, and Cater Allen employed him because he had strong links to funds and companies in the US and news agency giant Bloomberg.

Bloomberg was, and still is, the top news agency and data service for the financial markets and also has a widely used 'chat' system. All dealing rooms have Bloomberg connectivity, and this was followed in later years by a dedicated TV news channel.

Skip was to introduce US companies to Cater Allen for trade execution in London and to introduce clearing business.

His other brief was to market Cater Allen using his Bloomberg contacts. He set about networking and introducing an American fund to us, which started to trade directly via the LIFFE floor.

Skip was very flamboyant; he always had a bow tie, he frequently had brightly coloured shirts and always wore checked trousers and jackets. He had very 1930s-style spectacles with wire rims and resembled a character from *Harry Potter*.

Early in his association with Cater Allen, Skip invited everyone for a Saturday evening at his rented farmhouse in Tenterden, Kent.

Alison and I set off on the drive from Welling, armed with a map, and having arrived at Tenterden we struggled to find the farm.

We ended up at the end of a dirt track that stretched down between fields, and we only found the farm house after I had spotted Jonathon York and his girlfriend in their car, and we followed them.

As the car bumped and slowly navigated this winding mud track, we could see the lights of a house in the distance, and I was unconvinced that this dapper American had rented something so far from civilisation.

But as we got closer, we could see several cars already parked alongside the house, and two golden Labradors bounded out to greet us, both wearing bow ties, so then we knew we had the right house!

I climbed out my car and started talking to Yorkie about the journey when two vans followed down the track, parked up and unloaded a mountain of Chinese food from the local restaurant in Tenterden High Street.

We went inside and were welcomed by Skip and his wife, we spotted Mark Dyer and his wife, Philip Plumber, Smudger Smith, Dicky Gibbs, Reg DeSouza and others from Cater Allen already drinking.

We were all given a tour of large farmhouse, with its huge Aga and old beams and olde world charm that had convinced Skip to rent it.

The drink flowed, and there was way too much Chinese food being kept warm in the Aga and on various candlelit hotplates.

Skip then revealed three huge round boxes which were cheesecakes he had ordered and had flown in from America.

They were from a place called simply the 'Cheesecake Factory' and were three different varieties. I love cheesecake, and these were awesome. I had a slice from all three and was completely full after the mountain of Chinese food, but I totally understood why Skip had them flown in, although I hate to think what it must have cost.

A few weeks after the visit to Skips farmhouse, Skip invited Yorkie and I to meet two representatives from Bloomberg after hours.

Skip was flying to the Warsaw Stock Exchange in Poland with these two gentlemen, and he asked Yorkie and I to explain to them what Cater Allen had to offer Polish-based funds and trading companies they expected to meet while there.

After the two guys from Bloomberg had left, and more alcohol had been consumed, Skip suggested we move on to the American Bar at the Savoy Hotel.

We jumped into a black cab and arrived at the Savoy.

I had walked past the Savoy on my frequent visits to Covent Garden, but I had never been inside. Skip took charge, walking us up to the American bar and ordering whiskies all round. The glasses we were provided with contained doubles.

Both Skip and Yorkie downed theirs in no time and before I had taken a sip from my first glass another glass arrived. I have never been incredibly good with alcohol, and I knew I was in trouble when I headed off to the toilet and walked straight into a glass panel.

As I staggered back, deciding it was time to go, I said goodbye to Skip and Yorkie and headed for the exit.

As always with top hotels, the porter immediately offered me a cab. I glanced at my watch, and it was 11 pm. I nodded at the porter who gestured to the waiting black cab, and as it pulled up he opened the door for me.

I fell onto the back seat, and the driver asked, 'Where to?' I replied, 'Charing Cross station.'

The driver did not flinch – he said nothing, he drove the few hundred yards to the Strand, indicated left, went another few hundred yards, indicated left, and pulled up outside Charing Cross station.

In my drunken stupor, I had totally forgotten the Savoy is next door to the station. I was so embarrassed I tipped the driver ten pounds.

Cater Allen never looked back on Skip's employment with anything other than embarrassment.

His tenure was not long, and his departure was as abrupt as his joining. The rumour was that Cater Allen had unwittingly paid for Skip's wedding and that any income he had generated was vastly outstripped by the amount of expenses they had paid.

In September 1996, LIFFE merged with the LCE, coffee, cocoa, and sugar all moved into the LIFFE stable of contracts. The commodity markets continue to operate at their bespoke St Katharine Docks home.

By the end of 1996, LIFFE was by far the biggest futures exchange in Europe, followed by the MATIF in Paris and the Deutsche Terminbörse (DTB) in Frankfurt. The DTB was an electronic exchange founded in 1990 and the predecessor to Eurex.

LIFFE's most-traded product was the Bund contract, which was the ten-year German government bond. The DTB offered an identical product and, as an electronic exchange, it had a much lower cost base, but LIFFE had the all-important market liquidity.

Mid-1996 to mid-1997 was the high-water mark for the LIFFE market and its trading floors. At this moment, it looked invulnerable.

September 1996 marked my return to the USA.

This time, Alison and I booked a Virgin holiday to Miami. As part of the package, we had tickets for the huge Disney theme park, a trip to Universal Studios and tours to the Miami Seaquarium and Cape Kennedy.

The two-week trip was something we were both looking forward to. We packed our bags and headed off.

The hotel we were staying in was on International Drive, commonly known as I-Drive, which is a major 11.1-mile thoroughfare in Orlando and the city's main tourist strip. It has all manner of restaurants and bars and a high density of hotels and holiday apartments.

Our modest, mid-range hotel complex had a large outside pool and was handily placed for all the tours and sights we had planned. We had a two-day pass for both Disney and Universal Studios, which we could use at any time during our two-weeks stay. Shuttle buses ran from all the way down International Drive to the various parks and attractions.

We spent our first day relaxing and then set off for Disney the following day.

Disney was a huge, sprawling park. Apart from the more obvious child-friendly attractions, such as the Magic Kingdom itself, there was plenty to keep adults entertained, including a zoo and aquarium, as well as Epcot, which was a park in itself.

Conventional wisdom dictated that you arrive on the very first transit to the park, join the guests who were staying in the onsite hotels and accommodation, and quickly enjoy all the rides you wanted to do before the main rush.

Alison and I decided that we were not that bothered about rushing and arrived at 10 o'clock, joining the mass of tourists as we slowly worked our way around. We had decided to return to Epcot using our second day pass in the second week of our holiday.

Disney Orlando brings forth the hidden child in adults, and we contently queued for the majority of the rides.

The most memorable was Space Mountain. We joined the back of the queue, noting that we had walked past the 40-minute wait marker. As soon as we had joined the back of the queue, a group of about a dozen pensioners joined behind us.

They were all from the UK and were as excited as any group of children would have been. As the queue slowly snaked forward, various warning signs popped up saying, 'If you suffer from a heart condition, we do not advise you take this ride.' This caused a couple to drop out.

Other signs, which identified various medical conditions, kept reducing their numbers until just three of the pensioners remained behind us. This included a very chatty lady from Brighton, queuing directly behind me.

I was wearing my Charlton FC football shirt, which marked me out as a Brit abroad, and so Alison and I were soon conversing with the lady and the couple with her.

When we finally arrived at the ride itself, the 'rocket' we were getting into was unusually designed for three passengers, sitting one behind the other. Alison took the front position, I sat behind her, and the old lady from Brighton sat behind me.

Space Mountain was a roller coaster but in total darkness, with just the 'rockets' themselves illuminated, along with various planets and sites dotted around the ride. As is the custom with most roller coasters the start involved a long, steep climb as the 'rocket' went higher and higher.

The difference with this roller coaster being that in the pitch black you couldn't see what was coming. Once the 'rocket' reached the top of the 'mountain' without warning, we plunged at high speed and the ride began.

The old lady behind me was whooping and screaming with joy at each twist, turn and plunge, and I couldn't help but laugh my head off at her enjoyment as we shot around the ride.

When we finally entered the lit 'landing zone' to disembark, all those pensioners who had dropped out of the queue, and a bunch of others who had not fancied the ride anyway, gave the lady a round of applause as she climbed out and excitedly told them she had loved it. I only hope that I am that game at her age.

That evening, Alison and I headed out for a meal. We had already picked out an Italian restaurant a short walk from our hotel, and another that we would try out later in the trip was an IHOP (International House of Pancakes). But on our second evening in Orlando, we headed for a Chinese we had also spotted.

We sat down, ordered drinks, and were provided with the menu.

Unlike in the UK, there were no set meal options, and so we worked through, picking assorted dishes as we would have if we were at home. The waiter came over to take the order and we went through the list of dishes we wanted. After the fourth dish, he stopped us, saying, 'You must be from the UK.' When we confirmed we were indeed from the UK, he explained that unlike the UK, each dish here was a meal in itself and 'American sized.'

We went back to the menu, ordering a shared rice and side dish and one main dish each. He was spot on – if we had actually ordered as we had intended we would have been eating it for days!

Next day we went shopping. No holiday with Alison was complete without a day of shopping.

On this occasion, it wasn't clothes Alison was after. Alison and her sister Hannah had researched cosmetics designed for Afro Caribbean skin that you couldn't get in the UK.

We caught the shuttle bus to a huge, covered shopping mall, and I resigned myself to being the pack mule for the day. I did buy a pair of Caterpillar boots that were a fraction of the price I would pay in the UK.

Alison spent the day buying shoes, a couple of dresses and several carrier bags full of cosmetics.

I had no idea how she was going to get it all home, and when we arrived back to the hotel at dusk, dragging her shopping through the lobby, I am quite sure everybody else was thinking the same thing. We ended up having to buy another suit case to bring it all home.

The following day was our first time at Universal Studios and what I fully expected to be my highlight of the trip. It was a sweltering day, and we arrived earlier than we had for Disney, taking a cab instead of the shuttle bus, which was scheduled to pick up from five hotels and a good half an hour behind us.

We entered unsure which way to go first. We headed down Main Street, looking at our park map and decided to work our way clockwise, making sure we got back in time for the scheduled *Blues Brothers, Pet Detective* and *Terminator* shows as well as the Backlot Tour.

We started with the *King Kong* ride, the *Earthquake* ride, and the *Jaws* ride. *Jaws* was a boat ride, and what made the Universal Studio rides exceptional fun were the 'cast' members – these staff were all frustrated actors and really got into their roles. When we were on the boat and our guide shouted 'Shark,' her feigned panic really did sweep you into the experience.

We left the *Jaws* ride and headed over to the *Back to the Future* ride to check the waiting times. At 30 minutes, we knew it was tight to get back to Main Street for the *Blues Brothers* show.

As it turned out, the wait was less than 30 minutes, and having listened to the preamble film from Doc Brown, we entered a garage and climbed into the Delorean car that waited. The car had seating for four adult passengers, and Alison and I were lucky enough to be in the front.

We didn't know what to expect as the gull wing doors closed. The garage filled with smoke, and suddenly the car started making a load of noise. The garage doors in front of us opened, and then the car jumped forward and started flying. It lurched, banked, and jolted as it continued its flight, the illusion completed by a vast screen that totally filled your field of vision. With the hydraulics pitching the car left, right, back, and forward, the illusion was highly effective and believable.

I had never been on anything like it, and I was impressed by it. Judging by the screaming and laughing, Alison felt the same. By the time the ride ended, we were hooked and looking forward to the rest of the day.

We rushed into Main Street where an expectant crowd waited. The big *'Blues mobile'* pulled up and the 'Blues Brothers' got out. A number of what we had thought were fellow guests scattered around us turned out to be 'cast' members.

What followed was an impromptu street concert of the *Blues Brothers* songs and music, which spontaneously started out around us. If you loved the film, you couldn't help but love this, and the two main actors looked exactly like Dan Aykroyd and John Belushi, and the woman stepping in for Aretha Franklin and singing 'A Little Respect' was fantastic.

Once the Blues Brothers had climbed back into their beaten-up Blues mobile, Alison and I decided lunch was required and there were lots of choices. We headed for the 1950s-style diner on Main Street, grabbed a table and excitedly consulted the map to plan out the rest of our day.

After our lunch, we headed back out into the sunshine and the 'Art of Making Movies' show, followed by a walk around the 'Boneyard' which was a collection of memorable props from films, including sharks from *Jaws*, Ecto 1 from *Ghostbusters* and dinosaurs from *Jurassic Park*.

There was a Wild West show, which was in an open theatre with a Wild West town set and included trick shooting and horse riding. After that, we did the Backlot tour before heading back to Main Street for the *Pet Detective* act, with a particularly good Jim Carey impersonator aided by numerous birds and animals.

The finale for the day was a stunt act, which took place on the lagoon next to the *Jaws* ride, and after that we retired for the day, having exhausted ourselves. We had a couple of chill-out days and a trip to SeaWorld before heading off for another highlight – Cape Canaveral.

There were no scheduled shuttle launches while we were there, but there was still an amazing amount to see. This trip was on a coach as it was a longer journey than previous hops to the local parks. This meant a series of pickups from other hotels and resorts before we finally set off.

The John F. Kennedy Space Centre is located on Merritt Island in Florida, and since December 1968 it has been NASA's primary launch centre of human spaceflight. It was the place from which the Apollo, Skylab and Space Shuttles were launched.

As we approached the Cape, we drove down a long, straight road, through a 'marsh' area of land that surrounds the Kennedy Space Centre. The driver advised us that we would not see any fences or security away from the access road. This was because the Cape had a great unpaid security team in the snakes and alligators that lived there.

Much of the installation is a restricted area, and only nine per cent of the land is developed. The remaining ninety one percent of the site is an important wildlife sanctuary. The surrounding land is home to American alligators, wild boars, eastern diamondback rattlesnakes, the endangered Florida panther and Florida manatees.

As we pulled up at the Kennedy Space Centre, you couldn't help but notice the vast Saturn V rocket lying on its side on a purpose-built cradle. It was vast and rusting.

Seeing these rockets on the television launching the Apollo capsules to the Moon was one thing but seeing this huge miracle of engineering at the very place from which it was launched, was very humbling.

Close by was a memorial to the 1986 Space Shuttle Challenger disaster, set in a large pool into which an alligator had already made itself at home.

The trip into the vast assembly shed where the huge Saturn V rockets had been constructed was followed by a trip around a mock Space Shuttle.

We then went to see the various command and landing modules from the Apollo and Genesis space programs. The highlight was a visit to the Apollo mission control room.

That night, we went to the Hard Rock Café for our evening meal and then spent a couple of days relaxing before our return to Disney and the Epcot Centre.

Epcot was what I considered to be an 'adult' Disney – it had rides, but the main attraction was a trip around the various 'Lands' of Mexico, China, Germany, Italy, America, Japan, Holland, the UK and Canada, with miniature versions of the main landmarks from each country and food and drink from each.

After that there was a Zoo and 'Future World.' It was a full day, and I was determined to have the currywurst, complete with an authentic potato salad, while in the German exhibit.

We made a return to Universal Studios in our final days making an afternoon trip to the *Back to the Future* ride, taking in the *Terminator* show, which we had skipped the first time, and making a point of watching the *Blues Brothers* in action again, before loading up on gifts and heading back.

On our return home, we decided to do something incredibly special on our next trip to America and find another suitable escorted coach tour.

As always, the high of a really good holiday is followed by that surreal feeling when you get onto the train and head back to the office to work.

The legend that was Mark 'Tumble' Dyer never ceased to amaze and delight us in the office. We had been hearing for weeks that Mark had ordered a Range Rover Discovery. With a special paint job and air conditioning, it was a bespoke car, and he was practically counting down the days until delivery.

Each and every conversation he had with clients resulted in groans from all the desk traders when Mark hit them with the line, 'Have I told you about my Range Rover Discovery?'

It was a relief when the weekend finally came for the cars delivery, and Tony La Roche sent Mark off early on the Friday to collect it from the local Sevenoaks showroom.

On the Monday, Mark came in and sat down, but there was no mention of the car. 'Yorkie' was immediately on the case as everyone smelt a rat. What followed was one of the most bonkers stories of my career.

Mark had picked up his car on the Friday and had driven it the short distance back to his home. That Saturday was a sunny day, and so Mark told his wife he was going to take the 'Range Rover' for a spin.

The area around Sevenoaks in Kent has a lot of small, winding country lanes, and Mark happily headed off.

After 15 minutes or so, he got stuck behind a cyclist. A Range Rover Discovery is a large 4x4 off-road car and much wider than Mark's previous BMW, so he waited for his chance to overtake, crawling behind the cyclist for a frustratingly lengthy period of time before easing slowly past.

Having been crawling along for so long, and with a clear road ahead, Mark put his foot down. After a few minutes, and approaching a zig-zag section, Mark slowed and then could hear an annoying thumping noise. The thumping was persistent, and so Mark started speeding up, at which point the noise stopped.

When he slowed down again, the thumping returned. Mark consulted his dashboard, looking for any warning lights, then tried speeding up again, at which point the thumping stopped. But when he slowed down again, it returned – if anything, louder.

Mark looked in the driver's side mirror and saw nothing, but when he craned his neck and looked in the nearside mirror, he was shocked to see the cyclist he had passed back down the road.

He pulled over and got out to find the bicycle wedged firmly into his rear bumper and the cyclist lying on the grass verge, covered in sweat and incapable of speech.

Mark managed to yank the bike free and asked the cyclist if he was OK. The man nodded, enquiring as to why Mark had not heard him banging on the car roof whenever the car had slowed sufficiently for the poor man to take a hand off the handlebars.

At this stage in his story, everyone in the office were doubled up laughing, but Mark hadn't finished.

Having checked again that the cyclist was OK, Mark set off for home and promptly told his wife. Mark's wife immediately instructed him to report the incident to the police.

Mark drove the short distance to Sevenoaks police station.

He walked in and related the tale to the uniformed PC at the front desk. Once he had finished, the PC suggested Mark wait for a moment while he made sure they had not received any report of the incident or complaint from the cyclist.

Then the PC returned, accompanied by a uniformed sergeant and plain-clothes detective. With people now queuing behind Mark, the uniformed sergeant asked Mark to tell the story again.

As Mark came to the end of the tale once more, he said he could see the PC and sergeant laughing, as were the people behind him. Mark looked at Tony LaRoche sitting next to him and said, 'They were just not taking me seriously, Tony.'

With that, once again, the office fell around laughing.

Mark departed Sevenoaks police station and never heard any more about it – not from the police anyway. Needless to say, the desk traders in the office never let him forget it.

Another anecdote about Mark's Range Rover Discovery was when he told local trader Mike Clarkson, who was in the office for a meeting with Tony La Roche, about his new car. Mark pulled the glossy brochure out of his desk to show Mike, who nodded and said, 'Nice car.'

Mike promptly sat next to Mark, flipped through the brochure, and dialled the phone number of the showroom. He then calmly asked the salesperson on the other end of the phone about the price of the top-of-the-range model.

Mark was silent. Mike then asked about personalised number plates, and then Mark's jaw dropped as Mike calmly told the salesperson he wanted to buy three identical cars, promptly providing his credit card details in order to place a deposit. He finished the call by saying he would pop in and complete the order over the weekend.

As Mike hung up, Mark went bright red and asked, 'Why three?'

Mike smiled and replied, 'One for me and one each of my boys, Sam and Erick, as a little present.' Sam and Erick were local traders who worked for Mike on the LIFFE trading floor.

As an example of one-upmanship that typified the floor traders of the time, it has never been beaten.

This is not the only example of local trader excess.

Matthew Constantine, our gilt options trader, was so successful he owned a flat in the exclusive Cheyne Walk in Chelsea. His success was not limited to trading – it has to be said he was a handsome individual and was effortlessly successful with many of the girls on the LIFFE trading floor.

This combination of good looks and charm culminated in an appearance on Cilla Black's successful TV show *Blind Date*.

Matthew, however, was not the shark that some of his fellow traders were. Inevitably, when Matt decided to finish with a young lady he would pay them off.

His usual requests were for extravagant gifts or trips, and these payments would often be in the thousands of pounds. Each time, Matthew would call me and set up a payment from his clearing account.

On a memorable occasion, Matthew phoned the office and told me he wanted to make a transfer from his account. I grabbed a piece of paper and told him to continue. He gave me the bank details of where he wanted the money to go and then he told me the account name, which was an airline.

I immediately concluded he was taking a young lady on another romantic trip, until he gave me the amount, which was in excess of £25,000. I choked, 'Bloody hell, Matt, are you buying the plane?'

Matthew replied, 'Yes.'

He had bought himself a second-hand two-seater light aircraft and promptly started to pay for flying lessons. Matt succeeded in gaining his pilot's licence, and along with his powder-blue Aston Martin car, he lived the type of bachelor life that would have looked ludicrous if shown in a film or TV show.

Christmas 1996 saw Alison and me celebrating with her family. By this stage, I had met all of her siblings with the exception of her sister Emma and her husband Mel.

Alison had arranged a formal sit-down meal in Sutton where her mother and sister Hannah lived. We were joined by her sister Carla and brother Ryan. Ryan being the youngest in the family, was in his way even more outrageous than Hannah.

All of Alison's sisters were attractive and yet quite different.

Ryan was extremely attractive to the fairer sex, and as he worked for a fashion manufacturer, as a sales agent to a number of West End fashion boutiques, he was never short of interest from ladies. Ryan's 'long time' girlfriend, Maria, was just eighteen when she fell pregnant and had given birth to a baby girl, who at this stage was 18 months old. Alison's Mum had not been impressed and, along with his sisters, had concluded that getting pregnant had not been an accident and was designed to 'trap' Ryan.

But having a daughter had certainly not trapped Ryan – he just continued living his life, even though he seemed to dote on his baby daughter, and he continued his relationship with Maria, but it was a casual arrangement.

Carla was also a single mum and had split from the little boy's dad, who never got a mention. Of all Alison's siblings, Carla was the one I knew the least and was the one Alison had the least to do with. Alison always classified Carla as a 'user,' and whatever the history was between them I was never enlightened.

Our Christmas night out was very relaxed, and I was told it was it was the first time they had gathered in such numbers since they had started to leave home. My presence as the only non-family member did not seem to be an issue for any of them.

1997

1997 saw a return to insecurity.

Cater Allen had never really recovered from the Baring Brothers fallout. Once again, the balance sheets of companies operating in the financial markets had come under increasing scrutiny. But the real issue was a huge change in the financial markets themselves.

LIFFE had maintained its reliance on 'open outcry' as its primary trading methodology, and it was not alone as the huge US exchanges did the same. But the complacency of these international exchanges hinged on the simple fact that no market had ever lost its ownership of market liquidity and open interest once a contract was established.

The German DTB market, however, had two huge advantages over LIFFE. It was fully electronic, and by this stage had deployed screens to most of the major players in the markets. Not having the cost of maintaining a trading floor gave the DTB a much lower cost base, and it had started to 'give away' its trading by not charging exchange fees on the Bund contract, which it hoped to wrestle from LIFFE.

The other big advantage the DTB had was the nationalistic support of its central bank, which had started to apply political and regulatory pressure on the big German banks to transfer their trading in the Bund from LIFFE to the DTB exchange.

At this early stage in 1997, the DTB had less than 25 per cent of the liquidity in the Bund market, and so the LIFFE market did not consider itself to be at any risk.

Alison came home one evening in early 1997 and told me that I was finally going to meet her sister Emma. Alison had arranged for us to go to Tottenham, where Emma lived with her husband Mel and their two young sons. I had no idea what to expect, nor why it had taken me so long to meet them.

We travelled by train to central London, then by Tube to Tottenham and walked to the big modern block of flats where they lived. Emma met us at the door and invited us in. We went through to the kitchen, and Alison and Emma just started talking, so I was feeling increasingly like a spare wheel. Emma realised this and suggested she take me into the lounge to introduce me to Mel.

At this stage, I had no idea he was in the flat as he had made no attempt to introduce himself on our arrival, and I had not seen any sign of her children.

Emma led us into the lounge where Mel was watching a live football match. He stood as we came into the room and reached out a hand, which I shook. Mel kissed Alison on the cheek. The two young boys were playing with Lego on the floor.

Emma asked if I wanted a lager, and Mel confirmed he wanted another one.

Mel asked if I liked football, and I told him I was a season ticket holder at Charlton. He confessed his team was Tottenham, but he also followed Stoke City because his twin brother played for them. As Emma brought the lagers in, Mel stood and lifted his two sons up and calmly deposited them in the hallway, shutting the door behind him as he returned to his seat.

The conversation between myself and Mel was limited to events in the match, and I felt distinctly awkward.

Once the football was over, the girls came in, the children were allowed back in, and everyone seemed to relax a little. We chatted about the family and work and then Emma brought in some food to eat. After that we were on our way home.

One Sunday, weeks later, I sat down to read the *News of the World*, which was my usual Sunday paper. I maintain I bought it for the good football coverage and not its usual scurrilous sex exposés.

I was turning the pages of the paper when this picture leapt out at me – it was of Mel or his twin brother. As I read on in horror, I could not believe what I was reading. Mel's twin brother had been in a relationship with an *EastEnders* actress.

The article was about the twin confessing that he and his brother Mel had regularly swapped places on unsuspecting girls. It said that they were so identical that the girls simply never knew they were with the twin. This included not only the actress concerned but it clearly stated in the paper that the twin had slept with his brother's wife – Alison's sister Emma.

I called Alison into the lounge and showed her the article. She immediately phoned her mum and her sister Hannah, who rushed out to buy a copy of the newspaper.

Nothing more was ever said about it, but it was not the only familiar person to be pictured in the newspapers that year.

One morning, I was at the station, travelling to work and about to buy my usual *Daily Express*, when I saw the front cover of the *Daily Mail*. On the front page was a picture of Robin's ex-wife, Victoria Eastman, in a WPC uniform.

It turned out that the PC who Victoria had cheated with, causing Robin's divorce, had also been married. In an attempt to prove that his wife was having affairs, he had given Victoria a list of car number plates to check on the police national computer database. This unofficial search of the PNC database had become known and both had been dismissed from the force. Their claim of unfair dismissal had resulted in a court case. Victoria was front-page news.

In June 1997, all the Cater Allen staff were gathered at the 7 Birchin Lane offices, and we were told that Cater Allen Bank was in talks with Abbey National about a takeover. It was stated that one of the preconditions for that takeover was that Cater Allen divest itself of its futures trading interests. As a fearful silence descended, we were told that talks were taking place with a number of interested parties, but the most likely would be a takeover of Cater Allen Futures by MeesPierson.

This meant another batch of sleepless nights worrying about whether I would have a job in the coming months. On the plus side we were told by Danny Beckett that if we were made redundant we would get a generous year's redundancy money.

In the intervening weeks, a sizeable percentage of the Cater Allen LIFFE floor team received alternative employment offers from floor trading companies. This meant floor staff were keen to take any redundancy money on offer, safe in the knowledge they could then immediately jump into these new pre-arranged jobs.

When we finally had confirmation from Danny Beckett that a deal had been concluded with MeesPierson, a series of interviews were held.

On the LIFFE floor, David Morgan, the owner of David Morgan Futures, which was a local trading company associated with MeesPierson, and Roderick Weerts, the Dutch LIFFE floor manager for MeesPierson, held interviews with the floor trading brokers, local traders and admin staff.

MeesPierson was already the biggest clearer of locals on the LIFFE floor, and so the majority of our local traders were happy to make the move.

The floor staff that had lined up lucrative deals elsewhere, and wanting the redundancy, deliberately did badly in the interviews and got their wish.

MeesPierson had two separate divisions: MeesPierson Derivatives (MPD) was a broking entity and had its own LIFFE floor team and back office. MeesPierson ICS (ICS) was a clearing company for local traders, both individuals and companies like David Morgan Futures and Hills Independent Trading, as well as corporate entities and institutions.

In the Cater Allen back office, Trevor Kemp had already decided he did not want to move to MeesPierson and excluded himself from the interviews. In a surprising career change, Trevor had been accepted by the Church of England as a trainee vicar.

David Peart and I were to be interviewed by the director in charge of the Operations department at MeesPierson, a gentleman by the name of Paul White.

David Peart had been lined up to join MPD as the head of their back office. I had my fingers crossed that I would join him, but Paul White had other ideas and told me that he was setting up a new 'customer services' department at ICS and that my experience would be ideally suited to this role.

However, it was made clear that initially David and I would continue to service the existing Cater Allen business until the end of the year to give continuity to our institutional customers and local traders. A slow integration was envisaged as the clients transferred over to the new SunGard GMI statements.

Everything continued as usual at Cater Allen's Birchin Lane office for a while.

That was until the day David Peart was summoned to MeesPierson's office in Camomile Court, just off Houndsditch and Liverpool Street. David headed off for what he believed was a meeting to discuss our eventual move to MeesPierson's Camomile Court office.

After an hour, I received a phone call from David asking me to head off to Camomile Court myself, and so I set off for the walk down Gracechurch Street. As I entered the ground-floor reception and approached the receptionist, David exited one of the lifts and walked towards me, none too happy.

'What's going on?' I asked.

David looked at me, frustrated. 'I've just had another interview! This time with Roderick Weerts.'

I couldn't believe it – both of us had been offered positions, so what was going on?

David shrugged and headed out the door. Just as he vanished, another lift opened, and the imposing figure of Roderick Weerts strode out the lift towards me. In his clipped Dutch accent, he asked, 'Kevin Parker?' I nodded, and he gestured for me to follow him.

We travelled silently in the lift to the second floor, and all the while I was getting more nervous and annoyed. I followed Roderick to the right and through a door, onto a large open-plan office. All around, the atrium glass offices looked out onto the open floor.

The office was much bigger than Czarnikow's and certainly massive compared to Cater Allen's.

There were lots of employees walking around and working away on PCs, and it looked to be a busy environment.

I followed Roderick into an office, and he gestured to the chair the other side of the desk as he closed the glass door behind us.

In his suit trousers, braces, and loud tie, he looked like a dapper senior management figure and actually reminded me slightly of Nick Grason at Czarnikow. But whereas I always enjoyed Nick's dry wit, Roderick's Dutch directness rubbed me the wrong way.

He cupped his hands behind his head, looked me straight in the eye and said, 'So, tell me, why should we offer you a job?'

I could feel the rage bubbling and just couldn't help myself as I replied, 'Well, it seems to me that you need me more than I need you. The difference between clearing companies boils down to their service levels, and MeesPierson has a reputation for providing poor customer service levels. My understanding from Paul White was that you were setting up a customer services department to resolve this very issue and that I was a good fit for this department due to my broad experience.'

I am not sure what Roderick expected, but this was certainly not it. I could see I had upset him as he went red and started to stutter. 'Ya, ya. Well,' he said, 'I'm terribly upset to hear that.'

He stood and started pacing as he continued, 'We have worked hard on our service, and I understood we offer a particularly good service.' With that, he just went out the door and left the office.

I watched him go and assumed he was going to bring someone else into the meeting, maybe Paul White. I waited and waited. I could see people passing, some looking in at me, and I started to feel increasingly out of place.

After fifteen minutes, and with no sign of Roderick coming back, I picked up the phone on the desk and called Cater Allen. David Peart took the call, and I explained what had occurred, causing him to laugh and pass the phone over to Danny Beckett, who happened to be in the office.

Danny was responsible co-ordinating the move over to MeesPierson and he knew Roderick well, as Roderick was his opposite number on the LIFFE floor. He advised me to leave the office and return to Birchin Lane.

As I walked back down Gracechurch Street, I was convinced that I had just talked myself out of a job.

I walked down the corridor at Birchin Lane and into the office where Danny waited. He asked me to go through the meeting with him again with a big smile on his face. As I finished my tale, I said to Danny, 'If that man is the one deciding if I have a position at MeesPierson or not, then I would say I'm out of work.'

Danny told me not to worry, he had been told that both David and I were having our contracts picked up and we were getting continuity of service again.

Danny concluded that as I had service going back sixteen years, and David more than that, that this constituted a financial risk to MeesPierson, and for this was reason Roderick had felt compelled to get involved.

However, as far as Danny was concerned, it was not Roderick's decision as we were office-based staff. This gave me a level of comfort, although this meeting had unsettled both David and myself.

As the move to Camomile Court came closer, we learned that none of the office based directors and desk brokers were joining us at MeesPierson. This meant David and I would be saying goodbye to people who we had worked with at Czarnikow.

Graham 'Pinky' Stewart took retirement.

Prash Laud and Dicky Gibbs joined Bank Austria, Philip Plumber went to Merrill Lynch, Cliff Healy went to Crédit Agricole, Tony La Roche retired, and Mark Dyer joined Mellon Bank.

Yorkie was in a relationship with a young lady called Mel from HICA, a Kiwi by birth, and they had decided to head off to New Zealand. Smudger Smith joined Anglo Irish Bank.

David and I had a lunchtime beer soon after our run-in with Roderick at Camomile Court, and we discussed the possibility of setting ourselves up as a local clearing entity. We were confident that if we found a general clearing member to support us that we could provide a great service to the local traders.

We decided to sound out the key players. The biggest of which was still our old ex Czarnikow colleague Cliff Donovan, a personal friend of David's. We took him for a beer, and he confirmed he would be more than happy to support us.

We had to be careful to ensure that our discussions did not feedback to MeesPierson, and so we selected the locals very carefully. Next on our list were gilt locals John Arnold and Richard Taylor. They confirmed they had no loyalty to MeesPierson, and they would be happy to join us wherever we went. Next up was Mike Clarkson – likewise, he said he was onboard and more than happy to bring his team of Sam and Erik.

With these local traders secured, we had the nucleus of a viable business. We were confident that once we were up and running, we could convince others to join us. We kept this option as a plan B and waited to see what happened next.

When the time finally came for us to leave Birchin Lane, David and I found ourselves set up in a corner of the second floor, sitting with the MeesPierson computer support staff. This included Ray Bell, one of the old Czarnikow computer support team.

On a daily basis, David and I were handed the computer reports and we continued to service the Cater Allen locals and clearing clients. That said, a couple of our biggest clearing clients quickly decided they could not make the move with us.

JP Morgan Sydney had stubbornly refused to transfer their clearing business to JP Morgan Europe because they preferred the service Cater Allen had provided. They conceded defeat when the new clearing papers from MeesPierson arrived.

Likewise, Dresdner Luxembourg also said they could not move with us to MeesPierson under the same internal political pressure to consolidate their clearing internally.

Another casualty of our move to MeesPierson was our long association with Harris Futures who themselves were in the midst of being taken over by JP Morgan.

MeesPierson had their own US clearing operation which meant we had been forced to give Harris Futures notice.

I finally had to say goodbye to Denni Machi and Jennifer Johnson. I was obviously upset at having to say goodbye to Denni, but she assured me that if she got a job at JP Morgan, it would increase her chance of at least one more visit to London.

Staff at JP Morgan moved frequently between the US and the European headquarters of JP Morgan in London. That made me feel a little better about it. But sadly, it never happened, and I lost contact with her.

David and I began our spell as Cater Allen in exile, and Ray Bell quickly introduced us to his colleagues – Moira, a South African lady in her mid-thirties, Svetlana, a slightly prickly Russian lady, Dave Rivers, an elderly gentleman, who was the company's main phone technician, and Marcus DeSilva, who seemed to be managing procurement for the company supplying IT and communications hardware. They all were very pleasant, and David and I soon felt at home.

The biggest benefit of sitting where we had been located, apart from being left alone to get on with the work, was a blonde vision who appeared from time to time. This young lady was extremely attractive, and every now and again would appear and vanish into a little office behind us.

Ray Bell spotted the fact that David and I would stop working whenever she appeared and laughingly told us that her name was Carol Deebank and that in the office behind us was John, her boyfriend. Ray added we should join the queue, as they all had a bit of a crush on Carol.

Every generation has a 'Do you remember where you were when you heard ...,' whether it be the death of John F Kennedy, Elvis Presley, or John Lennon. For my generation it was the death of Diana, Princess of Wales.

On Sunday, 31 August 1997, I remember exactly where I was – behind the wheel of my Nissan with Alison next to me. We were heading for Sainsbury's in Bexleyheath, having had another of our Saturday evenings down the Thai Dynasty the night before.

It was 10.30ish, and we had not listened to any news before getting in the car.

The music had been solemn, and I was only half listening when the newsreader stated that Lady Diana had been killed.

I looked at Alison, who looked straight back at me. 'That can't be right,' I said as I turned it up, and we waited for them to repeat it.

We parked up in the Sainsbury's car park, and sure enough the news was repeated.

We listened, stunned, as the radio confirmed that in the early hours of 31 August 1997, Diana, Princess of Wales, died from the injuries she sustained in a car crash in the Pont de l'Alma tunnel in Paris. Her partner, Dodi Fayed, and the driver of the Mercedes Benz, Henri Paul, had been pronounced dead at the scene.

We walked around the supermarket in a sort of trance. Everybody was talking about it, and there was this huge aura of disbelief.

When we got back to the house in Wordsworth Road, we turned on the television and sat and watched the newsfeeds as reaction from around the world started to arrive. Alison was in tears as full details started to emerge.

Alison was not a royalist, but she had a high opinion of Diana, as a style icon and the first real media celebrity.

The funeral took place on the following Saturday, 6th of September, and the country came to a stop.

Like millions of others, we watched the events unfold on the television: the two boys, Harry, and William, walking behind the coffin; the funeral ceremony, including the controversial speech by Diana's brother Charles Spencer, Elton John singing his hit 'Candle in the Wind' with the bespoke lyrics, and the flowers being thrown from motorway bridges as the car carrying her coffin headed off to the Spencer estate and her final resting place. It was a highly charged emotional weekend.

By October 1997, the DTB had started to make significant inroads into the LIFFE market's hold on its flagship Bund contract it had claimed more than 50 per cent of the market's open interest.

The LIFFE exchange finally started to fight back by cutting its exchange fees on the Bund contract in an effort to hold on to the market share it still maintained.

One of the benefits of joining a company that was clearing a large number of the local traders was that MeesPierson had been compelled to establish an electronic trading facility in Nicholas Lane. This was just a stone's throw from our old Cater Allen offices in Birchin Lane.

This basement facility had DTB terminals deployed for traders, and as the Bund volume migrated from LIFFE to the DTB, more LIFFE traders started to switch to screen based trading. This put our new employers ahead of most of its competitors in terms of facilitating electronic trading.

This did not mean that a successful floor trader was guaranteed to be a success on a screen – they were hugely different animals.

Equally, some traders who had never been able to make an impression on the old trading floors were able to excel on the electronic trading screens.

At Cater Allen, we had a local trader called Graham Weaver who had been a mediocre floor trader but was able to make a good living on the APT screen.

Screen trading in its infancy had its pitfalls and was open to what became known as 'fat finger' trading errors. A fat-finger error is a keyboard input error or mouse mis click in the financial markets, whereby an order to buy or sell is placed of far greater size than intended, for the wrong stock or contract, at the wrong price, or with any number of other input errors.

Many catastrophic examples of this unfolded in the years to come, but in these early low volume days, the DTB exchange was keen to foster good relations and increase confidence and volumes, and so would quickly 'reverse' or cancel trades that resulted from obvious input errors.

As electronic trading became more advanced, automated systems deployed by companies started to catch fat-finger errors before they could reach the market. The larger the size of the mistaken order, the more likely it was to be spotted and cancelled.

Large scale errors were impossible on the traditional open outcry markets. Before electronic trading, erroneous orders were known as 'out-trades' and were cancelled as a matter of course. Erroneous orders placed using computers were much harder or impossible to prevent.

There were many who still believed in these early days of electronic trading that the tried-and-tested open outcry trading method would be preferred by market users and would see off the challenge from electronic trading platforms.

David Peart and I decided to investigate further the prospect of establishing ourselves as a local clearing company by visiting MeesPierson's rival Dutch clearing company KAS Clearing.

David made the appointment, and one evening we headed off to their office. We were directed into the boardroom, which had a huge painting of the England 1966 World Cup squad at one end of the boardroom table, which we both thought a little strange for a Dutch company.

Moments later, a tall, young gentleman stepped into the boardroom and introduced himself as William Den Haag.

We sat down and explained our recent move from Cater Allen and that we had some key, high volume locals willing to support us if we decided to start our own business. He listened intently, and when we finished he confirmed that KAS would be more than willing to help us if we decided to make the move.

We left feeling happy that plan B was looking viable, and we would take a view in the new year.

MeesPierson held an annual company Christmas party, and this was the only event at which all the staff got together. The ex-Cater Allen staff were placed together on one table, and, unlike Czarnikow, MeesPierson's invitation included partners, which meant that Alison was able to attend.

The event was at a hotel in Paddington and was a formal sit-down meal followed by the inevitable dancing.

Alison was happy to be meeting up with Ray Bell again, as they had got along very well at Czarnikow.

Once we arrived at the hotel, we consulted the large table planner that was on a noticeboard to find the table number we were on, and then I pointed out to Alison the table Ray was on.

After a complimentary drink in a reception area, we were asked to head to the tables in the main event hall.

Alison managed to hide away until Ray took his seat, and then she rushed over and put her hands over his eyes, much to the amusement of the others on his table. Ray gave up guessing, and he was shocked when the hands were removed from his eyes and he finally saw Alison, resplendent in her dress. Alison returned to our table laughing, telling me that they agreed to meet up later to have a chat and dance.

The event was a tremendous success, giving the ex-Cater Allen staff a chance to meet our new colleagues in a social setting.

The food and the dancing afterwards was a terrific opportunity to mingle. The handful of ex-Czarnikow staff attending meant Alison was not totally amongst strangers.

During our brief time at MeesPierson, David and I had been able to find a position for my old boss Paul Thompson's youngest son Daniel.

He had been employed on the 'clearing desk' that managed all the matching on TRS across the various exchanges and markets.

Daniel was working with Jack Kottenugh, who cleared the options markets and as such was a great mentor with years of experience.

Daniel attended the Christmas party on the Cater Allen table and had managed to bring along a very glamourous, obviously older lady as his partner for the evening.

As he lived in Essex, along with a high number of the staff who had attended, the company had laid on a coach to take them all home.

The following week, I was told by Paul Thompson, after he phoned me to make sure Daniel had behaved himself, that his youngest son had 'borrowed' his elder brother Dean's girlfriend for the night.

I had to admire his ingenuity.

What I did not tell Paul was that based on the gossip we had heard from others on the coach that Daniel and his "borrowed" date had been getting along a little too well, given the circumstances.

1998

As we entered 1998, the DTB was in the midst of a battle to wrench the remaining liquidity in the Bund contract away LIFFE.

The shift of Bund volume that had started gradually hit a 'tipping point' that began in early 1998, reducing LIFFE's share of the Bund financial futures contract to just ten per cent.

This was a hammer blow to the LIFFE market, as the Bund represented about a third of its business. The LIFFE exchange, which had turned in a profit of £57m in 1997, reported a loss of £64m in 1998.

Prior to the loss of the Bund contract, the LIFFE exchange had been investigating plans for an enlarged trading floor and offices on a site near Spitalfields Market, but these plans were now cancelled as it struggled with the loss of its flagship contract and the income that it had provided.

This was the first time any financial futures exchange had lost market liquidity on an existing contract, and it sent shockwaves through the industry.

The inevitable move away from the traditional open outcry markets and towards screen-based trading had begun.

The LIFFE market hurriedly supplied an electronic trading room for local traders and corporate floor traders to trade on their APT platform after the floor trading ceased for the day.

After Christmas, Paul White started to apply pressure for me to begin my new role in customer services at MeesPierson ICS and for David to take on his head of clearing role at MeesPierson Derivatives.

This meant passing the Cater Allen business onto the internal clearing teams.

As part of this handover, I had a meeting with the head of accounts at MeesPierson, a gentleman called Rod Fitzpatrick.

As Rod and I were discussing passing the reconciliation of the Cater Allen clearing accounts to the internal team, the managing director of MeesPierson, Peter Koster, knocked on the door. Peter apologised for interrupting and told Rod he wanted to introduce him to a new member of staff who would be bringing business to the company.

The appearance of the lanky, smiling man who stepped into Rod's office sent shivers of panic down my spine. It was none other than William Den Haag, the same man who David and I had spoken to at KAS Clearing.

To give William his due, he said nothing when Rod introduced me. He shook my hand with a smile and then was promptly led on by Peter.

I quickly made my excuses to Rod and dashed round to David Peart to warn him before he bumped into William.

That was the end of any thoughts David and I had of going it alone.

If KAS Clearing was imploding, then we were better off staying put.

Added to that, the move of the Bund liquidity onto the DTB had now put a question mark over the future of the LIFFE floor and the local traders to whom we had spoken.

My new role in MeesPierson ICS customer services put me alongside three other members of staff: Roger Little, Alan Byrne, and Barry Allen. All three were long-standing staff members.

Like Czarnikow, staff rarely resigned from MeesPierson, and this created a familiar family feeling in the office.

My new job was to be the "call centre" for all customer queries. This meant consulting with all of the other departments internally.

MeesPierson cleared a substantial number of clients, including a high percentage of the local trading companies. In fact, it owned a shareholding in key local trading companies including David Morgan Futures and Hills Independent Trading.

MeesPierson also oversaw derivatives clearing for large institutional and fund management companies.

The clearing desk managed all the TRS matching and settlement for futures and options, as well as amending and correcting trades in the GMI clearing system.

At Cater Allen, we had one member of staff devoted to this role full-time, but at MeesPierson there was a team of twelve individuals split into two teams. One team started at 8 am and went through until 2 pm, and the other started at 1 pm and finished at 8 pm.

MeesPierson cleared equities, something new to me. The equities clearing desk had a team of half a dozen staff managing the clearing and settlement of equity trades, predominantly on the London Stock Exchange (LSE).

MeesPierson had its own LSE membership and CREST settlement account but used agent banks for its European settlement. The equity settlements team managed all the reconciliation of these accounts and also managed any corporate actions, mergers, and takeovers, as well as dividend processing.

There was a two-man futures reconciliation department managing the reconciliation with the exchanges as well as the clearing accounts MeesPierson held on the US exchanges. This two-man team was directly alongside customer services.

The change from the smaller, bespoke, all-encompassing role to a focus on customer services, presented a completely new challenge for me. I considered that I was uniquely qualified for this role as, with the exception of equities, I had performed all the functions required in clearing and settling trades and I understood the entire process.

Alan Byrne dealt with 'public order members.' These were financial companies and institutions that were members of the LIFFE exchange and were authorised to clear on behalf of their customers. These exchange members required the clearing services of a general clearing member, in this case MeesPierson ICS.

With the vast number of clearing clients, we were fielding a high level of calls from day one. But by shielding the clearing and settlements desks from client contact, the new customer services desk quickly proved its worth and everything started to become more efficient.

Providing the clients with a dedicated customer services team also created new commercial opportunities, especially in the era of electronic trading, where new products were coming thick and fast.

With improved communication fostering better relationships with the client base, the customer services team were ideally placed to identify client interest in new markets and contracts and pass this information to the commercial director.

Having a customer service team that reported to the head of clearing operations now appeared to create a potential conflict of interest.

This was on the basis that if clients had issues with the clearing or settlement services and were threatening to leave, our reporting line was to director responsible for these areas. For this reason, the customer services teams reporting line was changed from operational to the commercial line and director, William Den Haag.

In March 1998, MeesPierson announced that it was selling its MeesPierson Derivatives brokerage arm to American grains giant Archer Daniels Midland (ADM), and this meant my old boss David Peart, who was the head of clearing for MPD, was heading off with them.

Because of the overlaps between the MeesPierson divisions, a handful of staff were given the opportunity to transfer between the entities before the sale was finalised. I was one of these people, as was Steve Kent on the reconciliations team.

I had a chat with David Peart and a meeting with William Den Haag and Paul White. William and Paul explained that with the almost inevitable move from the traditional open outcry markets to the new era of screen-based trading that huge changes were going to follow.

The thinking within MeesPierson at the time was that broking and offering execution services to big funds and banks would end. In the screen trading age, it was assumed that these companies would become members of the exchanges and would execute their own trades on the markets.

This was the commercial thinking behind the sale of the MeesPierson Derivatives entity to ADM.

I was told that my role as head of customer services at MeesPierson ICS was valued and that my career would be more secure if I turned down the option to transfer to ADM.

I decided to follow that advice, while Steve Kent took the other view and accepted his transfer.

In May 1998, my football team, Charlton Athletic, managed to get themselves into the play-offs for promotion to the Premier League. Their first obstacle was a play-off semi-final against Ipswich Town. The first leg was played at Portman Road in Ipswich on 10 May 1998.

An early own goal from Ipswich's Jamie Clapham decided the ill-disciplined match in which nine yellow cards were shown, including two to Charlton's Danny Mills, who was dismissed in the 73rd minute. The match ended 1–0 and secured Charlton's eighth consecutive clean sheet.

The second leg was played three days later at Charlton's home ground, The Valley, and once again ended in a 1–0 Charlton victory, meaning they won the tie 2–0 on aggregate and had qualified for the play-off final.

At this time, David Morgan, the owner of our local trading subsidiary, David Morgan Futures, was a fellow shareholder in Charlton Athletic. David Morgan Futures frequently sponsored Charlton games, and they owned a corporate box at The Valley. I was very keen to secure my ticket to the play-off final against favourites Sunderland.

I asked my dad if he fancied going to the match, and he immediately said he would and asked if I could get a ticket for his cousin, my uncle, John Rodgers, who lived in Ruislip.

As a season ticket holder, I was permitted to buy up to four tickets, and so, on the day the tickets went on sale to season ticket holders, I travelled to The Valley to join the queue and was able to secure three tickets. The tickets were in the Olympic circle at Wembley Stadium, which was high and gave a perfect view of the pitch.

Sunderland had ended the season in third position, and Charlton had finished fourth. It was estimated that a win would be worth up to twenty million pounds to the successful team.

On Saturday, 25 May 1998, I drove my car to Kingsbury, where I had planned to park behind my old flat in the high street and catch the Jubilee Line Tube back to Wembley.

As I parked up, dressed in my Charlton shirt and scarf, I had not expected to see any other fans before arriving at Wembley Park station. I was wrong –coach loads of Sunderland fans were being dropped at Kingsbury with the same idea of avoiding the usual gridlocked roads around the stadium itself.

This meant boarding a Tube train with rowdy Wearsiders, but they were very friendly, and playful banter flowed. The Sunderland fans were keen to tell me that Kevin Philips and Niall Quinn would win the game for Sunderland. I only hoped the trip back to collect my car was going to be as friendly.

I got off the train and onto the packed platforms with all the other football fans heading for Wembley Way.

I had agreed to meet dad and John Rodgers in the ground, having sent dad the tickets days beforehand. Mum and dad had travelled from Southampton to stay the weekend at John's house.

I was surrounded by fans wearing the red and white of Sunderland.

As I walked towards the stadium I was approached by a young lady with a clipboard, who exclaimed over a microphone, 'I've found one!' Holding onto my arm and leaning in so she could be heard over the chanting and singing she said, 'Would you please agree to a quick interview with Sky Sports. We've been looking out for a Charlton fan wearing a shirt!' I agreed and was led to a group of Sunderland fans surrounding a TV camera.

The lady explained they would be interviewing a Sunderland fan that they had previously selected and then me and that we would be live on the Sky Sports television channel.

Looking directly into the camera, the lady started to talk, explaining she was in Wembley Way and with a fan from each team.

Going to the Sunderland fan first, she asked if he was confident of a win, to which he replied yes and promptly cheered by the surrounding Sunderland faithful. He was then asked for a prediction, and he replied two-nil, Kevin Philips, and Niall Quinn one goal apiece.

Then the camera came to me. I replied I was quietly confident, and I gave her my prediction two-one to Charlton, Clive Mendonca scoring both Charlton's goals.

With that, the interview finished, and with slaps on the back from the Sunderland fans, I headed off for the turnstiles. I never did get to see or track down this short interview.

Both our predictions were far away from the ultimate result.

This was my last ever visit to the 'old' Twin Towers Wembley, where I had attended amazing and historical events.

My love affair with the old Wembley was crystallised that day, in what many believe was the second-best game of football the stadium ever witnessed, the ultimate being England's 4–2 World Cup final win against Germany.

The match was played in front of 78,000 spectators and was refereed by Eddie Wolstenholme. Clive Mendonca opened the scoring for Charlton midway through the first half, before Niall Quinn equalised early in the second.

Kevin Phillips then scored his 35th goal of the season to put Sunderland ahead, but Mendonca doubled his tally with fewer than 20 minutes of the match remaining.

Niall Quinn restored Sunderland's lead two minutes later, before a Richard Rufus header for Charlton, five minutes from the end of regular time, meant the score was 3–3 sending the game into extra time.

Nicky Summerbee then gave Sunderland the lead for the third time, before Mendonca completed his hat-trick, the first player to do so in a play-off final. Extra time ended with the game drawn at 4–4, so the result was to be determined by a penalty shootout.

Both teams scored their first five spot-kicks before the shootout moved to 'sudden death.'

Michael Gray stepped forward to take Sunderland's seventh penalty, but his weak strike was saved by the Charlton goalkeeper Saša Ilić, and Charlton had won the game 7–6 on penalties.

Charlton were into the Premier League, and I could not have been more hyped up and full of pride.

The fantastic efforts of the Valley Party and our return to The Valley, the development of The Valley itself, and the brilliant job Alan Curbishley had done building the team. These events had led to increased crowds and revenues generated for the club – all of this had coincided with my involvement with Charlton FC. I felt honoured to have been along for the ride with my fellow supporters, club members and shareholders.

I looked forward to renewing my season ticket and watching Premiership teams like Manchester United and Liverpool visiting The Valley the following season.

In June 1998, the LIFFE market stepped up its electronic trading offering by replacing its ageing APT trading platform with CONNECT.

CONNECT offered the opportunity for third-party trading platforms to connect to the exchange and offer direct market access (DMA) to registered traders and exchange members.

This open trading architecture sparked a rush of third-party trading platforms seeking approval from LIFFE as authorised DMA providers.

Platforms such as EasyScreen, Realtime Systems (RTS) and Trading Technologies (TT) applied for access to LIFFE. The process of being an authorised vendor required successful conformance testing and dummy market trading before being approval was granted.

CONNECT initially was only available when open outcry ceased daily on the LIFFE market floor in the same way as the APT predecessor used to. But it was obviously LIFFE's belated attempt to cover both bases and would start trading alongside the open outcry pit trading.

In July, Alison and I booked our most adventurous holiday in America. Returning to our old friends Kuoni, we booked a coast-to-coast escorted bus tour.

Once again starting in New York, but this time travelling along the old Route 66 via Pittsburgh, Indianapolis, Kansas, Oklahoma, Texas, New Mexico, Arizona, Santa Monica, Las Vegas, and San Francisco, and finishing in Los Angeles. On route, we would see the Hoover Dam, the Grand Canyon and Death Valley.

It looked to be an amazing adventure, and at the end of the tour there were two additional options: a flight down to Miami for a couple of days or a two-day extended stay in LA at the Beverly Hills Hilton.

Having done our holiday in Florida the year before we did not want to take that option.

Alison is the only person I ever met who stayed up every year to watch the Oscars from start to finish, the chance to stay in a hotel that had staged the Oscars and offered the 'Homes of the Rich and Famous Tour' was too good to miss. So, we opted for the stay at the Beverly Hills Hilton.

I had to ask for an extended holiday, as the trip was just a day short of three weeks – we were leaving on Wednesday, 23rd of September and due to return on 13th of October.

In August, I was once again at the annual Plumstead Anti-Racist Festival on behalf of Charlton Athletic FC. As always, the supporters club assisted the Charlton community team with a large stall at the event.

We made up goody bags with old football programmes, pens, pictures of the team and various freebies.

The CAFC community team, assisted by members of the Charlton ladies football team, provided football training and five-a-side games to the local children throughout the day.

Ben Tegg, Wendy Perfect and I represented the supporters club, and we handed out the goody bags in our Charlton shirts and assisted the community support team by supplying food and drinks and retrieving numerous stray footballs. We also had to organise the next batch of children who wanted to join in with the football training.

The weather was good, and Plumstead Common was full of stands offering food and drink, arts, music, bouncy castles, face painting and events. From midday, a huge stage started with live music, and the event went on until the late afternoon. There were big crowds all day, and by the time we packed up and loaded the Charlton community minibuses, we were all tired out.

As the community transit vans drove off, the last few of us – Ben, myself, and a couple of the Charlton ladies football team – went off to buy well-earned drinks and listen to the acts on the stage before heading off.

As September arrived, Alison and I were extremely excited about our pending trip to the USA. We finally set off for Heathrow Airport and our flight to New York. We only had an overnight stay in New York this time as the timetable was hectic.

Having rested overnight in our hotel, we were introduced to our guide, Eric, and our driver for the trip, a colourful Puerto Rican called Joe, who took an instant liking to Alison. Alison and I were the youngest people on the trip, the vast majority being in their fifties and sixties.

Once again, we had a mix, with couples from Germany, Japan, Australia, and New Zealand, and about a dozen people from the UK, including a Scottish family of four. We even had six Americans who had signed up for the coach tour.

Along the way, we had lots of stops and events, including the Hoover Dam, a cowboy ranch in Texas where we indulged in a spot of line dancing and a native American Indian reserve where we were treated to traditional singing, dancing, and food, including buffalo.

The most memorable part of the tour was the Grand Canyon. It was an awe-inspiring natural phenomenon on a scale that just blows your mind.

Our tour guide, Eric, indulged in what was obviously a well-rehearsed trick. Having lined us up alongside one of the many viewing points at Grand Canyon to take pictures, he advised us to watch a standing stone which was about five feet from the edge of the canyon. He then promptly launched himself from the vast cliff edge to land on the standing stone.

Not just our party, but also the dozen or so other coach tours collected at the site clicked away at him until he jumped back. That night, we stayed at a local ranch and went horse riding along, and at points down, the side of the Grand Canyon.

We headed off to Death Valley for more photo opportunities, again taking in the vast open desert, the colours, and the heat, which were awe inspiring.

In San Francisco, we saw the Golden Gate Bridge and took a boat trip out to Alcatraz prison.

The short hop to Los Angeles meant a stop to see the Hollywood sign as well as the Mann's Chinese Theatre and the historic Hollywood Walk of Fame with all the stars in the pavement. Walking along the Walk of Fame, stopping to read all the names of the famous Hollywood actors and actresses.

But we did not get to see anyone famous on the day.

When we got to the last day of the tour, the coach did a miniature version of the official star-spotting coach tour of Beverly Hills, driving past famous stars' houses. Then, with the afternoon free, we made the trip to Rodeo Drive which was another must-do in Alison's itinerary.

Rodeo Drive is advertised as one of the world's most exclusive luxury destinations and the shopping choice of the rich and famous wishing to indulge in luxury items, high-end and exclusive fashion, and all the top brands.

Thankfully, we were just window shopping, and Alison restrained herself, although we took pictures along the way. Once again, sadly we did not spot anyone famous as we walked down this exclusive shopping street.

I should explain that as brilliant as the tour was, it was full on, and by the time we got to Los Angeles we were tired out, and I for one was just looking to relax for our last couple of days.

That afternoon, the coach headed off to airport hotels to drop the vast majority of the tour off for their various onward flights the next morning. Most were flying home; the others had opted for the Miami extension.

Alison and I, as the only ones opting to extend our stay in Los Angeles, were the last onboard as Joe drove the huge coach towards the Beverly Hills Hilton. We arrived at the hotel late in the afternoon, and as we got off the luxury coach that had been our companion from New York, we said goodbye to Eric and Joe.

The hotel porters were on us in double-quick time, taking our bags from the huge coach.

The big American hotels are always hot on service, but at the Beverly Hills Hilton this seemed to be turbo charged. As the coach pulled away, our bags were on a trolley, and we were quickly but courteously escorted to the check-in desk by a steward.

The receptionists were all stunning and looked like aspiring young actresses waiting to be discovered.

The young lady waiting to serve us was no different. I handed over our Kuoni paperwork, I really had not noticed anything unusual around us, my attention fully on this attractive lady behind the desk.

Alison, however, had been taking in everything ultra-excited to be in this hotel.

As I talked to the young lady on the reception desk, Alison was suddenly trying to get my attention with subtle taps and elbow jabs. I thought it was because I was being too attentive to the young lady behind the desk.

The receptionist asked for our passports, and I pulled them out my jacket and handed them over. Then, this rich, distinctive voice next to me said, 'I thought you were English. Nice to be checking in with fellow countrymen.'

The voice was awfully familiar, and so I glanced to my right, and I realised why Alison had been jabbing me for five minutes – standing right next to me was none other than James Bond star Sir Roger Moore.

I was stunned in disbelief, doing a double-take, but Roger didn't miss a beat. 'Are you here for the event?' he asked.

'No,' I said, 'my girlfriend and I are just finishing off our holiday and we're traveling back home on Tuesday.'

In very typical Roger Moore style, his eyebrow went up. 'Oh well, you did very well to get a room at all then. It's going to be remarkably busy tonight. Are you into a bit of star spotting?'

At this point, Alison could stay silent no more, and had practically elbowed past me. 'Oh yes, Roger, that's why we chose to extend our stay at this hotel – to see all the stars homes and hopefully spot someone famous. But I doubt we'll top this!'

This prompted Roger to give us a warm smile. 'Very nice of you to say that. But tonight, Whitney Houston and Mariah Carey are hosting a charity function, so you don't need to find the stars – they'll all be coming to you, here!'

Alison nearly fainted on the spot, and at this stage the poor receptionist, who had been waiting patiently to regain our attention and give us our room key, jumped in.

By the time I had finished with the receptionist, Roger Moore had moved away. He gave us a little wave, turned to us, and said, 'Enjoy the rest of your holiday.' Then he headed off towards the lift in front of him.

Our room was in a separate wing to the left of the reception desk, and Alison was buzzing as we walked in.

We had just met Roger Moore. Who else might we see?

Where could we go to get the best view of all these celebrities?

Did I think the hotel would mind us standing in reception? Alison was in full celebrity meltdown.

We unpacked and started to discuss whether we were going to be able to get an evening meal at the hotel that night.

Then the bedside hotel phone rang. I picked it up, and it was the reception desk asking if we could go back to the desk to collect something.

I surmised it was something from Kuoni about tour and options during our short stay at the hotel.

It was a fair walk back to the reception desk, and when I got there I was handed a sealed envelope. As I ambled back towards our room, I opened the envelope, and two badges came out.

We found out later, after a bit of investigation, that Roger Moore had secured two press passes for us.

As the cars delivering the stars to the event pulled up, they all stopped just outside reception for a press photo.

Now, Alison and I were going to be there, with the paparazzi, taking pictures and mixing with the celebrities.

We had an absolutely magical evening.

We saw the two divas first – Whitney Houston, who arrived with Bobby Brown and their young daughter, and then Mariah Carey, who, it has to be said, loved to pose for the pictures.

Alison and I stood out because we were obviously not part of the press pack, so many of the stars appeared to make a point of stopping in front of us to enable us take a picture.

Following on from the hosts, Whitney, and Mariah, was the pop star known as Prince, Anthony Quinn, Stephanie Powers, Lauren Bacall, Jane Russell, Robert Wagner, Charles Bronson, Leslie Nielsen and so many others.

Some of the guests who arrived that night we didn't know or recognise.

These were domestic US TV stars from *NYPD Blue*, *Law and Order* and other shows that were big at the time. We just took our cue from the press pack around us, and if they got excited and took pictures, so did we.

But the most delightful of all the people we saw that night was Juliet Mills and her daughter Melissa.

Whitney Houston, Bobby Brown and Kristina

On hearing our accents, both Juliet and Melissa stayed and talked for a good ten minutes, wanting to hear all about our trip and how we had managed to get in amongst the press pack.

Mariah

I have plenty of pictures and memories from that night.

The following morning, we scoured the local papers and found out that Roger was more than just a guest – he was at the event

Robert Wagner and daughter Courtney Brooke

Juliette Mills and Daughter Melissa Caulfield

to receive the 'Lord & Lady Olivier Humanitarian in Arts' award.

The event itself was the fourth Annual International Achievement in Arts awards, and Roger's award was presented to him by Carroll Baker, with whom he starred in *The Miracle* in 1959.

When we finally boarded the plane for our flight home, both Alison and I were still in disbelief.

We had hoped to see a star if we were lucky, but to have the who's who of Hollywood stop within touching distance of us, stopping for photos, had been something neither of us could have dreamed of.

The architect of our great evening, Sir Roger Moore, became a firm favourite of mine thereafter. I considered writing to thank him on so many occasions, but I never did.

When he sadly passed away on 23 May 2017, I did leave a tribute on a website, giving a brief version of the above, but it still did not feel enough.

On 6th May 2020, I sat down and wrote a letter to his daughter Deborah and sent it to her via her agent. A week later, I got a card back with a delightful note thanking me for telling her about my meeting with her very gracious and amazing father.

Returning to Welling after our holiday also meant a return to Camomile Court and MeesPierson ICS.

Waiting for me when I got back into the office was my new line director, William Den Haag. William told me that we had three new accounts transferring from his old company KAS Clearing. They were Rosenthal Collins UK, Prime International and Seaport Clearing.

All three were LIFFE floor-based local collectives, and I was due to have a meeting with the head of Rosenthal and Prime International. However, Roger Little was taking on Seaport.

It turned out that both Rosenthal Collins UK and Prime International were London-based branches of Rosenthal Collins in the US. I was told that Mr Rosenthal and Mr Collins no longer got along and had set up rival LIFFE floor operations.

As a mirror of their US bosses' enmity, the London-based bosses of these rival UK-based operations also did not like each other.

Giving me both entities to account manage appeared to be a tongue-in-cheek bit of mischief from William.

The Rosenthal Collins UK entity was run by a very colourful American called Freddy Boyers.

Fred was an overly aggressive individual, and he seemed to enjoy that notoriety. Rosenthal UK had already made use of our electronic trading room in Nicholas Lane and had traders trading on the DTB exchange.

Prime International had offices next to Cannon Street station and the LIFFE exchange and was managed by the flamboyant but likeable Sean Conley.

Sean's head of operations was a gentleman called Mike Tindal. Prime had a number of local traders on the LIFFE floor under the watchful eye of their floor manager, Mike Wakefield.

These two accounts injected a huge amount of volume and work into my daily routine. But I was now starting to get more involved in the commercial side of the business, bringing in a new clearing account called Tradition.

Tradition had their offices just around the corner from our offices in Camomile Court, and the account had been secured after a cold call from the Tradition CEO Jeff Adler. I quickly visited their Bishopsgate office and we sat down to discuss their clearing requirements.

Tradition was a trading operation with no LIFFE floor presence and was, like many companies that were springing up, anticipating the end of open outcry and a full move to screen trading.

Jeff and I quickly built a rapport, and I promised to send a full commercial proposal.

I walked back to the office, sat down with William, and we worked out a clearing package. I was able to email Jeff with a full proposal that day.

We had subsequent meetings, including one with Paul Pealing from the MeesPierson clearing desk, and within a fortnight Jeff Adler signed the papers and Tradition opened its clearing account with MeesPierson.

I felt a huge amount of satisfaction with landing my first account, and Tradition was to quickly to be followed by GFI, a brokerage company.

I could feel my role changing, but I wasn't ready to give up on my account management function. I was keen to perform both a sales role and keep my hand in on the customer services side, where I felt at home.

As 1998 came towards a conclusion, MeesPierson established a fully equipped electronic trading 'arcade', as they had become known, on the sixth floor of Camomile Court.

This was to provide trading positions for the growing number of electronic traders. The 'arcade' was a major investment decision on behalf of the company.

The increasing amount of price data required by the trading systems and additional volume of trading data meant the company had to install huge, fixed communications lines from the office to the respective trading exchange data hubs – not one but two, as the exchanges required a backup line for resilience and to tick a box with the regulator.

There were servers required on the ends of these lines, and the trading systems often required state-of-the-art PCs to be deployed.

Many trading systems required multiple screens, meaning the video cards in the PCs needed to be more expensive quad cards. Traders also needed news services such as Reuters or Bloomberg, so multiple PCs were required by each trader.

This in turn meant a new support department was established, this was an Information Technology support team for the electronic traders. This team not only supplied and supported the hardware in terms of PCs and screens but also functioned as a point of contact for the growing numbers of trading platforms that were connecting to the markets.

Each platform had its own eccentricities and requirements, but as always traders tended to be tribal and not inclined to switch between platforms. Once they started trading on a specific platform and became familiar with its functionality, they stuck with it.

The other change that was essential to companies supporting electronic trading was related to risk control. Risk management on the trading floors was hugely different from what was required on the new trading screens.

All of this additional investment and increased staff costs needed to be recovered, and so as part of the commercial arrangement, each trader or trading group in an arcade was charged a monthly 'desk fee,' billed at the start of each month.

In the early 'Wild West' era that existed in electronic trading, risk management was very rudimentary as the trading platforms concentrated all their development resources into the actual trading systems.

Risk management was different on all the trading platforms and controlling this new trading risk was down to the risk staff watching multiple screens, in multiple formats, and trying to spot anyone running into negative equity.

New companies were springing up in and around the City of London to house and offer trading positions to traders.

This included all of the major local trading companies on the LIFFE floor who had now reconciled themselves to the ultimate closure of the trading floor and the transition to screens.

Sussex Trading, David Kyte Futures, David Morgan Futures, and Hills Independent Traders were joined by new companies popping up all over the City – Saxon Trading, Candlestick Trading, Griffin Trading, Schneider Trading, Pelican Trading, and Vantage, to name some of them.

All of these new companies needed a general clearing member to support them and to supply the DMA. This meant even more work for the screen-based trading IT support team.

MeesPierson, as an established screen-based trading supplier, quickly captured a big market share in supporting these new companies.

This meant a lot of new relationships and customer service support for us to deal with. We were working very closely with the MeesPierson risk department. A weekly meeting was established between the departments so we could exchange notes and manage any issues or concerns.

In the early days, the traders became very territorial about their trading methodology. If they had a system that worked for them, they did not want anyone else to see what they were doing.

This was emphasised one day when I took a call from the sixth floor about a trader called Simon Chan.

Simon spent his entire day trading the DTB Bund with headphones on, hunched over his screen. Next to him was an American trader called Chris Fosberg, who, Simon had convinced himself, was shadow trading him, copying his trading pattern.

I was invited up to the sixth floor trading arcade by the IT support team who told me that Simon Chan had asked them if he could 'pop' into the office over the weekend. They had given him permission, and as I looked at the IT support team I could see they were trying not to laugh.

I asked what the problem was, and they told me that Simon had 'built a bloody shed.'

I walked out on the trading floor, and I could see smirking and laughing traders, and sure enough Simon had nailed huge wooden panels either side of his desk.

Needless to say, we had to convince him that this was not acceptable, and the wood had to go; otherwise, we were quite sure the shiny new sixth-floor trading arcade would end up looking like a string of beach shacks standing next to each other.

The inevitable happened on 21 December 1998 when a gentleman by the name of John Ho Park was trading the Bund contract from Griffin Trading's office in London.

Griffin was clearing via an agreement with MeesPierson. Park was losing money and started to chase the market, increasing the scale of his trading as he tried to recover his growing losses.

Unlike Nick Leeson's trading at Baring Brothers, this trading and the growing losses should have been visible to anyone monitoring risk. If they were monitoring, they didn't stop him, and the losses mounted.

The next morning, due to the losses John Ho Park had accumulated on the Griffin account, MeesPierson's risk department issued a margin call for five million deutsche marks, payable the next day.

On the morning of the next day, 23rd December, Griffin answered the margin call by wiring five million deutsche marks from its Bank. The loss far exceeded any funding John Ho Park had in place and effectively wiped out the funds all the other Griffin traders had on their accounts.

As a result, the Securities and Futures Authority (SFA), which was the UK regulator and successor to the AFBD, stepped in and suspended all trading at Griffin.

The losses led to the bankruptcy of the company. Rogue trader John Ho Park was banned from working in the City by the SFA. In the crackdown that followed, the SFA also banned managers who were working for Griffin at the time.

MeesPierson itself had a smaller but similar incident when a trader called Stephen Humphries lost all the money he had on his account. The next day, he turned up on the sixth-floor trading arcade as normal, took his trading position and started trading again.

MeesPierson's risk department saw him start trading on the risk screen and immediately phoned the sixth floor to instruct the staff to stop him.

Matthew Parsons walked out onto the arcade and told Stephen to stop trading and to head down to the second floor to talk to the risk department about refinancing his account.

Stephen said he would finish and head down, so Matthew Parsons walked back to his office. No sooner had he sat down in his chair when the phone rang. It was the risk department saying, 'Have you spoken to him?'

Matthew said, 'Yes, he's on his way down.'

'No,' risk replied, 'he is trading again!'

Matthew and Neil McKenzie rushed out onto the trading floor, and sure enough Stephen was back at his desk trading. Matthew manhandled Stephen off the trading floor while Neil sat at his trading terminal and closed out the trades.

Matthew propelled Stephen into the lift and hit two, where the head of the risk department was waiting for him. As the lift doors opened, the head of risk was in no mood to discuss refinancing. Stephen Humphries was escorted off the premises and his account was closed.

MeesPierson had a change of managing director the position was taken by William Den Haag, who had enjoyed a meteoric rise since he joined from KAS. Paul White was transferred from director of operations to commercial director and became my new line manager.

The customer services team of Alan Byrne and myself was complemented with two new arrivals, Joanne Christoforou and Melinda Eason. At the same time, Roderick Weerts joined the commercial team, as he was co-ordinating the increasing move of traders from the LIFFE trading floor onto the screens.

Not all traders were ready or willing to embrace the screens some elected to stay on the LIFFE floor, moving to contracts where the trading floor maintained liquidity. Others decided to move down to the IPE floor where there was no indication of a move towards screen trading.

1999

In early 1999, MeesPierson was approached by a group of traders who had lost all their money at Griffin.

These traders came armed with their trading statements showing that they had been trading good volumes of trades and had been very profitable before John Ho Park had struck.

At this point in time, the SFA was still investigating the demise of Griffin, and all the funds remained suspended.

The dozen or so traders crammed into Paul White's offices explained that they had no idea if they would be getting anything back from Griffin, but obviously they traded for a living and had not been able to trade since Christmas.

The traders all had impressive records but letting them open accounts and start trading without any money meant that MeesPierson would be backing them all with company money.

MeesPierson had recently moved the last of the traders from the Nicholas Lane basement facility and relocated them onto the sixth floor of Camomile Court, so this office was now empty.

We told the assembled traders that we would get back to them, and internal discussions were held at MeesPierson with William den Haag and the risk department.

The following day, we called the traders back in and gave them a proposal: if they contracted as one entity and accepted the Nicholas Lane office as their trading office and traded conservatively until such time as they were self-financing, then MeesPierson would back them.

The deal was agreed, and the traders told us that they would be trading under the name of MacFutures. MacFutures would go on to become the biggest electronic trading group in London.

Not long afterward I received an unexpected phone call from my old Czarnikow/Cater Allen colleague Richard 'Dicky' Gibbs. Dicky told me that the Bank of Austria LIFFE floor trading operation were looking for a new home for their business.

Dicky, Prashant Laud and Reg de Souza had all gone to work at Bank Austria after leaving Cater Allen.

Bank Austria had decided that with the Bund volume now on the screen-based Eurex exchange (the DTB had rebranded as Eurex in 1998 after the merger with the Swiss Options and Financial Futures Exchange) and increasing doubts about the viability of the LIFFE trading floor, they were closing down their LIFFE operation.

Prashant Laud agreed to bring the two principals running the Bank Austria brokerage operation to Camomile Court and introduce them to us. I arranged the meeting with Paul White, and we agreed a date.

When Prash arrived at the ground-floor reception of Camomile Court, I went down to bring them up to Paul White's second-floor office. Prash looked unchanged from his days at Cater Allen – smart in his usual suit, shirt, and tie.

The same could not be said of the two young gentlemen he had with him. One was very tall and thin with long, black, shoulder-length hair, a knitted black woolly hat on his head and a long, black trench coat. The other was a shorter man with wavy, sandy hair, a casual jacket over a blue V-neck jumper and casual black chino trousers.

Prash and I shook hands, and then Prash introduced the taller of the two visitors as John Ruskin and the shorter one as Lee Hughes. I led the three of them to the lifts and we went up to the second floor.

As we approached Paul's office, William was leaning into the office talking to Paul. William looked at the three visitors trailing behind me, and with a nod he left, making his way round the corner to his own office.

John and Lee explained that they had six brokers including the three of them and that they had a good institutional client base. Bank Austria had promised that they would continue to support their old team by using them exclusively for their LIFFE and Eurex execution.

John and Lee were confident that once they were established in a trading room they would be able to attract other brokers from the LIFFE floor. Paul listened as the guys explained that they would need a phone recording system, six desks and six TT trading terminals but could make do with two Bloomberg terminals.

The main thing they needed from us was a brokerage invoicing service and 'factoring.' Factoring was required for brokerage operations because the big banks were extremely poor payers, sometimes taking up to nine months to pay for a month's execution services.

Factoring was a credit facility that enabled a broker to be paid monthly in advance of these invoices being paid. MeesPierson would pay out 80 per cent of the invoiced amount in advance under the terms of the deal.

MeesPierson had a dedicated brokerage invoice department and this team had long-established relationships with their opposite numbers at all the big banks and institutions, and they were well versed in chasing up and getting these invoices paid.

The important thing was to make sure the invoices were correct when sent, and this meant an accurate reconciliation of the trades that were 'given-up' by the executing broker to the client's clearing account.

Paul White agreed to work on a commercial proposal for this brokerage business, and we took the guys on a tour of the sixth floor to show them the trading arcade where they would be sitting if we concluded a deal.

We eventually escorted them out of the building, and as we returned in the lift, Paul was not very enthusiastic, saying he was not sure they had enough volume and income to make it exciting.

As we headed for Paul's office, William was waiting for us. 'Ya, who were those scruffy people. We're surely not signing them up are we?' William asked. Paul explained they were a potential brokerage client, but William was not impressed. 'We sold MPD because we don't think brokerage is sustainable when the floor goes.'

After William had gone, Paul's attitude changed. If William did not want them signed up, Paul was going to do all he could to sign them.

Paul and I sat down and worked out a commercial proposal, which I sent to John and Lee.

A commercial deal for a brokerage operation could not be on a 'pence per lot' basis that we applied to traders. It had to be a percentage split of the commission the brokerage team generated.

We offered a commission split weighted in the broker's favour, with a move to a more beneficial split on any monthly income over £100,000. This was net of the monthly costs we would be charging for the desks and systems deployed for them on the sixth floor.

We sent the proposal to John and Lee, and they quickly accepted on the understanding that we would review the profit split after six months. John and Lee were confident they would quickly attract additional brokers.

When it came time to issue an official contract, John Ruskin told me that they would contacting as Cube Financial.

Within weeks, Cube Financial was up and running on the sixth floor of Camomile Court.

On the morning of Friday, 18 June 1999, protestors started arriving in the City of London.

This was the beginning of a very heavily advertised protest that enabled a large number of varied protest and pressure groups to come together and attempt to disrupt working in the City of London, and in particular the financial services sector.

All around the City in the days before the event, a concerted publicity campaign was conducted, using colourful stickers and thousands of posters. These posters encouraged workers to phone in sick and stay away from the City.

An 18-minute promotional video was made and distributed globally via the internet. This video was called 'Squaring up to the Square Mile,' and it was accompanied by a 32-page pamphlet produced by a group called Reclaim the Streets and Corporate Watch.

This document went into huge detail, giving information on the major financial institutions in the City of London. The pamphlet included an A3 map of the City of London, showing exactly where these businesses were located. Everyone recognised this document to be a list of targets for the protestors to concentrate on.

The police had been monitoring all the internet and email traffic across all the various protest groups, and they had made it clear they were gearing up for the worst-case scenario.

That morning, the Metropolitan Police started turning up by the vanload and parking in side streets, ready to lend a hand to the City of London Police if required.

The City of London Police had been in contact with all the businesses in the City, telling them to expect trouble and issuing guidance that included recommendations that staff should dress down for the day, buildings should be secured, and extra security should be employed.

MeesPierson was no different – we all came to work in jeans and casual clothes for the day, and the reception area was locked down, with the metal grill pulled across the front entrance, leaving only one door open for use.

As my train pulled into Cannon Street, the vast majority of my fellow passengers were dressed down, and although I could see some protestors carrying rucksacks and placards, I did not see any trouble.

When I arrived at the office, I was told that at London Bridge and Liverpool Street, a group of protestors had been using high-powered 'super soaker' water pistols filled with white emulsion paint, targeting anyone wearing a suit. Whether this was true or not I never found out.

The start of the protest was incredibly quiet.

The first thing we heard at Camomile Court was a mix of horns and cycle bells as a group of forty or so cyclists pulled up at the major road junction outside our building. The crossroad between Liverpool Street (A10) and London Wall was brought to a halt as these cyclists fanned out to block all four exits. Flanked by four motorcycle police who obviously had instructions not to interfere, the cyclists blocked the road for 15 minutes before heading off to block another junction elsewhere.

This was 'Reclaim the Streets,' and as an initial taster we were not that impressed. This part of the day's events had been advertised as a critical mass bicycle ride designed to bring the City of London traffic to a standstill in the morning rush hour. We decided that if that was the best they could manage then we had little to worry about.

We knew from the pamphlets that had been distributed that a large march through the city was scheduled for midday.

On the televisions dotted around our floor we watched the Campaign Against the Arms Trade's hundred or so supporters stage a 'die-in' outside the Bank of England and the Royal Exchange (the old LIFFE floor). They were heckled by some of the local workers, but the watching police kept the two sides apart.

Then the television news coverage switch to a peaceful human chain which was formed around the Treasury. Other coverage showed protestors abseiling down Tower Bridge. Banners were hung from office blocks, and more than three thousand people danced and partied near Liverpool Street station.

Protestors were reported to have walked into City branches of NatWest, Lloyds and Friends Provident. They handed out leaflets to staff and customers and tried to padlock themselves to bank furniture.

Once secured with chains and padlocks, these protestors remained, and the bank branches were forced to close to customers.

Other Protestors scaled the Friends Provident building, unfurling a huge banner. Campaigners said that they aimed to bring home to those involved at every level of the financial industry the implications of their involvement with the arms trade.

The main march was still to come, and the protestors were gathering in carnival-style in and around Liverpool Street, just outside our office. A number of us decided to go out for lunch and to take in the atmosphere.

I left the office with Mark Mootoo, a very tall, stocky guy who worked on the clearing desk, Paul Willis, our flamboyant head of compliance, Sara St Angelo, who had recently moved from the LIFFE floor where she had worked as an admin clerk and now worked in compliance, and my colleagues Alan Byrne and Jo Christoforou.

We mixed and mingled with the mass of gathering protestors and were handed pamphlets declaring 'Food not Bombs.' People were singing, dancing, and waving flags in the sunshine and we were handed free samosas by a catering truck called the 'Veggie Catering Campaign.' At first, we were a bit dubious about eating them, until we saw other people tucking in.

We could hear music, and heading through the crowds was a samba band, so we stopped to listen to them for a while. There was the thick, sickly smell of cannabis floating around, but the majority of the crowd was friendly and just enjoying themselves.

People were walking around the crowd handing out carnival masks that seemed to be in assorted colours. One large lady came up to Paul Willis to offer him one of these masks, and she told him he may need it later as it was to hide his face from the 'pigs and CCTV.'

It was the first ominous indication that some people were expecting trouble with the police. We just found it amusing that, out of all of us, the woman had picked on Paul Willis to offer the mask – he was hardly an obvious anarchist or potential troublemaker.

We went to the White Hart, which was a local public house in Liverpool Street, and grabbed some drinks and food before heading back to the office. We believed from what we had seen and witnessed that there was a good chance the day was likely to pass off trouble-free.

As we arrived back at MeesPierson's office, we could hear the level of noise increase in the streets outside and the sound of drums and chanting as the marches prepared to set off. We knew that four separate marches were planned, but we did not know where they would be going.

As well as the television coverage we were kept up to date via the phones and numerous emails that were flying around the City between the various financial companies.

For example, there was a rumour that as one of the marches had passed Deutsche Bank, that their trading desk up on the fourth or fifth floor had opened the windows and dropped handfuls of photocopied fifty-pound notes down like confetti onto the protestors below. The bizarre response was that one of the protestors superglued himself to the main entrance door of the bank.

Later, we heard that all around the route, protestors had superglued their hands to doors of banks and financial institutions to try and stop people entering and exiting. The police merely called the fire brigade, and while they waited for them to turn up, the companies opened other doors for people to use or, in one case, just made the protestor walk back and forth as people used the door.

The first spark of violence occurred near to our office. A breakaway march from the planned four pre-arranged routes started to head down London Wall where the Met Police had parked a number of vans carrying riot police on standby.

Three riot police vans were immediately surrounded, and the demonstrators began dancing on top of them.

In an effort to quickly redeploy these police vans, one of them reversed and hit a woman, breaking her leg. This caused the protestors in this breakaway group to erupt in anger and start to attack the retreating vans. Demonstrators sat down in front of police vans and another male protestor was injured after he fell in front of one of vans.

These events were quickly communicated via phone to the other four marches, and trouble was now erupting all around the City, as branches of Starbucks, McDonald's and other multinational chains became targets.

The earlier scenes of carnival and peaceful protest against world debt, the arms trade and financial institutions now turned into a full-scale riot.

At this stage, we were told that the LIFFE floor itself was a primary target, and we started to get distressed phone calls from admin clerks on the LIFFE floor who wanted to leave before the protestors arrived. But by now, the best advice was to stay where you were and, more importantly, to stay off the streets.

Between two and three o'clock, the various marches came together, and an estimated five thousand people converged on the Lower Thames Street entrance to the LIFFE market. A fire hydrant was set off, symbolising the freeing of the Walbrook, graffiti messages were sprayed, and CCTV cameras were disabled.

This was the moment when a small but determined group of protestors broke into the LIFFE markets main entrance, smashed up the reception area and then tried to charge up the now-disabled four escalators that led up to the LIFFE trading floor itself.

What followed became folklore thereafter. These protestors had simply not done their homework. They had fallen for the widely held belief that the City was populated by chinless wonders who would run away at the first sight of a group of aggressive, burly protestors.

They were in for a very nasty surprise.

In what is now known as the 'Battle of the LIFFE Floor,' a large group of incredibly angry East Enders, Essex Boys and South Londoners moved from the LIFFE trading floor, resplendent in their multicoloured corporate trading jackets, and placed themselves at the top of the escalators.

These traders were truly angry – angry that their livelihoods may be ending as the electronic trading became more established and accepted; angry that despite trying to make the most of the days that were left to them on the trading floor, here was a group of scruffy vandals attempting to smash up their place of work and stop them trading.

Whatever these deluded protestors thought they were going to achieve when they ran up those escalators, came to violent and bloody end at the top of them. I was not there myself, but I have heard first-hand accounts from traders that were.

As fast as the protestors could go up the escalators, they were sent back down even faster. They were punched, kicked and unable to get past the determined group of LIFFE traders positioned at the top of the four escalators.

The hundred plus protestors made several attempts to storm the LIFFE trading floor, but with the restriction of charging up four escalators and into the waiting two dozen traders who hurled them back down, the result was inevitable. The beaten and bloodied protestors eventually retreated to the bottom of the escalators and traded insults with the LIFFE traders at the top, who challenged them to try again. They didn't and the protestors retreated back out into the streets.

That day saw some of the worst public disorder since the 1990 Trafalgar Square poll tax riots. Many people were injured as the police used water cannons and baton-charged the demonstrators on horseback.

By now, there were running battles in side streets with a hardcore of protestors hurling stones and bottles, breaking into buildings, throwing out files, setting fire to papers and breaking ground-floor windows.

By 4 pm, the McDonald's restaurant in Cannon Street had been gutted, with chairs ripped out, glass broken, graffiti daubed on walls and food thrown in the street.

A car showroom was trashed in Lower Thames Street, and police brought in heavy reinforcements and tried to move the protestors.

The battles raged down Broken Wharf and Upper Thames Street, with several hundred police charging every few minutes on horse and on foot. The police used CS gas and slowly succeeded in pushing the protestors down Lower Thames Street and finally out of the City of London.

In the aftermath, the remaining protestors gathered peacefully in Trafalgar Square.

By this time, the markets had shut, and our day had ended. I was able to join my colleagues in a nervous walk towards the train stations for our trip home. Cannon Street station was still shut at six o'clock, but I was able to make my way to London Bridge station and catch a train home from there.

Once again, the train was a mix of City workers and homebound protestors, and an eerie silence was what I remember most about that journey.

On the Monday, the streets around the City had been cleaned up. Boarded-up windows and graffiti were all that remained of the Stop the City riot.

The Bank of England and Royal Exchange buildings and many of the elegant and historical buildings had been covered in graffiti. I hoped that the damage was just superficial, and the offending paint could be removed quickly.

On 1ˢᵗ August 1999, I was once again helping Charlton Athletic at another annual Plumstead Anti-Racist Festival. This one was named 'Many Hearts, One Beat' and the main stage this time was to be graced by disco music royalty The Real Thing.

It was a balmy day, and as usual as I walked down towards our area to help set up the stand and the football training pitch. Fellow supporters club member Ben Tegg met me.

Ben had done so much work for the Kick It Out campaign with Charlton Athletic that Kick It Out had employed him full-time to co-ordinate their national campaign with football clubs.

Following their brilliant play-off win in May 1998, Charlton had been unable to hang on to a place in the Premiership, and so the season ahead was back in the First Division.

The club was keen to maintain momentum and continued to collaborate with the supporters club on these types of local events. They were so keen that Ben told me excitedly that the club had tasked a couple of the first team to join us on

Plumstead Common, although Ben had no idea who might be coming.

As usual, Charlton's ladies team had sent five of their number down to join the community support team, and we quickly had the stand set up and football training started.

This year, we had fewer match day programmes to give out as the Premiership programmes from the previous season had sold out for most of the big matches.

We did however have enough programmes, pens, pencils, team photos and various bits and pieces to make up enough goodie bags for the kids who did the football training.

The Charlton stand attracted a great deal of interest that year, and this increased substantially when Keith Jones, the club captain at the time, turned up at the stand.

A quick game of five-a-side was set up, and Benn Tegg could not contain himself, saying, 'I'll never get another chance to play football with Keith Jones.' With two of the ladies team and three lucky kids on one side, and Keith and Ben on the other side with three kids, this very strange game of five-a-side was played out on Plumstead Common.

After the game, Keith Jones happily signed autographs and had pictures taken numerous times with the kids and their parents. Keith Jones stayed for well over an hour before calling it a day.

This was the high-water mark of Charlton's involvement with the supporters club.

In the 1999/2000 season, Charlton went back up to the Premiership as champions of the First Division and stayed in there until the 2006/2007 season when they were relegated back down.

Changes at the top of the club and this prolonged spell in the Premiership meant the club soon forgot about the Valley Party, Target 10,000, City Addicks and all the help the supporters club had provided.

They even dispensed with the 'fans director' from the board.

This was to be my last event as a member of the supporters club.

However, Ben Tegg maintained his links and was at the forefront of the campaign to remove Belgian businessman Roland Duchâtelet as the club owner after his disastrous tenure of ownership from 2014 to 2019.

During this spell, the football club was starved of funding, sold all its best young talent, and slumped to the third tier of English football.

It was no surprise when the television coverage of a protest march of Charlton fans, before the kick-off of a home match, showed Ben Tegg at the very front of the march. I am pleased to say that Ben and the supporters helped remove Roland Duchâtelet, and to this day Charlton Athletic is still my team.

In 1999, my parents moved home once again, this time to a new build in Kingsmead Ashford. This left my grandmother, still loving New Forest life in her bungalow, as the remaining Parker in Dibden Purlieu.

Having my parents in Kent meant that they were a 45-minute drive away. With Robin now living in a very quirky old house in East Farleigh, just outside Maidstone, we were all local for the first time since we had lived together as a family in Froghall, Dibden Purlieu.

On 6 August 1999, a rogue trader bankrupted another electronic trading room.

This time it was Sussex Futures, a company set up by the much-respected local trader John Sussex.

John was a 'day one' trader, meaning he had started his LIFFE floor trading career on the very first day the exchange traded at the Royal Exchange. John had shared his success, funding local traders and then setting up his own floor trading company.

Sussex Futures, like many other local trading companies, had opened a trading arcade to house its traders as the old floor-based open outcry markets had slowly closed and moved onto the electronic trading platforms. These local trading arcades now competed with each other for business, and local traders were already, at this early stage, losing all their money at one arcade and then days/weeks later popping up at another one.

The same trader that MeesPierson had kicked out, Stephen Humphries, had signed up at Sussex Futures, and on 6th August 1999 had managed to bankrupt the company in just 1 hour and 32 minutes of trading.

However, he did not walk away this time.

Sussex Futures took him to court, and in what was to be a landmark case, he was jailed.

The court heard that despite the mounting concern of senior executives at Sussex Futures, 24-year-old Stephen Humphries had repeatedly lied about his trading position as his losses rose.

In the case held at Southwark Crown Court in London, the court was told that Humphries had fled the offices of Sussex Futures, but by that time the company was £750,000 in the red.

Despite the best efforts of the staff to limit the losses left by these positions, the company ended up closing with £2.3 million, costing the jobs of twenty traders. This was despite John Sussex injecting over half a million of his own money in an attempt to save the company.

By 3ʳᵈ September 1999, the LIFFE exchange achieved a small victory by winning the lion's share of the Euribor contract. This was a euro-denominated short-term interest rate. In an attempt to stop history repeating itself, the new contract was listed on the LIFFE CONNECT trading system.

A trading system war was developing as Europe's other exchanges were adding features to their own electronically traded Euribor contracts in hopes of carving out increased market share at London's expense.

In November 1999, LIFFE closed its last three main futures 'pits' on the floor of LIFFE exchange as the futures markets moved onto the LIFFE CONNECT trading platform.

All that remained on the trading floor, which had once been home to thousands of traders, was a few options pits. The system development that would see these remaining trading pits migrate was ongoing at this time.

Since its early appearance as the AFBD and now the SFA, compliance in the City of London was becoming an all-devouring monster, demanding more staff and systems to deal with the relentless amount of rules and red tape that was being forced onto the companies offering services in the financial industry.

MeesPierson, like all companies that offered clearing services and effectively held client money, was a prime target for these new regulations.

The customer services and commercial team were having to work ever closer with the MeesPierson compliance team to keep the current client paperwork up to date and also to ensure that new clients had the current paperwork required.

To deal with this, a weekly meeting was now held between the commercial team and compliance. Paul Willis, the head of compliance, and his team which consisted of Carol Deebank, June Allen, and Sara St Angelo.

These meetings and increased my contact with Carol Deebank and had given me the opportunity to get to know her better and we enjoyed the occasional lunch hour and evening out, usually in the company of Alan Byrne or members of the clearing desk.

At home, Alison and I were carrying on much as we had since she had moved in.

My parents became increasingly concerned that we were like 'an old married couple' despite the fact we were not married. We were good friends, we got along, but something was missing, and we just coasted along.

Increasingly, we went our own separate ways, with Alison going to the gym most nights and contenting herself with watching *Sex and the City* and *Friends* on TV, while I contented myself with increasing numbers of nights out with my colleagues at MeesPierson.

As the decade headed towards a conclusion, there was mounting panic about a potential 'data bomb,' and it was feared that computer systems could shut down and crash.

Information technology experts and senior business managers with responsibility for their organisations' computer systems were growing increasingly anxious about how their computers would handle the critical time movement from 23.59 hours on 31/12/1999 to 00.01 hours on 1/1/2000.

The problem was that most computer systems used two-digit data fields to recognise dates. For example, 1 April 1997 was typically recognised as 01/04/97. Two-digit data fields were set to move from 31/12/99 to 01/01/00, and the worry was that computers would recognise the final two digits as representing the year 1900, instead of the year 2000. The question was what would they do?

Entire project teams were set up to try to identify where problems might occur and how the date change might affect existing computer programs. MeesPierson was no different, assigning the project to a dedicated millennium team.

It was with a lot of trepidation that everyone went home on Friday, 31 December, wondering what mess we would come back to. In the end, nothing happened, the computers coped with the change.

Alison and I spent New Year's Eve 1999 together, alone at Wordsworth Road. Little did we know that we would not be together at the end of 2000.

THE END

When I started this book, I had to decide where would be a good place to finish. The millennium and the end of trading on the LIFFE floor seemed as good a place as any.

That is not to say there was nothing of note that happened after 2000, but things were never the same.

On Friday, 24ᵗʰ November 2000, the last of the LIFFE trading pits were closed as the options contracts transitioned onto LIFFE CONNECT.

Many of the traders who refused to move onto the trading screens had already moved down onto the IPE floor or the LIFFE commodity contracts where coffee, cocoa and sugar continued trading on the trading floors.

With the demise of the LIFFE trading floor, the number of trading arcades continued to grow, with regional offices opening up. The remaining traders displaced by LIFFE were now either trading electronically or had given up on trading altogether. Many retired, some became taxi drivers and others opened businesses like restaurants or in one case a wine warehouse.

Of those who did make the move to electronic trading, many did not last long and lost their money. Electronic trading was a hugely different animal and required different skill sets.

In order to continue growing, the trading arcades needed new blood, and many started 'trainee trader' programs. These were designed to teach the fundamentals of electronic trading to people who had never traded before.

MeesPierson decided to reconsider its position in the market and asked Paul White, as head of commercial in London, to present to the main board in Amsterdam his vision of the future and where MeesPierson could, and should, be focusing their attention.

When Paul returned, he was demoralised – not only did the MeesPierson Board not accept his vision of the future, he was so unimpressed with them that he felt his position was untenable.

Paul focused his attention on the IPE floor, where the influx of ex-LIFFE locals meant that MeesPierson was now the biggest clearer of locals on the trading floor and it also enjoyed a flourishing brokerage business.

Paul employed Carol Deebank from the compliance department as his assistant. Eventually, Paul resigned from MeesPierson and accepted a position at ADM, where he knew all the senior management from their time as MeesPierson Derivatives.

Paul managed to convince 90 per cent of the MeesPierson IPE floor team to join him at ADM.

Such was the size and importance of the oil team that Paul established on the IPE floor that ADM were soon the second largest, in terms of traded volume, on the market.

Inevitably, the IPE exchange started to investigate a move to electronic trading and set up a 'transition committee' that would manage the project and reflect the views of the exchange membership.

With this potential move to screen trading looming, Paul White convinced the senior directors of ADM that he would need to start the process of establishing a trading arcade to protect his business.

However, if ADM were going to seriously look at investing in a trading arcade, it seemed sensible to not restrict it to just energy products. ADM agreed provisionally to support the project.

Paul employed Mark Limbert as the project manager, and then, with the project well underway, Paul gave me a phone call.

At this point in time, MacFutures had evolved from the small group of traders we had supported from Griffin, and they had set up their own trading arcade. MacFutures had become a member of both the LIFFE and Eurex exchanges and quickly established the biggest trading arcade in the UK with hundreds of traders.

Cube Financial had expanded substantially and now had its own broking floor at the Royal Mint, with hundreds of brokers trading on all the major international financial markets. By offering a commission share deal, they had been able to encourage brokers and broking teams to join them from major banks and established themselves as the biggest independent broking team in Europe.

With these two examples of what could be achieved, combined with changes of staff at MeesPierson which had made me increasingly uncomfortable. I was more than interested in joining Paul White at ADM and assisting in setting up a new arcade business.

For the first, and only time, in my career, I resigned from MeesPierson on 20 September 2002 and accepted a position at ADM. This meant joining my old boss and mentor David Peart and my old colleague Paul 'Ollie' Collister who were also working at ADM.

I quickly set to work and signed up another new trading arcade called Atlas Futures as a clearing client at ADM.

Paul, and I started negotiations with traders and trading groups interested in taking space in our new proposed trading arcade.

With sufficient interest in place, we searched for suitable office space in the City. We found it in Lower Thames Street – an ideal empty floor with all the right connectivity – and we returned to ADM with the plan and to secure the required funding.

At the last-minute, ADM pulled the plug on us – in the background, a political war had broken out. Paul White had become so successful that his income, based on the profit he was making for the company, was upsetting some senior directors.

Also, the proposed trading arcade was so broad in scope that it would inevitably compete with other profit centres at ADM. The resulting dispute meant that proceeding at ADM was no longer possible, and Paul decided to back the project himself.

He established a company called White Circle Trading, until someone spotted that this would inevitably be shortened to WC Trading. Quickly, the company was rebadged as Xconnect Trading.

We now needed a clearing company, so we went back to our old friends at MeesPierson, and a deal was agreed.

Most of the oil business that Paul had taken to ADM stayed there while the trading floor remained open.

Xconnect played the long game, knowing that the IPE floor would be closing, and the business would follow LIFFE onto the screens. When it did we would be waiting with a new trading arcade.

During the political infighting with ADM, we lost the option on our Lower Thames Street office.

An alternative was quickly found in Old Jewry, where we were able to sublease a floor with 7,000 square feet of space from Anglo Irish Bank. Xconnect opened for business.

In March 2004, New York-based giant Refco Group purchased MacFutures for an undisclosed sum.

MacFutures by this time had offices in Gibraltar and Sydney in addition to its London headquarters and was clearing two hundred traders accessing the global futures markets. Under the terms of the deal, MacFutures operations became a division of Refco, and the key traders who had established and owned the company were financially rewarded.

In November 2004, the New York Mercantile Exchange (NYMEX) exchange decided to challenge the IPE and gambled that there was no real appetite in the London oil community for a move to electronic trading. They petitioned to the UK regulator to open an exchange trading floor in London.

While they were waiting for this to be approved, they opened a temporary trading floor in Dublin.

Xconnect had a sufficient amount of oil brokerage business to make a presence on the Dublin NYMEX floor viable and applied for membership. We ordered and registered Xconnect floor trading jackets from a supplier in Chicago, and we promptly sent our team to Dublin.

The NYMEX Dublin floor administration was managed by Gill Hyde (now Fenton after marrying her long-term boyfriend), who I had stayed connected with. Gill had joined us during our brief period at ADM and now agreed to join the Xconnect floor team in Dublin.

On 16th February 2005, the IPE trading floor was invaded by 35 Greenpeace activists in an attempt to disrupt trading. Once again, you have to ask, did Greenpeace do any homework before deciding this was a clever idea?

Surely the experience of the Stop the City protestors and the 'Battle of the LIFFE Floor' would have told them what to expect.

Timed to coincide with the signing of the Kyoto global warming treaty at 2 pm, the activists entered the IPE floor armed with foghorns, alarms, and whistles in an attempt to disrupt the trading.

Three Greenpeace climbers hung a banner from the roof declaring, 'Climate change kills. Stop pushing oil.'

More than a dozen people were injured when angry traders pulled a large metal bookcase on top of protestors. In the brief fighting that followed, the IPE traders drove the protestors off of the trading floor.

One protestor said later that he was a veteran of such events and had even faced a Texan SWAT team but had never witnessed the level of violence and hostility that took place that day on the IPE trading floor.

Afterwards, it was confirmed that police had taken twenty-seven people into custody, all of whom were demonstrators. Police attempted to get copies of the IPE trading floor surveillance tapes, but the system had experienced a 'fault' during the disturbance, and no footage was available.

Trading on the floor of the IPE ceased just months later on 7th April 2005.

NYMEX eventually got permission from the SFA to open a trading floor, and the business was moved from Dublin to a new trading facility off Finsbury Square on 12th September 2005. This NYMEX London trading floor closed on

9ᵗʰ June 2006, and many felt the delay in establishing a presence in London was the ultimate cause of the failure.

Cube Financial reached an agreement to sell their business to Refco in September 2005.

Just two weeks after the sale was agreed, Refco ran into financial problems which quickly became common knowledge. Technically solvent at that time, Refco's clients started to flee, and levels of confidence among customers, and indeed employees, were shattered.

On 18ᵗʰ October 2005, Refco filed for Chapter 11 bankruptcy in the US, and by then over half of Refco's customer business had jumped ship. It was too late to save Refco.

John Ruskin and Lee Hughes managed to move Cube Financials' business to NewEdge Group in a brilliant manoeuvre that meant they had no interruption to their business. Subsequently, a sale was agreed, and NewEdge purchased Cube Financial from John and Lee.

On 19ᵗʰ October 2010, I was invited to join a young lady called Anna Tokareva onboard HMS Belfast for the dedication of recently installed replica masts.

Let me rewind a little – Anna Tokareva is a Ukrainian national who, I am pleased to say, is now a naturalised UK citizen.

Employed by Xconnect as an accountant back in 2007, Anna's family lived in Sumi in Ukraine.

On a particular flight back from visiting her family, Anna was seated next to a lady flying to the Russian Embassy in London. They started chatting and the lady explained to Anna that she had been tasked with co-ordinating the visit of Russian veterans of World War 2 to the dedication ceremony of replacement masts on HMS Belfast.

The Russian dockyards had built the masts as a thank you to the Royal Navy for the supply convoys during WW2. The original masts on HMS Belfast had rusted and needed replacing.

Anna explained that she worked close to where HMS Belfast was moored and that was the moment the lady asked if Anna would be willing to help on the day. Hardly any of the Russian veterans could speak English, and Anna's help with interpreting would be greatly appreciated. Anna explained that she did not think she would be able to get the time off of work.

On the day of the ceremony itself, Anna quietly asked my opinion. I really could not see Paul White objecting, but Anna refused to ask him and went back to work.

Twenty minutes before the ceremony was due to start, Anna asked me to meet her outside the Xconnect office in Old Jewry. I went down to the ground floor and out the door and was duly kidnapped by Anna and piled into a black cab.

I have to explain that Anna is prone to these last-minute moments of madness, and before I knew what had happened, we were at the bottom of an access ramp up to HMS Belfast.

What I was not prepared for was the security.

A line of guests and both British and Russian WW2 veterans were making their way up the gangway. At the top of the gangway were two ladies armed with clipboards who were ticking off names. Next to them were two police officers armed with machine guns.

As I looked around, I could see armed security on the bank of the Thames and onboard HMS Belfast itself. As charming as Anna is, I could see no chance of us blagging our way onboard.

Just as I was about to tell Anna we should turn around, she started chatting to a group of Russian veterans, complete with berets and medals. They were delighted to find this charming, attractive young lady who could speak Russian, and before I realised it we were making our way up the gangway towards the ladies with the clipboards.

Once the veteran sailors Anna was talking to had arrived at the top of the gangway, they gave their names, and Anna waited and chatted with each in turn as they were slowly ticked off the list. Once done, the ladies with the clipboards looked at Anna, who promptly declared she was helping the Russian embassy with the interpreting, and then she pointed at me and said calmly that I was with her.

With a queue behind us, and against all the odds, we were waved onboard.

We followed the directions to the open area of the deck where the ceremony was due to take place, and Anna spotted the lady she had met on the plane. Before I knew what was happening, we were part of the Russian embassy delegation.

The event was much bigger than I had expected, with ambassadors, dignitaries, and British MPs all around us, as well as the group of fifty-plus war veterans.

Anna was called over to join the British and Russian sailors who had started trying to converse with each other and needed her help translating.

Just as I was starting to feel like a spare wheel, I was presented with the reason for the armed security – right next to me was the Duke of Edinburgh. That was when I spotted the TV camera pointing right at me.

My heart sank as I realised the entire event was being shown on national television.

In my mind, I could see my boss Paul White about to take a bite into his cheese-and-pickle sandwich seeing me appear on the television in his office, standing on HMS Belfast, next to the Duke of Edinburgh, instead of being in the office next door working, as I surely should have been.

Getting off of HMS Belfast was not an option during the ceremony itself, and Anna by now was having her picture taken with a gang of veteran sailors and having a wonderful time. We stayed for the entire ceremony with the clock ticking.

Even when the formalities were over and the Duke of Edinburgh had departed, Anna was still interpreting, and I finally had to intercede, pointing to my watch. When Anna finally looked at her watch, the colour drained from her face, and we quickly excused ourselves, rushed back down the gangway, and jumped into a cab back to the office.

If our prolonged absence had been noticed, nothing was mentioned, and so Anna and I put our heads down and kept quiet.

Not long after that, I was co-opted onto a business trip to Moscow.

Two of our brokers, Jason Wynch and Simon Spender, had a big client called Renaissance Capital based in Moscow.

These two characters could not have been more different.

Jason would not have looked out of place in a James Cagney movie – he was a 'geezer,' dapper in dress but not someone you would want to cross. Simon would have been at home at Czarnikow in the early days – a public schoolboy, polite and softly spoken.

When Paul White had been approached about the trip to Moscow, it was on the basis that the existing business would be cemented and hopefully expanded.

Anna was recruited once again in the role of an interpreter, but Jason got cold feet, explaining that he and Simon would be going on 'gentlemen's' evenings out and he feared there was not enough work to keep Anna occupied.

This was the moment I was recruited to join the trip to maximise its commercial potential. I set about calling Renaissance Capital and arranged a series of meetings with the clearing and settlements team, as well as other trading desks we were not in contact with.

We also planned to present Renaissance with the prospect of taking direct market access via Xconnect.

On the 28th of October, I had to attend the Russian National Tourist Office in person in order to have my passport stamped with a visa.

The four of us met up at Heathrow Airport on the 7th of November 2010 for the British Airways flight to Moscow.

Our week in Moscow was a revelation. We were booked into a hotel that seemed aptly named given who we were visiting – The Renaissance Moscow Monarch Centre Hotel. Renaissance Capital was based in a new commercial centre located just off of the Moskva River, and this meant a cab ride or a trip on the Moscow subway, which I was keen to do at least once.

The trip was not overly successful commercially.

We had all the meetings and were received very well, but Renaissance had a clearing relationship with JP Morgan and seemed reluctant to really give Xconnect a chance.

That said, Jason and Simon achieved their objective of cementing themselves with the client, and I got a ride on the Moscow subway.

We also met pop group "Slade" on the last night, as they were staying in the same hotel – less lead singer Noddy Holder, who had retired.

Apparently Slade are still huge in Russia!

UPDATES

I lost contact with Steve Dickinson, my old friend from Applemore School, after his marriage in 1989.

However, when my brother Robin joined the Met Police and Steve found out, they met up. At this stage, Steve was in charge of the robbery squad, and he offered Robin a position, which he declined.

Steve went on to become a detective chief inspector of the Specialist Crime Directorate before his retirement.

David Peart, my boss at the end of our time at Czarnikow and at Cater Allen, has since retired.

We are still in touch and enjoy the occasional beer in the City.

Barry Fontera, our American trader at Czarnikow, joined Goldman Sachs when Czarnikow sold us to Cater Allen. Barry had an amazing first year at Goldman Sachs, making them a fortune, and as a result became a partner.

David Peart told me that Goldman Sachs had made a huge mistake, and what they should have actually done was got rid of Barry the following year. David felt that from this point on, Barry would always be right, and the markets would always be wrong.

As usual, David was spot on because the following year Barry and Goldman Sachs parted company.

Barry always said he wanted to buy a ranch and settle down, playing his guitar and riding his Harley Davidson. I hope that is exactly what he is doing now.

The Hon. Ralph Daniel Beckett became the head broker at Odey Asset Management after the LIFFE floor closed.

I met up with Danny in the West End, flanked by Simon Spender, to try and establish a broking line with Odey.

Danny told me he had the best job in the City – he sat in the middle of the asset and fund managers who fed their market orders to him, and he pushed these orders out to the market.

Where possible, Danny used our old colleagues Tim Clark and Ian 'Burger' Hughes for execution. Danny has since retired.

Sean Conley, the MD of Prime International London, became a good friend.

He stayed in London after the LIFFE floor closed before personal issues forced him to return to Chicago.

Before he departed, I was given permission by MeesPierson to treat him to an evening out of his choice.

He chose to go to a 'soccer match.' MeesPierson had a corporate box at Chelsea, and as luck would have it, Chelsea were playing Charlton in a Premiership clash. I booked the box and told Sean to invite who he wanted.

As a surprise, I set off for The Valley and purchased a Charlton shirt with 'Conley' emblazoned on the back. As we sat down for our meal at the ground, I presented him with the shirt which he insisted on wearing for the duration of the evening.

Every year when we exchange festive greetings, Sean mentions he still has the shirt, and I am sure he has the only Charlton Athletic shirt in the USA.

He was a compliance officer for British Petroleum in Chicago before retiring in 2020.

My brother Robin worked his way up to sergeant in the Met Police before taking retirement.

He now happily lives in Norfolk with his wife Monica and my parents in an adjoining property.

The era of the trading arcades proved to be short and not very sweet.

The vast majority of 'click' traders were 'day traders,' meaning they entered the trading session without positions and ended the day without positions.

Once the market was fully electronic, algorithmic trading models started being deployed. These electronic monsters could consume and analyse vast amounts of data, and in a microsecond could spot trading opportunities with more efficiency than human traders.

When the LIFFE market had opened in 1982, the London and Essex Barrow Boys had ruled. Now the shoe was on the other foot, and the algorithmic trading models meant the vast army of day trading 'click' traders could no longer make a living.

As fast as the trading arcades had sprung up after floor trading ceased, they vanished, with only a vastly reduced number of technical 'directional' traders still able to make a living from trading.

On the personal side, in June 2000, I enjoyed an evening date with Fionnuala, the personal assistant of MeesPierson's managing director.

I was keen to meet again, but she was off on a two-week safari holiday, so I had to wait for her return before booking a second date.

The second date was even better than the first, and before long we were living together in Wordsworth Road, Welling.

It was quickly decided that we should buy a house together, and so I sold Wordsworth Road, and on 30th March 2001 we moved to a house in Hadlow Village just outside Tonbridge.

Fionnuala is a Dubliner, and with her family based in Ireland, we decided it was too complicated to organise a traditional wedding.

We found a solution with my old friends at Kuoni and booked a wedding holiday in Australia.

On 14th June 2002, Fionnuala and I married at the Radison Treetops Resort, Port Douglas, Queensland, Australia.

Our honeymoon was spent travelling the east coast of Australia on our way back down to Sydney for the flight home.

We now have two children, Liam, and Tara, and we live happily in Ashford, Kent.

The City is no longer the dynamic exciting place it was when I started back in 1981. Regulation, automation, and the political fallout from Brexit have all played a part in this change.

Before the trading floors opened, the City was a closed shop, a haven for the rich and public-school-educated elite.

The trading floors were a great leveller.

An individual from a comprehensive school could earn as much as, if not more than, a privately educated director.

Indeed, I remember a director from Cater Allen Bank venting to Graham 'Pinky' Stewart along these very lines when a couple of the floor locals cleared more than he did one year.

In many ways, the City has started the process of returning to the 'closed shop' that operated before the larger trading floors opened.

All that remains of days when multicoloured trading jackets could be seen walking the streets of the Square Mile is a lot of really good memories, a handful of lifelong friendships, and a statue of a LIFFE trader that for many years stood outside Cannon Street station.

This statue has been recently moved down to Lower Thames street, near to where the entrance of the LIFFE floor was located before its closure.

I am thankful that I worked in the City during this exciting period in its history.

Outside Totton College.
Charlotte, Nick, Lisa and Me

Hannah, Alison's Mum and
Alison at Woodbrook Road

Tour driver Joe and Alison

Our wedding at
Port Douglas